Sidney Perley

Principles of the Law of Interest

As Applied by Courts of Law and Equity in the United States and Great Britain

Sidney Perley

Principles of the Law of Interest
As Applied by Courts of Law and Equity in the United States and Great Britain

ISBN/EAN: 9783337207427

Printed in Europe, USA, Canada, Australia, Japan

Cover: Foto ©Suzi / pixelio.de

More available books at **www.hansebooks.com**

PRINCIPLES

OF THE

LAW OF INTEREST

AS APPLIED BY

COURTS OF LAW AND EQUITY

IN THE

UNITED STATES AND GREAT BRITAIN;

AND THE TEXT OF

THE GENERAL INTEREST STATUTES

IN FORCE IN THE

UNITED STATES, GREAT BRITAIN AND THE DOMINION OF CANADA.

BY

SIDNEY PERLEY

OF THE MASSACHUSETTS BAR.

BOSTON:
PUBLISHED BY GEORGE B. REED
Law Publisher
1893

PREFACE.

Having, in his practice, repeatedly had occasion to examine the law of interest, the writer has noticed that little attention had been given to this important branch of the law, — a branch, too, that is broader in its application than almost any other. The need of a general knowledge of the law of interest was so apparent that for several years past he has continued his examination of the cases bearing upon the whole subject, and at the request of the publisher has compiled the result of his researches for the use of the bar. There are nearly seven thousand decisions cited, and these comprise all the cases of value that have been decided to the time of the examination of the proof-sheets.

On many questions in the law of interest there is such a diversity of opinion that it is impossible to harmonize the decisions. To settle those points statutes should be passed. And when the great dissimilarity of the statutory laws that already exist is considered, the passage of general statutes seems imperative. Because the interest statutes of the different states are so unlike, it is deemed necessary to insert the text of those that are more general.

The writer has the satisfaction of knowing that he has endeavored to do his work well, and trusts that it will be useful to the bar.

SIDNEY PERLEY.

Salem, Mass., June 7, 1893.

CONTENTS.

CHAPTER IV.

CHAPTER V.

CHAPTER VI.

CHAPTER VII.

CHAPTER VIII.

CHAPTER IX.

CHAPTER X.

CHAPTER XI.

CHAPTER XII.

CHAPTER XIII.

THE LAW OF INTEREST.

CHAPTER I.

DEFINITION AND HISTORY OF INTEREST.

INTEREST is the compensation that one person gives for the use and profit of another's money, *or*, the legal damage he is obliged to pay to another person who has lost the use of his money through the payor's act or negligence, although the payor may not have received any benefit therefrom.[1] The word *interest* is derived from the Latin words, *inter*, between, and *esse*, to be; and has reference to the time between the receiving and the paying back the money for which period only interest is allowed.

The word *interest*, used in this connection, is comparatively modern. The original term was *usury*. For the last three centuries the latter term has been applied only to the excess of interest above the maximum legal rate allowed, that is, illegal interest, and the word as early used has become obsolete. The term *interest* is broad and means all interest, whether the rate is legal or usurious.

In early times, in conformity to the canons of the church, all interest whatever upon money loaned was prohibited.[2] To take it was, also, *in foro conscientiæ*, punished as a crime next to that of murder, and if the guilty parties had been habitual receivers of interest all of their estate was

[1] 53 Mich. 453 (1884).

[2] 1 Wils. (Eng.) 290 (1750).

forfeited to the king.[1] In one of the earliest law books extant,[2] it is lamented as "an abusion of the common law" that the offender was not likewise deprived of Christian burial. Our Savior seems to have favored the taking of interest;[3] though it was forbidden in the Mosaic law among the Jews themselves,[4] it, however, being provided that they might "lend upon usury" to a stranger.[5] This feeling against the taking of interest for the use of money was strengthened, probably, by the communism which sprang up in the early Christian church.

Judge Woodbury of New Hampshire said:[6]—

> "The prejudices on this subject have doubtless been embittered by the circumstance, that, anciently, Jews were the principal money-lenders; and such is still the extent of those prejudices as hardly to be accounted for, except on the belief that interest is prohibited by the scriptures as a moral offence, or that associations are continued, which have some connection with the fulfillment of the prophecy against the persecuted race of Israel."

The Koran also prohibited the taking of interest, and England, France and Turkey enacted express laws against it.[7] Aristotle, Pothier and Domat condemned all interest, the latter declaring "that every Covenant, or Commerce, whereby Intereſt is taken for a Loan, whatever pretext is made uſe of to colour it, is a criminal Uſury, most piouſly condemned by the Law of God, and that of the Church, and moſt juſtly puniſhed by the Ordinances."[8] The same writer, in speaking of interest among the Romans, said:—

[1] 13 Tex. 279 (1855).

[2] "Mirror of Justices," 191, 248. This was published in Old French long before the Conquest, but the author is unknown.

[3] Matt. xxv: 27; Luke xix: 23.

[4] Ex. xxii: 25; Lev. xxv: 36, 37; Neh. v: 7, 10; Ps. xv: 5; Prov. xxviii: 8; Isa. xxiv: 2; Jer. xv: 10; Ezek. xviii: 8, 13, 17; xxii: 12.

[5] Deut. xxiii: 19, 20.

[6] 2 N. H. 42 (1819).

[7] 13 Tex. 279 (1855).

[8] 1 Domat, b. 1, tit. 6, p. 131.

"It was prohibited at *Rome* in the firſt Ages of the Commonwealth, and long before the Goſpel was known there; and it was even more rigorouſly prohibited than Theft. Since whereas the Puniſhment of Theft was only the double of the thing ſtollen, that of Uſury was the quadruple.[1] Thus Uſury was looked upon among the *Romans* as a very pernicious crime."[2]

On the contrary, Lord Bacon said that "that opinion must be sent to Utopia;" Holland allowed the receipt of interest; and Solon, Locke, Turgot, Bentham and others also contended against the old view.

Notwithstanding the anathemas of the church, and the punishments and forfeitures of the state, interest could not be suppressed. There were always people ready to lend and others to borrow, and the lender would not let out his money unless he received some recompense for its use, and the borrower needed it so much that he would pay rates that would induce the lender to run the risk of detection and conviction. The community, therefore, instead of being benefited by these prohibitory laws, was seriously harmed.

It seems to the writer that a principal cause of the more common allowance of interest that followed was the increase in the amount of personal property. In early times a man's possessions consisted principally of real estate, and the articles that could be loaned were those of necessary use and therefore not expected to be loaned in the mercantile sense; but in these later days, when chattels are so abundant that they are the most common subject of trade, pay for the use of them seems only proper.

The first statute passed in England which rendered the taking of any interest lawful was enacted in 1545.[3] But it is not known whether it was the outgrowth of more en-

[1] *Tacitus* 6 *annalium, anno urbis* 786.

[2] 1 Domat, b. 1, tit. 6, p. 128.

[3] 37 Henry VIII, ch. 9.

lightened views as to the justice, honesty and advantage of letting money at interest, or the dictate of policy, which concluded that, as the vice could not be suppressed, it would be better to tolerate it, with many and severe restrictions. From that time the courts of England and other countries gradually broke down the old barriers by allowing interest in a class of mercantile actions and in a few isolated cases, and, after about a century, interest was sanctioned by the courts in a large number of contracts.

As interest obtained an increasing support in England, the people in the new world correspondingly grew in favor of it. Its allowance has now become very general as to subject matter, relating to nearly every contract, simple, special and contract of record, and to many torts.

CHAPTER II.

CONTRACTUAL INTEREST.

INTEREST is allowed by law only on the ground of a contract, express or implied, or as damages for breach of a contract, or violation of a duty.[1] The law does not of its own accord give interest before a debt is due; such interest must be created by agreement of the parties.[2] Therefore, interest is divided into two great and well defined classes, the first being that of contractual interest, and the second interest allowed as damages. Contractual interest exists only by agreement of the parties, while interest as damages is allowed by law in cases where there has not been, and in many instances where there could not be, an engagement to pay it, it being simply damages for the detention of a debt in proportion to its amount and the length of time it has been detained. Again, contractual interest is not given as damages, nor as the incident of the debt, *pro tanto* it is the debt itself,[3] a substantive part of it,[4] as much so as the principal, for both were contracted

[1] 15 L. R., Ch. D. (Eng.) 169 (1880); 49 L. J., Ch. (Eng.) 769 (1880); 43 L. T., N. S. (Eng.) 229 (1880); 28 W. R. (Eng.) 818; 22 Conn. 386 (1853); 3 Harr. (Del.) 528 (1843); 46 Mich. 193 (1881); 40 Minn. 512 (1889). Interest was early allowed as damages in England, at common law, on mercantile securities. 4 M. & P. (Eng.) 589 (1830); 6 Bing. (Eng.) 709 (1830).

[2] 64 Tex. 94 (1885); 1 H. & M. (Va.) 211 (1807).

[3] 11 Pa. St. 282 (1849).

[4] 11 La. 409 (1837); 12 Har. (24 Pa. St.) 310 (1855).

for, and can be recovered as a matter of right;[1] while interest that is given as damages is simply incidental to the debt, and does not follow it as of right.[2]

Contractual interest is created either expressly or impliedly.

1. EXPRESS CONTRACTS FOR INTEREST.

Interest is created expressly when the parties to the contract agree in terms that interest shall be paid. This is usually done, when the contract is in writing, by adding the words "bearing interest," "with interest," or, "with interest on the same." If the contract is silent as to interest it bears no contractual interest.[3]

It may be a contract for the payment of interest on money to be loaned, or for money already loaned, although in the latter case it is not strictly a contract to pay interest.[4]

Contracts for interest have the same elements as other contracts.

(*a*) *The contract.* The contract for interest, unless the statute law makes it incumbent upon parties to put such agreements into writing, may be oral.[5] But if a written contract says nothing about interest, interest cannot be added to it by an oral agreement made at the same time;[6] neither can the rate of interest be thus reduced,[7] nor the interest be agreed to be paid at stated times;[8] though oral agreements made after maturity, whether they be to create

[1] 110 U. S. 174 (1883).

[2] 110 U. S. 174 (1883).

[3] 8 Bush (Ky.) 276 (1871).

[4] 21 Minn. 530 (1875).

[5] 6 Mart. (La.) 276 (1819); 7 La. 520 (1835); 13 Tex. 279 (1855).

[6] 2 Mart. (La.) 78 (1811).

[7] 79 Mich. 564 (1890); 80 Mich. 249 (1890).

[8] 56 Md. 433 (1881).

new engagements to pay interest,[1] or to change the rate or times of payment,[2] are good and binding.

Like other contracts the agreement for the payment of interest must have a valuable consideration to support it.[3] The consideration of the principal part of the contract will sustain the interest clause of the agreement; but if the contract to pay interest is separate it must have a separate consideration: as, for instance, a promise to pay interest from its date on a non-interest-bearing debt already due. In such a case, the use of the money is held to be a valid consideration.[4] A promise of forbearance to enforce the collection of the principal will also support an engagement to pay such interest.[5] A definite promise of forbearance or extension of time for an engagement to pay a larger rate of interest,[6] or to make more frequent payments of interest,[7] is a valid consideration. But an agreement after maturity, in consideration of the payment of a part of the note, to pay interest on the balance is without consideration.[8]

Interest is to be paid in the same kind of money as the principal.[9]

The rate per cent may, or may not, be agreed upon, and if it is it must be included in the contract. The rate agreed upon will govern unless it is contrary to statute law, or is unconscionable.[10] Parties sometimes, in their haste, simply

[1] 1 Kas. 285 (1863).

[2] 12 Stew. (N. J.) 376 (1885).

[3] 36 O. St. 361 (1881).

[4] 5 Mart., N. S. (La.) 40 (1826).

[5] 6 S. C. 485 (1875).

[6] 15 Kas. 591 (1875).

[7] 36 O. St. 361 (1881).

[8] 1 Kas. 285 (1863).

[9] 64 Pa. St. 63 (1870).

[10] 8 Ir. R., Eq. (Ire.) 571-R (1873); 150 Mass. 524 (1890). In the latter case five per cent per month was held not to be unconscionable.

add to contracts the words "with six per cent;" and in such cases the courts construe it to mean that they bear interest at six per cent interest per annum.[1] Parties can agree beforehand what the rate shall be after maturity, although the contract carries no interest before maturity.[2] If the rate is not agreed upon, the legal rate will be implied.[3] For a statement of the law in general relative to the rate of interest see chapter five.

If no time is stated in the contract when interest is to begin to run, it will commence at the time the contract is made;[4] because, without that stipulation, interest as damages could have been collected from its maturity, and, again, the promise is to pay the interest when the principal is due, which of course must relate to prior interest, if to any. In this respect there is no difference between a demand note and one payable at a future day certain.[5] The same rule applies also to a note which stipulates that if it is not paid at maturity it shall bear interest — the interest will run from the date of the contract.[6] The courts have also decided that a note dated January 8, 1838, bearing "interest from the first day of January last," means from January 1, 1837;[7] and, in another case, where it was stip-

[1] 63 Ind. 432 (1878); 28 Iowa 516 (1870); Walk. (Miss.) 207 (1825).

[2] 2 Puls. (Me.) 282 (1876); 3 Puls. (Me.) 540 (1877).

[3] 1 Ark. 454 (1842); 9 Col. 228 (1886); 15 Col. 320 (1890); 11 La. Ann. 684 (1859).

[4] 1 Starkie (Eng.) 452 (1816); 79 Ala. 475 (1885); 2 Ark. 115 (1839); 4 Ark. 210, 408 (1842); 5 Ark. 166 (1843); 8 Cal. 145 (1857); 67 Cal. 127 (1885); 24 Conn. 500 (1856); 7 La. 479 (1834); 19 La. Ann. 472 (1867); 49 Miss. 95 (1873); 6 Mo. App. 577 (1879); 1 Zab. (N. J.) 18 (1847). 701 (18[illegible]); Add. (Pa.) 323 (1797). So on an instalment note, also. 113 Mass. 50 (1873).

[5] Hempst. (U. S., C. C.) 155 (1831); 1 Lit. (Ky.) 160 (1822).

[6] Mor. (Iowa) 294 (1843); 1 Iowa 204 (1855); 8 Mart. (La.) 716 (1820).

[7] 1 McM. (S. C.) 301 (1841).

ulated that the principal was to become due on January 1, 1836, and that it should carry interest "from 1835," the court held that interest was to be paid from January 1, 1835.[1] Another and more recent case was where a note, dated March 4, 1885, was made payable "on the 5th March after date," which the Georgia court construed to mean on the face of it that it became due March 5, 1886.[2]

When a note bears interest after maturity, it runs from the day of maturity, and not from the last day of grace.[3]

Interest as a general rule runs until the principal is paid;[4] but it may be barred,[5] temporarily or permanently, and while it is barred it does not run. Contractual interest exists and accrues during the period mentioned in the contract only,[6] and if the time is unlimited it runs until the principal is paid. A note, however, payable one day after date, with interest from date at a certain rate is deemed to be a contract for interest after the maturity of the principal.[7]

Interest is never payable at more than one time, or before the maturity of the principal, unless there is an express agreement to that effect.[8] This is true in both contractual interest and interest allowed as damages. But if the contract reads "with interest to be paid annually;"[9] or, "with the annual interest till the principal is paid;"[10] or, "with

[1] 8 Port. (Ala.) 497 (1839).

[2] 88 Ga. 298 (1891).

[3] 62 Miss. 369 (1884).

[4] 67 Mich. 605 (1888).

[5] See chapter four.

[6] This rule is subject to modification in some courts. See chapter five.

[7] 14 S. C. 341 (1880).

[8] 21 Conn. 388 (1851); 31 Pac. Rep. (Kas.) 1092 (1893); 10 Md. 32 (1856); 2 Mass. 568 (1803); 3 Mass. 221 (1807); 3 Zab. (N. J.) 200 (1851); 7 Barb. (N. Y.) 452, 560 (1849); 5 How. Pr. (N. Y.) 11 (1849); 1 Binn. (Pa.) 152 (1806); 16 Vt. 44 (1844).

[9] 5 Red. (Me.) 75 (1852); 1 Strob. (S. C.) 426 (1847).

[10] 3 Conn. 445 (1820); 42 Mich. 439 (1880).

interest annually,"[1] the interest is payable annually, whether the principal is due or not.[2] Such interest is payable at the end of each calendar year, reckoning from the time the interest began to run on the contract.[3] And the principle is the same if the parties agree to pay the interest at the end of every month, etc.,[4] where the statute fixes the rate per annum, contracts being legally made for payment at the rate, before the principal becomes due, at periods shorter than a year.[5] When interest is made payable annually upon a fixed date, the fact that the first instalment falls due within a year is not a departure from the terms established.[6]

An agreement that interest shall be paid annually does not extend beyond the maturity of the instrument, without an express stipulation to that effect. Where a note is payable within a year "with interest from date payable annually," it is held to be a contract to pay interest annually after maturity;[7] the reason being that in order to give the words "payable annually" any force and effect it is necessary to construe them as a promise to pay the interest annually until the note is fully paid. The contract would therefore be to pay the interest annually after as well as before maturity.

It is sometimes a nice question whether the words "per annum," or other words of similar import, refer to the time when interest is payable or to the rate per cent.[8] As, for instance, a note with interest at "six per cent. per annum" is not payable annually; the words "per annum" simply in-

[1] 49 Iowa 101 (1878).

[2] 61 Ga. 275 (1878); 34 Ind. 115 (1870).

[3] 34 Ind. 115 (1870).

[4] 1 R. I. 298 (1850).

[5] 1 Wall. (U. S.) 384 (1863); 5 Paige Ch. (N. Y.) 98 (1835).

[6] 37 Mich. 87 (1877).

[7] 19 S. C. 85 (1882).

[8] 39 Mich. 182 (1878).

dicate that the rate named is that by the year.[1] It is the same if it reads "with ten per cent. annually."[2]

(*b*) *Variance.* Where there is a variance between two instruments which form a single transaction, as a note and a mortgage, the courts are not in harmony as to what is the proper practice to follow. There are two manifest rules extant. One is to regard the two instruments as one transaction, and construe them together.[3] As where a note gives interest and the mortgage is silent; in which case the mortgage is bound for the payment of the interest.[4] So where the mortgage stipulated that the interest should be payable monthly, the note being silent as to when interest was payable, interest was held to be payable monthly.[5] The other rule is, that a mortgage is to be regarded merely as a security of the note, and that it is not security for anything more than the amount due by the note; as, where the note is silent as to interest, and the mortgage carries interest, none will be allowed.[6] A mortgage is valid for the interest of a note, if it does not mention it in terms;[7] but, the Michigan court has decided that a mortgage which says nothing about interest or time of payment is due as soon as given, although it is really security for a time note not due.[8]

In case of a discrepancy in the amount of interest named in a bond and coupon attached, the amount named in the

[1] 61 Mo. 403 (1875).

[2] 16 O. St. 348 (1865).

[3] 8 Kas. 456 (1871).

[4] 7 La. 479 (1834).

[5] 46 Iowa 357 (1877).

[6] 130 Mass. 88 (1881). The Massachusetts court allows oral evidence to be admitted to show which paper expresses the real agreement. 130 Mass. 88 (1881); 134 Mass. 593 (1883).

[7] 7 La. 479 (1834).

[8] 40 Mich. 1 (1879).

bond has been held to control.[1] The holder of such coupon, after its severance from the bond, was also not allowed to recover the sum named in the coupon, if larger than that named in the bond as the interest, without showing that he or some prior holder of the severed coupon, acquired the same in good faith, before maturity and without notice of the error.[2]

(c) *Interest on a contingency.* A contract may be made payable on condition that if paid at maturity no interest shall be charged, but if not then paid that it shall bear interest;[3] and in such a case interest will be allowed from the date of the instrument.[4] The same meaning is given to the contract when it simply says "ten per cent. if not paid when due."[5] Interest is recoverable from its date on a contract to pay a sum by several instalments "without interest, but with interest if not punctually paid," should there be a breach of the agreement to pay.[6]

A contract may stipulate that if, where interest is to be paid at certain times, an instalment of interest is not paid when due, the whole note shall become due.[7] In such a case the creditor can only collect the interest that has accrued.[8] But if interest on a contract is to be paid annually, and if not so paid to be added to the principal, the mortgage given to secure it could not be foreclosed

[1] 7 Spauld. (Me.) 462 (1885).

[2] 7 Spauld. (Me.) 462 (1885).

[3] 1 Kelley (Ga.) 469 (1846); 1 Blf. (Ind.) 69 (1820), 213 (1822); 11 Ind. 392 (1858); 17 Ind. 10 (1861); Harp. (S. C.) 397 (1824).

[4] 1 Kelley (Ga.) 469 (1846); 1 Blf. (Ind.) 69 (1820), 213 (1822); 11 Ind. 392 (1858); 17 Ind. 10 (1861)

[5] 91 Ill. 609 (1879).

[6] 3 McC. (S. C.) 180 (1826).

[7] 17 Ind. 10 (1861). A mortgage given to secure the debt could then be foreclosed. 9 Iowa 29, 114 (1859); 22 Iowa 445 (1867); 68 Iowa 412 (1886); 19 Kas. 165 (1877).

[8] 93 N. C. 51 (1885).

for the interest if it were not so paid.[1] A case slightly different from that is one where interest is to be paid annually, but if not so paid to bear interest. Such an agreement does not give the debtor the option of paying the interest when it is due or adding it to the principal as he chooses.[2]

In Virginia, the stipulation that if the interest is not paid when due the principal shall immediately become due,[3] and, also, that back interest shall be the penalty for not paying punctually,[4] are both relieved from in equity. Other courts also generally grant relief from penalties.

(*d*) *Effect of interest on maturity.* A stipulation to pay interest after maturity, if the note is not then paid, does not operate to extend the time of payment;[5] but it is to compel punctual payment, or to obtain compensation for the delay.[6] Though, as a general rule, the receipt of interest in advance upon a note is, *prima facie*, a binding contract to delay the time of payment; and no suit can be maintained against the maker during the period for which the interest has thus been paid,[7] whether the rate is the same or not.[8]

The Kansas court holds that the payment of interest in advance beyond the time agreed on will release a non-consenting surety;[9] but in Massachusetts and Missouri it is held that such an implied agreement is not sufficient to

[1] 67 Iowa 676 (1885).

[2] 76 Iowa 474 (1888).

[3] 5 Munf. (Va.) 495 (1817). This case was affected to some extent by statute.

[4] Gil. (Va.) 172 (1820).

[5] 2 Ball & B. (Ire.) 381 (1813); 35 Iowa 582 (1872).

[6] 2 Ball & B. (Ire.) 381 (1813).

[7] 37 Ga. 384 (1867); 43 Ind. 163, 393 (1873); 10 N. H. 318 (1839); *contra*, 57 Mo. 337, 399, 503 (1874).

[8] 43 Ind. 163, 393 (1873).

[9] 22 Kas. 363 (1879).

discharge a surety[1]— to accomplish that there must be an express contract.

Where a note is, by its terms, made payable on demand, and interest in advance for a certain period is paid at the time of making it, but not indorsed, oral evidence of a contract for delay, made at the time, cannot be admitted, as it would contradict the written contract.[2]

Interest may be received in advance, with a reservation, by agreement, of the right to sue within the time.[3]

The Missouri court holds that the payment of interest after the maturity of a note is not, by itself, evidence of an agreement for an extension of it;[4] but the taking of a renewal note from the principal debtor and receiving interest upon it from its date to its maturity will constitute such an agreement; and will discharge the surety upon it.[5]

The same court holds that usurious interest paid, or agreed to be paid, in advance, will not discharge a surety.[6]

(*e*) *Effect of interest on negotiability.* Making a note bear interest after its maturity does not affect its negotiability.[7] Neither does adding to it a stipulation that if it is not paid when due and a suit is brought thereon, the maker will "pay ten per cent. on the amount due," affect it.[8]

(*f*) *Alteration.* The alteration of a material part of a contract renders it void.[9] Such an alteration must be made

[1] 138 Mass. 53 (1884); 57 Mo. 357 (1874).

[2] 10 N. H. 318 (1839).

[3] 37 Ga. 381 (1867); 10 N. H. 318 (1839).

[4] 57 Mo. 357 (1874).

[5] 65 Mo. 562 (1877).

[6] 57 Mo. 399, 503 (1874).

[7] 23 Kas. 402 (1880).

[8] 32 N. E. Rep. (Ill.) 495 (1892).

[9] 17 S. C. 464 (1882). Adding the word "paid" before "annually," where a note reads "at six per cent. annually," is a material alteration. 16 O. St. 348 (1865).

in the body of the instrument to have that effect.[1] A memorandum made on the back of a note that the rate of interest shall be less, by agreement of the maker and holder, is not an alteration, and will not release the surety, though he were ignorant of the memorandum.[2]

(*g*) *Indorsers' and guarantors' liability.* Indorsers and guarantors of bills and notes are liable for the interest on them the same as the drawers and makers.[3]

Where a note is payable on time, with interest annually till its maturity, and no demand is made for the annual interest as it becomes due, or, if made, no notice thereof is given to the indorser, he if notified of non-payment when the note falls due, will be liable for the whole amount, both principal and interest, the interest being regarded as incidental to the debt rather than a part of it.[4] But a suit for such interest cannot be maintained against an indorser before maturity of the note unless proper demand therefor has first been made upon the maker.[5]

(*h*) *Present worth.* The present worth of a debt bearing interest for a definite period, and written for the amount loaned, is its face value. But if a note is written for an amount covering both principal and interest, or for the principal alone, when it carries no interest, the worth of such notes at any time before their maturity can be ascertained by dividing the face value of the instrument by the amount of one dollar for the time to elapse before its maturity at the rate of interest that the note bears, and the quotient will be the value of the instrument at that time.[6]

[1] 135 Mass. 514 (1883).

[2] 131 Mass. 77 (1881).

[3] 16 L. J., Exch. (Eng.) 3 (1846); 16 M. & W. (Eng.) 99 (1846); 2 Col. 596 (1875); 59 Ga. 840 (1877).

[4] 1 Appl. (Me.) 31 (1811).

[5] 24 Atl. Rep. (Vt.) 136 (1892).

[6] 17 Kas. 518 (1877).

(*i*) *Accrued interest.* Interest that has accrued during life goes to the personal representatives of a deceased person, who enjoyed a life interest in the estate, and not to the remainder-man.[1]

(*j*) *Apportionment.* Interest upon notes of individuals and incorporated companies, whether secured or not, accrues from day to day, and when to be appropriated to income may be apportioned between the days upon which it is stipulated to be paid; and when received it is to be credited to the income for the time during which it accrued.[2] But this rule does not apply to interest on United States bonds, or bonds or certificates of a state, county, city, town, railroad or other public or *quasi* public corporation, in absence of statute or express agreement.[3]

(*k*) *Insolvency.* Contractual interest should be allowed against an insolvent estate.[4] The proper manner is to add such interest to the principal of the debts, because this interest is as much due, and part of the debt, as the principal; to allow the principal only of debts not drawing such interest; and in cases of debts not yet due, not bearing interest, to make a rebate of interest for the unexpired time from the date of the failure, commission,[5] or decease of the insolvent, as the case may be.[6] If there is a surplus of assets, it is allowed to the creditors as interest for the subsequent time.[7] The decree of the commissioners is regarded as a judgment, and in granting the surplus as interest it will be allowed upon the aggregate of principal

[1] 87 Ky. 140 (1888); 8 S. & R. (Pa.) 299 (1822).

[2] 6 Spauld. (Me.) 172 (1884); 121 Mass. 178 (1876).

[3] 121 Mass. 178 (1876).

[4] Cooke's B. L. (Eng.) 181, 182; 2 B. & Ald. (Eng.) 305 (1819); 9 La. 64, 265 (1836).

[5] Cooke's B. L. (Eng.) 535.

[6] 2 Bl. Ch. (Md.) 376 (1830); 4 Met. (Mass.) 317 (1842).

[7] Cooke's B. L. (Eng.) 535.

and interest together found due by the commissioners and not upon the principal alone.[1]

In Maryland, on judgment debts against an insolvent debtor, interest is allowed until the property is sold to pay debts.[2]

(*l*) *How interest is transferred.* The assignment of the principal of a debt carries the interest.[3]

(*m*) *Payment.* A debtor is liable to pay interest by virtue of his contract, whether he made it or not.[4]

In settling a debt, on which there have been no payments, simple interest should be reckoned from the time it began to bear interest until the time of settlement or rendering of decree.[5] For the method of reckoning interest in partial payments, see chapter seven.

If an instalment of interest due on a note is paid by a note for the amount due, it is a mere substitution of one note for another, and will not generally be regarded as a payment of the interest, even if it be indorsed on the note as paid, and the holder can recover it on the original note even against subsequent incumbrancers of the security, if they have not been misled thereby.[6] But if a note bearing a higher rate of interest than the mortgage be given for the interest due on the mortgage, it will be construed as a binding agreement for forbearance, and received as payment it will be treated as such as far as the mortgage title or lien is concerned.[7]

In the absence of a special agreement to that effect, in-

[1] 65 Ga. 189 (1880).
[2] 73 Md. 80 (1890).
[3] 68 Tenn. 539 (1873).
[4] 1 Dev. Eq. (N. C.) 520 (1830).
[5] 80 Ill. 96 (1875).
[6] 16 Conn. 260 (1844).
[7] 23 Mich. 224 (1871).

terest cannot be collected on partial prepayments made on a contract payable on time, without interest;[1] neither can one be compelled to receive a part payment so as to stop interest on that part,[2] although the holder receives interest-bearing notes instead of the money, at their face value, no credit being given for the interest that they include.[3] This is the rule because the time of payment is part of the contract, and for the benefit of both parties.[4] So if one pays the entire debt before it is due he cannot have a rebate for interest.[5] But where the creditor collects a part of the amount due through legal proceedings he cannot afterward claim interest on that part from the time it is paid by the debtor.[6]

If the interest is not paid when it is due, the security can be sold and payment obtained thereby, if such is the agreement. If the mortgagee is a void corporation, it cannot foreclose the mortgage, but a receiver can demand an accounting for the secured debt. Such accounting should be with interest, after allowing all payments made on the loan.[7]

So a mortgage can be foreclosed if interest is payable annually, and is not so paid.[8] But the foreclosure of a mortgage of land for less than ten dollars interest, without calling upon the mortgagor for payment, whereby costs are made to many times that amount, is oppressive and entitled to no favor.[9]

[1] 7 Virg. (Me.) 70 (1870).

[2] 3 Paige (N. Y.) 400 (1832); 7 How. Pr. (N. Y.) 44 (1852); 5 O. 262 (1831).

[3] 1 Spauld. (Me.) 233 (1880).

[4] 7 Johns. Ch. (N. Y.) 7 (1823).

[5] 1 Gr. (N. J.) 171 (1839).

[6] 3 Paige (N. Y.) 400 (1832); 7 How. Pr. (N. Y.) 44 (1852).

[7] 45 Mich. 501 (1881).

[8] 44 Mich. 19 (1880).

[9] 47 Mich. 169 (1881); 48 Mich. 341 (1882).

Payments of interest made one day, or even two days after they become due are no defeasance of the undertaking, if the creditor accepts them without objection.[1]

In foreclosing a mortgage for an instalment only, where the whole sum is not due and the court orders the sale of the whole property, no interest should be allowed beyond the time when the proceeds should become applicable to the payment of subsequent instalments not then due.[2] If the payment of the mortgage is delayed by litigation, interest continues to run till the date of the judgment.[3]

The court will order a debtor to pay the contractual rate, although his lands are in the hands of a receiver at the creditor's instance.[4]

Where a note secured by mortgage is indorsed with an agreement to pay a higher rate of interest in the future it is a mere personal undertaking, and the mortgage is good only for the rate originally agreed upon as against third parties;[5] between the mortgagor and mortgagee, however, the land is charged with the new agreement.[6] So, a more general rule is, that property subject to a mortgage for principal and interest due under one contract is not subject to interest growing out of a subsequent agreement for the payment of the mortgage.[7]

When a deed says that the land is free of all incumbrances except a mortgage for a certain sum named, interest due and to become due on the mortgage note is included by the law.[8]

[1] 1 Russ. & M. (Eng.) 178 (1830).
[2] 8 Blf. (Ind.) 465 (1847).
[3] 77 Iowa 699 (1889).
[4] 83 Va. 715 (1887).
[5] 31 Mich. 265 (1875); 45 Mich. 253 (1881)
[6] 34 Mich. 302 (1876).
[7] 5 Mart., N. S. (La.) 207 (1826).
[8] 130 Mass. 460 (1881).

If a mortgagee stipulates to pay interest on certain debts, he must pay the interest from the date of the mortgage, and not from the time the debts become or will become due.[1]

"Post-due interest" is interest which has matured and is collectible.[2]

(*n*) *The governing law.* The law in force when the contract is made governs as to the rights of parties relating to contractual interest.[3] As to which law governs when a contract is made in one jurisdiction and is to be performed in another, see chapter nine.

II. IMPLIED CONTRACTS FOR INTEREST.

An implied contract for interest arises when the parties make no express agreement for interest, but from the circumstances the law infers that they contracted in reference to a tacit understanding between them. Such contracts may arise in several ways.

(*a*) *Previous dealings.* A promise to pay interest may be implied from previous dealings between the parties.[4] So may the rate be thus implied.[5] But where, by express agreement, more than the legal rate has been paid two or three times only there is no implication that such rate is to be paid in the future.[6] Where one purchased goods at more than the legal rate of discount from time price for cash, in rescission of the sale he cannot claim interest at that rate.[7]

[1] 14 Iowa 22 (1862).

[2] 12 Mo. App. 261 (1882).

[3] 17 Neb. 491 (1885). See Chapter nine.

[4] 5 Geo. (Miss.) 528 (1857).

[5] 1 Camph. (Eng.) 50 (1807); 3 Wash. (U. S., C. C.) 350 (1818); 33 Ala. 459 (1859); Kirby (Conn.) 207 (1787); 39 Ill. 307 (1866); 8 Iowa 163 (1859); 2 Pen. (N. J.) 548 (1809); 4 Wend. (N. Y.) 483 (1830); 50 Wis. 628 (1880); *contra*, 13 Tex. 279 (1855).

[6] 8 Cal. 522 (1857); 3 Hun (N. Y.) 254 (1874).

[7] 5 Rob. (La.) 5 (1843).

(*b*) *General usage.* An implied contract to pay interest may be inferred from the usages of the trade governing the business in which both parties are engaged.[1] Also, where parties have been accustomed to pay and receive interest upon such or similar securities.[2] So an agreement to pay interest on a running account for goods sold may be inferred from the course of dealings between the parties, where it is the usage of the merchants in the neighborhood, and the practice of the creditor, to charge interest in such cases; and this was known to the debtor at the time of the dealing.[3]

If a merchant is in the general practice of charging interest to his customers, after a limited period of credit, those who deal with him with knowledge of it are bound to pay interest;[4] but knowledge by the purchaser of such a practice will not be presumed.[5]

(c) *Admission.* If, in an account stated, a party charges himself with interest at a certain rate it will imply a promise to pay interest at that rate.[6] So, if a debtor gives his bond for such an account, he will be bound by it.[7]

(*d*) *Acceptance of accounts.* The rate per cent may be established by acceptance, without objection, of accounts rendered, in which the implied rate is charged.[8]

[1] 39 Ill. 307 (1866); 1 Dall. (Pa.) 315 (1788); 3 W. & S. (Pa.) 271 (1842).

[2] 2 Campb. (Eng.) 486, n. (1810); 1 Rose (Eng.) 399 (1813); 1 Stark. (Eng.) 487 (1816); 4 C. & P. (Eng.) 124 (1830). And this rule is extended even to an implied promise to pay interest upon interest, when it has been paid for a considerable length of time upon a consolidated sum of principal and interest. 1 Ball & B. (Ire.) 375 (1810).

[3] 1 Barb. (N. Y.) 235 (1847); 3 N. Y. (3 Comst.) 502 (1850); 1 Dall. (Pa.) 315 (1788).

[4] 4 Wend. (N. Y.) 483 (1830); 8 Wend. (N. Y.) 109 (1831).

[5] 1 Barb. (N. Y.) 235 (1847).

[6] 21 Neb. 605 (1887).

[7] 2 Desau. (S. C.) 623 (1808).

[8] 5 Geo. (Miss.) 528 (1857).

CHAPTER III.

INTEREST ALLOWED AS DAMAGES.

IN the preceding chapter was explained the difference between contractual interest and interest allowed by the law as damages in the absence of a contract to pay it. In this chapter will be treated the principles of law governing the last-named division.

In ancient times, parties could not even make agreements for the payment of interest, and it was long after such contracts began to be regarded as legal that the courts were willing that interest should be given as damages for the detention of a debt in any case, unless there was an express agreement therefor. Now, in the United States, interest is very freely allowed, but in England the practice is much narrower. There is a feeling against allowing interest as damages, because the creditor is dilatory in not bringing an action to recover his debt. This has given rise in England to an idea that the creditor ought to try to collect his debt before he is given interest on it, which influences the decisions of the courts there to a considerable degree.[1] That is, they regard interest as real damages.[2] This is true, without regard to the form of the debt, whether it is a contract bearing interest, or otherwise.[3]

[1] 2 B. & Ald. (Eng.) 305 (1819); M. & M. (Eng.) 228 (1828).
[2] 69 Ala. 117 (1881).
[3] 2 C. & P. (Eng.) 88 (1825); 3 Bing. (Eng.) 353 (1826).

Interest is allowed either of course on certain claims, or because of the conduct of the parties.[1] But no contract bears interest before it is due and payable, except by express agreement.[2]

Interest allowed as damages is regarded as such and not as interest,[3] and it is the only damage allowed by the common law for the detention of a debt.[4] It will generally not be denied if it does not appear that either party should be punished.[5] In some states it must be assessed as damages,[6] and though it is then called "interest" it is not a material error.[7]

Some courts hold that interest as damages is entirely a creature of statute,[8] and that if the statute of the state does not allow it the courts cannot give it; and there is certainly much reason for the position, as at the old common law even express contracts for interest were not allowed, and later it was allowed where there was an express contract to pay it,[9] and as damages only in those cases authorized by statute. But the courts soon made it a matter of common law, and to-day in nearly every jurisdiction it is allowed where it is deemed proper under and by virtue of precedents that have been slowly established. In Iowa, the practice is so broad that interest is chargeable upon all debts unless there is a contract between the parties to the contrary;[10] and parties can agree, even orally, that a debt

[1] 3 Binn. (Pa.) 295 (1811).
[2] 64 Tex. 94 (1885); 1 H. & M. (Va.) 211 (1807).
[3] 2 Col. 70 (1873).
[4] 12 Cal. 107 (1859).
[5] 51 N. W. Rep. (Mich.) 356 (1892).
[6] 2 Zab. (N. J.) 424 (1850).
[7] 38 Mich. 172 (1878).
[8] 66 Ind. 1 (1879); 3 Cush. (Miss.) 95 (1852); 3 Tenn. 268 (1813); 42 Tenn. 378 (1865); 2 Tex. 232 (1847); 37 Tex. 315 (1872).
[9] 1 Scam. (Ill.) 167 (1832); 13 Ill. 544 (1852); 86 Ill. 384 (1877).
[10] 63 Iowa 275 (1884); 67 Iowa 654 (1885).

shall not bear interest after it is due.[1] It is allowed in actions of contract[2] much more freely than in tort,[3] because in the latter claims the amount due is generally uncertain.

The right to interest as damages, rests upon default in payment, and not the use of the money due;[4] and it makes no difference whether that which is due is money or chattels,[5] or whether it is due under an implied or express contract.[6] If it is a contract to deliver chattels, the amount of money represented by the chattels is the amount due.[7]

If payment is delayed by circumstances over which the debtor has no control, as when a debt is garnished or trusteed, he is not chargeable with interest during such period of inability.[8] So when debtor dies.[9]

In discretion of jury. In England, the jury are allowed to give damages for the unjust detention of a debt, due diligence to collect it, on the part of the creditor, having first been shown; and the court can order what rate it thinks is just.[10]

In the United States, there are a few instances where courts have allowed the jury the privilege of giving interest in certain cases, at their discretion. These are among those cases where there is no usage, no precise time of payment fixed, no account rendered and no demand made.[11]

[1] 79 Ky. 277 (1881).
[2] 1 Utah 55 (1871).
[3] 7 Mart. (La.) 710 (1820).
[4] 5 Cow. (N. Y.) 331 (1826), 587 (1825); 6 Binn. (Pa.) 159 (1813).
[5] 3 McC. (S. C.) 498 (1826). *Contra*, no interest is allowed on costs of a judgment payable in tobacco. 2 Brev. (S. C.) 99 (1806).
[6] 3 McC. (S. C.) 498 (1826).
[7] 52 Pa. St. 363 (1866).
[8] 1 Jones (Ire.) 51 (1834).
[9] 2 R. I. 558 (1850).
[10] 43 L. J., Ch. (Eng.) 855 (1874); 7 L. R., H. L. Cas. (Eng.) 27 (1874). See Bunb. (Eng.) 119 (1722).
[11] 2 S. & R. (Pa.) 393 (1825).

In Kentucky and Maryland, it is in the discretion of the jury, free from the intervention of the court.[1] In Wisconsin, the jury are allowed, in their discretion, to give interest from the beginning of the action on damages to personalty.[2] The court in Tennessee holds, that in some cases a verdict for interest by way of damages, when the law allows none, should not be set aside.[3] So, the courts in New York and Utah will, under certain circumstances, allow the jury, in their discretion, to give interest.[4]

There are certain well established principles, however, which govern in the great mass of decisions, to wit: 1. The amount due must be certain; 2. The time when it is due must be certain; and, 3. The amount due and time of payment must be known to the debtor.

1. *The amount due must be certain.* The old common law requires that the debt be liquidated, or its amount be ascertained, before interest will be allowed;[5] but the rule has been so far modified, that if the amount is capable of being ascertained, that is to say, by calculation,[6] or

[1] 1 Mar. (Ky.) 43 (1817); 1 Lit. (Ky.) 358 (1822); 3 Mon. (Ky.) 369 (1826); 3 J. J. Mar. (Ky.) 306 (1830); 4 J. J. Mar. (Ky.) 244 (1830); 59 Md. 131 (1882).

[2] 34 Wis. 139 (1874).

[3] 1 Tenn. 106 (1799); 3 Tenn. 447 (1813); 24 Tenn. 103 (1844).

[4] 1 Johns. (N. Y.) 315 (1806); 2 Utah 230 (1878). Generally these are cases that arise *ex delicto.*

[5] 44 Cal. 239 (1872); 57 Cal. 356, 641 (1881); 63 Cal. 503 (1883); 76 Cal. 60 (1888); 56 Ga. 350 (1876); 3 Gilm. (Ill.) 626 (1846); 82 Ill. 134 (1876); 2 Blf. (Ind.) 312 (1830); Hardin (Ky.) 527 (1808); 1 Bibb (Ky.) 326, 443 (1809); 1 Mar. (Ky.) 580 (1819); 11 Bush (Ky.) 50 (1874); 5 Mart. (La.) 388 (1818); 6 Mart. (La.) 689 (1819); 13 La. 371 (1839); 139 Mass. 372 (1885); 8 Mo. 41 (1843); 4 Nev. 437 (1868); 7 Wend. (N. Y.) 109 (1831); 12 How. Pr. (N. Y.) 523 (1856); 7 Lans. (N. Y.) 381 (1873); 125 N. Y. 237 (1891); 1 Dall. (Pa.) 265 (1788); 29 Pa. St. 360 (1857); 1 McC. (S. C.) 419 (1821); Harp. (S. C.) 274 (1824); 2 Speer (S. C.) 594 (1844); 1 Tex. 102 (1846); 2 Hen. & M. (Va.) 603 (1808).

[6] 20 N. Y. 463 (1859); 1 Abb. Pr., N. S. (N. Y.) 121 (1865); 50 Barb. (N. Y.) 62 (1867); 44 Wis. 458 (1878).

determined by reference to ordinary market rates [1] it will carry interest. A claim should be regarded as liquidated when rendered if no objections are made to it within a reasonable time,[2] or after the time the debtor promises to pay it if he accepts the bill.[3] It is not necessary at common law that the account be put into writing to liquidate it.[4] A disputed claim is liquidated when a certain sum is agreed to be due.[5] So, a memorandum check given in settlement of accounts and for immediate payment bears interest.[6]

When there is no contract, usage, time fixed for payment, or account rendered, it is not usual to allow interest.[7]

An unliquidated account will not bear interest[8] until suit is brought to recover it, that is, from the date of the writ,[9] unless there is an express or clearly implied agreement that it shall do so.[10] The court in Wisconsin

[1] 20 N. Y. 463 (1859); 50 Barb. (N. Y.) 62 (1867).

[2] 3 Rob. (La.) 361 (1842); 15 Johns. (N. Y.) 409 (1818); 7 Wend. (N. Y.) 441 (1831); 121 N. Y. 230 (1890).

[3] 68 Wis. 312 (1887).

[4] 2 Kelley (Ga.) 370 (1847).

[5] 35 Barb. (N. Y.) 282 (1861). A *bona fide* dispute as to the amount of the debt is no bar to accruing of interest. 108 Pa. St. 55 (1884).

[6] 10 Rich. Eq. (S. C.) 441 (1859).

[7] 3 Harr. (Del.) 528 (1843).

[8] 46 Mich. 193 (1881); 53 Mich. 421 (1884); 3 Cow. (N. Y.) 393 (1824); 5 Cow. (N. Y.) 587 (1825); 7 Wend. (N. Y.) 178 (1831); 10 N. Y. (6 Seld.) 189 (1854); 17 Barb. (N. Y.) 454 (1854); 20 N. Y. 463 (1859); 50 Barb. (N. Y.) 62 (1867); 3 Hun (N. Y.) 218 (1874); 60 N. Y. 106 (1875); 6 Hun (N. Y.) 175 (1876); 22 Hun (N. Y.) 412 (1880); 123 N. Y. 291 (1890); 125 N. Y. 237 (1891); 2 Speer (S. C.) 536 (1844); 30 S. C. 305 (1888); 32 S. C. 57 (1889); 2 Call (Va.) 358 (1800).

[9] 39 Cal. 662 (1870); 46 Conn. 586 (1879); 61 Iowa 693 (1883); 3 Rob. (La.) 361 (1842); 3 La. Ann. 88, 562 (1848); 12 Pick. (Mass.) 547 (1832); 9 Gray (Mass.) 237 (1857); 13 Allen (Mass.) 326 (1866); 47 Mich. 499 (1882); 62 N. Y. 316 (1875); 39 Hun (N. Y.) 303 (1886); 46 Hun (N. Y.) 258 (1887); 4 Dall. (Pa.) 463 (1806); 5 Rich. (S. C.) 295 (1852); 1 Wash. (Va.) 172 (1793); 37 Wis. 149 (1875); 51 Wis. 407 (1881); 60 Wis. 240 (1884).

[10] 53 Mich. 421 (1884).

holds that interest is not recoverable on any unliquidated demand previous to the finding of the jury,[1] because the amount due is not fixed before that time. The court in South Carolina once held the same view, but long since adopted the prevailing one.[2] The court in Louisiana rather leans against the allowance of interest where the amount due is uncertain. In some cases it has held that interest should not be allowed until judgment;[3] in others, that it should not be allowed even after judgment;[4] and again that interest in such cases should be left to the discretion of the court.[5]

If property sold must be first appraised in order to find the sum due, interest will run from the time of the appraisal only.[6] But, in cases where the debtor is to fix the amount, and he is in default for not having taken the requisite steps, interest is allowed from the time of the default.[7]

2. *The time when the debt is due must be certain.* Interest is generally allowed where it is the legal duty of the debtor to pay over money, deliver property, or perform service, without a previous demand, from the time of default.[8] This is true even if the duty to pay without a demand is an implied one.[9] The fact that the right to sue is indefinitely postponed beyond maturity does not affect the

[1] 44 Wis. 158 (1878); 55 Wis. 271 (1882).

[2] 2 Bay (S. C.) 233 (1799).

[3] 6 La. Ann. 569 (1851).

[4] 4 La. 128 (1832); 7 La. 131, 365 (1834), 596 (1835); 8 La. 569 (1835); 11 La. 236 (1837). See 1 La. Ann. 382 (1846).

[5] 3 La. 140, 149 (1844).

[6] 128 Ill. 88 (1889).

[7] 20 N. Y. 463 (1859); 50 Barb. (N. Y.) 62 (1867).

[8] 3 Harr. (Del.) 528 (1843); 82 Ill. 134 (1876); 9 Pick. (Mass.) 368 (1830); 1 Johns. (N. Y.) 276 (1806); 4 Wend. (N. Y.) 313 (1830); 6 Barb. (N. Y.) 643 (1848); 5 Den. (N. Y.) 135, 470 (1848); 2 N. Y. (2 Comst.) 141 (1849); 11 N. Y. (1 Kern.) 80 (1850); 108 Pa. St. 55 (1884); 4 McC. (S. C.) 59 (1826). The court in 12 Mart. (La.) 365 (1822) says that interest is generally due from judicial demand only.

[9] 9 Pick. (Mass.) 368 (1830); 152 Mass. 141 (1890).

right to recover interest from the time the debt is due.[1] So a cash sale will bear interest from the day of sale, though the day of payment may be postponed until a particular event transpires.[2] If a conveyance is to be made before the money is paid, interest will run from the time the conveyance is made.[3] So, on a contract to pay a stipulated sum for work to be done, interest is allowed from the time the work is finished.[4]

Interest as damages generally begins to run from the time when the debt is due and payable.[5] This is true at both law and equity.[6] The converse of this rule is also true, that when a liquidated sum is unjustly withheld it bears interest from the time it began to be so withheld.[7] So, in an agreement to pay by instalments, interest runs on each instalment from the time it becomes due;[8] and it is allowed from the time an agreement on the part of the payor is fully carried out; as on the consideration of a contract not to object to the probate of a will, when it will run from the day the will is proved.[9] When a definite sum

[1] 11 Rich. (S. C.) 125 (1857).

[2] 26 Ga. 465 (1858).

[3] 24 Ind. 299 (1865).

[4] 5 Rich. (S. C.) 295 (1852); 7 Rich. (S. C.) 124 (1854).

[5] 2 B. & P. (Eng.) 337 (1800); 5 Ves. (Eng.) 801 (1801); Coop. (Eng.) 29 (1805); 17 Ves. (Eng.) 27 (1810); 2 Port. (Ala.) 451 (1835); 22 Ala. 343 (1853); 25 Ala. 152 (1854); 64 Ala. 210 (1879); 67 Ala. 253, 310 (1880); 19 Ark. 16 (1857), 690 (1858); 69 Ill. 521 (1873); 74 Ill. 158 (1874); 3 Mart., N. S. (La.) 185 (1824); 6 La. 727 (1834); 2 Rob. (La.) 471 (1842); 4 Minn. 528 (1860); 35 Mo. App. 511 (1889); 2 Dutch. (N. J.) 398 (1857); 9 Vr. (N. J.) 531 (1875); Bat.'s Mart. & 2d. Hay'd (N. C.) 185, 191, 207 (1798); 22 O. St. 372 (1872); 64 Pa. St. 411 (1870); 66 Pa. St. 132 (1870); 130 Pa. St. 37 (1889); 2 Speer (S. C.) 591 (1844); 34 Vt. 2 (1861); 37 Vt. 285 (1864); 53 Wis. 188 (1881).

[6] 5 Ves. (Eng.) 801 (1801); 17 Ves. (Eng.) 27 (1810); 64 Ala. 210 (1879); 67 Ala. 253, 310 (1880).

[7] 64 Pa. St. 411 (1870).

[8] 3 Ves. (Eng.) 133 (1796); 78 Ill. 440 (1875); 37 Mich. 402 (1877).

[9] 35 Barb. (N. Y.) 282 (1861).

is to be paid out of the proceeds of a certain mine, interest is allowable at the expiration of a reasonable time if work is not commenced;[1] and where a note is made payable "in January," interest thereon will not run until the month has entirely elapsed.[2]

If no time of payment is fixed, interest will run from demand.[3] The Massachusetts court recently decided that where the defendant agreed to pay the plaintiff a yearly salary, but no time was fixed for its payment, interest could not be recovered until payment was demanded.[4] So, where a mandamus is granted for payment of a school order, when it is such a settled demand as would sustain a recovery of interest at law.[5] Also, where by mutual mistake of parties the whole sum due has not been paid at settlement, or too much has been received, interest on the amount not paid or overpaid is recoverable from demand only, unless it was taken or retained unjustly.[6] It is a well settled rule in Virginia, that when no day of maturity is named in a bond or note given for the payment of a debt, it is due and payable on the day of its date, and bears interest from date, though no interest be reserved.[7] Also, in Texas, it is held that interest should run from delivery of the note if no time is fixed for payment.[8]

[1] 59 Cal. 484 (1881); 20 Minn. 527 (1874).

[2] 2 Mar. (Ky.) 267 (1820).

[3] 5 Ves. (Eng.) 801 (1801); 17 Ves. (Eng.) 27 (1810); 1 Hodges (Eng.) 251 (1835); 2 Bing. N. C. (Eng.) 167 (1835); 2 Scott (Eng.) 334 (1835); 4 L. R. Eq. (Eng.) 250 (1867); 36 L. J., Ch. (Eng.) 806 (1867); 71 Ala. 145 (1881); 19 Ga. 537 (1856); 15 Pick. (Mass.) 500 (1834); 9 Gray (Mass.) 401 (1857); 47 Mich. 499 (1882); 63 Mich. 79 (1886); 54 N. W. Rep. (Neb.) 308 (1893); 20 N. Y. 9 (1859); 1 Dall. (Pa.) 52 (1781); 4 Dall. (Pa.) 289 (1803); 51 N. W. Rep. (Wis.) 319 (1892).

[4] 32 N. E. Rep. (Mass.) 663 (1892).

[5] 51 Mich. 184 (1883).

[6] 51 Pa. St. 465 (1866).

[7] 28 Grat. (Va.) 840 (1877); 87 Va. 599 (1891).

[8] 13 Tex. 316 (1855).

Claims payable on demand. On claims payable on demand, interest is allowable from and after a demand,[1] the service of the writ in a suit brought to recover the debt being such a demand.[2] Part payment of a demand note is equivalent to a demand.[3] A check is deemed to be payable on demand so far as its bearing interest is concerned.[4] But a debtor cannot claim that interest should not be allowed prior to demand, when he, by absenting himself, or otherwise, prevents a demand being made.[5]

Credit. Interest as damages never begins to run until the principal sum is due and payable. There must be a real default first.[6] Therefore, if any credit is given, the claim does not bear interest until the time of credit expires.[7] If credit is given, but its length cannot be proven, interest can be recovered only from and after a demand,[8] or, from

[1] 6 Mod. (Eng.) 138 (1705); Minor (Ala.) 417 (1826); 5 Conn. 222 (1824); 71 Iowa 92 (1887); 2 Bibb (Ky.) 471 (1811); 4 Bibb (Ky.) 246 (1815); 1 Mar. (Ky.) 66 (1817); 1 Mon. (Ky.) 209 (1824); 6 Dana (Ky.) 7 (1837); 9 La. 444 (1836); 12 Mass. 4 (1815); 15 Pick. (Mass.) 500 (1834); 1 Met. (Mass.) 112 (1840); 138 Mass. 151 (1884); 12 N. H. 474 (1841); 3 N. J. L. (2 Pen.) 419 (1808); Bat's Mart. & 2d Hay'd (N. C.) 191, 207 (1798); Add. (Pa.) 137 (1793); 16 S. & R. (Pa.) 264 (1827); 1 McC. (S. C.) 370 (1821); 2 Bail. (S. C.) 276 (1831); 28 Vt. 135 (1855); 2 W. Va. 332 (1867); *contra*, 1 Camph. (Eng.) 50 (1807); 18 Ala. 300 (1850).

[2] 18 Ala. 300 (1850); 38 Iowa 325 (1874); 2 Bibb (Ky.) 471 (1811); 4 Bibb (Ky.) 246 (1815); 1 Mon. (Ky.) 209 (1824); 1 Met. (Mass.) 112 (1840); 12 N. H. 474 (1841); 11 Wend. (N. Y.) 477 (1833); *contra*, 1 Mart., N. S. (La.) 130 (1823).

[3] 15 Iowa 279 (1863).

[4] 122 Ind. 534 (1889).

[5] 2 Keyes (N. Y.) 21 (1865).

[6] 3 La. Ann. 338 (1848); 19 La. Ann. 299 (1867).

[7] 4 Harr. (Del.) 130 (1844); 5 Mart. (La.) 300 (1818); 3 Mich. 560 (1855); 50 N. W. Rep. (Neb.) 265 (1891); 30 N. H. 511 (1855); 8 Vt. 258 (1836); 22 Vt. 191 (1850). The Louisiana court says, that there must be a demand upon the debtor to make him liable for interest. 8 Rob. (La.) 207 (1844); 1 La. Ann. 325 (1846).

[8] 3 Mich. 560 (1855); 30 N. H. 511 (1855).

the beginning of the suit brought to recover the debt.[1] The time of credit can be stipulated, or it can be presumed from the custom of the trade or region.[2] In the Massachusetts case of *Bromfield v. Little*,[3] decided in 1764, it was held that there was at that time no custom of merchants in this province to charge interest after a year on the price of goods sold, which would raise an implied contract to pay the same. The chief-justice said: —

"This case is of much importance to the community. 'Tis agreeable to natural equity that interest should be allowed; and I am glad it is growing into a custom; but the rule is that both parties ought at the time of contracting to understand it so, and I doubt whether it is so general as that it can be supposed in this case."

The courts of Maine are decidedly opposed to limiting the length of credit by custom. In the case of *Amee v. Wilson*[4], decided there in 1842, interest was not allowed on a bill of articles charged on account after the expiration of six months from the time of their delivery, by proof "that the usual term of credit on the purchase" of such articles at the place of the sale "was six months with interest after." It was decided that the plaintiff was entitled to such interest only by proof of an agreement to pay it, or by proof of a demand of payment. In this case, in his opinion, Justice Shepley said, that

"One is entitled to have his rights determined by his own contract or by the law; and he cannot without proof be considered as agreeing to any usual term of credit."[5]

Evidence is not admissible to show a custom of merchants in the city of another state allowing them to charge

[1] 1 Bush (Ky.) 225 (1866); 2 Dall. (Pa.) 193 (1792).

[2] 3 Hous. (Del.) 32 (1864); 8 Iowa 163 (1859); Quincy (Mass.) 108 (1764); *contra*, 9 Shepl. (Me.) 116 (1842); 5 Heath (Me.) 457 (1855).

[3] Quincy (Mass.) 108 (1764).

[4] 9 Shepl. (Me.) 116 (1842).

[5] 9 Shepl. (Me.) 116 (1842); 5 Heath (Me.) 457 (1855).

interest on their accounts, when the courts of that state have refused to recognize the custom.[1]

3. *The debtor must know the amount and time when it is due.* The sum due must be known to the debtor,[2] and he is chargeable with interest thereon from the time it came to his knowledge;[3] but the allowance of interest is not erroneous, though there is no evidence of notice to the defendant that the condition of his contract had been performed.[4] The debtor is obliged to pay interest even if he had no notice, provided he is to blame for not receiving notice.[5]

So interest is chargeable on a balance of accounts only from the time that the party against whom the charge is made has notice of the deficiency on his part.[6]

Allowed in settlement. A demand is justly and equitably entitled to interest, though it cannot be recovered at law; and a settlement allowing interest is valid, even as against creditors of the debtor.[7]

Rate. In England, it would seem that the court can vary the rate per cent as they deem it to be consistent with justice.[8] In the United States the legal rate is always allowed,[9] unless parties agree what the rate shall be after maturity of the claim, which they can do if they please.[10]

[1] 2 Blf. (Ind.) 312 (1830).

[2] 57 Cal. 356, 641 (1881); 63 Cal. 503 (1883).

[3] 2 Ves. Ch. (Eng.) 365 (1751); 2 Burr. (Eng.) 1085 (1760); 2 W. Bl. (Eng.) 761 (1761); 3 Wils. (Eng.) 205 (1771); 13 Ill. 592 (1852); 22 Pick. (Mass.) 291 (1839); 3 Caines (N. Y.) 226 (1805); 1 Hayw. (N. C.) 4 (1791), 173 (1795); 1 Ames (4 R. I.) 285 (1856); 2 Ames (5 R. I.) 63 (1857); 16 R. I. 213 (1888).

[4] 34 Mich. 328 (1876).

[5] 20 N. Y. 463 (1859).

[6] 12 Johns. (N. Y.) 156 (1815); 3 Cow. (N. Y.) 393 (1824).

[7] 10 N. Y. (6 Seld.) 202 (1854).

[8] 43 L. J. Ch. (Eng.) 855 (1874); 7 L. R., H. L. Cas. (Eng.) 27 (1874).

[9] 13 Ark. 563 (1853).

[10] 2 Col. 70 (1873).

Not allowed if included in principal. Where, upon the evidence, it is clear that the consideration of a contract was excessive because of an agreement to make it so on account of slow and precarious payment, interest ought not to be allowed, as the damages for delay are included in the amount due.[1]

Demand for principal includes interest. When interest is a legal consequence of a debt, even without such a stipulation in the contract, a demand for the principal is a demand for both principal and interest, that is, the interest is included in the demand.[2]

I. RELATING TO PERSONS.

The law of interest allowed as damages generally applies alike to all individuals, and to those corporations that are regarded as persons. But there are exceptions arising out of a person's office or position, and the law declares that persons having such relations shall be regarded differently from the common individual. These exceptional persons are those holding property in their hands, and acting as trustees, or in a public office. The rules of law in regard to them vary to some extent, but there are certain principles which run through them all. The first class of such persons, alphabetically, is that of

(*a*) *Administrators.* Good faith and diligence on the part of administrators of the estates of deceased persons are indispensable. They must so conduct themselves as not to subject the estate to unnecessary expense, charge, or loss;[3] and when an administrator manifestly intends to

[1] 4 Bro. P. C. (Eng.) 539 (1723).

[2] 8 Mart., N. S. (La.) 608 (1830).

[3] 60 Ga. 316 (1878); 10 Vt. 192 (1838).

do his duty fairly he will not be held liable for interest on slight grounds.[1]

Collection of assets. Upon receiving their appointment, they must proceed to collect the debts due to the estate. Even if the money be well invested and drawing interest, they will not, for that reason, be charged with interest, which may have been thus lost.[2] Neither, says the court in California, will they be liable to pay interest lost, if they take from a bank money that is drawing interest, when they had money with which to pay debts.[3] So, where a sale is made on credit, bearing interest, under an order of court, it is not improper for the administrator to receive the money after the sale was made, and before the money became due, thus stopping the interest.[4]

Payment of debts. Administrators must pay debts, especially those bearing interest, as soon as possible. If the sums received by them are large, and they cannot be immediately applied to extinguishing claims against the estate, they should be deposited where they can be readily available and productive, if that can be done with safety, or without subjecting the administrators to hazard. But if the sums received are small and the debts against the estate are large, it may not be feasible to apply the sums in payment of the debts, and if they are not so applied the administrators are not chargeable with interest thereon.[5] If the court orders an administrator to pay a certain claim, it bears interest from and after that time, whether it did before or not.[6]

[1] 4 Gill & J. (Md.) 453 (1832); 2 Dev. & Bat. Eq. (N. C.) 400 (1839); 101 N. C. 461 (1888).

[2] 41 N. H. 355 (1860).

[3] 44 Cal. 584 (1872).

[4] 4 Gill & J. (Md.) 453 (1832).

[5] 78 Ala. 73 (1884); 10 Vt. 192 (1838).

[6] 70 Cal. 184 (1886); 74 Cal. 567 (1888).

In case an administrator pays a debt of the estate in full, believing that the estate is solvent, after a decree of insolvency, he can recover interest on the amount overpaid only from and after demand.[1]

As soon as an administrator is in funds to a sufficient amount debts due to him must be considered as paid, they being allowed to carry interest no longer.[2]

Administrators are liable for interest on all illegal disbursements,[3] even if they are made to themselves.[4]

Investment of assets. Administrators must not keep the money that they have in their hands and which they have collected unemployed for an unreasonable length of time.[5] They must pay debts with it, or put it at interest.[6] The rule is that they are not chargeable with interest on the fund in their hands unless they have retained it more than a year from their appointment, from which time interest begins to run.[7]

Administrators are dealt with much more leniently than executors and trustees, as the former handle the funds simply for the winding up of the estate, while executors

[1] 3 Pick. (Mass.) 261 (1825).

[2] 2 Hill (S. C.) 340 (1834).

[3] 6 Geo. (35 Miss.) 321 (1858); 2 Hill (S. C.) 468 (1834).

[4] 5 Cush. (Miss.) 767 (1854).

[5] 22 Ala. 478 (1853); 50 Ark. 217 (1887) (in this case the administrator retained the assets between one and two years); 32 Cal. 424 (1869); 42 Cal. 288 (1871); 11 Gill & J. (Md.) 185 (1840); 10 Md. 352 (1856); 25 Mich. 428 (1872); 41 N. H. 355 (1860); 1 Ashm. (Pa.) 305 (1822); 4 Desau. (S. C.) 65 (1809), 463 (1814), 555 (1815); 61 Vt. 254 (1888). In the last cited case the length of time was several years. *Contra*, Lit. Sel. Cas. 475 (1821).

[6] 31 Ala. 227 (1858); 66 Ala. 35 (1880); 76 Ala. 509 (1884); 4 Heath (Me.) 15 (1854); 44 Miss. 170 (1870); 41 N. H. 355 (1860); 1 Johns. Ch. (N. Y.) 620 (1815).

[7] 30 Ga. 463 (1860); 4 Gill & J. (Md.) 453 (1832) (in which thirteen months were allowed); 40 Miss. 256 (1866); 6 S. C. 83 (1874); 11 S. C. 139 (1878).

and trustees, as a general rule, hold the property for the purpose of obtaining an income, something more than the mere closing up of the affairs of the deceased.

If an administrator has wantonly kept funds idle, he is chargeable with interest;[1] but a mere neglect to invest money which he may be called upon to pay over to the distributee at any moment, is no ground for charging him with interest, if the money is kept ready to be paid over when called for.[2]

Where an administrator is ordered by the court to let out the money, but refrains from doing so because he deems it unsafe on account of the unsettled condition of the country, he is chargeable with interest on the money after six months from the time he received it.[3] If he retains money under the sanction of the court and parties interested to meet some future contingences he will not be liable for interest.[4] So, when he cannot find the heirs, and the court refuses him the right to invest it.[5]

Administrators should not be charged with interest if the amount of money on hand is reasonable.[6]

If they act reasonably in making a loan, but fail in collecting the interest, they are not responsible for it, unless they could have collected it.[7]

They must not speculate with the funds;[8] and if, through their negligence, a note is lost, they are liable for interest at the rate named in the note.[9]

[1] 2 Dev. & Bat. Eq. (N. C.) 400 (1839)

[2] 11 Paige (N. Y.) 142 (1844).

[3] 66 Ala. 35 (1880).

[4] 3 Gill & J. (Md.) 20 (1830).

[5] 26 Md. 495 (1866).

[6] 98 Mo. 262 (1889). In the case cited 61 Vt. 254 (1888), the amount retained for several years was seven hundred dollars. It was decided to be unreasonable.

[7] 72 Cal. 335 (1887).

[8] 40 Miss. 256 (1866).

[9] 6 Geo. (Miss.) 321 (1858); 44 Miss. 170 (1870).

Pending proper litigation, administrators are not liable to pay interest on the fund when they have made none.[1] But, if they set up a claim to the funds in their hands, they are liable for interest pending litigation, if the case is decided against them.[2]

They are not liable for interest on funds due to distributees residing in a country which is at war with the country of the administrators.[3]

Profits. Administrators must account for all interest that they receive, be the rate what it may,[5] even though they realize it from a misappropriation of the funds of the estate.[6] So, if they speculate with the funds, and are successful.[7]

Mingling funds. If administrators mingle the funds of the estate with their own money, they are liable for interest,[8] besides forfeiting all pay for services in caring for it.[9]

Misapplication of funds. If administrators misapply the funds, they will be liable for interest thereon.[10]

Private use of funds. Administrators must not use the money of the estate in their own business;[11] if they do, the heirs or creditors can elect to take the profits they have made or legal interest.[12]

Compound interest. If administrators are very culpa-

[1] 44 Ga. 652 (1872).
[2] Rich. Eq. Cas. (S. C.) 452 (1831).
[3] 78 Va. 12 (1883), 665 (1884).
[4] 30 Ga. 463 (1860); 4 Blf. (Ind.) 115 (1835); Dud. (S. C.) 48 (1837).
[5] 2 Geo. (Miss.) 578 (1856).
[6] 73 Mo. 569 (1881).
[7] 6 Geo. (Miss.) 321 (1858); 44 Miss. 170 (1870).
[8] 10 Ala. 900 (1846); 73 Cal. 515 (1887).
[9] 42 Miss. 221 (1868); 56 Vt. 261 (1883).
[10] 93 N. C. 488 (1885).
[11] 31 Ala. 227 (1858); 10 Md. 352 (1856); 6 Geo. (Miss.) 321 (1858); 44 Miss. 170 (1870); 41 N. H. 355 (1860); 101 N. C. 461 (1888).
[12] 39 Cal. 597 (1870).

ble,[1] or use the funds of the estate in their private business, and refuse to give an account they must pay compound interest;[2] but if they simply mingle the money with their own they are only chargeable with simple interest.[3]

Accounts. The probate court should exercise equitable control over interest in administrators' accounts.[4] An account stated by one administrator is binding upon all, and the balance will bear interest from the time it is signed.[5] If the court has once settled the question of interest on the items of an account it will not be reopened; otherwise, it will be.[6] An administrator is only liable for interest on the balance of principal in his hands up to the date of the decree at the close of the administration account;[7] but after the settlement of the account the balance which may include interest carries interest on the whole from the time of settlement.[8] If interest is charged on the debits in an account, the credits should be allowed interest.[9] *Rests.* An administrator's accounts should be reckoned with annual rests;[10] and if he retains the balance unnecessarily interest should be allowed thereon.[11] In Georgia, it has been held that if the administrator has been grossly negligent in not making returns of the condition of the estate in his hands, interest should be compounded against him every six years on balances in his hands.[12]

Interest on distributive shares. After an administrator

[1] 11 Ill. 1 (1852); 87 Tenn. 172 (1889).
[2] 1 Johns. Ch. (N. Y.) 620 (1815).
[3] 10 Ala. 900 (1846); 73 Cal. 515 (1887).
[4] 98 Mo. 262 (1889).
[5] 1 Hayw. (N. C.) 101 (1794).
[6] 6 Pick. (Mass.) 422 (1828).
[7] 31 S. C. 463 (1889); 4 Grat. (Va.) 293 (1848)
[8] 70 Pa. St. 183 (1871).
[9] 87 Tenn. 172 (1889).
[10] 17 Fla. 820 (1880); 19 Fla. 300, 373 (1882).
[11] 52 Iowa 665 (1879); 8 S. & M. (Miss.) 682 (1847).
[12] 6 Ga. 265 (1849); 8 Ga. 417 (1850).

has completed the settlement of the estate, it is his duty to turn over to the heirs or the court the balance of the personal estate, after paying debts and charges of administration, within a reasonable time;[1] and if he does not do so the court in Connecticut holds that he will be chargeable with interest from the time of the settlement,[2] or order of distribution,[3] although he has kept the funds on deposit, unemployed.[4] The general rule is that he will not be charged with interest if he has not received it, until a demand is made, and payment refused;[5] but when a definite sum is ordered to be paid to a distributee on settlement of the estate, no demand is necessary to make it bear interest.[6] If an heir is absent, a reasonable time will be given in which to find him; and in one case[7] six months from the confirmation of the administrator's account was allowed.

Interest on advances. The general rule is that administrators cannot recover interest on money of their own that they have paid out for the benefit of the estate, because it is in their power to put themselves in possession of cash from the funds, and the law does not expect them to advance money out of their own pocket for the benefit of the

[1] 31 Pa. St. 44 (1857).

[2] 15 Conn. 115 (1842). In this case, there had been no demand made by the heirs, they being at the time of the settlement, and long afterward, minors, having no guardian.

[3] 67 Cal. 279 (1885).

[4] 75 Ala. 162 (1883); 76 Ala. 535 (1884); 78 Ala. 73 (1884). In 1853, the Alabama court decided that an administrator was not properly chargeable with interest on money in his hands if he showed that he had not used it; but peculiar circumstances caused a different application of the rule, probably. 22 Ala. 478 (1853).

[5] 2 Lit. (Ky.) 346 (1822); 5 Mon. (Ky.) 578 (1827); 2 J. J. Mar. (Ky.) 201 (1829); 11 Paige (N. Y.) 441 (1845). A distributee, residing with the administrator, having been unreasonably tardy in the assertion of her right in the estate, interest was not allowed during the time she resided with the administrator. 5 Rich. Eq. (S. C.) 31 (1852).

[6] 87 N. C. 196 (1882).

[7] 24 Pa. St. 498 (1855).

estate.[1] If interest were allowed in such cases freely, administrators would be tempted to use a great deal of their private funds in this way. But in cases of emergency, when the estate is materially benefited by it, they can recover interest on such advances,[2] providing they act reasonably in converting the estate into money.[3] So, administrators have no right to borrow money of other persons for the use of the estate; and if they do they will not generally be allowed interest paid on it in their accounts.[4]

Estates of deceased administrators. An administrator of a deceased administrator is not bound to make interest on the funds of the original estate in the hands of the first administrator at the time of his death; or for the time that the second estate is unrepresented.[5] But if the second administrator uses the funds of the first estate, or is guilty of wilful neglect, he must pay compound interest.[6] This rule also applies to administrators *de bonis non.*[7]

(*b*) *Agents, attorneys and factors.* Agents are not responsible to their principals if they follow their instructions;[8] neither are they generally liable to pay interest on funds in their hands if they have conducted themselves in a reasonable manner and with due diligence;[9] and the same rule applies to attorneys.[10]

[1] 9 Mass. 37 (1812).

[2] 31 Ala. 227 (1858); 60 Ala. 557 (1877); 11 N. J. L. (6 Halst.) 44 (1829).

[3] 8 Vt. 365 (1836).

[4] 5 Nev. 189 (1869).

[5] 2 Hill (S. C.) 560, and notes (1835).

[6] 10 Ala. 900 (1846).

[7] 6 S. C. 83 (1874).

[8] 5 Johns. Ch. (N. Y.) 534 (1821).

[9] 1 Met. (Mass.) 112 (1840); 6 Johns. Ch. (N. Y.) 353 (1822); 4 Dall. (Pa.) 286 (1803); *contra*, 44 Ala. 627 (1870), unless some contract or usage releases them from paying interest.

[10] 12 Ga. 564 (1853); 26 Vt. 544 (1854). 2 Leigh (Va.) 650 (1831) decides that attorneys are not bound to pay interest on debts lost through their negligence.

Courts early held that after a reasonable time an agent was liable to pay interest on the money received for his principal.[1] So, with an attorney in later times in Georgia and Illinois.[2] The Massachusetts court decided many years ago that, if agents unnecessarily neglect to inform their principals of the receipt of money, they are liable for interest from the time when they should have communicated such information.[3] The general rule, however, seems to be that a demand is necessary to make an agent liable for interest on money received for his principal, in the transaction of the business of the principal,[4] unless the agent has received special instructions to remit the money as fast as it is collected,[5] or is in default in neglecting to render his account.[6] The same rule applies to attorneys.[7] An agent is also bound to make a reasonable, speedy and prudent investment of funds sent to him by his principal for that purpose, and if he does not do so he will be chargeable with interest.[8] So, if an agent fraudulently converts to his own use money he has collected he must pay interest from the time of such wrongful conversion;[9] or, if he has converted that which has been given to him to invest forthwith, he is liable for interest from its receipt, without

[1] Quincy (Mass.) 5 (1762); 3 Desau. (S. C.) 497 (1812); 4 Desau. (S. C.) 110 (1810); 5 Call (Va.) 118 (1804).

[2] 34 Ga. 173 (1865); 77 Ill. 337 (1875).

[3] 9 Pick. (Mass.) 368 (1830).

[4] 31 Ind. 156 (1869); 31 Iowa 49 (1870); 1 Met. (Mass.) 112 (1840); 4 Jones Law (N. C.) 155 (1856); 98 N. C. 550 (1887); Bail. Eq. (S. C.) 226 (1831). The court in Louisiana holds that interest runs from a judicial demand only, unless the agent employed the funds in his own business, or there has been a real prior default. 15 La. Ann. 17 (1860).

[5] 2 Kelley (Ga.) 370 (1847).

[6] 8 Ves. (Eng.) 48 (1802); 66 Ala. 424 (1880); 26 Vt. 544 (1854).

[7] 26 Vt. 544 (1854).

[8] 40 Conn. 464 (1873); 1 Dev. Eq. (N. C.) 520 (1830).

[9] 77 Ill. 337 (1875); 31 Ind. 156 (1869).

a demand.[1] Agents are also chargeable with legal interest if they use the funds in their own business.[2] This rule also applies to attorneys.[3]

Mixing funds. Mixing the principal's money with the agent's private funds does not make him liable to pay interest, unless he uses it.[4]

Liability for sub-attorney. An attorney is bound to pay interest on a sum collected, if he sends the claim for collection to another attorney, without orders, and the second attorney embezzles it.[5]

Special damages. If, on account of an undue detention of his money by an agent, a principal is obliged to borrow money at a greater than the legal rate of interest, the agent is not liable to pay more than the legal rate, unless the bill seeks to recover the profits he has made, if any, and he has made more than the legal rate. In case the profits exceed the legal rate, the full amount of the profits can be collected.[6]

Profits. All the interest which an agent receives on the money of his principal must be accounted for,—it belongs to the principal, and not to him. He must make no profit beyond compensation for his services.[7]

The law presumes that an agent has collected the interest on interest-bearing securities in his possession, and he must prove that he has not received it, else he will be charged with it.[8]

[1] 9 Gray (Mass.) 66 (1857).

[2] 104 Ind. 562 (1885); 6 Johns. Ch. (N. Y.) 353 (1822).

[3] 26 Iowa 482 (1868); 6 Johns. Ch. (N. Y.) 353 (1822).

[4] 39 L. J., N. S., Eq. (Eng.) 369 (1870); 60 Vt. 410 (1888).

[5] 24 Kas. 600 (1880).

[6] 137 Mass. 487 (1884). In this case the agent was the treasurer of a corporation.

[7] 24 Conn. 267 (1855); 1 Dev. Eq. (N. C.) 520 (1830); *contra*, 8 Ves. (Eng.) 48 (1802).

[8] 60 Vt. 410 (1888).

Practice. When a discharged agent has retained money of his principal, and notified him of it, the question of recovery of interest, says the Illinois court, is for the jury under proper instructions, and it is error for the court to compute interest and direct the jury to allow it.[1]

Accounting. If an agent has stipulated to account to his principal semi-annually, he is liable to pay interest on all sums of money received and not accounted for at the stipulated times.[2] Annual rests are also allowable, but not after the relation of principal and agent has ceased.[3] Compound interest is allowed only when agents use the money in their business.[4]

The balance of a factor's account, struck after termination of dealings with his principal, does not bear interest until demand, in the courts of South Carolina.[5] The courts of Louisiana, however, hold that a balance struck and account rendered by a factor to his principal, and acquiesced in by him, draws interest from that time, though it may contain interest,[6] but otherwise if it is not acquiesced in.[7]

An attorney is not chargeable with interest on so much of the money in his hands as he is entitled to receive for his services and disbursements.[8]

Interest should be charged only on the balance.[9] If, however, the agent is charged interest on the receipts, he must be credited with interest on his commissions[10] and disburse-

[1] 60 Ill. 149 (1871).
[2] Dud. Eq. (S. C.) 85 (1837).
[3] 9 Jur., N. S. (Eng.) 267 (1863); 32 L. J., Ch. (Eng.) 540 (1863); 11 W. R. (Eng.) 411; 32 Beav. (Eng.) 86 (1863).
[4] 39 L. J., N. S., Eq. (Eng.) 369 (1870).
[5] Harp. (S. C.) 274 (1824); 1 Hill (S. C.) 400 (1833).
[6] 4 La. Ann. 160 (1849); 29 La. Ann. 679 (1877).
[7] 11 La. Ann. 217 (1857).
[8] 9 Conn. 15 (1831).
[9] 3 Hun (N. Y.) 283 (1874).
[10] 95 N. C. 358 (1886); 47 Pa. St. 485 (1864).

ments.[1] Interest is allowed on attorneys' claims for services and costs when they are liquidated.[2] But the costs are not liquidated by being taxed and included in the judgment.[3]

Interest is also allowable as damages for the non-payment of commissions when earned;[4] which in case of a real estate agent is the time the contract is made between the vendor and vendee.[5]

Advances. An agent can collect interest on advances and disbursements made for the principal,[6] and on money advanced to the principal at his request,[7] from the time the money was advanced.[8] So, on advances made by attorneys.[9] If a certain rate of interest is stipulated to be paid for advancements that rate must govern until the advance is paid.[10] Interest and commissions cannot both be charged for money advanced.[11]

Liens. An agent, entitled to retain property for his indemnity, although he disposes of it without authority, is not chargeable with interest on the avails of that property, during the continuance of his lien,[12] because he could not be compelled to pay it to the principal while the lien existed.

(*c*) *Assignees of bankrupts and insolvents.* Such assignees are allowed a reasonable time in which to settle the es-

[1] 36 N. Y. 255 (1867).

[2] 3 Hun (N. Y.) 218 (1874); 6 Hun (N. Y.) 475 (1876).

[3] 23 How. Pr. (N. Y.) 45 (1861).

[4] 38 Mich. 172 (1878).

[5] 8 Vr. (N. J.) 437 (1874).

[6] 3 Campb. (Eng.) 467 (1813); 1 Dana (Ky.) 309 (1833); 8 Rich. (S. C.) 287 (1855).

[7] 2 Beav. (Eng.) 359 (1840); 1 Bail. (S. C.) 620 (1830).

[8] 19 Tex. 216 (1857).

[9] 19 Ark. 487 (1858).

[10] 20 Tex. 772 (1858).

[11] 1 Hill (S. C.) 400 (1833); Riley (S. C.) 215 (1837).

[12] 3 Conn. 171 (1819).

tate.[1] After that time they are liable to pay interest on the money in their hands, if they have made, or, under certain circumstances, might have made it productive.[2] They are not bound to invest the funds under ordinary circumstances,[3] as their business is to settle the estate immediately.

The assignee's own note, when included in the assignment, should be reckoned as cash received at the time it falls due.[4]

Assignees are liable to pay interest if they mix the funds with their own, by depositing them in a bank in their own names, or otherwise.[5] This is true notwithstanding they are always ready to pay creditors.[6] This rule also refers to an assignment for the benefit of creditors.[7]

If an assignee mixes the funds with his own, neglects to settle his accounts, and when called into equity, fails to account satisfactorily, or show what he did with the funds, he is chargeable with interest with annual rests.[8]

After the collection of assets and proof of debts, they are chargeable with interest from the time when, by the exercise of diligence, they could have secured an order declaring a dividend.[9]

Advances. Assignees may be allowed interest on payments necessarily made before any funds come to their hands.[10]

[1] The court in Alabama allowed twelve months in 25 Ala. 363 (1854).

[2] 25 Ala. 363 (1854); 2 W. & S. (Pa.) 557 (1841); 3 S. C. 11 (1871).

[3] 68 Pa. St. 454 (1871); *contra*, 24 Pa. St. 487 (1855), which says that assignees must invest funds which they cannot apply.

[4] 25 Ala. 363 (1854).

[5] 32 Barb. (N. Y.) 587 (1860); 68 Pa. St. 454 (1871).

[6] 32 Barb. (N. Y.) 587 (1860).

[7] 32 Barb. (N. Y.) 587 (1860).

[8] 124 Ill. 391 (1888).

[9] 129 Ill. 1 (1889).

[10] Sax. (N. J.) 571 (1832).

(*d*) *Banks.* National banks in the United States are controlled by the United States laws.[1] Other banks are governed by the laws of the states by which they are incorporated.[2] Statutes vary their liability to some extent, but otherwise the rules of law regarding interest on their engagements are the same as those governing individuals.[3]

A clause in the charter of a bank limiting interest on discounts, does not apply after the breach of a contract.[4]

A banker is not liable at common law to pay interest upon money deposited,[5] although at the time of the deposit it was declared by the parties that interest should not be payable upon a certain event which did not happen.[6] But where deposits bear interest, after an acquiescence in accounts annually furnished by bankers, an agreement that the balance of principal and interest shall bear interest is presumed.[7]

(*e*) *Solvent estates.* The general rule is that where claims bear no contractual interest, no interest should be allowed on them before the date of the decease of the debtor, because the laches was the voluntary act of the plaintiff until the decease of the debtor when the creditor became necessarily subject to the delay ordinarily attending the settlement of estates. Hence, interest should be allowed on all claims after death, if the estate is solvent.[8] But interest is not allowed even then if the creditor delays the administration.[9] If the debt is unliquidated, the New York

[1] 44 Ind. 298 (1873); 52 Iowa 114 (1879).

[2] 49 Tenn. 173 (1872).

[3] 24 Conn. 147 (1855); 63 Tenn. 499 (1872).

[4] 9 Wend. (N. Y.) 471 (1833).

[5] 5 W. Va. 50 (1871). See 65 Hun (N. Y.) 342 (1892).

[6] 5 B. & Ad. (Eng.) 282 (1833); 2 N. & M. (Eng.) 120 (1833).

[7] 1 Ball & B. (Ire.) 428 (1810).

[8] 4 Met. (Mass.) 317 (1842); 11 Vt. 214 (1839).

[9] 41 Mich. 657 (1879).

court holds that it carries interest from judgment only.[1] In Texas, the approval of a claim by an administrator is deemed to be a sort of judgment, and the debt bears interest from that time.[2]

When the deceased had in his hands certain money for investment which belonged to his wife, and which he had mingled with his own, the estate should pay compound interest upon it.[3]

In England, if a testator devises his land for the payment of his debts, it is like a mortgage given to secure them, and will make simple contract debts carry interest as the land yields annual profits;[4] otherwise, however, if it is a general charge to pay debts, so far as it concerns simple contracts.[5]

(*f*) *Executors.* Executors are regarded as temporary custodians of the assets of the estate, holding them for distribution and not for investment.[6] They will not be charged with interest personally if they have acted reasonably, and have not made private use of the funds.[7] If they use the money in their private business, they must pay compound interest thereon,[8] as this is necessary in order to reach the profits which they ought to refund. If they simply allow the funds to be idle an unreasonable length of time, they will be charged with simple interest.[9]

[1] 19 Hun (N. Y.) 595 (1880).

[2] 9 Tex. 517 (1853).

[3] 104 N. Y. 618 (1887).

[4] 2 P. Wm. (Eng.) 26 (1722).

[5] Vern. & Scriv. (Ire.) 528 (1788).

[6] 40 Conn. 464 (1873).

[7] 13 Mass. 232 (1816).

[8] 10 Md. 352 (1856); 1 Johns. Ch. (N. Y.) 508, 527, 620 (1815); 5 Johns. Ch. (N. Y.) 441 (1821); 1 Dev. Eq. (N. C.) 373 (1830); 1 Binn. (Pa.) 194 (1806); 84 Pa. St. 51 (1877).

[9] 1 Johns. Ch. (N. Y.) 508, 620 (1815); 5 Johns. Ch. (N. Y.) 441 (1821); 2 Dev. & Bat. Eq. (N. C.) 155 (1838); 1 Binn. (Pa.) 194 (1806); 4 Desau. (S. C.) 65 (1809), 369 (1813) (for several years), 555 (1815); Harp. Eq. (S. C.) 224 (1824); 1 Munf. (Va.) 183 (1810); *contra*, 6 Jones Eq. (N. C.) 280 (1862); 101 N. C. 461 (1888); 1 Desau. (S. C.) 191 (1791).

If the sum they retain is reasonable in amount and they keep it on hand to pay debts with, or for a general settlement even, they will not be liable to pay interest thereon.[1]

They should deposit the money in a bank if one is convenient, and they are compelled to retain it for a considerable length of time, whether under order of court or not;[2] otherwise they may be liable to pay interest on it on the ground of keeping it an unreasonable length of time, even though they have received no income or benefit from it for themselves.[3]

If they mingle the funds with their own, or with those of a firm with which they are connected, it is presumed that the money is used in their own business, or in that of the firm, and that they received profit therefrom, and they will be charged with interest, although it is shown that they have received no benefit from it, because they might have invested the money and obtained interest thereon.[4] In such cases they will be charged simple interest only, though a court of equity may change the rate to a less per cent, as justice requires.[5] And, if they mingle and loan the funds with their own, in good faith, disclosing all the profits, and without fault or want of prudence, suffer some losses, but claim no deduction therefor, and nothing for their services, when such interest exceeds what they actually received on the funds, and the money has not been

[1] 2 Dev. Eq. (N. C.) 535 (1834).

[2] 21 Md. 432 (1863).

[3] 10 Md. 352 (1856); 21 Md. 432 (1863); 24 Pa. St. 180 (1854): 61 Vt. 254 (1888). In the latter case the executor kept the funds, amounting to seven hundred dollars, idle for several years, though he might have easily deposited them in a bank that was near, at four per cent interest. He was charged with that amount of interest therefore on equitable grounds.

[4] 52 Cal. 403 (1877): 66 Cal. 180 (1881): 83 Cal. 423 (1890).

[5] 24 Pa. St. 180 (1854): 61 Vt. 251 (1888).

used in business, trade or speculation, they will be charged only with simple interest.[1]

Investments. It was once doubted if executors were chargeable with interest, when the property was not directed by the testator to be put to interest, but it is now settled that they are.[2] As when a testator in his will directed that a certain sum of money should be taken from his estate and be retained in the hands of his executor for the purpose of paying certain annuities and legacies, to be kept at interest so long as such annuities and legacies should become payable, the executor was chargeable with interest on the fund, being credited with the amount paid on such annuities and legacies, and a compensation for his services.[3] When an executor was authorized by will to sell real estate, and invest the proceeds, he kept the money, failed to invest, and was held to pay interest with annual rests, compounded.[4] So where a will provided that the interest of a fund should be collected from time to time and invested, the court presumed that the executor did so, and held him responsible for interest.[5] And, although executors are not expected to pay so much attention to investments as trustees, yet they must not keep the funds unemployed for a great length of time. Six months has been held to be a reasonable time in which to make investments,[6] although the length of time will vary under different circumstances.

[1] 59 Vt. 348 (1887); also, 3 B. Mon. (Ky.) 645 (1843), where an executor, who used the funds of the estate to carry on a large manufacturing business of the testator, was required to pay interest on the funds so employed.

[2] 12 Conn. 350 (1837).

[3] 12 Conn. 350 (1837).

[4] 71 Ill. 72 (1873).

[5] 5 Dana (Ky.) 70 (1837).

[6] 2 Wend. (N. Y.) 77 (1828).

If executors mix trust funds with their own, or neglect to keep account of the investments and receipts of interest, they are chargeable with interest, as though they had kept the fund invested upon interest payable periodically,[1] under the New York practice.

Parol evidence is admissible against executors to rebut an equity arising out of their obligation to invest funds so as to make interest.[2]

If executors neglect to obtain an order to invest in bank stocks, they are not exempt from paying interest on the ground of laches in the beneficiary in not demanding payment.[3]

Where an executor is liable to be called upon at any time to pay a legacy, and there are no directions to put it at interest, he is not chargeable with interest, unless he has used the money in his business, or loaned it, or mingled it with his own.[4]

Where executors, instead of investing money for the benefit of the testator's widow for her life, as directed by the will, retain a debt due to the estate from themselves for the purchase price of land, and pay the interest, they are not accountable to the estate for interest on such debt.[5]

If they allow property to be taken and sold on execution, they will be responsible for interest from the date of the writ in the suit or proceeding in which it is sought to be recovered.[6]

Compound interest. An executor will not be charged with compound interest on the final settlement of his

[1] 2 Wend. (N. Y.) 77 (1828); 2 Barb. Ch. (N. Y.) 211 (1847).
[2] 2 Hill Ch. (S. C.) 146 (1835).
[3] 9 Rich. Eq. (S. C.) 279 (1857).
[4] 4 Harr. (N. J.) 108 (1842).
[5] 24 Atl. Rep. (Pa.) 621 (1892).
[6] 5 Pick. (Mass.) 65 (1827).

account in equity, unless it is clearly shown[1] that he has been guilty of such gross neglect that it would be evidence of a corrupt intention.[2] If an executor refuses to render an account of the use which he has made of the money in his hands, but claims it as his own, he is chargeable with compound interest, with annual rests, from the time when he ought to have settled his account.[3] Compound interest will also be allowed in a decree for an accounting, by way of damages, for persistently and wrongfully refusing to account.[4]

An executor has no power to bind the estate to pay compound interest, except when the principal sum originally due, with simple interest, is charged to the estate.[5]

Profits. Executors are not allowed to make any profit from the estate for themselves, or to become personally benefited thereby.[6] If they have made interest from the estate, they must pay it over to the parties entitled to receive it upon final settlement;[7] and so they may be obliged to pay more than compound interest, even.[8] If the interest received is usurious, will they be obliged to pay it over, when no action has been brought by the party who had paid it to recover it under a statute of usury? However that may be, they are personally liable to the statutory forfeiture, or other penalty, for receiving the usurious interest, though they, at the time of its receipt, supposed it to be legal interest.[9]

[1] 45 Barb. (N. Y.) 182 (1865).
[2] 38 Ala. 695 (1863).
[3] 10 Pick. (Mass.) 77 (1830).
[4] 40 Mich. 457 (1879).
[5] 85 Va. 76 (1888).
[6] 1 Pick. (Mass.) 530 (1823).
[7] 1 Vern. (Eng.) 197 (1683); 5 J. J. Mar. (Ky.) 35 (1835).
[8] 71 Pa. St. 106 (1872).
[9] 7 Allen (Mass.) 59 (1863).

Interest received on the amount of legacies goes into the general assets of the estate.[1]

Rate. Executors are always chargeable with at least the rate of interest that they have made.[2] If they have made less than the legal rate, when with due diligence they might have made at least that,[3] they will be liable to pay the legal rate.[4] So if the executors are silent as to what were the proceeds on the sale of a certain bond, the court will charge them with the highest market value of the bond, and the legal rate of interest.[5]

Liability of executors' executors. Upon the balance due at the time of an executor's death, interest will not be charged until some one is authorized to receive it.[6]

Accounting. There is no general rule charging executors with interest in accounting,[7] except that they are chargeable on annual balances,[8] that is, on such part of them as are necessarily kept in their hands for the purposes of the estate,[9] as to meet demands that will fall due within the current year, or if the amount of the balance is small.[10] They may be allowed interest on balances in their favor.[11]

Where an executor's account consists of many small items, commissioners are allowed to ascertain the amount for the year and reckon interest from the middle of the year on the whole of it.[12]

[1] 3 Harr. (N. J.) 59 (1840).
[2] 1 Pick. (Mass.) 530 (1823).
[3] 12 Conn. 350 (1837); 7 S. & R. (Pa.) 264 (1821).
[4] 24 Pa. St. 180 (1854).
[5] 53 Vt. 660 (1881).
[6] 9 Rich. Eq. (S. C.) 71 (1856).
[7] 1 Wash. (Va.) 246 (1793).
[8] 3 Desau. (S. C.) 241 (1811).
[9] 24 Pa. St. 335 (1855); 3 Desau. (S. C.) 241 (1811); Riley (S. C.) 38 (1837).
[10] 6 Leigh (Va.) 271 (1835).
[11] 3 Desau. (S. C.) 241 (1811); 2 Call (Va.) 102 (1799).
[12] 2 Dev. & Bat. Eq. (N. C.) 155 (1838).

If executors are not charged with interest the account may be surcharged;[1] and they may be charged with interest in the decree on the final account, though they had had a previous account confirmed in which they were charged with the principal without interest.[2] Executors are not charged with interest before decree, if the failure to account was the fault of the legatees, that is, the legatees can reap no benefit thereby.[3]

Executors are chargeable with interest on the balance of a former account settled by them in the court, although it was in part made up of interest on the balance of a still earlier account then settled.[4]

Executors are chargeable with interest on the sums ascertained to be in their hands, during the pendency of exceptions to their accounts.[5] After the final accounting, interest on the balance in their hands is allowed during the pendency of their appeal from an order disallowing their alleged credits for money paid on illegal claims.[6]

Rests in accounts against executors are not allowed except in particular cases.[7] If they greatly delay in accounting they will be charged with interest with annual rests.[8] There is no certain rule as to rests;[9] but they are generally allowed annually.[10]

Interest on distributive shares. When the time arrives for the executors to make a final settlement of the estate

[1] 3 Leigh (Va.) 348 (1831).

[2] 22 Pa. St. 445 (1854).

[3] 1 Munf. (Va.) 150 (1810).

[4] 10 Pa. St. 408 (1849); *contra*, 2 Hill Ch. (S. C.) 492 (1836); 1 Wash. (Va.) 246 (1793).

[5] 13 Pa. St. 575 (1850).

[6] 76 Mich. 318 (1889).

[7] 2 McC. Ch. (S. C.) 1, 185 (1827)

[8] 74 Cal. 199 (1887).

[9] 7 B. Mon. (Ky.) 176 (1846).

[10] 74 Cal. 199 (1887); 20 Fla. 262, 292 (1883).

they must do so; and if they pay within a reasonable time thereafter they will not be compelled to pay interest;[1] otherwise, they will be charged from the time when they should have paid it.[2] But if the settlement is delayed without negligence on their part they will not be liable for interest, unless they have used the funds or made profit from them.[3] If executors are ordered by the court to pay a share, they will be chargeable with the interest they have received on it from the time of the order.[4]

A residuary legatee is not chargeable with interest on notes given by executors for funds of the estate, after final settlement where they constitute part of the assets.[5] But such legatees are charged with interest on legacies though they are not demanded for many years.[6]

Executors are bound to inform a guardian of the exact sum due, and to pay it over without deduction or delay, and where they delay payment for several years, without just cause, they must pay interest.[7] But they must have notice that a guardian has been appointed.[8]

Executors' own debts. Executors have no right, on taking out letters testamentary, to make a rest in the computation of a debt due them from the estate, so as to charge interest on interest. But they may charge interest on interest that they would have received, but for the wrongful issuing of an injunction.[9]

Legacies. After a legacy becomes due, mere readiness

[1] 31 Pa. St. 44 (1857).
[2] 140 Mass. 351 (1885).
[3] 11 Pick. (Mass.) 371 (1831).
[4] 26 Iowa 525 (1868).
[5] 14 Ore. 171 (1886).
[6] 1 Grat. (Va.) 292 (1844).
[7] 1 Paige (N. Y.) 479 (1829); 28 Pa. St. 376 (1857).
[8] 3 Munf. (Va.) 198 (1812).
[9] 9 Paige (N. Y.) 461 (1842).

to pay it will not excuse the executor from paying interest upon it.[1] And where an executor determined not to pay the legacies until the estate could be made available without a sacrifice, he was obliged to pay interest on a general legacy to a married woman, although she had no trustee to act for her.[2] But an executor is not liable to pay interest on a legacy due to infant legatees, no time of payment being specified, until guardians are appointed and the executor is notified of such appointment, unless he has received interest on the money or might have received it without hazard.[3]

If an executor pays a legacy after it is barred by the statute of limitations, he must pay interest thereon from the time of the payment (misappropriation) of the money.[4] So, if he pays it to the wrong party;[5] or, pays a debt due, as he supposes, to himself, but which the court afterward disallows.[6] In the latter case, he is chargeable with simple interest while it is in litigation, and after that time with compound interest.[7]

At common law, a refusal by a legatee's husband to accept a legacy stops interest on it.[8]

Advances. A similar rule prevails as to the payment of interest on advances made by executors as on those by administrators. In some cases, executors are allowed interest on advances made by them under particularly necessitous circumstances,[9] as to prevent the foreclosure

[1] 24 Pa. St. 310 (1855).
[2] 13 Ala. 554 (1848).
[3] 9 Vt. 41 (1837).
[4] 71 Ala. 169 (1881).
[5] 19 Conn. 548 (1849).
[6] 49 Conn. 519 (1882).
[7] 49 Conn. 519 (1882).
[8] 4 Call (Va.) 605 (1803).
[9] 9 Virgin (Me.) 411 (1872); 90 Tenn. 359 (1891).

of a mortgage.[1] But, when there are funds of the estate that are subject to the executors' control, the policy of the law is against such allowance of interest,[2] and they are not allowed interest.[3] If such advance is made the executors should, as soon as they can do so, apply the money of the estate to the satisfaction of the claim which they have created against the estate in their own favor. So, on the same grounds, executors have no authority to borrow money for the use of the estate, and will not be allowed interest on it if they do borrow.[4]

Executors may receive compound interest on advances on the principle of rests.[5]

(*g*) *Garnishees, interpleaders, etc.* A garnishee occupies his position compulsorily, and without pay, and he is to be treated very leniently. If the claim is drawing contractual interest, the interest does not stop running when trusteed, it being a part of the debt, running right along during the pendency of the suit, until maturity, and passing to the principal defendant in the action.[6] In the case of interest that could be collected, if at all, as damages, the rule is different. In fact there is a multiplicity of rules that have been adopted by different courts. Some say there is no presumption, and that every case must stand or fall according to the facts, as in Ohio, where the garnishee, during the pendency of the process, is not thereby necessarily exempted from paying interest on the debt, the cause of exemption

[1] 10 Pick. (Mass.) 77 (1830).

[2] 10 Pick. (Mass.) 77 (1830).

[3] 20 Md. 282 (1863).

[4] 5 Nev. 189 (1869); 90 Tenn. 359 (1891), in which case usurious interest paid was not allowed.

[5] 16 Mass. 221 (1819).

[6] 1 Spauld. (Me.) 213 (1880); 56 Vt. 302 (1883). See 3 H. & M'H. (Md.) 124 (1793).

not being presumed, and the garnishee being compelled to show it like any other defence.[1] Most of the courts hold, however, that the money remains *in statu quo* during the pendency of the action, and the trustee is not liable to pay interest for that time,[2] provided that he has not used the money,[3] and there is no fraud, collusion, unreasonable delay, or litigation on the part of the trustee,[4] and that he is ready and willing to pay the amount due whenever required to do so.[5] In Missouri, the trustee must acknowledge his indebtedness and readiness to pay in court, if he would be relieved from the payment of interest.[6] In Alabama, Georgia, Iowa, Kentucky, Maryland and Virginia, he must pay the money into court;[7] and that is the safest thing for a trustee to do everywhere.[8] The court in Illinois holds that he must pay it into court or to the party entitled to it.[9]

So, when a trustee does not offer to bring the money into court, etc., but insists upon his own right to retain it as against both plaintiff and defendant he will be charged interest if it is decided that he has no right or title to it.[10]

[1] 9 O. St. 432 (1859).

[2] 15 W. R. (Eng.) 371; 9 Wheat. (U. S.) 738 (1824); 35 Ala. 143 (1859); 28 Cal. 539 (1865); 8 Pick. (Mass.) 260 (1829); 4 Met. (Mass.) 1 (1842); 5 Allen (Mass.) 356 (1862); 105 Mass. 340 (1870); 129 Mass. 322 (1880); 131 Mass. 294 (1881); 4 Halst. (N. J.) 8 (1827); 43 Pa. St. 488 (1862); 44 Pa. St. 82 (1862); 26 Vt. 119 (1853).

[3] 25 Iowa 336 (1868).

[4] 2 Dall. (Pa.) 215 (1793); 64 Pa. St. 63 (1870); 99 Pa. St. 317 (1882).

[5] 1 Ga. 38 (1846); 1 Spauld. (Me.) 213 (1880); 4 Mass. 170 (1808); 4 Met. (Mass.) 1 (1842); 9 Pa. St. 468 (1848).

[6] 9 Mo. 636 (1845).

[7] 30 Ala. 227 (1857), if he is not restrained from using it; 74 Ga. 4 (1884); 60 Iowa 510 (1883); 1 Dana (Ky.) 338 (1833); 1 Bland (Md.) 333 (1827); 4 Hen. & Munf. (Va.) 259 (1809).

[8] 64 Pa. St. 63 (1870)

[9] 56 Ill. 362 (1870).

[10] 7 Ala. 217 (1844).

Where a debtor promised his creditor that at the debt's maturity he would pay over the money to a trustee to await the result of a garnishee suit, and the debtor did not do so, he was held liable for interest.[1] So where two claimants of money agreed that the holder of it should deposit it in a bank to remain there, subject to a decision of the court. The money was duly deposited, but shortly afterward the holder took it out of the bank; and it was decided that he must pay interest on it.[2]

A party receiving funds deposited in court, to which he is entitled, is not chargeable with interest thereon.[3]

Using the funds. If the trustee uses the money or receives a profit from it during the pendency of the action, he should be charged with interest;[4] and it has been held, in the case of a bank, that there is a presumption that it has been used.[5] He will not be obliged to pay interest if he has simply mingled the funds with his own, provided he is able to pay at any time.[6]

Compound interest. If a garnishee uses the funds as his own, and has not on hand at times as much as he owed the defendant, therefore not being able to pay it at any moment when called upon, the Connecticut court holds that he must pay compound interest.[7]

Dilatory proceedings. If a garnishee simply answers, admitting an indebtedness, and submitting to the jurisdic-

[1] 16 Fla. 510 (1878).

[2] 3 Binn. (Pa.) 121 (1810).

[3] 18 Neb. 508 (1886).

[4] 20 How. (U. S.) 128 (1857); 35 Conn. 97 (1868); 40 Conn. 464 (1873); 1 Ga. 38 (1846); 25 Iowa 336 (1868); 19 S. W. Rep. (Ky.) 185, 841 (1892); 18 Me. 332 (1841); 45 Me. 542 (1858); 1 Spauld. (Me.) 213 (1880); 4 Mass. 170 (1808); 8 Pick. (Mass.) 260 (1829); 4 Met. (Mass.) 1 (1842); 9 Pa. St. 468 (1848); 3 Rand. (Va.) 434 (1825).

[5] 19 S. W. Rep. (Ky.) 841 (1892); 3 Rand. (Va.) 434 (1825).

[6] 40 Conn. 464 (1873); 4 Met. (Mass.) 1 (1842).

[7] 35 Conn. 97 (1868).

tion of the court, he can raise the question of his liability for interest while the debt is suspended by litigation. But when a garnishee interposes a dilatory plea, he cannot raise the question of his liability for interest during the pendency of the action.[1] But, pending a *certiorari* and bill in equity, even though the debtor has mixed the funds with his own and derived some benefit from them, he will not be chargeable with interest.[2]

Abatement of process. If the process is dissolved without the payment of the money to the creditor, the debtor cannot claim interest of the trustee during the time of the pendency of the action, because the debtor and not the trustee is the person who caused the funds to be locked up in the hands of the trustee.[3]

But a void process does not relieve the garnishee from paying interest.[4]

Payment. A trustee under the trustee process must regard his payment under the judgment in the suit as a partial payment made to his creditor and reckon interest accordingly.[5]

Interpleading. The plaintiff in an interpleader suit is not liable to pay interest after payment of the fund into court during the litigation between the defendants.[6] If the interpleading is defective, however, and the interpleader causes the rightful owner to be kept out of his money for some time, he must pay interest.[7]

Injunctions. If a debtor is estopped from paying a debt

[1] 30 Ala. 668 (1857).

[2] 3 Edw. (N. Y.) 512 (1841).

[3] 32 Ga. 20 (1861); 60 Iowa 510 (1883); 26 Vt. 119 (1853).

[4] 61 Ga. 106 (1878).

[5] 30 N. H. 531 (1855).

[6] 4 Cl. & F. (Eng.) 616 (1837); 11 Bli., N. S. (Eng.) 158 (1837); 52 N. W. Rep. (Mich.) 631 (1892); 4 Geo. (Miss.) 539 (1857).

[7] 69 Cal. 133 (1886); 44 Mich. 25 (1880).

by an injunction, interest is suspended from the service of the process while it remains in force, although he is not a party to the bill and it is inoperative.[1]

(*h*) *Guardians.* As long as guardians are reasonable in caring for the property of their wards they are not chargeable with interest.[2]

If they have kept funds unemployed an unreasonable length of time, when they might have made them productive, they will be charged with interest,[3] even if they do not use the money themselves.[4] If they convert the funds to their own use, they are chargeable with the highest rate of interest that they could have obtained.[5]

If the funds are lost through their negligence,[6] or they mingle them with their own[7] they must pay interest.

The court will allow fees paid to an attorney for services in recovering money put out at interest.[8]

Guardians should make their disbursements from the interest, and not from the principal of the funds, otherwise they will be charged interest on the interest received.[9]

Investments. Guardians must be allowed a reasonable time for investing the funds,[10] six months being generally

[1] 4 Halst. (N. J.) 3 (1827); 13 Wend. (N. Y.) 639 (1835).

[2] 18 Pick. (Mass.) 1 (1836); 1 Cush. (Mass.) 189 (1851); 17 N. H. 458 (1845); 41 Pa. St. 494 (1862).

[3] 12 Ala. 354 (1847); 1 Pick. (Mass.) 527 (1823); 45 Mich. 265 (1881); 43 N. H. 465 (1862); 2 Grant's Cas. (Pa.) 341 (1856).

[4] 55 Cal. 137 (1880).

[5] 90 Ind. 105 (1883).

[6] 40 Miss. 765 (1866).

[7] 53 Pa. St. 500 (1866).

[8] 29 Ga. 82 (1859).

[9] 29 Ga. 82 (1859); 6 Dana (Ky.) 6 (1837); 2 Grant's Cas. (Pa.) 341 (1856).

[10] 6 Dana (Ky.) 5 (1837); 18 Pick. (Mass.) 1 (1836); 45 Mich. 265 (1881); 31 Minn. 312 (1883); 43 N. H. 465 (1862); 60 N. H. 179 (1880); 4 S. & R. (Pa.) 112 (1818); 41 Pa. St. 494 (1862); 53 Pa. St. 500 (1866).

considered as about right.[1] If investments are made at less than the legal rate of interest, guardians are chargeable with the legal rate, unless the rate received is a reasonable one under the circumstances.[2]

Compound interest. Compound interest is allowed, not to punish, but to reach the profits, which under the facts disclosed the guardians have made.[3] As a rule they should not be charged with compound interest;[4] but if they have been guilty of gross delinquency, or malfeasance,[5] or have used the funds for their own profit,[6] they must pay compound interest, with annual rests.[7] A guardian is chargeable with interest on the accumulated balance of principal and interest annually, after deducting the necessary expenditures for the ward, unless he shows to the satisfaction of the court such equitable circumstances, as ought in conscience to acquit him of his accountability for such interest,[8] being unable to realize it.

If the sum of money on hand is small, however, only simple interest will be charged, as such careful attention

[1] 23 Pa. St. 44 (1854); 2 Grant's Cas. (Pa.) 341 (1856); 53 Pa. St. 500 (1866); 12 Grat. (Va.) 668 (1855).

[2] 33 Ill. 212 (1864); 41 Pa. St. 494 (1862).

[3] 52 Tex. 84 (1879).

[4] 56 Mich. 508 (1885); 73 Mich. 220 (1889); Hopk. (N. Y.) 424 (1825).

[5] 46 Ala. 153 (1871); 49 Ala. 237 (1873); 29 Ga. 82 (1859); 18 Pick. (Mass.) 1 (1836); 5 Pa. St. 87 (1847); 53 Pa. St. 500 (1866).

[6] 14 Ill. 1 (1852); Hopk. (N. Y.) 424 (1825); 4 S. & R. (Pa.) 112 (1818).

[7] 85 Cal. 98 (1890); 29 Ga. 82 (1859). In the latter case the court says that rests should be taken once in six years. In Kentucky, two-year rests are generally allowed (3 Met. (Ky.) 555 (1861), and if it is a testamentary guardian three-year (5 Dana (Ky.) 594 (1837).

[8] Law Repos. (N. C.) 230 (1815); 1 Rob. (Va.) 196 (1842); *contra*, 56 Mich. 508 (1885), which says that guardians are liable only for simple interest, unless there is shown such a state of facts as ought to make them chargeable for compound interest, and the burden of proving those facts is on the ward.

would not be given generally to a small sum as to a large one.[1]

A failure to make a return of interest received is not sufficient in itself to prove fraud, or to make the offending party chargeable with compound interest.[2]

Profits. Whatever interest guardians make or receive they must pay over to the estate, though it be compound interest.[3] If guardians use the trust funds in a trade or venture of their own, whether they keep them separate, or mix with them their private money, and notwithstanding difficulties may arise in the latter case in taking the accounts, the ward, if he prefers to do so, may insist upon having the profits made by, instead of legal interest upon the amount of, the trust funds so employed.[4]

Accounts. Guardians' accounts should be rendered annually;[5] the interest for each year being added to the principal; and the payments for debts and other charges against the estate should be taken annually from such sum, the balance being the new principal for the next year.[6] Guardians can make monthly rests if they wish, but they must adopt the same principle.[7] The balance of each account is carried forward and interest is allowed on that.[8]

The court in Pennsylvania says that a reasonable rule is to strike a balance of the money in the hands of the

[1] 1 Pick. (Mass.) 527 (1823).

[2] 29 Ga. 82 (1859).

[3] 47 Ala. 314 (1872); 73 Mich. 220 (1889); 17 N. H. 458 (1845); Hopk. (N. Y.) 424 (1825); 7 W. & S. (Pa.) 48 (1844); Sp. Eq. (S. C.) 309 (1843).

[4] 33 Ill. 212 (1864).

[5] 33 Ill. 212 (1864).

[6] 12 Ala. 354 (1847); 33 Ill. 212 (1864); 6 Iowa 123 (1858); 39 Iowa 681 (1874); 64 Iowa 391 (1884); 1 Pick. (Mass.) 527 (1823); 18 Pick. (Mass.) 1 (1836); 47 N. H. 88 (1866).

[7] 109 Mass. 252 (1872).

[8] 77 Wis. 666 (1890).

guardian at the end of every six months, and to charge him with simple interest on that, allowing a reasonable sum for contingent expenses;[1] but that the principle of rests must not be adopted if it is a mere omission or neglect to invest.[2]

If a guardian charges himself with compound interest in his annual accounts, it is an admission, and he should not be relieved from it unless good reason is shown.[3]

When items of money advanced are disallowed in the account, interest is allowed to the guardian to offset that charged to him on the other side of the account.[4]

If the question of interest has not arisen in a previous account with the court, the guardian can be charged with interest in a succeeding account; but, if the question has been put in issue and decided on the settlement of a former account it cannot be revised so long as the former decree remains in force.[5]

A guardian is not chargeable with interest on the funds in his hands while his account is pending before an auditor, and during the pendency of exceptions in court,[6] unless they have been filed at his instance, in which case he is.[7]

Approval of such an account by an interested party does not preclude him from afterward insisting upon interest.[8]

Termination of guardianship. At the termination of the guardianship, only simple interest is allowed on the

[1] 4 S. & R. (Pa.) 112 (1818). The court in Georgia also says that a guardian can retain at the beginning of each year enough money to cover the disbursements of that year. 29 Ga. 82 (1859).

[2] 41 Pa. St. 494 (1862).

[3] 4 Geo. (Miss.) 553 (1857).

[4] 152 Mass. 328 (1890).

[5] 18 Pick. (Mass.) 1 (1836).

[6] 46 Pa. St. 347 (1863).

[7] 23 Pa. St. 44 (1854).

[8] 18 Pick. (Mass.) 1 (1836).

balance remaining in the hands of the guardian; or on the money afterward received by him;[1] or after the infant ward marries an adult husband.[2] This money he is bound to pay over to his ward immediately after the termination of his duty.

If the guardian has died, compound interest should be computed only to his death, and simple interest afterward,[3] unless compound interest has been received.[4]

Where the guardian makes a final settlement, showing a certain amount due from him to his ward, and such settlement is approved by the court, the guardian and his personal representatives are estopped to deny the correctness of the report.[5]

Advances. When a guardian advances his own money in payment of debts or expenses of his ward, under such circumstances as render that course of proceeding proper, he is entitled to interest on the money so advanced.[6]

(*i*) *Indorsers.* Indorsers are liable for interest on notes as a matter of law;[7] and the holder can recover according to their tenor, whether he paid less for them or not.[8] But if a note has been assigned, the assignee cannot recover of the assignor more than the latter can collect of the maker, provided he is solvent.[9]

[1] 31 N. E. Rep. (Ill.) 589 (1892); 9 B. Mon. (Ky.) 441 (1849); 15 La. Ann. 417 (1860); 2 Dev. Eq. (N. C.) 478 (1833); 12 Grat. (Va.) 608 (1855); *contra*, 29 Mo. App. 595 (1888), where a guardian, who failed to account with the ward and settle for five years after maturity of the ward, was held to pay compound interest.

[2] 13 W. P. D. Bush (Ky.) 176 (1877).

[3] 14 Ill. 1 (1852); 1 Dev. Eq. (N. C.) 386 (1830).

[4] 1 Dev. Eq. (N. C.) 386 (1830).

[5] 31 N. E. Rep. (Ill.) 589 (1892).

[6] 13 Pick. (Mass.) 272 (1872).

[7] 50 Tenn. 223 (1873).

[8] 19 Johns. (N. Y.) 244 (1821).

[9] 39 Ill. 31 (1865).

(*j*) *Masters in chancery.* If masters in chancery receive the assets of the estate, and are ordered by the court to invest them, they must do so or else pay interest.[1]

(*k*) *Minors.* There is a difference of opinion as to whether infants can be compelled to pay interest, either by contract, or as damages. There is no general rule exempting them,[2] and yet the trend of the decisions is that they cannot be obliged to do so.[3] In the English case of *Fisher, ex'x, v. Mowbray*,[4] it was held that an infant can on no account bind himself in a bond with a penalty conditioned for the payment of interest as well as principal.

(*l*) *Municipal corporations.* Interest as damages on accounts in favor of the United States, towns, cities, counties, states and other similar corporations runs the same as it does ordinarily, in the absence of statutes to the contrary;[5] but such bodies and corporations are not obliged to pay interest, unless there are statutes to compel them.[6] The county board cannot allow it;[7] and no agent of such corporations can contract for interest unless statutes permit.[8] Interest is allowed, however, on money illegally exacted

[1] 1 Desau. (S. C.) 115 (1785); Harp. Eq. (S. C.) 47 (1824).

[2] 23 Vt. 378 (1851).

[3] 23 Vt. 378 (1851), which overruled 14 Vt. 405 (1842).

[4] 8 East (Eng.) 330 (1807).

[5] 48 Ga. 115 (1873); 56 Ill. 327 (1870); 91 Ill. 49 (1878); 95 Ill. 352 (1880); 66 Ind. 109 (1879); 127 Ind. 204 (1890); 2 Cush. (Mass.) 475 (1848); 10 Tex. 315 (1853); 30 Vt. 285 (1858).

[6] 127 U. S. 251 (1887); 1 Scam. (Ill.) 67 (1832); 11 Ill. 170 (1849); 2 Mich. 187 (1851); 37 Mich. 351 (1877); 71 Mich. 118 (1888); 52 Miss. 732 (1876); 53 Miss. 148 (1876); 64 Miss. 534 (1886); 2 Ired. Eq. (N. C.) 444 (1843); 36 O. St. 409 (1881); 13 Ore. 287 (1886); 18 S. C. 132 (1882); 15 Tex. 72 (1855); *contra*, 2 Dall. (Pa.) 101 (1788). The court in 1 Cush. (Miss.) 565 (1852) holds that the state is bound to pay interest if she claims it.

[7] 91 Ill. 49 (1878); 95 Ill. 352 (1880).

[8] 15 Tex. 72 (1855).

as a tax and paid under protest.[1] It has also been allowed in several instances after a demand has been made;[2] which in case of a state must be made on the legislature.[3] The court in New York held, in 1848, that this question of municipal corporations' liability for interest should be left to the discretion of the court, saying that there is no reason why interest should not be paid by the state.[4]

(*m*) *Officers.* A public officer, who retains money wrongfully, is chargeable with interest during such detention.[5] A defaulting revenue officer is bound to pay interest to the United States.[6] In Louisiana it has been held that a curator of a vacant succession must pay interest from the time the fund should have been paid into the state treasury, under a judgment order from court to do so.[7]

Tax collectors, who, after a reasonable time, unreasonably refuse to pay over the money collected, must pay interest[8] from the time it was demanded of them.[9] They are also chargeable with interest if they have converted or used the money.[10] This is not true, however, where a collector, who bid off the privilege of collecting the taxes of a town, which had voted to collect interest on taxes that were

[1] 40 Mich. 367 (1879).

[2] 5 Denio (N. Y.) 401 (1848); 67 N. Y. 87 (1876); 3 Yeates (Pa.) 102 (1800).

[3] 3 Yeates (Pa.) 102 (1800).

[4] 5 Denio (N. Y.) 401 (1848).

[5] 105 Ill. 560 (1883); 6 N. H. 456 (1833); 9 Johns. (N. Y.) 71 (1812); 4 Wend. (N. Y.) 675 (1830); 3 Binn. (Pa.) 123 (1810).

[6] 6 Binn. (Pa.) 266 (1811).

[7] 3 La. Ann. 353 (1848).

[8] Coxe (N. J.) 190 (1793).

[9] 3 Spauld. (Me.) 177 (1882); 13 Gray (Mass.) 321 (1859); 6 N. H. 456 (1833). 1 Call (Va.) 194 (1797) says not till judgment.

[10] 6 N. H. 456 (1833); 9 Johns. (N. Y.) 71 (1812); 3 Cow. (N. Y.) 393 (1824); 10 Wend. (N. Y.) 96 (1833).

unpaid at a certain date, from and after that time, pays over the whole amount of the taxes at the date named, from which interest was to run, and he afterward collects interest on those that were unpaid. In such a case, the collector and not the town is entitled to the interest.[1]

A collector is liable for interest on taxes, if they bear interest, even if illegally collected.[2]

A collector, when sued on his bond, is liable for interest from the time the taxes should have been paid over, whether he or his deputy duly collected them or not.[3]

Sheriffs, who receive interest on money collected on execution, are obliged to pay it over, as they are not allowed to make a profit on the money in their hands.[4] Where one took an interest-bearing note, running to himself, and approved by the attaching creditor, it was held that the sheriff had no right to retain for his own use the interest money that accrued on the note. He must hold the interest as a part of the proceeds of the sale.[5] But the New Hampshire court holds that sheriffs are not obliged to return interest that they receive on sales made on credit before the return day of the execution.[6]

A sheriff is not chargeable with interest before a demand, unless he has received it;[7] and a rule of court for him to pay the money into court, and a delay for several years after that is not a demand.[8] The court in Georgia, however, holds that a sheriff must pay over money collected

[1] 146 Mass. 476 (1888).

[2] 25 W. Va. 266 (1884).

[3] 36 Tex. 323 (1872).

[4] 52 N. H. 9 (1872); 38 Vt. 68 (1865).

[5] 4 Red. (Me.) 56 (1852); 21 N. H. 146 (1850).

[6] 30 N. H. 427 (1855).

[7] 13 Johns. (N. Y.) 255 (1816); 4 Wend. (N. Y.) 675 (1830); 2 Bail. (S. C.) 51 (1830); 42 Vt. 325 (1869).

[8] 21 Pa. St. 291 (1853).

within a reasonable time,[1] and the Delaware court, that he must pay interest from the time the money is payable.[2]

In a case where a sheriff sold land on execution, the purchaser entered, and took the rents and profits. He gave the sheriff a bond for the purchase-money, conditioned to pay on a day certain, "or according to order of the court." The creditor agreed that the money should be considered as in court, and it was decided that the sheriff was not chargeable with interest from the date of the bond to the final decree of court.[3]

Where sheriffs retain money, left in their hands during the pendency of an action to determine conflicting claims thereto, in disobedience to an order of court directing a deposit of the money in court, they may be charged with interest thereon.[4]

In an action against a sheriff, for the escape of a prisoner committed on execution, the rule of damages is the amount of the execution and costs, with interest from the time of the escape.[5] The Massachusetts court holds that he is liable for interest in such a case only from demand.[6]

A constable, who is negligent in serving an execution, is liable to pay interest on the amount of it.[7]

Treasurers. If a treasurer neglects to pay over money when he is bound to do so, whether to his successor or other party, he is chargeable with interest from that time.[8]

[1] 34 Ga. 173 (1865).
[2] 3 Harr. (Del.) 25 (1839).
[3] 4 Watts (Pa.) 59 (1835).
[4] 73 N. Y. 622 (1878).
[5] 3 Conn. 423 (1820).
[6] 14 Pick. (Mass.) 523 (1833).
[7] 1 Halst. (N. J.) 211 (1822); 4 Halst. (N. J.) 205 (1827).
[8] 73 Ala. 118 (1882); 14 Vr. (N. J.) 125 (1881); 15 Vr. (N. J.) 371 (1882); 21 Pa. St. 385 (1853).

If he defaults, he, or his sureties, must pay interest from the time of defalcation.[1]

(*n*) *Partners.* Where partners agree to invest equal amounts of money in the business, and one puts in a larger sum than the other he is entitled to interest on one-half of the excess of his share so advanced by him from the time of its appropriation to the use of the firm.[2] If one partner does not pay in his share he must pay interest thereon;[3] but the other partner cannot recover interest on his share that he has paid in, while the other was negligent.[4]

Where one partner furnishes the capital and the other his skill and labor, no interest should be allowed on the capital;[5] but if the business finally ceases to be carried on, and there is a loss, it is proper in ascertaining the liability of the partner not furnishing money, but liable for a loss, to charge interest on his share from the termination of the business.[6]

Where each member of a firm gives notice to a debtor not to pay the other member, it is held that such notice does not relieve the defendant from liability for interest on the debt.[7]

Withdrawing funds. In general, where articles of co-partnership permit the partners to withdraw certain sums annually, without containing any stipulation in re-

[1] 17 Cal. 504 (1861); 102 Ill. 540 (1882). The court in 63 Tex. 428 (1885) held that interest should begin at the first of the year succeeding the default.

[2] 17 Ala. 32 (1849); *contra*, 20 Ala. 747 (1852).

[3] 42 Kas. 247 (1889); 1 La. Ann. 138 (1846). In the latter case, it was allowed "from judicial demand."

[4] 11 Rich. Eq. (S. C.) 135 (1859).

[5] 11 Hun (N. Y.) 509 (1877).

[6] 19 Hun (N. Y.) 130 (1879).

[7] 51 Pa. St. 36 (1865).

gard to interest thereon, interest will not be allowed.[1] If a partner has overdrawn the funds, he will be chargeable with interest;[2] and if he has used the money and refuses to disclose the profits he has made, when called upon to account, he will be compelled to pay compound interest as a substitute for the profits he might reasonably be supposed to have made.[3] If a partner has made a wrongful collection and detention, he must pay interest from the time of the collection.[4]

Advances. A partner who advances money to his firm is not entitled to interest upon it,[5] unless an intent to allow it can be inferred from usage or from circumstances, or unless it is understood by the partners that it is to be allowed.[6] Where it is allowed, and it is not expressly or impliedly stopped running it will continue to accrue until the final settlement.[7]

Dissolution. A partner, who, on the dissolution of the firm, by death, or otherwise, holds the assets and property of the partnership, and is entrusted with the duty of winding up its affairs, is chargeable with interest, as between himself and his co-partner, or his co-partner's personal

[1] 1 Idaho 513 (1873); 11 Pick. (Mass.) 11 (1831).

[2] 133 Mass. 552 (1882); 1 Johns. Ch. (N. Y.) 167 (1815); 2 Johns. Ch. (N. Y.) 209 (1816); *contra*, 6 Jur., N. S. (Eng.) 600 (1860); Johns. (Eng.) 653 (1860); 29 L. J. Ch. (Eng.) 418 (1860); 8 W. R. (Eng.) 204. In the case of *Harris v. Carter*, cited 147 Mass. 313 (1888), the court would not allow interest on funds overdrawn because the partners had overdrawn them about equally, and there was no agreement to pay interest.

[3] 1 Johns. Ch. (N. Y.) 467 (1815); 2 Johns. Ch. (N. Y.) 209 (1816).

[4] 30 Kas. 1 (1883).

[5] 29 Cal. 655 (1870); 72 Ga. 154 (1883); 75 Ill. 190 (1874); *contra*, 56 Cal. 446 (1880); 3 Gilm. (Ill.) 626 (1846); 3 Bush (Ky.) 519 (1868); 129 Mass. 517 (1880).

[6] 43 Mich. 171 (1880); 1 McCart. (N. J.) 44 (1861).

[7] 1 McCart. (N. J.) 44 (1861).

representatives, if he mingles the money with his own, or neglects unreasonably to settle his account,[1] on the other partner's share of the balance,[2] from the time the balance is struck, if it is done within a reasonable time.[3] The partner against whom the balance is found must pay interest thereon.[4] If the surviving partner continues the business, using all the property, he must pay interest from the time of dissolution.[5]

Where an executor and his testator were partners prior to the latter's death, and the former, without separating the testator's portion of the firm property, as he should have done, continues to employ the same in the business, he is chargeable with compound interest upon the value of the testator's share.[6]

Accounting. As a general rule, interest is not allowed upon partnership accounts until after a balance is struck on a settlement between the partners, unless they have otherwise agreed or acted in their partnership concerns.[7] But interest is not allowed on balances struck annually, if they remain partnership assets.[8] Several courts hold, however, that in some cases interest should be allowed, and that there should be no strict rule, as it might work injustice.[9]

If a partner agrees to render an account on a certain day, and make settlement, but on the day appointed refuses

[1] 128 Ill. 209 (1889); 5 Dana (Ky.) 438 (1838); 124 Mass. 305 (1878); 4 Dall. (Pa.) 286 (1803).

[2] 21 W. R. (Eng.) 86; 70 Md. 465 (1889).

[3] 89 Ky. 628 (1889); 17 Pick. (Mass.) 519 (1836). 4 Ired. Eq. (N. C.) 223 (1846) says from dissolution.

[4] 2 Johns. Ch. (N. Y.) 209 (1816); 3 Bradf. (N. Y.) 99 (1854).

[5] 50 Mich. 401 (1883); 56 Mich. 276 (1885).

[6] 68 N. Y. 610 (1877).

[7] 44 Wis. 646 (1878).

[8] 52 N. W. Rep. (Iowa) 341 (1892).

[9] 2 Stew. (N. J.) 345 (1878); 64 Pa. St. 73 (1869).

and withholds the books, the court in Illinois makes him chargeable with interest on the balance found against him from that time.[1]

The payment on a partnership debt by the surviving partner cannot be applied to a higher rate of interest agreed upon between the survivor and creditor.[2]

Where a master, in stating an account between partners, adopted the mercantile usage of an interest account, it was allowed to stand, there being evidence that the parties had followed that usage.[3]

(*o*) *Receivers.* A receiver who violates his trust by mixing the trust-fund with his own,[4] or with other trust money, or deposits it in a bank to his private account,[5] or uses it for his own purposes, or loans it on his own account, should be charged with interest.[6]

(*p*) *Stakeholders.* The general rule is, that where a man holds money, which he is bound to produce at a moment's notice, he is not expected to invest it, and is not liable to pay interest even if he makes it,[7] until demand.[8] This rule applies to common stakeholders,[9] and to auctioneers.[10] So, where an insurance company was restrained from paying over money it was owing to one of the parties of the suit, it was held that the company was acting as a

[1] 81 Ill. 110 (1876).

[2] 17 S. C. 106 (1881).

[3] 2 Johns. Ch. (N. Y.) 209 (1816).

[4] 11 Paige (N. Y.) 520 (1845).

[5] 100 U. S. 153 (1879).

[6] 11 Paige (N. Y.) 520 (1845).

[7] 22 Conn. 386 (1853). He will be liable if he uses the money. 1 Dana (Ky.) 398 (1833).

[8] 13 Barb. (N. Y.) 556 (1852); 20 N. Y. (6 Smith) 9 (1859); 4 Tenn. 252 (1817).

[9] 22 Conn. 386 (1853); 2 Bradw. (Ill.) 30 (1878); 6 J. J. Mar. (Ky.) 581 (1831).

[10] 1 B. & Ad. (Eng.) 577 (1830); 22 Conn. 386 (1853).

stakeholder, and therefore was not liable to pay interest upon the money while it was thus retained.[1]

(*q*) *Stockholders.* Stockholders are generally liable only to the amount of their stock, and interest is not to be allowed thereon.[2] It is not error, however, in a suit to enforce the liability of a stockholder, to include in the judgment rendered interest from the date of bringing the suit, although the amount of recovery might thus exceed the original liability.[3] So, interest may also be allowed on calls for assessments on stock subscribed, after default.[4]

Interest runs against stockholders of a dissolved corporation from the filing of a bill against them.[5]

The agreement of a railroad corporation to pay stockholders interest on the amount of stock paid in prior to the time the road begins operations is not legal.[6]

Preferred stock bears interest from its date, and not from its delivery simply.[7]

(*r*) *Sureties and guarantors.* A surety on a bond becomes liable upon a breach thereof by the principal, and, although he cannot be charged with any interest that accrued before the breach, that is, beyond the amount of the face of the bond, yet the amount due at the time of the breach will bear interest even though the full amount of the bond is awarded as damages.[8]

The courts are divided in their opinion as to when interest against the surety should begin to run. Some say

[1] 15 W. R. (Eng.) 371; 131 Mass. 294 (1881).
[2] 1 Lad. (Me.) 40 (1857).
[3] 44 O. St. 318 (1886).
[4] 68 Ind. 288 (1879).
[5] 92 Ala. 388 (1890).
[6] 8 Gray (Mass.) 433 (1857), (ultra vires?).
[7] 28 S. C. 134 (1887).
[8] 1 Root (Conn.) 423 (1792); 9 Mon. 126 (1889); 3 Cow. (N. Y.) 151 (1824); 5 Cow. (N. Y.) 424 (1826); 18 N. Y. (4 Smith) 35 (1858).

from demand on the principal;[1] others, from demand on the surety;[2] others, from the time of the surety's default;[3] and still others say that on an executor's bond, the liability begins at the time when the executor's last account was settled in court.[4] In replevin, it is generally allowed from the date of the judgment against the principal.[5]

A guarantor is not generally liable for interest as damages accruing after breach.[6]

Discharge. If the principal makes a binding contract to delay the payment of a note having a surety without the knowledge and consent of the surety,[7] as to pay in advance interest for a longer time than the instrument runs, or, after it has become due, with the understanding that the time for payment shall be extended, it will discharge the surety;[8] but in order to have this effect the agreement must be binding upon the holder.[9] A mere promise by the maker will not be binding on any one.[10] Therefore, an agreement to pay usurious interest, or the payment of such interest in advance, as a consideration for extension of time of payment will not discharge the surety.[11] If the surety agrees, or performs acts that show his assent, to a

[1] 3 Spauld. (Me.) 384 (1882); 1 Mass. 308 (1805); 9 Mon. 126 (1889); 2 Rich. (S. C.) 99 (1845).

[2] 10 Mass. 371 (1813).

[3] 18 N. Y. (4 Smith) 35 (1858); 51 Barb. (N. Y.) 40 (1868)

[4] 2 Col. 578 (1875); 124 N. Y. 1 (1891).

[5] 1 McC. (S. C.) 28 (1821).

[6] 43 N. Y. 244 (1871); Rice (S. C.) 21 (1838); 10 Rich. (S. C.) 323 (1857); *contra*, 124 Pa. St. 58 (1889).

[7] 59 Miss. 39 (1881); 10 N. H. 162 (1839); 110 N. C. 311 (1892).

[8] 22 Kas. 363 (1879); 10 N. H. 162 (1839); 15 N. H. 119 (1844); 23 S. C. 588 (1885).

[9] 57 Mo. 357 (1874).

[10] 10 N. H. 162 (1839).

[11] 57 Mo. 399, 503 (1874); 50 N. W. Rep. (Iowa) 66 (1891). See *Sureties* in chapter ten.

postponement of the time of payment, he will remain liable.[1]

Recovery. A surety is entitled to receive from his principal the amount he has been compelled to pay (including interest) and interest thereon[2] at the legal rate[3] from the time he paid out the money.[4]

If one of several joint sureties has been compelled to pay the amount due, he can recover of the other sureties their proportionate shares of the amount and interest thereon[5] at the legal rate, even though the contract bore another rate.

(*s*) *Trustees.* Formerly, in England, trustees were regarded as gratuitous bailees, and there was required of them a corresponding degree of care; but now they are well paid for their services, especially in the United States, and their responsibility has proportionately increased. But against honest and faithful trustees interest is never charged beyond actual receipts.[7]

Trustees are not liable to pay interest on money that has gained no interest unless they have been negligent;[8] but if they might have made the funds productive, and were grossly negligent in letting them lie idle, or have used them,[9] or made interest they are liable for interest.[10] They will not be responsible for more than legal interest, even

[1] 10 N. H. 318 (1839).
[2] 16 Tex. 229 (1856).
[3] 82 Mo. 660 (1884); 29 Mo. App. 649 (1888).
[4] 2 L., M. & P. (Eng.) 107 (1851); 15 Jur. (Eng.) 86 (1851); 20 L. J. Q. B. (Eng.) 242 (1851); 74 Cal. 409 (1887); 29 Mo. App. 649 (1888).
[5] 5 Strob. (S. C.) 15 (1850).
[6] 77 Wis. 435 (1890).
[7] 89 Tenn. 63 (1890).
[8] 17 N. H. 458 (1845).
[9] 78 Va. 24 (1883).
[10] 1 Dev. Eq. (N. C.) 520 (1830).

if they might have obtained a larger rate,[1] unless they have received more.

If trustees have mingled the trust funds with their own to a large amount and for a long period, they are chargeable with interest, although they have made none.[2]

If they deny the trust, and claim in hostility thereto, they are chargeable with interest from the time of their receipt of the money, not being allowed to invoke the rule permitting trustees to have six months for the investment of the funds.[3]

These rules concerning trustees are well settled in the civil law of Rome, and in the common law of the United States, England, and most of the continental nations of Europe.[4] "This historical fact," says Chancellor Kent, "is calculated to inspire us with much respect for these principles, independent of their practical utility in securing the diligence and fidelity of trustees."

Investments. If trustees have kept money an unreasonable length of time before investing it they must pay interest out of their own pockets,[5] as the funds are then presumed to have been used for profit. They must make the funds productive.[6]

If the testator directs the investment of even a small sum, trustees must invest it, or pay interest.[7]

If trustees invest a small trust fund with their own money

[1] 2 B. Mon. (Ky.) 261 (1842).

[2] 128 Mass. 377 (1880); 35 N. Y. 185 (1866); 92 Pa. St. 407 (1880).

[3] 58 N. Y. 204 (1874).

[4] 1 Johns. Ch. (N. Y.) 620 (1815).

[5] 1 Ball & B. (Ire.) 385 (1810); 40 Conn. 464 (1873); 136 Mass. 60 (1883); 50 Barb. (N. Y.) 453 (1867); 89 Tenn. 63 (1890); 37 Tex. 565 (1872); 3 Call (Va.) 538 (1790); 78 Va. 24 (1883). In the Texas case, the retention of six hundred dollars for two years was deemed unreasonable.

[6] 5 Dana (Ky.) 132 (1837).

[7] 38 Pa. St. 466 (1861).

on loan at a certain rate per cent, they are not chargeable with a greater rate if it appears that the rate was common, and all that could be safely had in the neighborhood.[1]

Compound interest. Compound interest is not allowed in favor of trustees.[2] Interest against trustees is largely in the discretion of the court, which may compound it, at the highest rate.[3]

If trustees convert the funds to their own use, and they will render no account of them, nor divulge the amount of the profits they have made, or so mingle them with their own money that they cannot ascertain the profits they have made, they will be charged with compound interest.[4]

If trustees use the funds in their own business,[5] or are guilty of such gross delinquency as to constitute an intentional violation of duty,[6] they will be charged with interest properly compounded with rests.[7]

Profits. All profits that the trustees receive from the funds in their hands belong to the estate, and not to themselves.[8] They must make no profit beyond a reasonable compensation for their services.[9] If they have received compound interest, or usurious interest, they must account for it.[10] If they make use of the money in their business, and receive income from it, the *cestui que trust* can elect

[1] 50 Pa. St. 189 (1865).

[2] 5 Johns. Ch. (N. Y.) 497 (1821).

[3] 72 Mich. 456 (1888).

[4] 48 Conn. 207 (1880); 58 N. H. 566 (1879); 1 Johns. Ch. (N. Y.) 620 (1815); 5 Johns. Ch. (N. Y.) 497 (at page 517) (1821).

[5] 82 Ky. 573 (1885).

[6] 4 Barb. (N. Y.) 626 (1848); 2 Dev. & Bat. Eq. (N. C.) 325 (1839).

[7] 82 Ky. 573 (1885), biennial rests being allowed; 50 Barb. (N. Y.) 453 (1867); 2 Dev. & Bat. Eq. (N. C.) 325 (1839).

[8] 2 Dev. & Bat. Eq. (N. C.) 325 (1839).

[9] 2 Vern. (Eng.), 548 (1706); 40 Conn. 464 (1873); 2 Bland's Ch. (Md.) 324 (1803); 27 Md. 51 (1867).

[10] 16 How. (U. S.) 535 (1853).

whether he will receive the legal rate of interest or the profits that have been made by the trustees.[1]

Disbursements should be made first from the interest that has been received, and not from the principal.[2]

Advances. Trustees are allowed interest on advances made by them on account of the estate in cases of emergency.[3]

Accounts. Trustees should account for interest annually.[4] Mere negligence will justify rests in accounts; as well as a corrupt intent, or gross delinquency.[5]

Simple interest is to be allowed generally on the annual balances,[6] annual rests being made.[7]

When trustees refuse to account the court will adopt the most rigid rule for calculating interest, compounding it.[8] And the rule that generally prevails exempting trustees from liability for interest until the end of the year is not absolute.[9]

If items that should have been charged in a trustees' account are not thus charged, the court will order them to be treated as far as interest is concerned as though they had been reckoned in when they ought to have been.[10]

Distribution. After an order of distribution, trustees must pay the funds over to the parties entitled, or into the court; if they do not, they will be charged with interest,

[1] 2 Ves. (Eng.) 630 (1795): 2 Myl. & K. (Eng.) 655 (1834); 3 L. J., N. S., Ch. (Eng.) 200 (1834); 52 Tex. 84 (1879).

[2] 117 Mass. 41 (1875).

[3] 117 Mass. 41 (1875): 6 Halst. (N. J.) 44 (1829); 1 Binn. (Pa.) 488 (1808).

[4] 17 Fla. 593 (1880): 2 B. Mon. (Ky.) 261 (1842).

[5] 50 Barb. (N. Y.) 453 (1867): *contra*, 18 Ga. 8 (1855).

[6] 2 McC. Ch. (S. C.) 317 (1827): 8 S. C. 347 (1876).

[7] 55 Tenn. 417 (1874).

[8] 2 McC. Ch (S. C.) 214 (1827).

[9] 10 Rich. Eq. (S. C.) 356 (1858).

[10] 109 Mass. 511 (1872).

in the discretion of the jury,[1] or the court should allow it from and after demand.[2] So interest will be allowed generally on the balance in the trustees' hands that they should have paid over, it being presumed that the funds were used.[3] Interest will also be allowed against a trustee if distribution is delayed by his groundless exceptions alone.[4]

Practice. The question of laches is a question of fact for the jury.[5]

Interest will be decreed against a trustee, even though it is not prayed for, if the facts disclosed show that equitable interest should be decreed.[6]

II. RELATING TO SUBJECT MATTER.

The leading classes of cases as they relate to subject matter are as follows, viz.:—

(*a*) *Running accounts.* A running account is one that consists of items on the part of the creditor only, or with both debit and credit items.[7] Parties can, of course, agree on the manner in which interest shall be charged and credited in accounts;[8] but if there is no agreement, and the account is unliquidated, that is, if no balance has been agreed upon, running accounts do not generally bear interest.[9] The mere fact that an account is unliquidated is

[1] 2 Gill (Md.) 439 (1845).

[2] 2 Dall. (Pa.) 182 (1792).

[3] 3 B. Mon. (Ky.) 153 (1842).

[4] 45 Pa. St. 394 (1863).

[5] 37 Tex. 305 (1872).

[6] 16 Md. 446 (1860).

[7] 6 Johns. (N. Y.) 45 (1810); 2 Wend. (N. Y.) 501 (1829).

[8] 2 Paige (N. Y.) 207 (1830); 1 Dall. (Pa.) 315 (1788); 2 Wash. T. 228 (1884).

[9] 1 H. Bl. (Eng.) 303 (1789); 9 Price (Eng.) 134 (1821); 2 Port. (Ala.) 451 (1835); 20 Ark. 410 (1859); 46 Conn. 586 (1879); 2 Blf. (Ind.) 312 (1830); 17 Kas. 18 (1876); 1 Bibb (Ky.) 443 (1809); 2 Rob. (La.) 360

often, though not always a decisive objection to the allowance of interest, and the objection is much stronger when no sum has been named by either party as the amount to be charged until after a controversy has arisen.[1] If there is a usage of merchants to charge interest on a running account, it is valid,[2] if it is known to the debtor at the time the dealings occurred;[3] but knowledge of the usage is not presumed.[4] Where the creditor reckoned a running account, charging interest on both sides, and rendered it to the debtor, who made no objection within a reasonable time, interest was allowed accordingly.[5] But the simple rendering of an account does not liquidate it if the acts of the parties show that they do not consider it settled.[6] If an account has once been stated and agreed to between the parties, such settlement is conclusive, and neither can open it for the purpose of charging interest on

(1812); 2 Cush. (Mass.) 475 (1848); Coxe (N. J.) 176 (1793); 6 Johns. (N. Y.) 45 (1810); 3 Johns. Ch. (N. Y.) 587 (1818); 4 Cow. (N. Y.) 496 (1825); 5 Cow. (N. Y.) 587 (1825); 6 Cow. (N. Y.) 193 (1826); 2 Wend. (N. Y.) 501 (1829); 4 Barb. (N. Y.) 36 (1848); 7 Lans. (N. Y.) 381 (1873); 4 Ired. Eq. (N. C.) 223 (1846); 2 Ore. 321 (1868); 1 Dall. (Pa.) 265. 313 (1788); 3 Rich. (S. C.) 376. 380 (1832); 2 Hill (S. C.) 468 (1834); 1 Rice (S. C.) 21 (1837); 1 Spears (S. C.) 209 (1843); 1 Tex. 102 (1846); 5 Vt. 177 (1832); 2 Wash. T. 228 (1884); *contra*, 18 S. C. 1 (1882). From verdict only, says 2 Bay (S. C.) 233 (1799). In Tennessee, interest is allowed on separate items from maturity. 18 Tenn. 458 (1837).

[1] 46 Conn. 586 (1879).

[2] 4 Ired. Eq. (N. C.) 223 (1846). Evidence to prove a custom of merchants in a city of another state allowing them to charge interest on accounts is not admissible when the courts of that state refuse to recognize the custom. 2 Blf. (Ind.) 312 (1830).

[3] 1 Barb. (N. Y.) 235 (1847); 3 N. Y. (3 Comst.) 502 (1850).

[4] 1 Barb. (N. Y.) 235 (1847).

[5] 3 Cal. 231 (1853); 74 Cal. 60 (1887). In the latter case, it was charged from thirty days after the date of each item.

[6] 6 Johns. (N. Y.) 45 (1810); 2 Wend. (N. Y.) 501 (1829); 4 Ired. Eq. (N. C.) 223 (1846).

either side, either at law or equity.[1] The Iowa court decides, however, that, if it is discovered that the account has been reckoned with short rests, the settlement will be reopened and only simple interest allowed.[2]

Courts state the principle in these two ways: that interest must be allowed on the balance of a running account from the time when it ought to have been paid;[3] or, from the time when the defendant had notice of the deficiency on his part.[4]

The foregoing rules only apply, however, to those cases where there is no stipulated period of credit, and where the balance may vary from time to time.[5] If there is at the time of the dealings a general practice of the creditor of charging interest to his customers, after a limited period of credit, those who deal with him with knowledge of the fact are bound to pay it;[6] but knowledge of the practice is not presumed.[7] So if a certain time is fixed for payment, interest is allowed from that time.[8]

Some courts hold that though no stipulated term of credit appears, it is to be presumed that the parties contracted in view of a reasonable time of credit and therefore the law infers that a reasonable time was allowed for the payment of the account, and they leave the facts in each case to determine the question.[9]

[1] 61 Cal. 401 (1882).

[2] 32 Iowa 187 (1871).

[3] 12 Fla. 640 (1869); 86 Ky. 668 (1888); 5 Vt. 177 (1832).

[4] 12 Johns. (N. Y.) 156 (1815); 3 Cow. (N. Y.) 393 (1824).

[5] 8 Vt. 258 (1836).

[6] 4 Wend. (N. Y.) 483 (1830); 8 Wend. (N. Y.) 109 (1831).

[7] 1 Barb. (N. Y.) 235 (1847).

[8] 6 Binn. (Pa.) 159 (1813). *Contra*, unless expressly or impliedly promised. 3 Brev. (S. C.) 506 (1814).

[9] 33 Ala., N. S. 459 (1859); 22 Pick. (Mass.) 291 (1839); 2 Pen. (N. J.) 518 (1809); 2 Vt. 536 (1830); 40 Vt. 251 (1867). In the last-named case, the court says that it has not followed the English or New

It is generally held that parties should settle their mutual and running accounts at least once a year, and on that basis the courts allow interest on the balance from such time as the settlement should have been made between the parties whether it was made or not.[1] Such annual rests are allowed in merchants' accounts,[2] but not on ordinary unliquidated accounts,[3] and in settlement of mortgage debts when rents have been received by the mortgagee.[4] If the interest is to be paid semi-annually, the rests should be semi-annual.[5] Some courts hold that the time for drawing annual balances is January first of each year.[6] Such annual rests are not allowed after mutual dealings have ceased,[7] except under a specific agreement.[8] This rule of rests is not only valid and sanctioned by the law, but computation by them is even directed by the courts;[9] in the Massachusetts courts, however, to be so treated,[10] it must be an open and mutual account current. The Alabama

York practice. The court, in the case cited 23 Vt. 706 (1851), says that it would not assume that by the universal custom in Vermont six months is the longest period of ordinary credit, as understood between merchants and their customers, and that it is the custom to charge interest from and after that time, or semi-annually.

[1] 33 Ala., N. S. 459 (1859); 38 Vt. 492 (1866); 48 Vt. 52 (1875); 60 Vt. 473 (1887).

[2] 3 Wash. (U. S., C. C.) 350 (1818); 136 Mass. 60 (1883); 2 Johns. Ch. (N. Y.) 209 (1816). Pennsylvania allows it only with the assent of the customer. 10 S. & R. (Pa.) 257 (1823); 16 S. & R. (Pa.) 257 (1827).

[3] 4 Cow. (N. Y.) 496 (1825): 2 McC. Ch. (S. C.) 200 (1827).

[4] 110 Mass. 273 (1872).

[5] 5 Pick. (Mass.) 146 (1827).

[6] 58 Vt. 576 (1886).

[7] 3 Wash. (U. S., C. C.) 396 (1818).

[8] 11 Met. (Mass.) 240 (1846).

[9] 11 Ves. jr. (Eng.) 92 (1805): 13 Eng. L. & Eq. (Eng.) 140 (1852); 16 How. (U. S.) 535 (1853); 18 Pick. (Mass.) 1 (1836); 1 Johns. Ch. (N. Y.) 620 (1815).

[10] 10 Pick. (Mass.) 398 (1830); 124 Mass. 212 (1878).

court is strongly opposed to this rule, contending that such rests are not allowed by law, and that no custom or agreement to that effect can alter the law.[1] In that state, the court holds that the account is closed at the date of the last item, and that the balance draws interest from that time.[2]

In the case of annual rests, the Vermont court holds that a demand at the end of each year is not necessary.[3] Other courts affirm that it is, and that such balances will bear interest only after a demand.[4]

Interest is not chargeable on book debts,[5] except by virtue of special custom, usage[6] or agreement,[7] unless they are due at the end of each year,[8] when the presentation of a bill or demand of payment is not necessary.[9] The custom of charging interest must be sanctioned by the purchaser.[10] In absence of proof of such an agreement or custom interest is not allowed,[11] except for items of cash advanced,[12] unless a bill is rendered or demand is made.[13]

There is no objection to charging interest on both sides of an account.[14]

[1] 2 Port. (Ala.) 351 (1835).

[2] 46 Ala. 653 (1871). See 26 Atl. Rep. (Vt.) 67 (1892).

[3] 30 Vt. 285 (1858); 36 Vt. 46 (1863); 60 Vt. 473 (1887).

[4] 4 Dall. (U. S.) 286 (1803); 2 Cush. (Mass.) 475 (1848); 26 N. H. 85 (1852).

[5] 1 Dick. (Eng.) 305 (1757); 32 Conn. 482 (1865).

[6] 1 Dall. (Pa.) 315 (1788).

[7] 32 Conn. 482 (1865); 6 Johns. (N. Y.) 45 (1810); 2 Wend. (N. Y.) 501 (1829).

[8] 68 Ga. 831 (1882).

[9] 38 Vt. 492 (1866).

[10] 1 Speer (S. C.) 249 (1843).

[11] 32 Conn. 482 (1865).

[12] 6 Caines (N. Y.) 226 (1805); 2 Wend. (N. Y.) 413 (1829); Riley (S. C.) 215 (1837).

[13] 46 Conn. 586 (1879); 62 Ind. 359 (1878); demand must be made or suit begun, 8 Fla. 161 (1858); 3 Rob. (La.) 270 (1842); 71 Mo. 495 (1880); 76 Mo. 68 (1882).

[14] 3 Cal. 231 (1853).

Interest may be charged on an account[1] when the settlement of it has been long delayed.[2] The court in Nebraska holds that unsettled accounts bear interest after six months from the last item.[3] In Pennsylvania, there is a binding custom to charge interest on book accounts for goods sold and delivered, from the end of six months after delivery.[4]

The general rule of casting interest in partial payments is not applicable to a running account.[5]

In Mississippi, the jury may allow interest on open accounts,[6] but it is not absolutely due.[7] In Pennsylvania, interest on running accounts is within the allowance of the jury only, in their discretion.[8]

Interest upon items of which the debtor was ignorant through the creditor's fault is not allowed;[9] as where parties settled from time to time, and an item had been overlooked by both parties when they settled. Upon such an item no interest is allowed, if a suit is afterward brought to recover it.[10]

It is not proper to add the interest to the principal each year, and thus obtain interest upon interest, unless the parties have so agreed;[11] and a custom of a creditor, known and acquiesced in by a debtor, to charge interest on accounts after the end of each year, is evidence of an agreement to

[1] 63 Ind. 31 (1878).

[2] 75 Ind. 307 (1881).

[3] 15 Neb. 326 (1883); 30 Neb. 613 (1890).

[4] 30 Pa. St. 346 (1858).

[5] 8 Fla. 211 (1858).

[6] 1 Cush. (Miss.) 298 (1852).

[7] Walk. (Miss.) 20 (1818); 2 Geo. (Miss.) 51 (1856); 4 Geo. (Miss.) 529 (1857).

[8] 10 S. & R. (Pa.) 257 (1823).

[9] 3 Wms. (29 Vt.) 151 (1857); 30 Vt. 285 (1858).

[10] 3 Wms. (29 Vt.) 154 (1857).

[11] 3 H. & M. (Va.) 89 (1808); 31 Vt. 679 (1859); *contra*, 1 Bald. (U. S., C. C.) 536 (1832).

pay interest.[1] The Vermont supreme court said, "no custom of merchants, however uniform or long standing, will justify a court, in Vermont, in allowing a party to cast interest upon interest on a running account."[2] It is, however, allowed in England under a custom of forwarding accounts, quarterly, half yearly, or yearly to the debtor, who acquiesces in them by his silence.[3]

(*b*) *Account stated.* The mere act of striking the balance of an account between two parties does not entitle the party in whose favor the balance is, to interest from that time, unless the money is to be then paid,[4] or a demand is then or afterward made.[5] It carries interest from the time it is stated;[6] and in England the jury may give interest from that day in their discretion.[7] If the account has been rendered and acquiesced in, interest will be allowed from that time;[8] and it must be of the whole account between the parties.[9] The latter statement is true of all accounts if they would bear interest on settlement.[10] Another rule is that interest is chargeable from the time the debtor has notice of the deficit in the account at accounting;[11] and so

[1] 8 Iowa 163, 182 (1859); so on bank accounts, 9 Iowa 313 (1859).

[2] 13 Vt. 430 (1841); 58 Vt. 576 (1886).

[3] 2 Ves. (Eng.) 15 (1792); 2 Anst. (Eng.) 496 (1795); 3 Campb. (Eng.) 467 (1813); 1 Starkie (Eng.) 487 (1816); 5 B. & Ald. (Eng.) 34 (1821).

[4] 6 Esp. (Eng.) 45 (1806); 2 Campb. (Eng.) 429 (1810); *contra*, 2 Red. (Me.) 256 (1850).

[5] 3 Campb. (Eng.) 468, 472 (1813); 42 Ill. 225 (1866); 22 Pick. (Mass.) 291 (1839).

[6] 67 Mich. 277 (1887); 1 Hayw. (N. C.) 104 (1794); 1 Desau. (S. C.) 537 (1797).

[7] 2 W. Bl. (Eng.) 761 (1771); 3 Wils. (Eng.) 205 (1771).

[8] 8 Fla. 214 (1858); Dud. (Ga.) 218 (1832); 26 Ill. 54 (1861); 18 Ill. 198 (1868); 69 Ill. 624 (1873); 14 Bradw. (Ill.) 593 (1883); 3 Rob. (La.) 361 (1842): *contra*, 1 Ball & B. (Ire.) 428 (1810).

[9] 40 Iowa 117 (1874).

[10] 18 Mich. 25 (1869).

[11] 12 Johns. (N. Y.) 156 (1815).

if no notice is had, if the defendant is to blame for not receiving notice.[1]

The balance of a stated account is principal whether it includes prior interest or not.[2]

Interest is allowed where it has been customary between the parties to allow it in similar cases.[3]

An account stated by one administrator is binding upon all;[4] and an executor's account is a stated account if all parties agree to it.[5]

An account stated cannot be re-opened to discover what is in it;[6] and so the rate of interest charged therein cannot be changed, unless mistake is shown.[7]

(c) *Advancements.* What shall be included in advancements made by a parent to a child while both are living is not always clear. Much depends on circumstances. Articles of use are generally included, and not articles of luxury.[8] They are usually given for the support of a child who goes away from home, and who thus receives the benefit of his share, while the other children enjoy their shares by residence with the parent.[9] So advancements do not bear interest,[10] even though the child gives notes bearing interest to evidence the fact that he received the money.[11] In Tennessee, interest is computed on advance-

[1] 20 N. Y. 463 (1859).

[2] 1 Baldw. (U. S., C. C.) 536 (1832); 88 Cal. 384 (1891); 70 Pa. St. 183 (1871).

[3] 1 Campb. (Eng.) 50 (1807).

[4] 1 Hayw. (N. C.) 104 (1794).

[5] 7 Yerg. (Tenn.) 172 (1834).

[6] 70 Pa. St. 183 (1871).

[7] 76 Ga. 200 (1886).

[8] 2 McC. Ch. (S. C.) 90 (1827).

[9] Bail. Eq. (S. C.) 154 (1830).

[10] 35 Ala. 293 (1859); 17 Mass. 356 (1821); 3 Pick. (Mass.) 450 (1826); 135 Mass. 71 (1883); Sax. (N. J.) 685 (1832); 1 Stock. (N. J.) 572 (1853; 128 Pa. St. 269 (1889).

[11] 35 Ala. 293 (1859); 3 Pick. (Mass.) 450 (1826).

ments from the time of the ancestor's death;[1] but the court in South Carolina holds to the contrary.[2] Generally, advancements will carry interest from the time the property is ready for distribution,[3] the time being, as a general rule, one year after the ancestor's decease.[4] Advancements made to distributees when their shares are due are not technically advancements, and do not bear interest.[5]

For a statement of the law of interest on advancements made by administrators, agents, assignees, executors and trustees, see those subjects.[6]

(*d*) *Alimony.* Interest is allowed on alimony.[7] Where a decree for a sum of money in lieu of alimony was made, and, if not paid, execution was to issue twenty days from date of the decree, it was held that interest ran from the end of the twenty days and not from the date of the decree.[8]

(*e*) *Annuities.* Annuities begin at the death of the testator, if no other time is mentioned in the will, and consequently the first payment is due one year from the testator's decease, from which time, if it is not then paid, interest upon it will begin.[9] It makes no difference whether it is interest or principal, either will bear interest after a year.

[1] 85 Tenn. 124, 430 (1886).

[2] Bail. Eq. (S. C.) 154 (1830).

[3] 18 Ga. 177 (1855); 32 Ga. 530 (1861); 1 Jones Eq. (N. C.) 233 (1854).

[4] 128 Pa. St. 269 (1889).

[5] 52 Miss. 291 (1876); 42 Hun (N. Y.) 592 (1886).

[6] Administrators, page 33; agents, page 40; assignees, page 44; executors, page 47; and trustees, page 75.

[7] 19 Kas. 159 (1877).

[8] 2 Smith (Me.) 428 (1873).

[9] 3 Atk. Ch. (Eng.) 579 (1747); 7 Ves. (Eng.) 89 (1802); 1 Harr. (Del.) 330 (1845); 6 Mass. 37 (1809); 128 Mass. 575 (1880); 5 Binn. (Pa.) 472 (1813); 3 W. & S. (Pa.) 437 (1842); 9 W. & S. (Pa.) 530 (1840); Bail. Eq. (S. C.) 274 (1831); *contra*, 1 Dick. (Eng.) 178 (1743), 278 (1755), 305 (1757).

The Delaware court holds that the question of allowing interest upon arrears of an annuity is, in a court of equity, discretionary with the court, depending upon equitable considerations arising out of the circumstances of each particular case.[1]

There is no certain rule; the most frequent instances where it is allowed being where interest is necessary for maintenance.[2]

If an annuity is bequeathed by a man to his wife in lieu of claims on his estate, interest is allowable on it if it is in arrears.[3] So, if it is given in lieu of dower.[4]

(*f*) *Betterments.* Interest is allowed on betterments from the time of the acceptance of the report of referees at *nisi prius*, when exceptions are taken to the acceptance of the report,[5] as for a verdict.

(*g*) *Bills and notes.* Bills and notes do not carry interest as damages, it is obvious, until after maturity, and they are payable,[6] but they do then, even though there is an agreement not to sue till later.[7] To draw interest before that time there must be an express agreement therefor. In England, if there is no agreement to pay interest on a note, its allowance is in the discretion of the jury.[8]

Demand. No demand is necessary to enable a holder to collect interest on a note payable at a day certain from and after that day.[9] If the note or bill is payable on demand, it will not begin to carry interest as damages until

[1] 1 Del. Ch. 368 (1831).

[2] 2 Atk. (Eng.) 211 (1741).

[3] 4 Desau. (S. C.) 422 (1814).

[4] 1 Harr. (Del.) 106 (1832).

[5] 6 Hub. (Me.) 337 (1863).

[6] 5 Ves. (Eng.) 801 (1801); Coop. (Eng.) 29 (1805); 3 Dev. & B. (N. C.) 70 (1838).

[7] 3 N. C. 70 (1838); 5 Humph. (Tenn.) 405 (1844).

[8] 17 L. T., N. S. (Eng.) 325.

[9] 2 Smith (Me.) 54 (1873).

an actual demand has been made,[1] as it is not payable until then, unless a contract or usage requires it;[2] service of the writ, in an action to recover the principal of the note, being such a demand.[3] So, interest on an "I. O. U." does not begin to run until a demand.[4]

Instalment notes. When by the terms of a promissory note it is payable by instalments, and on the failure to pay any instalment all the subsequent ones shall become due immediately, interest begins to run on the whole amount of the note from the first default.[5]

(*h*) *Bonds and recognizances.* The general rule is that the penalty of a bond limits the amount that can be recovered;[6] so, on a bail recognizance;[7] but interest as damages may carry it beyond that amount.[8] If the whole amount is due upon it at the time of the breach of the condition of the bond, interest as damages begins to run against the principal and sureties[9] for detaining the debt from the time of the breach, the amount[10] of the bond being regarded as liquidated damages.[11] It is a question of law

[1] 6 Mod. (Eng.) 138 (1705); 18 Ala. 300 (1850); 54 Ala. 71 (1875); 8 Bradw. (Ill.) 69 (1880); Add. (Pa.) 137 (1793); 1 McC. (S. C.) 370 (1821). In Louisiana, interest on bills is due only from judicial demand, at common law. 8 Rob. (La.) 207 (1844).

[2] 15 Pick. (Mass.) 500 (1834).

[3] 18 Ala. 300 (1850); 15 Pick. (Mass.) 500 (1834).

[4] 151 Mass. 115 (1890).

[5] 4 Esp. (Eng.) 147 (1802).

[6] 1 Salk. (Eng.) 154 (1707); 5 Cow. (N. Y.) 424 (1826).

[7] 3 Hous. (Del.) 49 (1864).

[8] Show. (Eng.) 15 (1698); 1 C. E. Gr. (N. J.) 59 (1863); 13 Grat. (Va.) 351 (1856).

[9] 12 Allen (Mass.) 243 (1866); 10 Leigh (Va.) 281 (1839).

[10] Even if it is for the payment of a less sum. 7 T. R. (Eng.) 124 (1797).

[11] R. & M. (Eng.) 105 (1824); 1 Paine (U. S., C. C.) 661 (1824); 4 Day (Conn.) 30 (1809); 10 Conn. 95 (1834); 26 Conn. 42 (1857); R. M. Charl. (Ga.) 12 (1819); 34 Kas. 43 (1885); 2 G. & J. (Md.) 254 (1830); 12 Allen (Mass.) 243 (1866); 8 N. H. 491 (1837); 3 Cai. (N. Y.) 49 (1805); 15 Wend. (N. Y.) 76 (1835); 18 N. Y. (4 Smith) 35 (1858); 1 Watts (Pa.) 365 (1833); 1 McC. Ch. (S. C.) 100 (1825).

and not one for the jury.[1] Interest is, however, also recoverable beyond the penalty in England[2] on a bond conditioned to account for moneys to be received;[3] and where the plaintiff is kept out of his money by writs of error;[4] or, if delayed by injunction;[5] or, if the recovery is delayed by the obligor.[6] But these exceptions are not allowed in the administration of the debtor's assets where his other creditors might be injured by allowing the bond to be rated beyond the penalty.[7]

Appeal bond. A party is entitled to interest in an action on an appeal bond as well as though he proceeded on the judgment.[8]

Bail bond. No interest can be recovered on a bail bond conditioned for the appearance of a person to answer to an indictment for forgery.[9]

Replevin bond. In New Jersey, the court allows interest on a replevin bond from the date of the judgment for the return of the goods.[10] In South Carolina, the court holds that interest is not recoverable on a replevin bond;[11] but in Maryland it is held that the question should be left to the discretion of the jury.[12]

Back interest. A bond, conditioned to pay certain bills and interest on them from date if not paid on a certain

[1] 3 Cai. (N. Y.) 49 (1805).

[2] 1 Dick. (Eng.) 408 (1769), 514 (1775); 2 Ves. jr. (Eng.) 301 (1793); 6 Ves. (Eng.) 411 (1801).

[3] 2 T. R. (Eng.) 388 (1788).

[4] 2 Burr. (Eng.) 1094 (1760).

[5] 1 Vern. (Eng.) 349 (1685).

[6] 1 Vern. (Eng.) 349 (1685); 6 Ves. (Eng.) 73 (1801).

[7] 5 Ves. (Eng.) 329 (1800).

[8] 8 Wheat. (U. S.) 691 (1823); 9 Mon. 126 (1889).

[9] 127 U. S. 212 (1887).

[10] 1 Zab. (N. J.) 411 (1848); 3 Zab. (N. J.) 736 (1852); 8 Vr. (N. J.) 179 (1874).

[11] 2 Bay (S. C.) 408 (1802).

[12] 2 G. & J. (Md.) 450 (1830).

day, only carries interest from the time the bills became due or were payable.[1] So, a judgment on bonds made payable at a day subsequent to their date, with interest from a prior day, "if not punctually paid," was enjoined as to the back interest,[2] because it was secured by a penalty.

From what time allowed. If a penal bond is payable on demand, it carries interest only from demand, or date of the writ.[3] There are many rules relative to the time when interest on a bond begins to run, but the best one perhaps is that which fixes the obligor's liability for interest when he is bound to pay the principal.[4] In New York, it is held that, on a bond conditioned to pay over a certain sum of money, interest not being mentioned, nor time of payment, or that it is payable on demand, interest is chargeable from date.[5] Other rules are as follows: interest is allowed on a school commissioner's bond for failure to collect, on the amount claimed, from the time when by reasonable diligence he could have realized the money.[6] On a bond to pay a debt merely, a surety is not bound to pay interest until he has been in default himself.[7] On a penal bond to pay a definite sum if possession of certain land was recovered, interest was allowed from the time possession of the land was taken, and not from the time of the judgment merely.[8] A jail bond carries interest from the date of the judgment.[9] So, in a suit against a surety

[1] 1 H. Bl. (Eng.) 227 (1789).
[2] Gilm. (Va.) 172 (1820).
[3] Minor (Ala.) 417 (1826); 82 Ga. 33 (1888); 2 Mo. App. 123 (1870).
[4] McM. Eq. (S. C.) 103 (1841).
[5] 1 Duer (N. Y.) 369 (1852); 11 N. Y. (1 Kern.) 406 (1854).
[6] 1 Gilm. (Ill.) 347 (1844).
[7] 6 La. Ann. 51 (1851).
[8] 4 Dana (Ky.) 176 (1836).
[9] 2 Vt. 517 (1830).

on a bail bond,[1] and on a recognizance;[2] in the latter from the time of the forfeiture.[3] In a suit on an administration bond, interest is allowed from the time that the judge of probate passes his decree fixing liability.[4]

(*i*) *Bottomry.* When the risk is ended simple interest begins to run *ipso jure* without any demand. Interest on the marine interest or premium is not allowed by the civil law, but under the common law that rule is not of universal application,—the law and practice in France, however, being in favor of it. The better opinion is, that the maritime premium, as well as the sum lent, becomes due, the whole forming one aggregate debt, and that a delay in discharging it ought to be followed by the allowance of simple interest, as in other cases of debt.[5]

(*j*) *Damages.* In England and in some parts of the United States, the courts hold that damages bear interest generally from the time they are liquidated;[6] and they are liquidated when it is certain how much is due, and when it is due. They are not liquidated when one of the parties cannot alone render it certain how much is due;[7] that is, if property destroyed has a definite money value, susceptible of easy proof,[8] interest will be allowed from time of the loss.[9] The general American rule, however, is that interest shall be allowed from the time the wrong was

[1] 12 La. Ann. 720 (1857).

[2] 3 Hous. (Del.) 49 (1864).

[3] 21 Kas. 175 (1879).

[4] 1 Mass. 69 (1804).

[5] 3 Mas. (U. S., C. C.) 255 (1823); Marsh. on Ins. & Bot., b. 2, ch. 1, p. 752.

[6] Wms. Rep. (Eng.) 376, 377 (1717); 21 Ark. 349 (1860); 30 Minn. 115 (1883); 63 Mo. 99, 308, 367 (1876); 64 Mo. 47 (1876), 542 (1877); Pen. (N. J.) 652 (1810).

[7] 20 Ga. 561 (1856).

[8] 60 Conn. 125 (1891).

[9] 61 Iowa 618 (1883).

done.[1] Some courts allow interest on damages only from the time that the right of action accrued,[2] which, as a matter of fact, is always the time when the injury was done; others from the date of the writ;[3] and others not till judgment.[4] Where land is taken for railroads,[5] or highways,[6] or parks,[7] interest runs from the time the land is actually taken.[8] Other courts than those holding the above opinion differ to a considerable extent as to when interest should begin. Some say from the time the land is entered on;[9] others, from time the award is made, without demand;[10] others, from the time of the assessment;[11] and

[1] 75 Ala. 113 (1883); 79 Ala. 298 (1885); 50 Ark. 169 (1887); 9 So. Rep. (Fla.) 661 (1891); 68 Ga. 818 (1882); 81 Ga. 414 (1888); 55 Ill. 421 (1870); 74 Ill. 83 (1874); 86 Ill. 384 (1877); 6 Virg. (Me.) 600 (1870); 9 Virg. (Me.) 290 (1872); 11 Pick. (Mass.) 223 (1831); 64 Miss. 604 (1887); 13 Neb. 317 (1882); 23 Neb. 620 (1888); 25 Neb. 146 (1888); 63 Tex. 57 (1885); *contra*, 3 Scam. (Ill.) 193 (1841); 27 Iowa 22 (1869).

[2] 11 Vr. (N. J.) 11 (1878).

[3] 26 Wis. 295 (1870).

[4] 125 Pa. St. 24 (1889); 126 Pa. St. 1 (1889); 135 Pa. St. 437 (1890); 27 Pac. Rep. (Utah) 693 (1891); 5 Leigh (Va.) 598 (1833).

[5] 25 Fed. Rep. (U. S.) 886 (1885); 41 Iowa 52 (1875); 52 Iowa 613 (1879); 61 Iowa 637 (1883); 63 Iowa 443 (1884); 64 Iowa 753 (1884); 9 Virg. (Me.) 290 (1872); 105 Mass. 303 (1870); 125 Mass. 544 (1878); 127 Mass. 571 (1879); 13 Neb. 317 (1882); 28 Neb. 174 (1889); 17 Hun (N. Y.) 344 (1879).

[6] 91 Ill. 49 (1878); 93 Ill. 125 (1879); 108 Mass. 535 (1871); 116 Mass. 165 (1874); 23 Neb. 620 (1888); 14 N. H. 240 (1843). In the case last cited, a highway was laid out in 1837, but not opened till 1842. The plaintiff made no claim for land damages, but subsequently brought a suit therefor. He was allowed interest only from the time the road was opened, because "the damages could not be considered as detained before that time."

[7] 100 Ill. 75 (1881); 88 Tenn. 510 (1890).

[8] 34 Kas. 159 (1885); 1 Stew. (N. J.) 450 (1877); 25 Fed. Rep. (U. S.) 886 (1885). From demand only, says the court in 18 N. H. 75 (1846).

[9] 2 Pa. St. 340 (1845); 20 Pa. St. 240 (1853).

[10] 131 N. Y. 123 (1892).

[11] 41 Pa. St. 463 (1862).

others from judgment only.[1] In trespass for seizing personal property, interest is allowed from the time of the seizure.[2]

In an action of deceit in the sale of a farm, interest is allowed from the date of the conveyance,[3] if the mere difference in value does not make the damage good.[4]

If a statute awards special or stipulated damages, as for killing stock, no interest will be allowed,[5] even from date of the writ.[6]

On damages for personal injuries, no interest will be allowed before judgment,[7] as they do not have actual values.[8] It is allowed in Louisiana on the amount of damages on protested bills and notes.[9] In Missouri, interest was not allowed in an action for negligence, where the defendant could get no benefit from his acts.[10]

In an action for the breach of a contract, interest is allowed only from a demand,[11] or the beginning of the suit,[12] as the claim is unliquidated. So on the breach of a warranty of title,[13] the plaintiff is not allowed interest till the time of his eviction, provided he has had the profits of the land in

[1] 50 Wis. 78 (1880).

[2] 22 Ill. 493 (1859).

[3] 6 Virg. (Me.) 600 (1870).

[4] 43 Mich. 383, 623 (1880).

[5] 58 Iowa 625 (1882). See 13 Ala. 708 (1848).

[6] 11 Ired. L. (N. C.) 490 (1850).

[7] 17 S. W. Rep. (Tenn.) 882 (1891): 91 Tenn. 35 (1891).

[8] 81 Ga. 397 (1888).

[9] 2 Rob. (La.) 117 (1842); *contra*, 13 La. 357 (1839).

[10] 6 Mo. App. 594 (1879); 73 Mo. 33 (1880); 15 Mo. App. 577 (1884); 17 Mo. App. 177 (1885); 32 Mo. App. 350 (1888); 44 Mo. App. 396 (1891).

[11] 140 Mass. 517 (1886). The court in 64 Miss. 640 (1887) says from breach.

[12] 5 Rob. (La.) 192 (1843); 68 Mo. 268 (1878); 21 Tenn. 103 (1841).

[13] 27 Am. R. 13 (1877); 5 Rob. (La.) 217 (1843); 71 N. Y. 118 (1877).

the meantime.[1] So interest should not be allowed where land has been taken, so long as the plaintiff receives the rents and profits of the premises.[2]

Where a contractor agreed to build a house for another, to be paid for thirty days after it was finished, and it was not done on time, the owner forbidding further work, the contractor sued for what he had done, and was allowed interest from thirty days after the time when he would have completed the house if he had continued to work upon it.[3]

Interest is also allowed on damages for the breach of an executory contract to convey land.[4]

Interest may be recovered on the difference between the amount of the purchase money at a resale by an administrator and the amount bid by the purchaser at the first sale who failed to comply with the terms of the sale.[5]

Where goods are lost by a carrier, interest will be allowed on their value from the time of the loss.[6]

Where in a real action, judgment is to be entered for the demandant for the value of the land, if the entry of judgment on the verdict has been delayed at the request of the tenant, interest will be added to the price so estimated by the jury from the time of finding the verdict, and judgment be entered for the amount thus ascertained, in spite of a statute that judgment be rendered "for the sum so estimated" by the jury.[7]

Interest should be allowed as damages on a sum awarded to a defendant on an injunction, where the decree is in

[1] 52 Ark. 322 (1889).
[2] 8 Vr. (N. J.) 222 (1874).
[3] 9 Cush. (Mass.) 58 (1851).
[4] 11 Leigh (Va.) 261 (1840).
[5] 10 Rich. (S. C.) 60 (1856).
[6] 40 Ill. 249 (1866).
[7] 4 Greenl. (Me.) 297 (1826).

his favor, from the date of the final decree, the defendant having appealed, and the plaintiff not having been in default before.[1]

Interest should be allowed on damages for the infringement of a patent from the report of the master.[2]

Interest as a part of damages. Whether interest, *eo nomine*, is allowable in ascertaining the damages in actions of tort or not, all the authorities agree that the lapse of time from the commission of the wrong to the time of recovery may be considered in determining the damages,[3] whether interest is claimed or not; and whether or not the jury should take this fact into their consideration and add interest, is in their discretion.[4] The court may instruct the jury, says the supreme court of Florida, to allow interest as damages from the destruction of property;[5] but where interest is given as damages by a statute, the court will not allow interest on such damages.[6] The court has no right to add interest to the verdict of a jury in an action for damages,[7] as it is presumed that the jury reckoned it in[8] (it being an element of damage), which they can do if they wish.[9] The court should add interest on the verdict from the day the judgment is actually rendered,

[1] 36 Vt. 439 (1863).

[2] 141 U. S. 441 (1891).

[3] 68 Ga. 818 (1882); 4 Zab. (N. J.) 47 (1853); 125 Pa. St. 24 (1889); 126 Pa. St. 1 (1889); 135 Pa. St. 437 (1890); 56 Vt. 401 (1883).

[4] 1 M. & S. (Eng.) 169 (1813); 1 Harr. (Del.) 234 (1833), 149 (1836); 11 Pick. (Mass.) 421 (1831); 141 Mass. 126 (1886); 30 Minn. 18 (1882); 96 N. Y. 477 (1884); 32 N. E. Rep. (N. Y.) 44 (1892); 51 N. W. Rep. (So. Dak.) 601 (1893); 82 Tex. 104 (1891).

[5] 27 Fla. 1 (1891).

[6] 13 Ala. 708 (1848).

[7] 36 Iowa 121 (1872).

[8] 22 Iowa 49 (1867); 2 Spears (S. C.) 594 (1844). The clerk should add the interest whether the jury did or not, says 91 N. Y. 651 (1883).

[9] 22 Iowa 49 (1867); 33 Iowa 422, 502 (1871); 10 Rich. (S. C.) 382 (1857); 2 W. Va. 90 (1867); *contra*, 104 Pa. St. 306 (1883).

and not from the first day of the term;[1] and the Maine court holds that the jury should not be allowed to add interest subsequently to the date of the writ.[2] But the supreme court of the United States says that the allowance of interest in collisions and other cases of pure damage is in the discretion of the court.[3]

Costs. The circuit court of the United States is not bound to allow interest on costs awarded by the district court, although such costs are included in the decree of the circuit court.[4]

Compound interest. Where a contract provided for liquidated damages, on a breach and for yearly settlement, interest on the damages of each year, from the end of the year, should be allowed.[5]

Rests. In a breach of covenant of warranty of title in a deed of land, rests are not allowable in the computation of interest upon the amount of the consideration paid for the land.[6]

(*k*) *Debts of another.* The measure of damages in an action brought upon a promise to pay a debt of another, brought after the debt was due, but before any payment thereon, is the amount of the debt and interest.[7] Where the promise is to pay the debt, if it is not paid on a day named, the promissor is liable for interest from the day named, without notice of the non-payment.[8]

(*l*) *Deposits.* Mere depositaries are not chargeable with interest on the deposits in their hands.[9] It is al-

[1] 27 Pac. Rep. (Utah) 693 (1891); 15 W. Va. 628 (1879).
[2] 4 Heath (Me.) 287 (1855).
[3] 118 U. S. 507 (1886). See 53 Fed. Rep. (Me.) 948, 952 (1891).
[4] 118 U. S. 507 (1886).
[5] 86 N. Y. 618 (1881).
[6] 30 N. H. 531 (1855).
[7] 119 Mass. 500 (1876).
[8] 58 Ga. 54 (1877).
[9] 26 Vt. 100 (1853).

lowed, however, on purchase money remaining in the purchaser's hands to pay off incumbrances. It is also allowed on deposits made by a purchaser, either to a principal or an auctioneer, which he is entitled to recover,[1] in a suit against the vendor, by alleging special damage in the declaration.[2] If the suit is against the auctioneer, a demand upon him must be made.[3] If the purchaser has had possession of the premises, which have been of value to him, the vendors will be entitled to interest upon the purchase money as a remuneration for the occupation.[4]

Banks. At common law a banker is not liable to pay interest upon money deposited, although at the time of the deposit it is declared that interest shall not be payable upon a certain event which did not happen.[5] So a bank paying a check with a forged indorsement is not liable to pay interest on it.[6] A depositor in a national bank, when it suspends payment, and a receiver is appointed, is entitled to interest upon his deposit from the time of his demand,[7] even though it be interest on interest.

(*m*) *Dividends.* Interest is not allowed against corporations on dividends;[8] nor on profits of shareholders that have been retained a series of years;[9] but it is allowable in an action for dividends on preferred stock.[10]

[1] 3 Camph. (Eng.) 258 (1812); 1 Moore (Eng.) 322 (1817); 7 Taun. (Eng.) 592 (1817); 48 N. H. 273 (1869); 38 Vt. 559 (1866); *contra*, 5 Taun. (Eng.) 625 (1814); 1 M. & Rob. (Eng.) 143 (1831); 5 C. & P. (Eng.) 48 (1833).

[2] 1 Moore (Eng.) 322 (1817).

[3] 1 Moore (Eng.) 481 (1817).

[4] 4 Ala. 21 (1842).

[5] 2 N. & M. (Eng.) 120 (1833); 5 B. & Ad. (Eng.) 282 (1833).

[6] 81 Ga. 597 (1888).

[7] 94 U. S. 437 (1876).

[8] 6 Gill (Md.) 363 (1847).

[9] 6 La. 745 (1834).

[10] 84 N. Y. 157 (1881).

(n) *Dower, etc.* A widow is entitled in equity, when dower is assigned to her, to an account for rents and profits, or, if it be in money, to interest upon it.[1]

A widow's statutory interest in her husband's estate, when she waives the provisions of the will, will not bear interest until an effectual order for the payment of it has been made.[2]

Where a wife is deprived of the benefits of a settlement, among which is the enjoyment of the estate by her, if surviving, and her property is restored to her, she is entitled to interest from her husband's decease.[3]

(o) *Money fraudulently obtained.* Interest is allowed on money obtained by fraud from the time it was obtained.[4] So, if interest has been paid it can be recovered.[5]

Where a party receives unimproved lands in the set-off of a claim, through the fraud of the debtor, which contract he afterward rescinds, he can collect interest from the time of the original settlement, if he has had no rent or profits from the land, and tenders a reconveyance.[6]

(p) *Incumbrances.* The general rule is that particular tenants or tenants for life must pay the interest on incumbrances on the estate, as between themselves and the remainder-men.[7] And the incumbrancer is entitled to

[1] 2 Bail. (S. C.) 343 (1831); Rich. Eq. Cas. (S. C.) 378 (1832); 1 S. C. 119 (1869).

[2] 101 Mass. 40 (1869).

[3] Bail. Eq. (S. C.) 268 (1831).

[4] 1 Campb. (Eng.) 129 (1807); 2 Kelley (Ga.) 370 (1847); 35 Ga. 40, 136, 193 (1866); 85 Ga. 141 (1890); 11 Mass. 504 (1814); 118 Mass. 147 (1875); 144 Mass. 313 (1887); 12 Mo. App. 335 (1882); 3 Cow. (N. Y.) 393 (1824); 39 Hun (N. Y.) 519 (1886).

[5] 30 Mo. App. 10 (1888).

[6] 81 Ill. 15 (1875).

[7] 4 Ves. (Eng.) 24 (1798); 89 Ala. 273 (1889); 3 Bland's Ch. (Md.) 245 (1831); 5 Johns. Ch. (N. Y.) 482 (1821); Bail. Eq. (S. C.) 337 (1831); 1 Washb. R. P., 96, 257, 573; Story, Eq. Jur., § 487.

the arrears of interest against remainder-men, though by laches he omitted to obtain it from the tenant for life.[1] But the Vermont court has decided that there is no rule there requiring a dowress in an equity of redemption to pay interest.[2]

Legatees for life are bound to keep down the interest of a debt charged upon their legacies, and they may be compelled to contribute to its payment; but, they are not bound to surrender all the profits for the purpose of extinguishing it.[3]

(*q*) *Insolvency.* The only interest accruing before the bankruptcy or insolvency of the debtor that can be proved on a debt in insolvency is contractual interest.[4]

If there are several preferred creditors, and the assets are insufficient to pay the interest due them in full, they are to be paid proportionately as far as the money will go.[5]

There is no objection to adding interest generally to all claims from date of failure or death to the time of allowance of the claims, report of the commissioners or decree of distribution. It is proper enough to do it, but it can possibly have no perceptible effect if the estate is really insolvent.[6] It is immaterial to the creditors themselves, provided an equitable principle be adopted, whether interest stops at the time of the failure or death of the debtor, or at the time of the report of the commissioners, or the decree of distribution.[7] But the Connecticut rule

[1] 2 Madd. (Eng.) 457 (1816).

[2] 23 Vt. 248 (1851).

[3] 2 Dev. Eq. (N. C.) 420 (1833).

[4] Cox Eq. Cas. (Eng.) 219 (1790); 2 B. & A. (Eng.) 305 (1819); 18 S. C. 87 (1882).

[5] 1 Paige (N. Y.) 181 (1828).

[6] 13 Mass. 537 (1816); 4 Met. (Mass.) 317 (1842).

[7] 4 Met. (Mass.) 317 (1842).

is not to allow interest after the average is struck,[1] nor between the rendering of the report of the commissioners and the passing of the decree.[2]

If there is a surplus of funds, courts may add interest to the claims from the time of the commissioners' return to the decree of distribution;[3] and if any assets then remain, interest on their debts under the ordinary rules should be decreed to the creditors.[4] It is then a different question than it is when it arises between the creditors only.

Assignment. In an assignment for the benefit of creditors, the demands stated as a charge on the funds should include interest up to the time of selling the property, and realizing the proceeds.[5]

Interest on a claim is not suspended by the debtor placing it upon his schedule, when the creditor takes no part in the proceedings, although the debtor may obtain a respite.[6]

Where a debtor assigned his estate in trust, *inter alia*, to pay to certain persons the amount of their respective demands in full, the surplus to go to the debtor, and the creditors release, they are entitled to interest on their debts, if the fund prove sufficient.[7]

Whether interest is to be paid to a preferred creditor under an assignment depends upon the language used in the assignment.[8]

[1] Kirby (Conn.) 38 (1786); 21 Conn. 41 (1851).

[2] 21 Conn. 41 (1851).

[3] 4 Met. (Mass.) 317 (1842).

[4] 3 Ch. Rep. (Eng.) 64 (1670); 3 Brown's Ch. (Eng.) 436 (1792); 4 Met. (Mass.) 317 (1842); *contra*, 2 Wms. Rep. (Eng.) 27 (1722).

[5] 18 Pick. (Mass.) 360 (1836).

[6] 12 La. Ann. 833 (1857).

[7] 9 S. & R. (Pa.) 123 (1822).

[8] 6 W. & S. (Pa.) 223 (1843).

(*r*) *Judgments.* At common law formerly judgments did not bear interest;[1] but they generally do now;[2] even if it is otherwise agreed.[3] Judgments for costs also draw interest;[4] so on attorneys' fees stipulated in a mortgage.[5] A judgment on a bill for official fees, unless there has been a regular taxation as against the debtor, does not draw interest.[6] If part of the costs of a judgment is expressed to be payable in chattels, no interest will be allowed thereon.[7] Neither will interest be allowed on costs when payment has been delayed by error proceedings.[8] Interest cannot be collected on a judgment on a bond with penalty to perform covenants, when the jury find a verdict for a specific sum.[9]

A judgment for use and occupation does not draw interest.[10]

Some courts do not allow interest on the judgment if

[1] 17 Ala. 404 (1850); 2 Cal. 99 (1852); 7 Mart., N. S. (La.) 14 (1828), 425 (1829); 4 Met. (Mass.) 317 (1842); Walk. (Miss.) 214 (1826); 2 N. H. 169 (1820); 6 N. H. 567 (1834); 20 N. H. 34 (1849); 3 Hawks (N. C.) 36 (1824); 4 Dall. (Pa.) 251 (1802); 5 Binn. (Pa.) 61 (1812); 16 Pa. St. 151 (1851); 1 McC. (S. C.) 328 (1821); 4 McC. (S. C.) 212 (1827); 3 Rich. (S. C.) 376, 380 (1832).

[2] 3 Stew. (Ala.) 109 (1830); 7 Port. (Ala.) 110 (1838); 10 Ala. 867 (1846); 25 Ill. 95 (1860); 5 Kas. 70 (1869); 1 Mon. 66 (1868); 2 N. H. 169 (1820); 20 N. H. 34 (1849); Bat.'s Mart. & 2d Hay'd (N. C.) 182 (1797); 4 Dall. (Pa.) 251 (1802); 2 Brev. (S. C.) 99 (1806); 2 N. & McC. (S. C.) 395 (1820); 1 McC. (S. C.) 328 (1821); 3 Rich. (S. C.) 376, 380 (1832); 2 Spears (S. C.) 573 (1841); 7 Leigh (Va.) 346 (1836); 20 Wis. 602 (1866).

[3] 6 Binn. (Pa.) 435 (1814).

[4] 26 Ind. 123 (1890); 42 O. St. 82 (1884); 2 Brev. (S. C.) 99 (1806); 7 Leigh (Va.) 346 (1836); *contra*, 95 Pa. St. 481 (1880).

[5] 11 Kas. 381 (1873).

[6] 5 Denio (N. Y.) 355 (1848).

[7] 2 Brev. (S. C.) 99 (1806).

[8] 31 Neb. 816 (1891).

[9] 3 McC. (S. C.) 166 (1825).

[10] 8 Cal. 32 (1857).

the cause of action upon which it is founded was *ex delicto*;[1] so, in an action on a bond to recover damages;[2] and this is true in equity.[3] Other courts hold that interest should be allowed on judgments in tort as well as for any other cause, as the judgment liquidates the demand and makes it a debt of a certain amount.[4] A judgment on a claim in contract will bear interest,[5] whether the contract upon which it was founded did or not.[6]

A judgment against a garnishee will not be for interest if the writ does not claim it.[7]

Where a judgment is recovered on an open account, and the defendant pays it before an action of debt is commenced thereon, he is not liable for interest.[8]

Where the plaintiff is entitled to interest on the amount due him, from commencement of the action, he may include such interest in a judgment taken by default, although the damages were unliquidated and the interest was not specifically demanded in the complaint.[9]

Where there has been no delay by defendant, and, the action being on a penal bond, damages have been assessed to the full amount of the penalty, no interest is allowed.[10]

Interest is not taxable for delay on verdicts in tort.[11]

[1] 1 Mon. (Ky.) 150 (1824); 1 J. J. Mar. (Ky.) 95 (1829); 84 Ky. 462 (1886); 15 La. Ann. 504 (1860); *contra*, 18 La. Ann. 28 (1866); 15 Nev. 133 (1880); 2 Bay (S. C.) 193 (1798).

[2] 15 La. Ann. 504 (1860).

[3] 1 Mon. (Ky.) 150 (1824).

[4] 22 Wend. (N. Y.) 157 (1839).

[5] 3 La. Ann. 574 (1848); 15 La. Ann. 333 (1860); 2 Spears (S. C.) 573 (1844); 9 Tex. 517 (1853).

[6] 1 Hill (S. C.) 79 (1833); 9 Tex. 517 (1853); *contra*, 3 McC. (S. C.) 166 (1825).

[7] 3 Call (Va.) 455 (1803).

[8] 3 Rich. (S. C.) 376, 380 (1832).

[9] 68 Wis. 61 (1887).

[10] 1 Johns. (N. Y.) 343 (1806).

[11] 19 Wend. (N. Y.) 101 (1838).

Interest cannot be allowed on a judgment given for the balance of an account between the parties, when payments have been made for costs, and on other accounts.[1]

Demand. A demand of payment of the judgment is not necessary,[2] and need not be alleged or proved.[3]

Rate. The contractual rate is merged in the judgment, and from the date of the judgment the rate allowed is the legal rate[4] of the place where, and time when,[5] the judgment is sought to be enforced. There are some courts, however, that hold that the contract rate will be allowed on the judgment;[6] and if the judgment is founded on two contracts bearing different rates, interest should be given proportionately for both rates.[7] If a judgment is for interest only it bears the legal rate.[8]

Validity. The judgment need not state how much of it is principal and how much is interest.[9] In Louisiana and Nevada, it must state on its face that it bears interest.[10]

When interest begins to run. Interest on a judgment begins to run on the day when it is rendered or entered.

[1] 2 La. 512 (1831).

[2] 9 Virg. (Me.) 255 (1872).

[3] 129 Mass. 600 (1880).

[4] 32 Ark. 573 (1877); Breese (Ill.) 52, 83 (1824); 1 Scam. (Ill.) 137 (1834); 35 Ill. 152 (1864); 45 Ill. 178 (1867); 79 Ill. 532 (1875); 27 Iowa 349 (1862); 136 Mass. 344 (1884); 6 Neb. 356 (1877); 16 S. C. 15, 169 (1881); 20 Tex. 465 (1857).

[5] 26 Hun (N. Y.) 546 (1882).

[6] 5 Cal. 116 (1855); 6 Cal. 155 (1856); 9 Cal. 294 (1858); 28 Cal. 289 (1865); 32 Cal. 82 (1867); 14 Mo. App. 187 (1883); 25 O. St. 622 (1874). The court in 29 Cal. 165 (1865) said that the contractual rate should be allowed if it was prayed or pleaded for, otherwise not; but see the other California cases.

[7] 47 Iowa 477 (1877).

[8] 1 G. Gr. (Iowa) 66 (1847).

[9] 12 Ala. 54 (1847). It must state how much of it is principal, says the court in 1 Nev. 613 (1865).

[10] 12 La. Ann. 112, 116 (1857); 15 Nev. 313 (1880).

A decree of the orphans' court against an administrator, for the amount of which an action on his bond is brought, bears interest from the time of its rendition.[1] In equity, on a master's report, interest will be allowed from the day up to which he computed interest.[2] When a dividend is declared by a receiver the plaintiff is entitled to interest on the amount of his dividend from the time it was declared.[3] In Louisiana, if a judgment on a suit *ex contractu* does not state when interest begins to run, it will commence at the institution of the suit.[4]

A verdict bears interest only from time of judgment upon it;[5] but the court may enter a judgment *nunc pro tunc*, and thus make a verdict bear interest from its date.[6] An award, and, also, a master's report, if confirmed, bears interest from the time they are made;[7] and if an award is subsequently reduced in amount, interest is only given from the final allowance.[8] Where a report on an order of reference must be confirmed before a decree can be carried into effect, interest runs from the date of its confirmation.[9]

If the plaintiff, after obtaining a verdict, delays the cause by moving for a new trial, he can have interest only to the time of the verdict.[10] Where the delay is caused partly by each of the parties the plaintiff can only have interest

[1] 22 Ala. 692 (1853).

[2] 31 Ala. 288 (1858).

[3] 133 U. S. 433 (1889).

[4] 15 La. Ann. 333 (1860).

[5] 27 Ind. 527 (1867); 30 Pa. St. 340 (1858); 37 Pa. St. 465 (1860).

[6] 37 Pa. St. 465 (1860).

[7] 3 Ind. 86 (1851); 87 Ind. 475 (1882); 6 Dana (Ky.) 16 (1837); Hopk. (N. Y.) 314 (1824); 3 Hill (N. Y.) 426 (1841); 1 Yeates (Pa.) 480 (1795); 28 Pa. St. 211 (1857).

[8] 44 Hun (N. Y.) 117 (1887).

[9] 38 Mich. 1 (1878); 11 Hun (N. Y.) 385 (1877).

[10] 2 Cai. (N. Y.) 253 (1804).

during that portion of the period of delay caused by the defendant.[1]

When interest ends. Interest on judgments ceases at the return and confirmation of administrators', executors' and sheriffs' sales.[2] Defendants are not chargeable with interest after the return day of the execution, when enough has been raised by the sale of property to pay the interest to the time, unless delay in the payment of the money to the plaintiff has been occasioned by them.[3] So where land, encumbered by judgments, is sold by a sheriff, and the money paid into court for distribution, it is error to allow interest on the judgments after the sale.[4]

The adjudication of commissioners in insolvency is not in the nature of a judgment, so that the debts would bear the legal rate of interest after their return.[5] But if, after the return, for any reason, any money is left over it should be given to those to whom the court has ordered distribution, as interest.[6] In Rhode Island, the report of the commissioners is regarded as a judgment, ascertaining the sums due from the deceased at his death, and interest is allowed thereon as upon a judgment;[7] but though it is so regarded, how its effect can be any different than that of the rule in Massachusetts as stated in the preceding sentence it is difficult to perceive.

A decree binding all property without reference to the sale of any part in particular and distribution of the proceeds, has the same force as regards interest as judgments have when contending for money.[8]

[1] 2 Den. (N. Y.) 188 (1846).
[2] 4 Watts (Pa.) 71 (1835).
[3] 6 Watts (Pa.) 96 (1837).
[4] 25 Atl. Rep. (Pa.) 76 (1892).
[5] 139 Mass. 360 (1885).
[6] 4 Met. (Mass.) 317 (1842).
[7] 2 R. I. 60 (1851).
[8] 65 Ga. 189 (1880).

Decisions of the county court allowing claims against an estate are judgments, and will bear interest the same as common judgments.[1] So, are such claims when they are approved by the administrator, says the Texas court, that being a sort of judgment.[2]

Compound interest. Judgments generally carry interest on interest,[3] but if the supreme court simply affirms a judgment, it must not give interest on the aggregate of the principal and interest then due, but on the original judgment.[4] Where a judgment is given merely as a security, interest ought not to be calculated on the whole amount of the judgment if it contains both principal and interest, but only on the sum originally due.[5]

Lien. The lien of a judgment is good for interest which it includes, and which has accrued on it, as for the principal.[6] Where interest on a judgment cannot be enforced by execution, equity does not treat it as a lien in respect to interest upon it.[7] Interest which accrues after judgment on a cause of action bearing interest is no part of the recovery, or damages assessed.[8]

Audita querela. Interest on a debt, whose payment has been suspended by an *audita querela*, is not recoverable on the bond given for the prosecution of the *audita*.[9]

[1] 16 Ill. 83 (1854).

[2] 9 Tex. 517 (1853).

[3] 5 Cal. 416 (1855); 100 Ill. 276 (1881); 8 Mon. 312 (1889); 5 S. & R. (Pa.) 220 (1819); 13 Tex. 75 (1854); 12 W. Va. 143 (1877); 14 W. Va. 737 (1879); *contra.* 2 Ill. (1 Scam.) 137 (1834); 1 J. J. Mar. (Ky.) 166 (1829); 3 La. 431 (1832); 1 Gill (Md.) 372 (1843); 1 Nev. 613 (1865); 5 Binn. (Pa.) 61 (1812); 2 Hill (S. C.) 343 (1834). Such interest on interest is not compound interest, says the court in 2 Bl. Ch. (Md.) 306 (1830). See more citations in chapter six.

[4] 30 Pa. St. 340 (1858).

[5] 3 Dall. (Pa.) 506 (1799).

[6] 26 Hun (N. Y.) 546 (1882); 1 McC. Ch. (S. C.) 53, 100 (1825).

[7] 6 Paige (N. Y.) 88 (1836).

[8] 2 Strob. (S. C.) 113 (1847).

[9] 1 Root (Conn.) 372 (1792).

Appeal. In the case of a judgment on appeal, interest is to be calculated during the appeal,[1] but on the amount of the principal only.[2]

Reviving judgments. In reviving a judgment by a *scire facias*, interest on it is not to be reckoned for the time it has been dormant.[3] Where a judgment has been revived by repeated writs of *scire facias*, the plaintiff has the right to charge interest on the aggregate of principal and interest due at the time of rendering judgment on each writ.[4]

On a judgment on a *scire facias* against bail, the jury may give interest from the day the bail became fixed; that is, after the expiration of the time allowed *ex gratia* for the surrender;[5] but the plaintiff must not neglect to take out execution and proceed against the bail.[6]

Motion for new trial and exceptions. Where a plaintiff in an action of contract is delayed of his judgment by the unsuccessful motion of the defendant for a new trial, or when the defendant fails to establish his exceptions, the plaintiff shall always have interest on the sum found by the verdict, from the time of finding the same to the time of judgment.[7]

All judgments and decrees when stayed by injunction, or supersedeas, or appeal, bear interest, unless rendered on causes of action arising *ex delicto*, says the Kentucky court.[8] The United States circuit court, however, is not

[1] 2 Ill. (1 Scam.) 137 (1834); 6 Paige (N. Y.) 10 (1836); 21 Pa. St. 291 (1855).

[2] 2 Ill. (1 Scam.) 137 (1834).

[3] Bat.'s Mart. & 2d Hay'd (N. C.) 182 (1797); 4 Watts (Pa.) 341 (1835); 2 Mill (S. C.) 146 (1818); 1 McC. (S. C.) 171 (1821); 8 Vt. 156 (1836); *contra*, 15 Ga. 435 (1854).

[4] 5 S. & R. (Pa.) 220 (1819).

[5] Col. & C. Cas. (N. Y.) 65 (1798).

[6] 2 Johns. (N. Y.) 480 (1807).

[7] 25 Conn. 491 (1857); 6 Mass. 262 (1810). In Connecticut, there is such a rule of court. 18 Conn. 575. *Contra*, 37 Md. 443 (1872).

[8] 3 J. J. Mar. (Ky.) 103 (1829); 4 J. J. Mar. (Ky.) 410 (1830).

bound to allow interest on the costs awarded by the district court, although such costs are included in the decree of the circuit court.[1]

Review. Where a court of errors affirms the judgment of the court below, interest should only be given from the time of the affirmance of the judgment in the higher court.[2] The court in New York says, it is always in the discretion of the court, and will not be allowed if the costs are sufficient to cover the damage.[3]

When a plaintiff's verdict on review is less than his verdict in the original action, the defendant is entitled to judgment for the difference between the verdicts, and interest on the difference for the time between the verdicts, irrespective of the question whether he has paid the former judgment.[4] A judgment on review of a judgment that has been paid, the verdict being reversed, should contain the interest on the first judgment from the time it was paid to the time of the judgment on review.[5]

How collected. Executions must follow the judgments; that is, if a judgment gives interest the execution must.[6] Under a judgment at law, no interest subsequent to the date of the judgment can be recovered on execution;[7] but an action must be brought.[8] A levy on execution for such interest would be invalid.[9] When statutes give the authority to collect on execution interest on the judgment accru-

[1] 118 U. S. 507 (1886).

[2] 15 Johns. (N. Y.) 221 (1818); 4 Cow. (N. Y.) 53 (1825).

[3] 2 Wend. (N. Y.) 209 (1829).

[4] 54 N. H. 96 (1873).

[5] 54 N. H. 346 (1874).

[6] 1 Nev. 613 (1865); 14 Nev. 405 (1879).

[7] 1 Brev. (S. C.) 454 (1804).

[8] 2 Ves. Jr. (Eng.) 162 (1793); 15 N. H. 337 (1844). Statutes generally provide for interest on judgments accruing after their rendition to be collected on execution.

[9] 1 Nev. 613 (1865).

ing after the judgment was rendered, the levy on execution can be for interest only to the time of making the levy,[1] that is, when the levy is completed.[2]

Equity. The practice of allowing interest on judgments, etc., in equity varies somewhat from the practice at law. Equity will decree interest on a bond on judgment beyond the penalty against the principal debtor.[3]

A direction to a master to compute the amount due on a judgment in tort, is not a positive direction to compute interest upon it. The allowance of interest on such a judgment is not a matter of course in equity.[4]

Sureties on a replevin bond must pay interest on damages from the time of the judgment in the original action.[5]

Foreign judgments. Foreign judgments are generally held not to bear interest,[6] unless the original cause of action bore interest,[7] or by proof that the foreign state allows interest on judgments,[8] or by the terms of the judgment itself it bears interest.[9] In the latter case, the plaintiff need not show what the law of the place where the judgment was obtained is, because the interest is ascertainable from the judgment.[10] If it is settled that a foreign judg-

[1] 2 Heath (Me.) 423 (1854).

[2] 2 Allen (Mass.) 562 (1861); 9 Allen (Mass.) 147 (1864).

[3] 13 Grat. (Va.) 354 (1856).

[4] 3 Paige (N. Y.) 100 (1832); 5 Paige (N. Y.) 543 (1836).

[5] 14 Ore. 293 (1886).

[6] 4 Campb. (Eng.) 380 (1816); 2 Cal. 99 (1852); *contra*, 7 Col. 561 (1884); 25 Ill. 95 (1860), without any averment of the law of the foreign country; 129 Mass. 600 (1880), which holds that a foreign judgment is a liquidation of damages that will carry interest.

[7] 3 McC. (S. C.) 166 (1825); 3 Tex. 487 (1848). See the statutes.

[8] 20 Ala. 629 (1852); 2 Cal. 99 (1852); *contra*, Breese (Ill.) 298, 378 (1830); 25 Ill. 83 (1860), which allows interest on a foreign judgment without alleging that interest is allowed by the state where the judgment was recovered; 46 Ill. 69 (1867).

[9] 13 Ala. 722 (1848); Breese (Ill.) 298 (1830).

[10] Breese (Ill.) 298 (1830).

ment carries interest, the general rule is to allow the legal rate of the place where the action on the judgment is brought;[1] but if it is claimed that the rate of interest is different in the state in which the judgment was rendered, that fact must be averred and proved.[2]

(s) *Legacies.* A testator may order that interest be allowed upon a legacy, and from what time;[3] but, generally, it is allowed from the time when the legacy is payable,[4] availability of assets making no difference in the rule,[5] and no demand being necessary.[6] The period from which the statute of limitations begins to run and the time from which interest is payable are generally identical.[7] A legacy given to a grandchild, an infant, to be paid when the wife of the testator thought best, she dying about twenty years afterward, without paying it, no demand having been made, interest was allowed on the legacy from the death of the testator, the wife, who was executrix, being deemed a trustee for the child.[8] Where a particular legacy is due upon demand, a demand for the

[1] 38 Iowa 237 (1874); 5 Gray (Mass.) 9 (1855); 129 Mass. 600 (1880); 136 Mass. 344 (1884); *contra*, 72 Cal. 264 (1887), which allows the legal rate of the foreign state, if no rate is named in the judgment.

[2] 38 Iowa 237 (1874).

[3] 136 Pa. St. 374 (1890).

[4] 1 Cox (Eng.) 133 (1784); 9 Beav. (Eng.) 164 (1846); 15 L. J., N. S., Ch. (Eng.) 193 (1846); 10 Jur. (Eng.) 150; 12 L. T., N. S. (Eng.) 763; 34 Ga. 309 (1866); 106 Mass. 586 (1871); 20 Atl. Rep. (N. H.) 387 (1890); 2 Johns. Ch. (N. Y.) 614 (1817); 1 Barb. (N. Y.) 77 (1845); 12 N. Y. (2 Kern.) 472 (1855); 127 N. Y. 402 (1891); 5 Jones Eq. (N. C.) 4 (1859); 6 Jones Eq. (N. C.) 224 (1861); 62 Pa. St. 139 (1869); Bail. Eq. (S. C.) 274 (1831).

[5] 1 Sch. & Lef. (Ire.) 10 (1802); 106 Mass. 586 (1871); 58 Vt. 95 (1886).

[6] 2 Haml. (Me.) 204 (1889); 106 Mass. 586 (1871); *contra*, Pre. Ch. (Eng.) 161 (1701).

[7] 27 Beav. (Eng.) 448 (1857); 3 Jur., N. S. (Eng.) 1237 (1857); 27 L. J., Ch. (Eng.) 545 (1858).

[8] 1 Vern. (Eng.) 251 (1684).

principal is a demand for both principal and interest, without an express stipulation for interest.[1] The fact that the testator directed in his will that a legacy be paid "next after my lawful debts;"[2] or, "as soon as the same can be conveniently done from sales and collections of my property without sacrifice;"[3] or, "forthwith upon my decease;"[4] or, "as soon as possible,"[5] makes no difference in the rule. Neither would the simple fact that an infant legatee had no guardian,[6] nor a *feme covert* had no trustee,[7] make any difference. If a testator directs that legacies shall be paid within three years, interest does not begin to run until the end of three years from his decease.[8] Where legacies are to be paid out of the proceeds of real estate which was not to be sold for two years, interest does not run till the end of that time.[9] Neither does a pecuniary legacy bear interest when the settlement of an estate is protracted by litigation three or four years, when such legatee has had the benefit of it all the time.[10]

Interest, however, will not be decreed on a legacy, where it appears that, though not actually appropriated to the legatee, it has been lodged at a bank where he enjoyed the benefit of it by the banker's releasing to him in con-

[1] 17 La. 328 (1841).

[2] 106 Mass. 586 (1871).

[3] 106 Mass. 586 (1871).

[4] 3 Md. Ch. 526 (1850).

[5] 3 Md. Ch. 526 (1850).

[6] 106 Mass. 586 (1871).

[7] 13 Ala. 554 (1848).

[8] 106 Mass. 586 (1871). So, if it is to be paid "as soon as convenient," within three years. 2 Y. & Coll (Eng.) 525 (1837). *Contra*, 53 L. J., Ch. Div. (Eng.) 525 (1884); 50 L. T. N. S. (Eng.) 355 (1884). These two cases say that interest in such a case begins to run one year after the decease of the testator.

[9] Coke P. C. (Eng.) 97.

[10] 19 Conn. 408 (1849).

sequence the interest on a sum of equal amount due by him to the bank;[1] or if it has been brought into court, while it remains there, unless it is placed at interest by the court, when it will carry what it earns.[2]

Where a certain amount of money is given to children of the testator in one sum, to be divided between them equally, their shares do not bear interest from the end of one year after the testator's death as against each other.[3]

Specific legacies. Unless the terms of the will are otherwise, specific legacies bear interest from the testator's death,[4] though they are not to be paid or delivered until a future day.[5] So, if the legacy is to be paid out of certain assets drawing interest.[6]

General legacies. General, or pecuniary legacies begin to draw interest one year after the death of the testator,[7]

[1] Wall. Lyn. (Ire.) 358 (1785).

[2] 2 P. W. (Eng.) 27 (1722).

[3] 13 Rich. Eq. (S. C.) 180 (1867).

[4] 2 Ves. sr. (Eng.) 563 (1751); 1 Hous. (Del.) 382 (1857); 5 Geo. (Miss.) 510 (1857); 41 N. H. 391 (1860); 5 Jones Eq. (N. C.) 4 (1859); 3 W. & S. (Pa.) 30 (1842).

[5] 5 Geo. (Miss.) 510 (1857).

[6] 6 Jones Eq. (N. C.) 365 (1863).

[7] 1 Ves. sr. (Eng.) 209 (1749); 1 Ves. (Eng.) 367 (1791); 7 Ves. (Eng.) 89 (1802); 10 Ves. (Eng.) 333 (1804); 13 Ves. (Eng.) 333 (1807); 2 DeG., J. & Sm. (Eng.) 373 (1864); 49 L. T., N. S. (Eng.) 554 (1883); 24 L. R., Ch. Div. (Eng.) 616 (1883); 1 Sch. & Lef. (Ire.) 10 (1802); 1 Hous. (Del.) 382 (1857); 2 Haml. (Me.) 204 (1889); 106 Mass. 586 (1871); 149 Mass. 82 (1889); Walk. (Miss.) 179 (1824); 41 N. H. 391 (1860); 56 N. H. 191 (1875); 17 Stew. (N. J.) 506 (1888); 2 Dick. (N. J.) 179 (1890); 17 Hun (N. Y.) 341 (1879); 5 Binn. (Pa.) 472 (1813); 2 Pa. St. 388 (1845); 106 Pa. St. 268 (1884); 16 R. I. 98 (1889); 4 Rich. Eq. (S. C.) 254 (1852); 3 Munf. (Va.) 10 (1811). So, if it is to be paid "as soon as convenient." 152 Mass. 71 (1890). *Contra*, from the testator's decease. 39 N. H. 547 (1859); 2 Rand. (Va.) 409 (1824). The Alabama court says interest runs from eighteen months after the testator's decease, but statutes have probably affected the rule there. 13 Ala. 554 (1848); 55 Ala. 440 (1876).

though there is no one to receive them for many years.[1] So, on a legacy to a legatee in remainder, interest will begin one year after the death of the tenant for life.[2] If the time of payment of a general legacy is named in the will, interest will be allowed only from and after that time,[3] notwithstanding the fact that the legacies may be vested;[4] and when that period arrives the legatee will be entitled to interest even though the legacy be charged upon a dry reversion.[5]

This rule applies to similar legacies under a *feme covert's* will made in the exercise of a power of appointment.[6]

The rule is the same when applied to a legacy given to the wife in lieu of dower.[7]

Where only interest or income is given, it will begin to run at the decease of the testator;[8] and if it is given for the life of the legatee, it will run to the very day of his death, though it is "yearly interest" that is given.[9]

When a legacy is given payable at a future day with interest, and the legatee dies before it becomes payable, the arrears of interest up to the time of the legatee's death must be paid to his personal representatives.[10]

[1] 7 Grat. (Va.) 377 (1851).

[2] 3 Munf. (Va.) 10 (1811).

[3] 1 Vern. (Eng.) 261 (1684); 3 Atk. (Eng.) 101 (1744); 1 Cox Ch. (Eng.) 133 (1784); 4 Ves. (Eng.) 1 (1798); 69 Ind. 203 (1879); 4 M. & M'H. (Md.) 58 (1797); 1 Md. Ch. 152 (1847); 3 Md. Ch. 266 (1851), 526 (1850).

[4] Finch's Pres. in Ch. (Eng.) 337 (1712); 17 Ala. 396 (1850).

[5] 2 Atk. (Eng.) 108 (1740).

[6] 2 Hem. & M. (Eng.) 262 (1864).

[7] 45 L. R., Ch. Div. (Eng.) 496 (1890).

[8] 7 Ves. (Eng.) 89 (1802); 17 Stew. (N. J.) 479, 506 (1888); 2 Dick. (N. J.) 73 (1890); 55 Hun (N. Y.) 503 (1890); 2 Ames (5 R. I.) 353 (1858).

[9] 1 Del. Ch. 116 (1821).

[10] M'Cle. (Eng.) 141 (1824); 1 Del. Ch. 146 (1821).

The devisee of lands charged with a legacy is liable to pay interest on the legacy from the time it is payable, though payment is not demanded by the legatee.[1] A legacy payable out of a general fund in the hands of the executor is not a legacy charged on real estate.[2]

If the payment of a legacy is charged upon land of a deceased person, interest upon it runs from the death of the deceased;[3] but, says the Indiana court, legacies do not bear interest, with certain modifications of the rule, until they are payable.[4] However, if a legacy is charged upon the residue of an estate yielding rents and profits it bears interest from the death of the testator.[5] If legacies are made payable *in futuro*, out of the personal estate, the general rule is that no interest is allowed until after the day of payment.[6]

Where a legacy is charged with the payment of a certain sum, bearing interest from a given day, which is long before the death of the testator, it appearing that the legacy was advanced before the day specified for interest to accrue, it will be charged with interest from that day.[7]

A legacy payable by instalments, and the last instalment expiring before the testator's death, is to be considered as a legacy payable generally, and carries interest from one year after the testator's decease.[8]

A will charged the support of a person during life upon

[1] 6 Johns. Ch. (N. Y.) 33 (1822); 1 Paige (N. Y.) 32 (1828).

[2] 2 Johns. Cas. (N. Y.) 200 (1801).

[3] 3 Del. Ch. 269 (1869); 37 Vt. 562 (1865).

[4] 5 Ind. 18 (1854).

[5] 51 Ind. 277 (1875). The South Carolina court holds that the residuary legatee is liable if he knows that the interest on other legacies has not been paid or provided for. Bail. Eq. (S. C.) 274 (1831).

[6] 5 Ind. 18 (1854).

[7] 3 Jones Eq. (N. C.) 330 (1857).

[8] 9 S. & R. (Pa.) 409 (1823).

certain land which it had already charged with the payment of a pecuniary legacy to another person. A residuary legatee having become personally liable to pay the pecuniary legacy, it was held that it became due and payable at the expiration of the time limited for the payment of debts and legacies generally, and was not postponed until the death of the person whose support was charged upon the land.[1]

An executor is not charged with interest on a legacy to an infant until he has notice of the appointment of a guardian.[2]

Contingent legacies. Contingent legacies do not bear interest until they become payable.[3] Where a legacy was given to a girl on condition that she lived with the widow as long as the latter lived, interest was allowed from the time of the widow's death.[4]

What interest belongs to the residue. The interest of a fund that is held upon a contingency, from the death of the testator until the contingency happens, if there is no previous legatee for life, or if there is, what accrues after the death of such previous taker, will become a part of the residue.[5] But the interest that accrues during the time of such life interest, or until a specified contingency happens, belongs to such previous taker, and if he dies, or the contingency happens, without its having been collected to the day of his death, or the happening of the contingency, the uncollected interest which thus accrued, belongs to him, or, in case of his death, will pass to his personal

[1] 80 Wis. 509 (1891).

[2] 3 Munf. (Va.) 198 (1812).

[3] 4 Brown's Ch. (Eng.) 144 (1792); 65 Cal. 25 (1884); 2 Dev. Eq. (N. C.) 366 (1833); 44 Pa. St. 140 (1863); 16 R. I. 274 (1887).

[4] 23 Atl. Rep. (N. J.) 501 (1892).

[5] 2 Atk. (Eng.) 329 (1742); 4 Brown's Ch. (Eng.) 144 (1792).

representatives, and not become a part of the residue.[1] Interest in favor of the remainder-man does not begin to run until the death of the life-tenant.[2] It is immaterial whether the residue is only given generally, or directed to be laid out with all convenient speed, in funds or securities, or to be invested in lands.[3] But where the residue is directed to be laid out in land, to be settled on one for life, with the remainder over, and the testator directs the interest to accumulate in the meantime until the money is laid out in land, or otherwise invested on security, the accumulation ceases at the end of one year from the testator's death, and from that period the tenant for life is entitled to the interest.[4]

Maintenance. There is a great exception to the rule that general pecuniary legacies do not bear interest until a year has elapsed after the testator's death.[5] It makes no difference when they are payable, nor whether they are vested or contingent, general, particular, or residuary;[6] and this is true even if legacies are ordered to accumulate till the legatees are of age.[7]

This is the case of a parent and a legitimate[8] minor[9]

[1] 1 P. Wm. (Eng.) 500 (1718); 2 P. Wm. (Eng.) 419 (1727), 504 (1728); Ambl. (Eng.) 448 (1764); 1 Brown's Ch. (Eng.) 335 (1783); 5 Ves. (Eng.) 335, 522 (1800); 3 Mer. (Eng.) 335 (1816); 3 Myl. & C. (Eng.) 688 (1838); 8 L. J., N. S., Ch. (Eng.) 36 (1838); 2 Jur. (Eng.) 1029 (1838); 5 Jones Eq. (N. C.) 273 (1859).

[2] 81 Ga. 229 (1888).

[3] 6 Ves. (Eng.) 520 (1801).

[4] 6 Ves. (Eng.) 520 (1801); 2 Sim. & St. (Eng.) 396 (1825).

[5] 3 Ves. (Eng.) 10 (1795); 2 Johns. Ch. (N. Y.) 614 (1817).

[6] 1 Eq. Cas. Abr. (Eng.) 301 (1729); 48 Pa. St. 80 (1864).

[7] 1 Dick. (Eng.) 310 (1757).

[8] 15 Ves. (Eng.) 301 (1808).

[9] 1 Swans. (Eng.) 553 (1818); 15 Sim. (Eng.) 513 (1847); 16 L. J., N. S., Ch. (Eng.) 305 (1847); 11 Jur. (Eng.) 403 (1847).

child.[1] The exception is placed upon the ground that it must have been the intention of the parent to have the interest paid as means of support of the infant from time to time, when the will made no other provision for it.[2] The rule means that when a testator gives a pecuniary legacy to his child, and no other arrangement, or only a trifling provision, is made for the maintenance of the child in the will, he shall be allowed interest on the legacy from the decease of the testator,[3] whether a time of payment is stated in the will or not.[4] It extends to adopted children,[5] and to those infants to whom the testator has put himself *in loco parentis*,[6] though he is not under any legal obligation to support them;[7] but it does not apply to other relatives.[8] Where a testator has voluntarily entered into

[1] 2 Vent. (Eng.) 346 (1671); Pre. Ch. (Eng.) 337 (1712); 1 Atk. (Eng.) 507 (1738); 2 Atk. (Eng.) 211 (1741); 3 Atk. (Eng.) 102 (1744); 1 Ves. sr. (Eng.) 209 (1749); 3 Ves. (Eng.) 283 (1796); 4 Ves. (Eng.) 1 (1798); 15 Ves. (Eng.) 301 (1808); 1 Russ. & M. (Eng.) 555 (1830); Taml. (Eng.) 476 (1830); 6 L. J., N. S., Ch. (Eng.) 116 (1837); 8 L. J., Ch. (Eng.) 141; 17 Jur. (Eng.) 1044 (1853); 4 Del. Ch. 44 (1868).

[2] Prec. Ch. (Eng.) 337 (1712); 5 L. J., N. S., Ch. (Eng.) 120 (1836); 9 Hare (Eng.) 649 (1852); 25 Vt. 127 (1853).

[3] 2 Vent. (Eng.) 346 (1671); 4 Del. Ch. 44 (1868); 5 Ind. 18 (1854); 20 Atl. Rep. (N. H.) 387 (1890); 17 Stew. (N. J.) 479, 506 (1888); 6 Paige (N. Y.) 298 (1837); 2 Rich. Eq. (S. C.) 68 (1845).

[4] 3 Md. Ch. 526 (1850).

[5] 41 N. H. 391 (1860).

[6] 7 L. J., N. S., Ch. (Eng.) 118 (1838); 12 L. J., N. S., Ch. (Eng.) 120 (1843); 7 Jur. (Eng.) 572 (1843); 3 Md. Ch. 526 (1850); 79 N. Y. 136 (1879); 48 Pa. St. 80 (1864).

[7] 79 N. Y. 136 (1879).

[8] 3 Ves. (Eng.) 10 (1795); 6 Ves. (Eng.) 546 (1801); 12 Ves. (Eng). 461 (1806); 15 Ves. (Eng.) 301 (1808); 49 L. T., N. S. (Eng.) 554 (1883); 1 Sch. & Lef. (Ire.) 1 (1802); 4 Geo. (Miss.) 126 (1857); 2 Johns. Cas. (N. Y.) 200 (1801); 2 Dev. Eq. (N. C.) 366 (1833); 2 Pa. St. 221 (1845); Rich. Eq. Cas. (S. C.) 297 (1832); *contra*, 1 Con. & L. (Ire.) 284 (1842); 2 Dr. & War. (Ire.) 133 (1842); 4 Ir. Eq. R. (Ire.) 339 (1842); 6 Paige (N. Y.) 298 (1837).

a bond with a parish to pay a weekly maintenance for a natural child as his son, and has continued such payments up to his death, he is deemed to have placed himself *in loco parentis*.[1]

Posthumous children. In the case of a child *in ventre sa mère* at the time of the death of the father, interest is allowed only from its birth.[2]

If a child is already supported by his parent, not being the legitimate natural child of the testator, or if he is of sufficient ability to discharge this moral obligation, a legacy to such child does not carry interest from the testator's death, even though maintenance be immediately given; so that the interest will accumulate for the child's benefit until the principal becomes payable.[3] Nor is a legitimate child entitled to interest in the way of maintenance, if he has a maintenance, although it may be less than the amount of the interest on the legacy.[4] So a person maintaining an infant legatee is not chargeable with interest on the legacy.[5]

Express maintenance. The rule as to presumed interest for maintenance is never applied if the testator expressly gives maintenance;[6] as where a will says that the income of a certain amount is for the maintenance of

[1] Coke P. C. (Eng.) 96; 2 Keen (Eng.) 598 (1838); 7 L. J., N. S., Ch. (Eng.) 118 (1858).

[2] 2 Cox Ch. (Eng.) 425 (1796).

[3] 3 Atk. (Eng.) 399 (1746); 1 Brown's Ch. (Eng.) 387 (1781); 3 Brown's Ch. (Eng.) 60 (1789), 416 (1791); 4 Brown's Ch. (Eng.) 223 (1793); 4 Ves. (Eng.) 498 (1799); 4 Madd. (Eng.) 275 (1819). The principal may be used if the interest is insufficient, says the court in 4 Johns. Ch. (N. Y.) 100 (1819).

[4] 3 Md. Ch. 526 (1850).

[5] 2 Rob. (Va.) 492 (1842).

[6] 1 Cox (Eng.) 133 (1788); 37 L. T., N. S. (Eng.) 201 (1877); 5 L. R., Ch. Div. (Eng.) 837 (1877); 47 L. J., Ch. (Eng.) 118 (1877); 25 W. R. (Eng.) 507; 26 W. R. (Eng.) 65; 2 Ames (5 R. I.) 353 (1858).

the legatee.[1] Such interest will begin at the death of the testator;[2] and whether the parent is able to support the child does not come into the question.[3] So, on legacies to a natural child of the testator, with directions to apply a competent part of the interest for maintenance.[4] It is the same, also, where an intention, though not expressed is fairly inferable from the will that the legacy shall be for the maintenance of the child.[5] A limited allowance for maintenance, however, does not exclude an implied gift of interest on a contingent legacy during the period for which maintenance is not provided.[6]

Rate. Where maintenance or interest is given by the will, and the rate specified, the legatee will not, generally, be entitled to claim more than the rate specified;[7] but he is entitled to no more than will support him.[8]

Legacies in general. If a legatee has a claim against the estate, the offset should be made as of the time of the death of the testator, if the question of interest is involved, says the Massachusetts court.[9] The Iowa rule is, that a general legatee's claim will bear interest until the legacy is payable.[10]

Where a statute provides that executors shall pay the taxes on the estates in their hands, and a will orders

[1] 1 Beav. (Eng.) 271 (1839); 3 Jur. (Eng.) 101 (1839).

[2] 3 Ves. & B. (Eng.) 183 (1814); 8 L. R., Eq. (Eng.) 119 (1869); 41 L. J., Ch. (Eng.) 699 (1872); 36 N. Y. 15 (1866); 34 How. Pr. (N. Y.) 115 (1866).

[3] 4 Brown's Ch. (Eng.) 223 (1793); 3 Ves. (Eng.) 730 (1798).

[4] 3 Swans. (Eng.) 689 (1786); 2 Russ. & M. (Eng.) 343 (1831).

[5] 1 Swans. (Eng.) 561 (1818).

[6] 2 L. R., Eq. (Eng.) 479 (1866).

[7] 3 Ves. (Eng.) 283 (1796).

[8] 12 Beav. (Eng.) 357 (1849); 13 Jur. (Eng.) 737 (1849); 18 L. J., N. S., Ch. (Eng.) 169 (1849).

[9] 145 Mass. 239 (1887).

[10] 70 Iowa 368 (1886).

that a certain sum should be set apart for the benefit of the testator's sister during her life, the interest therefrom to be paid to her "as her absolute property," and that after her decease such sum should remain in the testator's estate for distribution, no part of such interest can be used to pay the taxes on the principal sum, or the expense of its management, but the expense must be paid from the general assets of the estate.[1]

Compromise. In the case of the compromise of a will, the legatees and heirs to get certain sums each and the remainder to be divided equally between them, no interest should be allowed to the legatees.[2]

Rate. Where legacies bear a conventional rate of interest by the will, they bear the legal rate after they become payable.[3] In England, legacies payable out of personal estate are generally allowed five per cent interest, but if payable out of real estate only four per cent, because real estate is esteemed to be a better security.[4]

Compound interest is not allowed on a legacy,[5] unless the failure to pay arose from the fault of the executor.[6] So, a devisee of lands charged with the payment of legacies is liable for simple interest only.[7]

Law of what place governs. The law of interest on legacies is that of the place where the estate is being settled.[8]

[1] 33 N. E. Rep. (Ind.) 361 (1893).
[2] 128 Mass. 203 (1880).
[3] 2 Desau. (S. C.) 170 (1803).
[4] 3 Atk. (Eng.) 402 (1746).
[5] 4 Rand. (Va.) 181 (1826).
[6] 106 Mass. 586 (1871).
[7] 66 Cal. 157 (1884).
[8] 38 L. T., N. S. (Eng.) 215 (1878); 26 W. R. (Eng.) 326, V. C. B.

Contest of will. The fact that the legatee attempted, at great cost to the estate, to set the will aside does not change these rules.[1]

Legacy of a debt. Interest is presumed to be included in the legacy of a debt.[2] So a gift by will of a note carries with it the interest that is due upon it.[3] A legacy given in payment of a debt bears interest from the death of the testator.[4]

Tender. If a legatee will not receive the legacy when it is tendered to him, he cannot recover interest upon it after that time.[5] So a refusal by a legatee's husband to accept a legacy stops the running of interest upon it.[6]

(*t*) *Mechanics' liens.* A sum of money due for labor or materials, or both, for which a mechanics' lien has been filed, does not bear interest,[7] except from the date of the petition to enforce the lien,[8] if no claim is made for it in the petition.[9] If the word "interest" is inserted in the bill when the materials are sold for cash, interest will be allowed from the time the delivery of the articles is completed.[10]

There may be an item in the account that would generally carry interest; if so, interest will be allowed upon it.[11]

(*u*) *Money had and received.* Interest as damages is

[1] 51 Ind. 277 (1875).

[2] 2 Mart. N. S. (La.) 446 (1824).

[3] 2 Dev. Eq. (N. C.) 488 (1834).

[4] 17 Stew. (N. J.) 479, 506 (1888).

[5] 10 Md. 352 (1856).

[6] 4 Call (Va.) 605 (1803).

[7] 20 S. C. 555 (1883).

[8] 141 Mass. 280 (1886). From the time of filing the petition, says the court in 2 Allen (Mass.) 605 (1861).

[9] 1 Bradw. (Ill.) 94 (1878).

[10] 50 Md. 133 (1878).

[11] 1 Ore. 183 (1855).

not generally allowed on money had and received[1] by one who believes it to be his due, or for another person,[2] until it has been demanded by the party entitled to it,[3] and in suing for the money the demand must be alleged.[4] If there has been no demand, the interest begins to run from the date of the writ only.[5] This rule applies to cases of money lent, where there is no contract for interest;[6] also to money paid by mistake,[7] or on a void execution.[8] In the last-named case it can be collected from the final judgment.[9]

Interest is allowed on money had and received if there is a contract to that effect, either express, or one that can be implied from the usage of trade, or from special circumstances, or from written securities for the payment of the principal at a given time.[10]

[1] 7 D. & R. (Eng.) 201 (1825).

[2] 9 S. & R. (Pa.) 109 (1823.)

[3] 15 East (Eng.) 223 (1812); 3 Stark. (Eng.) 132 (1822); 5 C. & P. (Eng.) 498 (1833); 46 Ala. 282 (1871); 19 Conn. 548 (1849); 4 Blf. (Ind.) 21 (1835), 164 (1836); 15 Pick. (Mass.) 500 (1834); 3 Met. (Mass.) 34 (1841); 4 Met. (Mass.) 181 (1842); 14 Allen (Mass.) 59 (1867); 1 Stew. (N. J.) 315 (1877); 1 Dall. (Pa.) 52 (1780); 1 S. & R. (Pa.) 176 (1814); 1 Bail. (S. C.) 201 (1829); *contra*, 64 Ala. 193 (1879); 1 Conn. 32 (1814); 3 Caines (N. Y.) 266 (1805); if liquidated, 1 McC. (S. C.) 449 (1821). The court in 1 Dall. (Pa.) 349 (1788) says, that where one has received money of another, and has retained it with the owner's consent, he ought to pay interest on it, the same as for money lent.

[4] 14 Allen (Mass.) 59 (1867).

[5] 100 U. S. 119 (1879); 15 Pick. (Mass.) 500 (1834); 129 Mass. 67 (1880); 28 N. H. 561 (1854).

[6] 11 Met. (Mass.) 124 (1846); *contra*, 1 Binn. (Pa.) 488 (1808); 17 S. C. 313 (1881).

[7] 19 Conn. 548 (1849); 83 Ga. 627 (1889); 31 Minn. 201 (1883); 24 N. H. 417 (1852); 1 Dall. (Pa.) 52 (1781); 1 McC. (S. C.) 97 (1821).

[8] 19 Conn. 548 (1849); *contra*, 1 Pick. (Mass.) 211 (1822).

[9] 2 Root (Conn.) 156 (1794).

[10] 15 East (Eng.) 223 (1812); 3 Stark. (Eng.) 132 (1822); *contra*, 1 Campb. (Eng.) 50 (1807); not an implied agreement, 2 Scott (Eng.) 135 (1835); 2 Bing. N. C. (Eng.) 77 (1835).

There are many cases where interest is allowed from the day the money is paid without a demand;[1] as, for instance, where a purchaser has paid the price for land, when interest will be decreed to him till he recovers either the money or the particular land;[2] or, where purchase money has lain dead when the vendor could not make a title;[3] or, where the consideration has failed;[4] or, on purchase money remaining in the purchaser's hands to pay off incumbrances,[5] unless the purchaser has the use of the property, when he cannot claim interest;[6] or, on a void judicial sale on execution;[7] or, where the plaintiff paid a debt that had been paid by another party who was liable to pay it, but, without knowing it had been paid;[8] or, where the defendant received rents under an implied trust for his co-tenant;[9] or, when the attorney of one of the parties in an interpleader suit, pending the litigation, on his own motion, is paid over the fund in dispute;[10] or, where a husband during coverture received money belonging to the *corpus* of the wife's separate estate upon the express condition that it be invested;[11] or, where the money was simply loaned

[1] 64 Ala. 193 (1879).

[2] 64 Ala. 193 (1879): 1 Paige (N. Y.) 244 (1828).

[3] 32 L. R., Ch. Div. (Eng.) 454 (1886); 50 Ind. 403 (1875).

[4] 2 Root (Conn.) 46 (1793); 50 Ind. 403 (1875); 3 Bibb (Ky.) 529 (1814); 5 J. J. Mar. (Ky.) 310 (1831); 16 Md. 190 (1860): 7 Met. (Mass.) 438 (1844); 6 Allen (Mass.) 549 (1863). From demand, says the court in 85 Ga. 141 (1890). This is true, even though collusion on the part of the purchaser was the cause of a sale's being set aside. 154 Mass. 51 (1891).

[5] 1 Sch. & Lef. (Ire.) 132 (1803).

[6] 28 Ga. 289 (1871): 4 Dana (Ky.) 66 (1836); 16 La. 35 (1840); 8 Rob. (La.) 157 (1844); 9 Rob. (La.) 458 (1845); 11 C. E. Gr. (N. J.) 202 (1874).

[7] 10 Neb. 130 (1880).

[8] 2 Root (Conn.) 405 (1796).

[9] 23 Ala. 316 (1853).

[10] 87 Ala. 387 (1888).

[11] 30 Ala. 113 (1857).

to him, interest is recoverable from his death;[1] or, if there was coercion or other improper conduct on the husband's part, the jury may give interest for a period before his death.[2] Where money is advanced on a contract, only a part of which is fulfilled, interest is allowed on the excess advanced.[3] So interest is allowed on advances made under a contract, without an express agreement, to pay it;[4] but a commission is a fair compensation for the use of the name and credit of an acceptor, and interest is not then allowable on advances to take up an acceptance, when there is no agreement to pay any.[5] Where the amount recovered does not adequately compensate for the damage interest is given.[6] Where the purchase money was paid, and the title failed, interest was allowed in one case from the time the vendor was notified of the purchaser to reclaim the consideration.[7] Where a vendor caused delay, and the interest exceeded the rents, the purchaser is permitted to elect, to pay the interest or to relinquish his right to the rents.[8]

It is not necessary where a party desires to rescind a contract by the repayment of money paid thereon that he also pay interest on the amount.[9]

When specific performance is decreed in favor of the vendor, he is entitled to receive interest on the purchase money from the tender of the deed, when the purchaser is in possession, and has not put the vendor in default.[10]

[1] 3 Whart. (Pa.) 48 (1837).

[2] 3 Whart. (Pa.) 48 (1837).

[3] 76 Ill. 484 (1875); 3 C. E. Gr. (N. J.) 401 (1867).

[4] 46 Mich. 239 (1881); 3 Cai. (N. Y.) 266 (1805); 5 Cow. (N. Y.) 587 (1825); 15 N. Y. (1 Smith) 397 (1857).

[5] 10 La. 295 (1836).

[6] 44 Mich. 157 (1880).

[7] 1 N. M. 19 (1852).

[8] Hoffm. (N. Y.) 71 (1841).

[9] 52 Iowa 137 (1879).

[10] 21 Barb. (N. Y.) 381 (1855).

One who has received rents and profits of land, and obtained interest on them, not being entitled to them, as against a judgment-debtor having an equitable right of the property, for the satisfaction of his debt, and to the rents and profits that they may be so applied, is chargeable with interest, on accounting for the rents and profits, although he resisted the claim in good faith.[1]

If an executor, through a third person, buys land belonging to the estate and the sale is set aside, and the deed cancelled, he will not be allowed interest on the money paid.[2]

In an action to recover contribution to a general average, interest will run from the time that the money upon which the average arose was advanced.[3]

If the defendant is a wrong-doer in obtaining or detaining money, interest is allowed on it from the time of the wrongful obtaining or detaining.[4]

Where one has money of another in his hands, and uses it, he cannot avoid payment of interest upon it by answering that he does not know what profit he has made by its use. In such a case he is at least liable for interest while it was so employed.[5]

These rules of law on money lent and money paid apply when the money forms matters of account as well as when they are detached transactions.[6] But rests are not allowed if there is no wrongful obtaining or detention.[7]

Rate. The holder of collateral paper is liable for interest at the legal rate from the collection of the same,

[1] 46 Barb. (N. Y.) 579 (1866).
[2] 5 Ore. 93 (1873).
[3] 8 S. & R. (Pa.) 103 (1822).
[4] 11 Met. (Mass.) 121 (1846).
[5] 8 Ala. 632 (1845).
[6] 9 R. I. 32 (1868); 10 R. I. 501 (1873).
[7] 91 N. Y. 74 (1883).

which he applies to his own use, though the paper bore a higher rate.[1]

Money disbursed by a mortgagee bears the same rate of interest as the original loan.[2]

(*v*) *Money paid for the use of another.* Interest as damages is allowed on money paid on account of, or for the use and benefit of, or at the request of another from the time of payment,[3] without proof of a demand,[4] and at the legal rate.[5] As where one was compelled to pay damages for injuries received by the default of another;[6] also, on costs and taxes when a mortgage is redeemed, after it has been foreclosed.[7]

Where a tenant in common is obliged to pay and does pay off an incumbrance, he can recover interest at the same rate as he pays;[8] and interest on the aggregate of principal and interest that he has paid is allowed from actual demand, or service of writ.[9]

When the owner of a building pays a judgment on a mechanic's lien, he is entitled to interest on the amount paid from the date of the judgment.[10]

Where money expended by a husband in permanent

[1] 4 Geo. (Miss.) 467 (1857).

[2] 2 Anstr. (Eng.) 551 (1795).

[3] 2 P. & D. (Eng.) 408 (1839); 1 Mack. (D. C.) 314 (1881); 63 Iowa 275 (1884); 67 Iowa 651 (1885); 1 Adams (Me.) 574 (1856); 13 Mass. 218 (1816); 1 Pick. (Mass.) 118 (1822); 2 Met. (Mass.) 168 (1840); 146 Mass. 148 (1888); 1 Mo. 718 (1827); 48 Hun (N. Y.) 253 (1888); 2 N. & McC. (S. C.) 493 (1820); 7 Rich. (S. C.) 23 (1853); 40 Vt. 35 (1867); *contra*, solicitor's bill of costs, 5 Jur. N. S. (Eng.) 637 (1859); 4 DeG. & J. (Eng.) 104 (1859).

[4] 2 Met. (Mass.) 168 (1840).

[5] 15 Iowa 181 (1863).

[6] 1 Mack. (D. C.) 314 (1881).

[7] 146 Mass. 148 (1888).

[8] 97 Ill. 237 (1881); *contra*, 12 C. E. Gr. (N. J.) 82 (1876).

[9] 4 Ired. Eq. (N. C.) 1 (1845); 46 O. St. 66 (1888).

[10] 43 Mo. App. 369 (1891).

improvements on land, which is his wife's separate estate, is charged on such land, in an action by a creditor of the husband, interest will be allowed on such money only from the commencement of the action.[1]

(*w*) *Partitions.* Interest should be decreed on a sum of money assessed for equality of a partition.[2]

(*x*) *Penalties.* Interest is not generally chargeable on penalties, as on the annual penalty for bastardy,[3] until the service of the writ.[4]

Interest is allowed, however, where it is necessary to protect that which it was given to secure.[5]

Equity will relieve against a bond given for a penalty sum, with contract for interest from date, as it is secured by a penalty, and if it has been paid, equity will cause it to be refunded.[6]

(*y*) *Policies.* Insurance companies cannot be compelled to pay interest on policies until a loss is proved.[7] If a time is set in the policy when the amount due is payable, interest begins to run at that time.[8] If no time is stated, either in life or fire insurance, interest is allowed on the amount due on demand after it is payable,[9] and if there has been no demand, then from the date of the writ.[10]

[1] 14 S. E. Rep. (W. Va.) 410 (1892).

[2] Bail. Eq. (S. C.) 102 (1830).

[3] 14 Rich. (S. C.) 29 (1866), 177 (1867).

[4] 6 Rand. (Va.) 101 (1828).

[5] 55 Pa. St. 238 (1866).

[6] 2 Murph. (N. C.) 145 (1812).

[7] 1 Hall (N. Y.) 247, 261 (1828); 23 Wend. (N. Y.) 525 (1840).

[8] 71 Ala. 516 (1882); 10 So. Rep. (Fla.) 297 (1891); 80 Ill. 388 (1875); 153 Mass. 143 (1891); 10 Mon. 340 (1891); 6 O. 456 (1834).

[9] 98 Ill. 324 (1881); 111 Mass. 93 (1872); 138 Mass. 151 (1884); 153 Mass. 143 (1891). From notice of death in life insurance, says the court in 129 Ill. 298 (1889). From demand, if company waives the condition of payment, the court of Maryland decided in the case cited 20 Md. 40 (1862).

[10] 138 Mass. 151 (1884); 64 Mich. 372 (1887).

Where there has been a demand it must be alleged in the declaration.[1] If there is an express promise to pay, it is allowed on the promise.[2]

If the amount due on the policy is unliquidated, interest runs from the beginning of the suit.[3]

Interest on the amount due on an insurance policy should be computed at the legal rate of the place of payment provided for in the policy, and not at the place where suit is brought thereon.[4]

No interest is allowed to an insurance company on a premium note.[5]

(z) *Rent.* It has been suggested that rent itself is in the nature of interest, being given for the use of property, and that if interest were allowed upon it, it would be like enforcing the payment of compound interest when there had been no agreement for its payment.[6] This was the old view;[7] but, later, the courts have almost universally given interest on rent in arrears from the time it was payable in money;[8] and even if it were payable otherwise

[1] 138 Mass. 151 (1884).

[2] 93 Ill. 271 (1879); 98 Ill. 324 (1881).

[3] 4 Dall. (Pa.) 463 (1806).

[4] 16 S. E. Rep. (S. C.) 134 (1892).

[5] 37 Barb. (N. Y.) 630 (1862).

[6] 6 Col. 120 (1881).

[7] 10 B. Mon. (Ky.) 229 (1850); 2 Call (Va.) 253 (1800); 3 Hen. & M. (Va.) 463 (1809); 5 Munf. (Va.) 21 (1816).

[8] 5 Espi. (Eng.) 114 (1804); 5 Harr. (Del.) 123 (1848), 204 (1849); 8 Bradw. (Ill.) 367 (1880); 10 B. Mon. (Ky) 229 (1850); 6 G. & J. (Md.) 383 (1834); 141 Mass. 162 (1886); 1 Johns. (N. Y.) 183 (1809); 7 Wend. (N. Y.) 109 (1831); 2 Barb. (N. Y.) 643 (1848); 12 How. Pr. (N. Y.) 523 (1856); 1 Hun (N. Y.) 102 (1874); 58 N. Y. 323 (1874); 75 N. Y. 579 (1878); 6 Binn. (Pa.) 159 (1813); 4 Whart. (Pa.) 516 (1839); 2 Call (Va.) 249 (1800); 1 Grat. (Va.) 416 (1845); use of a negro, 12 G. & J. (Md.) 288 (1842); rent of a boat, 50 Barb. (N. Y.) 62 (1867).

9

than in money, but is not so paid.[1] If the amount due is unliquidated, interest will not be allowed.[2]

Some courts allow interest on rent only when it is secured by covenant;[3] while others will give it for use and occupation.[4] The South Carolina court will not allow it on a parol lease.[5]

Interest is allowed in an action of ejectment,[6] but no distress, following the general rule of interest, can be made for the interest only.[7]

The courts in Colorado and other places, holding the view that rent is a kind of interest, decide that, in equity, they may, in their sound discretion, impose interest upon rent when a party has been grossly delinquent, or intentionally contrary to his duty.[8] In Pennsylvania, the jury is generally allowed to give interest from the time the rent is distrained or sued for.[9] The court in North Carolina does not usually allow interest until an account is demanded; but if the possession has been *mala fide* it is allowed from receipt of the profits.[10]

Interest is not recoverable by way of damages in an

[1] 1 Johns. (N. Y.) 276 (1806); 4 Wend. (N. Y.) 313 (1830); 5 Denio (N. Y.) 135 (1848); 2 Barb. (N. Y.) 643 (1848); 2 Comst. (N. Y.) 135 (1849).

[2] 32 S. C. 57 (1889).

[3] 3 Dana (Ky.) 31 (1835); 4 Johns. (N. Y.) 183 (1809); 6 Binn. (Pa.) 159 (1813).

[4] 8 Cal. 32 (1857).

[5] 1 Strob. (S. C.) 250 (1847).

[6] 141 Mass. 162 (1886); *contra*, 63 Mo. 103 (1876).

[7] 6 G. & J. (Md.) 383 (1834); 1 Gill (Md.) 57 (1843); 2 Binn. (Pa.) 146 (1809).

[8] 6 Col. 120 (1881); 1 Cush. (Miss.) 398 (1852); 2 Yeates (Pa.) 72 (1798); 2 Binn. (Pa.) 146 (1809); 33 Pa. St. 435 (1859); 5 Rand. (Va.) 571 (1827).

[9] 4 Yeates (Pa.) 264 (1805).

[10] 2 Dev. Eq. (N. C.) 67 (1831).

action of debt for rent, says the Virginia court,[1] which allows it, however, on estimated rents and profits.[2]

A lessee is only obliged to pay interest on the rent that falls due during his tenancy; therefore, an assignee of a lease should pay interest only subsequent to the conveyance;[3] and a stranger, whose tenancy begins at the expiration of a written lease, is not chargeable with interest on the rent in arrears.[4]

(*aa*) *Replevin.* Interest is allowed on the value of replevied property from the time of the wrongful taking.[5] It is also allowed on the bond if the goods are not returned,[6] but not from a time anterior to its date.[7] If the goods are returned after judgment interest from the date of the judgment to the time of return is allowed,[8] in a suit on the bond for the conversion of the goods. The Maryland court holds that the question of interest on a replevin bond is exclusively for the jury.[9]

(*bb*) *Royalties.* On royalties on patents, etc., interest should run from the receipt of the proceeds of sales, etc.[10]

(*cc*) *Sales.* Interest on the price of goods sold will run from the day of sale if the amount is liquidated;[11] and

[1] 3 H. & M. (Va.) 463 (1809).

[2] 1 Rob. (Va.) 196 (1842); 26 Grat. (Va.) 36 (1875); *contra*, 5 Leigh (Va.) 561 (1834); 6 Leigh (Va.) 38 (1835).

[3] 33 Pa. St. 435 (1859).

[4] 1 Strob. (S. C.) 250 (1847).

[5] 54 Cal. 192 (1880); 63 Cal. 371 (1883); 8 Nev. 41 (1872).

[6] 35 Ill. 178 (1864).

[7] 3 Munf. (Va.) 277 (1812).

[8] 16 Ind. 374 (1861); 1 Zab. (N. J.) 411 (1848); 3 Zab. (N. J.) 736 (1852); 8 Vr. (N. J.) 179 (1874).

[9] 2 G. & J. (Md.) 430 (1830).

[10] 82 N. Y. 271 (1880).

[11] 30 Ala. 721 (1857); 31 Ala. 53 (1857); 36 Ark. 355 (1880); 69 Ill. 423 (1873); 6 Allen (Mass.) 221 (1863); *contra*, 10 Cush. (Mass.) 250 (1850); 36 Vt. 46 (1863), unless there is a custom among merchants to charge interest in similar cases, and the purchaser knows of it.

this is true, if it is a cash sale, although the day of payment is postponed until a particular event transpires.[1] If credit is given, interest will be allowed from its expiration.[2] If the term of credit is not agreed upon, then from demand.[3] If the price is not ascertained, interest will be allowed from the time it is.[4]

In Louisiana, there is a rule that interest cannot be claimed, under the custom of merchants, when the goods do not appear to have been bought for the purpose of trade, and the vendee is not a merchant.[5]

In a sale on credit, if the vendor refuses to give the purchaser possession, the purchaser is not compelled to pay interest during the time he is deprived of such possession.[6]

If there are any binding customs relative to the allowance of interest on goods sold and delivered at the place where they are sold the parties will be bound by them,[7] if they know of them.[8]

If it is agreed that over-due bills for sales of goods shall not bear interest, the seller cannot apply money paid on account to the satisfaction of interest that he has charged.[9]

[1] 26 Ga. 465 (1858), in which case the purchaser was a creditor, and agreed to pay when the estate was settled.

[2] 2 B. & P. (Eng.) 337 (1800); 13 East (Eng.) 98 (1810); 3 Taun. (Eng.) 157 (1810); 2 Campb. (Eng.) 480 (1810); 3 M. & W. (Eng.) 25 (1837); 6 Dowl. (Eng.) 163 (1837); Mur. & H. (Eng.) 274 (1837); 2 Port. (Ala.) 351, 451 (1835); 4 Harr. (Del.) 130 (1844); 3 Rob. (La.) 361 (1842); 4 Minn. 528 (1860); 30 N. H. 511 (1855); 3 Comst. (N. Y.) 502 (1850); 22 Vt. 191 (1850).

[3] 12 Barb. (N. Y.) 288 (1851); 11 N. Y. (1 Kern.) 97 (1854); 4 Dall. (Pa.) 286 (1803); 37 Wis. 149 (1875); 51 Wis. 407 (1881). The Louisiana court holds, from judicial demand. 1 La. Ann. 424 (1846).

[4] 1 Scam. (Ill.) 577 (1839).

[5] 7 Mart. (La.) 228 (1819).

[6] 2 Md. Ch. 516 (1850).

[7] Bat.'s Mart. & 2d Hay'd (N. C.) 26 (1794).

[8] 2 Dall. (Pa.) 193 (1792).

[9] 69 Wis. 527 (1887).

The following are general rules of equity. If the purchaser has not been in possession interest on the price is not recoverable.[1] If the purchaser is in possession of the estate, receiving the rents and profits, he is liable to pay interest on the unpaid purchase money,[2] although he was not to pay it until a subsequent day.[3] If the purchaser has the use of the premises, he cannot claim interest on the price paid if the title fails.[4] So, if a vendee enjoys an estate and withholds the purchase money until a dispute concerning the title is adjusted he is required to pay interest.[5] Interest is not allowed to an evicted vendee, who is not held responsible for *mesne* profits before the time of his eviction.[6]

A purchaser at a sheriff's sale is liable for interest from the day of sale on so much of his bid as is applicable to judgments other than his own.[7]

When a sale is rescinded, the vendee becomes entitled to interest on what he has paid from the delivery or tender of the property to the vendor.[8] Interest on a contract for the purchase of land runs from the tender of the deed.[9] Interest does not run on the price, after suit has been instituted against the vendee for the premises.[10] Also, when property having an income is sold, the vendee cannot avoid

[1] 2 Pa. St. 122 (1845).

[2] 12 Ves. (Eng.) 25 (1806); 3 H. L. Cas. (Eng.) 565 (1852): 16 Mich. 223 (1867); 20 Ore. 360 (1891); 6 Binn. (Pa.) 435 (1814); 64 Pa. St. 411 (1870); 27 W. Va. 1 (1885).

[3] 12 Ves. (Eng.) 25 (1806).

[4] 16 La. 35 (1840); 8 Rob. (La.) 157 (1844); 9 Rob. (La.) 458 (1845).

[5] 4 Bibb (Ky.) 273 (1815).

[6] 85 Tenn. 26 (1886).

[7] 12 S. C. 600 (1879).

[8] 5 La. 57 (1833).

[9] 8 Kas. 328 (1871).

[10] 3 La. 404 (1832).

the payment of interest, even when he has a right to require security against eviction, unless he makes a tender or deposit of the price.[1]

If, in the case of the purchase of property, the vendee seeks to escape the payment of interest on account of the default of the vendor, he must actually set aside the purchase money and appropriate it for the vendor, and notify him that the money is thus idle.[2] So, if a claimant is in the possession of and enjoying a fund.[3]

Interest cannot be recovered on the common count for goods sold and delivered.[4]

(*dd*) *Subscriptions.* Whether interest is allowed on subscriptions has not been very generally discussed. Where a subscription was made in aid of a railroad, interest on it was allowed from demand, or service of writ.[5] Again, where a person made a subscription to the capital stock of a railroad corporation, and failed to pay, he was charged with interest from the time of his default, and it was further held that he could not compel the company to issue the stock until he paid the interest as well as the principal.[6] Interest on a subscription for the erection of a building was allowed from the time the money was expended on account of it, in an Illinois case.[7] The court in Maryland holds that interest on subscriptions to stock is not recoverable as a matter of right.[8]

(*ee*) *Taxes.* Interest is not allowed on overdue taxes

[1] 13 La. Ann. 569 (1858).

[2] 27 W. Va. 1 (1885).

[3] 49 Mich. 631 (1883).

[4] 2 Bail. (S. C.) 173 (1831); *contra*, Harp. (S. C.) 393 (1824).

[5] 53 Mich. 458 (1876).

[6] 3 Hun (N. Y.) 401 (1875); 71 N. Y. 298 (1877).

[7] 91 Ill. 535 (1879).

[8] 55 Md. 399 (1880).

at common law.[1] When a tax sale is judicially pronounced to be void a reasonable time should then be given to the owner to pay the taxes.[2]

If taxes are paid under protest, the payor can recover interest thereon from the date of payment; but, if not paid under protest, only from demand, or the date of the writ.[3]

(*ff*) *Trover.* Interest is allowed in trover on the value of the chattels at the time when converted,[4] from that time,[5] or from demand, when a demand is necessary.[6]

In England, it was held in an action in trover, for a bill of exchange, that the jury might, in their discretion, include the amount of the interest in the damages, although there was no mention of interest in the declaration and no special damage alleged.[7]

In Kentucky, whether interest should be allowed from the time of conversion is left to the jury.[8] But, in Georgia, the jury cannot add interest to the value of the property as damages, if the property was illegally taken.[9]

[1] 65 Ala. 391 (1880); 70 Ga. 11 (1883): 87 Ky. 605 (1888): 89 Ky. 531 (1890); 2 Dutch. (N. J.) 398 (1857); 18 Vr. (N. J.) 75 (1885); 55 Tex. 157 (1880), 314 (1881).

[2] 8 Neb. 52 (1878).

[3] 4 Met. (Mass.) 181 (1842).

[4] 72 Ill. 148 (1874); 1 N. H. 451 (1818); 3 Zab. (N. J.) 342 (1852); 2 Dutch. (N. J.) 426 (1857); 3 Dutch. (N. J.) 637 (1858); 2 Johns. (N. Y.) 280 (1807); 8 Johns. (N. Y.) 446 (1811); 4 Cow. (N. Y.) 53 (1825); 7 Wend. (N. Y.) 354 (1831).

[5] 73 Ala. 70 (1882); 33 Cal. 117 (1867): 46 Cal. 323 (1873); 35 Kas. 225 (1886); 1 Met. (Mass.) 172 (1840); 134 Mass. 453 (1883); 139 Mass. 593 (1885); 140 Mass. 183 (1885); 142 Mass. 422 (1886): 85 Mo. 443 (1885); 47 N. H. 219 (1866); 2 Johns. (N. Y.) 280 (1807); 2 W. Va. 90 (1867); 68 Wis. 619 (1887).

[6] 49 Ga. 434 (1873); 35 Ill. 455 (1864); 52 Ill. 249 (1869); 20 N. H. 544 (1847).

[7] 2 C. & P. (Eng.) 558 (1827).

[8] 1 Dana (Ky.) 400 (1833); 14 W. P. D. Bush (Ky.) 658 (1879).

[9] 50 Ga. 444 (1873).

An odd case coming under this branch of the law of interest was that of a ship carrying specie. She became damaged, and some of the coin was taken to pay for repairing the vessel. The court held, in an action to recover the amount used, that interest upon it should begin to run when the vessel reached the place to which the specie was consigned.[1]

[1] Sprague (U. S., D. C.) 51 (1843).

CHAPTER IV.

HOW INTEREST IS BARRED.

INTEREST cannot be barred before it begins to run. So a release of interest indorsed upon a note which was never delivered to the releasee is inoperative.[1]

It is a general rule, that if a party is barred from recovering the principal of a debt, he is equally barred from recovering interest as damages on it, which is an accessory only, and must follow the nature of the principal.[2]

Mere readiness to pay the principal is not a bar to the recovery of interest upon it;[3] neither is the possession of the money with which to pay it, if it is not so used.[4]

If a contingent note, including interest to a given date, becomes due prior to that time by the happening of the contingency, the maker may defend to the extent of the unearned interest included therein.[5]

But interest on money secured by a trust deed, will not stop accruing on account of complications in the title to the land caused by attempted foreclosures of the trust deed.[6]

If the law prohibits the payment of the principal, in-

[1] 1 Jones Eq. (N. C.) 253 (1854).

[2] 8 Scott N. R. (Eng.) 147 (1844); 15 Q. B. (Eng.) 297 (1850); 19 L. J., Q. B. (Eng.) 405 (1850).

[3] 45 N. H. 211 (1864); 24 Pa. St. 310 (1855).

[4] 63 Cal. 113 (1883).

[5] 9 Iowa 434 (1860).

[6] 52 Ill. 504 (1869).

terest accruing during the existence of such prohibition is not demandable, and the rule is the same in courts of equity as in courts of law.[1]

It is no valid objection to a recovery of interest by the plaintiff that he was under a rule for trial or *non pros.*[2]

Where the fact of non-payment is ascribable to mutual misapprehension of the parties, as where a stakeholder could not discover from the indistinct direction of the owner as to whom the fund should be paid, or to the laches of the creditor, interest does not run from that time till the debt is demanded.[3]

Interest may be barred absolutely, or it may be only suspended for a time.

(*a*) *Act of creditor.* A *bona fide* effort to find the creditor is evidence to go to the jury on the question of barring interest due to him.[4] A debtor is not obliged to seek the creditor if he goes outside of the realm, and by so doing prevents the payment of the principal when it is due.[5] This evidence may be given to the jury under the plea of payment.[6] If the creditor was in the country when the debt became due, his subsequent absence, without leaving an agent, will not prevent interest from accruing.[7]

When a debtor, without fault on his part, is prevented from paying the debt at and after maturity, through the

[1] 2 Dall. (Pa.) 102 (1789).

[2] 2 Binn. (Pa.) 428 (1810).

[3] 1 S. & R. (Pa.) 176 (1814).

[4] 21 Pa. St. 310 (1855).

[5] 3 McC. (S. C.) 340 (1825): *contra*, 9 S. & R. (Pa.) 263 (1823), which holds that contractual interest is not to be abated because of the continued absence of the creditor at a distance from the state, and his not having been heard from for many years.

[6] 1 Root (Conn.) 178 (1790): 3 McC. (S. C.) 340 (1825): 1 Call (Va.) 133 (1797).

[7] Conf. (N. C.) 505 (1800).

act of his creditor or the law, interest should be abated during the time he is so prevented, and this the debtor should show by affirmative proof.[1]

(*b*) *Change of legal rate.* Interest as damages may be partly barred by a reduction of the legal rate by statute while the interest is running; the old rate being the extent of damages to the time when the new rate goes into effect after which the new rate controls.[2] This is also true where a contract allows "lawful interest for the time," —the rate will vary with the statute.[3] An agreement fixing the rate of interest on future dealings between the parties, terminates by the passage of a law making such rate usurious.[4]

(*c*) *Courts' order.* An order to pay money into court stops interest,[5] from the time the money is brought in.[6]

(*d*) *Garnishee process and interpleader.* Interest will not generally be allowed during the pendency of a trustee or garnishee process on a debt upon which no interest is due except as damages.[7] Otherwise, if the process is void.[8] If the proceeding was legal originally, the dismissal of the suit will not make the garnishee responsible for interest while the action was pending.[9] For exceptions to these rules, and a full discussion of the subject, see page 56.

[1] 26 Ark. 240 (1870).

[2] 42 Cal. 279 (1871); 44 Cal. 366 (1872); 46 Cal. 323 (1873); 63 Cal. 503 (1883); 5 Kas. 567 (1870); *contra*, 4 La. 87 (1832); 12 La. 530 (1838).

[3] 3 Vr. (N. J.) 423 (1868).

[4] 4 Geo. (Miss.) 299 (1857).

[5] 9 G. & J. (Md.) 80 (1837).

[6] 2 Bland's Ch. (Md.) 333 (1808).

[7] 32 Ga. 20 (1861); 5 Allen (Mass.) 356 (1862).

[8] 61 Ga. 106 (1878).

[9] 32 Ga. 20 (1861).

Interest is not allowed on a note during a contest to determine to whom it should be paid.[1]

(*e*) *Judgment.* Upon a judgment, generally, only the legal rate is allowed.[2] Thus a contract rate may be reduced.

(*f*) *Negligence.* Where a party has neglected to claim interest until after the settlement of a running account, or an award of a committee has been made,[3] he will not be allowed such claim. So he will not be allowed interest if he has been guilty of gross laches in delaying the prosecution of his claim.[4] Where A mortgaged some land to B, and subsequently to C, B entered, and afterward suffered A, the mortgagor, to receive the profits for several years, without the payment of interest on the mortgage, it was held that the interest that should have been paid during the time the premises were thus occupied by the mortgagor should not be charged on the land against C.[5]

So, if a trustee violates his trust, and the offended party delays for many years to bring his suit for recovery, interest will only be allowed from the commencement of the suit.[6]

(*g*) *Payment of principal.* The payment of the principal, interest not being claimed at the time by the creditor, generally bars a future recovery of it.[7]

[1] 8 Mart. N. S. (La.) 214 (1829).

[2] 20 Fla. 980 (1884); 65 Ga. 189 (1880); 74 Ga. 465 (1885); Breese (Ill.) 52, 83 (1824); 1 Scam. (Ill.) 137 (1834); 27 Ill. 349 (1862); 28 Ill. 201 (1862); 35 Ill. 152 (1864); 45 Ill. 178 (1867); 79 Ill. 532 (1875); 14 O. St. 367 (1863). See page 104.

[3] 17 Conn. 377 (1845).

[4] 110 U. S. 174 (1883); 5 Rich. Eq. (S. C.) 31 (1852).

[5] Pre. Ch. (Eng.) 30 (1691).

[6] 22 Ark. 1 (1860).

[7] 14 Cal. 171 (1859); 19 Conn. 529 (1849); 132 Ill. 550 (1890); 2 La. 518 (1831); 4 Hubb. (Me.) 481 (1861); 4 Pick. (Me.) 572 (1878); 11 Mass. 217 (1814); 103 Mass. 33 (1869); 71 Mich. 118 (1888); 8 Mo.

Where the defendant used a county's money from time to time to pay his own notes, and an expert reported the various sums due, but did not include the interest, the defendant's payment of those sums and his release by the plaintiff, the New Jersey court holds, does not estop the county from recovering the interest.[1]

From the fact that the sum sued for is precisely the amount of the interest, it must not be presumed that the principal, as such, has been paid.[2]

Receiving the principal and part of the interest as so much paid generally, and not as payment of the principal itself, does not preclude the recovery of the rest of the interest.[3]

One cannot be compelled to receive a partial payment so as to stop interest on that part, yet if the creditor collects a portion of the debt through legal proceedings he cannot afterward claim interest on that part from the time it was paid by the debtor.[4] See the law relating to partial payments in chapter seven, at page 167.

Contractual interest may, under peculiar circumstances, be recovered after the payment of the principal.[5] Where the maker of a note, bearing contractual interest overdue,

41 (1843); 3 Johns. (N. Y.) 229 (1808), 587 (1818); 5 Johns. (N. Y.) 268 (1810); 3 Cow. (N. Y.) 86 (1824); 15 Wend. (N. Y.) 76 (1835); 3 Edw. (N. Y.) 512 (1841); 11 Paige's Ch. (N. Y.) 142 (1844); 4 Hun (N. Y.) 429 (1875); 119 N. Y. 1 (1890); 95 N. C. 245 (1886); 22 Vt. 437 (1850); 26 Vt. 624 (1854); 56 Vt. 609 (1884); *contra*, 3 P. W. (Eng.) 126 (1731); 32 Ind. 328 (1869), overruling 8 Blf. (Ind.) 328 (1846); 56 Ind. 288 (1877).

[1] 7 N. J. L. J. 148.

[2] 5 Cow. (N. Y.) 331 (1826).

[3] 13 Wend. (N. Y.) 639 (1835).

[4] 7 Johns. Ch. (N. Y.) 7 (1823); 3 Paige (N. Y.) 400 (1832); 7 How. Pr. (N. Y.) 44 (1852).

[5] 15 Wend. (N. Y.) 76 (1835).

gave the holder a new note for the amount of the principal, the question of interest being left open, it was held, that under those circumstances, the interest could be sued for alone.[1] Also, where the maker of a note paid its principal and promised to pay the interest at a future day, the holder giving him the note for a particular purpose, it was similarly held.[2]

(*h*) *Statute of limitations.* Interest may also be barred by the statute of limitations. See chapter twelve for the law concerning the effect of the statute of limitations upon interest.

(*i*) *Tender.* When the exact amount in cash of the sum due is tendered to the creditor (not to his attorney at law[3]), and he refuses to receive it, the interest ceases.[4] If the debt is payable in chattels, they must be tendered.[5] The tender must be unconditional.[6] It must be a real tender at the place and time agreed, and not simply proposals to deduct on an account,[7] nor an appropriation by setting the money aside and telling the creditor what has

[1] 5 Scott (Eng.) 230 (1837); 4 Bing. N. C. (Eng.) 9 (1837); 3 Hodges (Eng.) 247 (1837); 1 Jur. (Eng.) 799 (1837); 135 Mass. 573 (1883).

[2] 2 Col. 711 (1875).

[3] 6 La. 17 (1833).

[4] 1 Ch. Cas. (Eng.) 29 (1663); 2 Ves. (Eng.) 678 (1795); 3 Campb. (Eng.) 296 (1812); 67 Ala. 310 (1880); 39 Cal. 61 (1871); 41 Cal. 133 (1871); 9 Col. 38 (1885); 35 Ga. 8 (1866); 86 Ill. 470 (1877); 96 Ill. 11 (1880); 5 Kas. 649 (1864); 6 La. 17 (1833); 42 Md. 192 (1874); 5 Pick. (Mass.) 106 (1827); 37 Mich. 158 (1877); 56 Mich. 332 (1885); 57 Miss. 410 (1879); 3 Binn. (Pa.) 295 (1811); 47 Pa. St. 353 (1864); 80 Pa. St. 116 (1875); 108 Pa. St. 55 (1884); on taxes, 39 Iowa 151 (1874); 37 Kas. 663 (1887).

[5] 39 N. Y. 481 (1868).

[6] 9 Col. 38 (1885); 17 Fla. 575 (1880); 1 Duv. (Ky.) 301 (1864); 3 Jones Eq. (N. C.) 126 (1856).

[7] 2 Ves. (Eng.) 678 (1795); 72 Ind. 567 (1880); 47 Pa. St. 76 (1864).

been done,[1] nor a mere statement that the debtor is ready to pay.[2] Nor will a real tender stop interest if the person making it has the use and benefit of the money from and after the time when it was made;[3] it must be continuing. The tenderer must also show that he had the right to make the tender;[4] but even then a mortgagee is not obliged to accept a tender from the holder of but a moiety of the equity of redemption, and when such a tender is refused the interest on the debt does not stop.[5]

A tender stops interest until the creditor asks for the money and no longer, if the debtor is not then ready and does not again tender it.[6] The amount tendered must be kept in readiness and paid into court if the tender is pleaded, according to the decisions in New Jersey.[7]

If payment, or tender, is prevented by the act of the creditor, he is not entitled to interest.[8]

But a tender does not stop interest on a note secured by a trust deed, where the debtor, after the tender, assails the validity of the claim and seeks to have the deed cancelled as a nullity.[9]

A refusal by the husband of a legatee, at common law, to receive a legacy stops interest on it.[10]

Where money is lent to be paid on a certain day, with

[1] 34 L. R., Ch. Div. (Eng.) 386 (1886).

[2] 71 Iowa 648 (1887).

[3] 2 P. Wm. (Eng.) 378 (1726); 62 Ga. 596 (1874); 84 Ill. 470 (1877); 96 Ill. 11 (1880); 1 Duv. (Ky.) 304 (1864); 3 Spauld. (Me.) 365 (1882); 11 Mon. 53 (1891).

[4] 139 Mass. 348 (1885).

[5] 3 Spauld. (Me.) 365 (1882).

[6] 84 Ill. 470 (1877); 42 Md. 192 (1874).

[7] 1 McCart. (N. J.) 168 (1861); 7 C. E. Gr. (N. J.) 56, 447 (1871); 8 C. E. Gr. (N. J.) 509 (1872).

[8] 1 Mar. (Ky.) 159 (1818).

[9] 60 Miss. 496 (1882).

[10] 4 Call (Va.) 605 (1803).

interest payable at stated periods, the borrower cannot, by tendering the principal before the date it is due stop the interest, for the time of payment is part of the contract, and for the benefit of both parties.[1]

In a certain case, the defendant was able, ready and willing to pay a note ever after it matured, with interest to the time of its maturity, and he had repeatedly offered to pay the amount due, to the proper person, upon the delivery to him of the note to be cancelled and the mortgage to be discharged, or a sufficient indemnity against any claim on account of said note and mortgage. The plaintiff could not surrender the note and mortgage, and it was held in equity that the defendant should not suffer from that, and, although it was not a lawful tender, yet it was sufficient to relieve the defendant from the payment of interest after such offer.[2]

In actions of tort the plaintiff is generally not entitled to interest on his damages, when he refused, before suit, to accept for damages a sum larger than he was entitled to, although no formal tender was made, the plaintiff by his suit putting off payment.[3] So, it was held in a Wisconsin case that interest was not recoverable on the balance of a disputed account found due to the plaintiff, where the defendant had previously offered to pay the amount so found due, which offer had been refused.[4]

In Massachusetts, it is held that a tender will stop conventional interest only above the legal rate.[5]

(*j*) *Waiver.* Parties may at any time waive the interest portion of a debt; but indulgence to the maker by

[1] 7 Johns. Ch. (N. Y.) 7 (1823).

[2] 55 N. H. 476 (1875).

[3] 58 N. H. 524 (1879).

[4] 21 Wis. 27 (1866).

[5] 139 Mass. 407 (1885).

extending the time of payment of a note is not a waiver of interest upon it.[1]

(*k*) *War.* The mere circumstance of war existing between two powers or nations is not a sufficient reason for abating interest on debts due from subjects of one belligerent power to those of another;[2] but a prohibition of all intercourse with an enemy during war,[3] rather than the fact that the money could not be profitably used because of the condition of the country,[4] furnishes a sound reason for the suspension of interest until the return of peace, and, therefore, as a rule, interest does not run during a formal war.[5]

The war of the Revolution began September 10, 1775, and ended March 10, 1783.[6] The civil rebellion in the United States commenced July 13, 1861, and terminated May 10, 1865.[7]

To stop interest, the parties must not only be enemies to each other, but be resident in their respective countries or states.[8] So interest on debts due from citizens of Texas to citizens of New York was not suspended during the

[1] 24 Tenn. 406 (1844).

[2] 2 H. & McH. (Md.) 161 (1798).

[3] 1 Pet. (U. S., C. C.) 496 (1818); 15 Wall. (U. S.) 177 (1872); 62 Ala. 58 (1878); 11 Bush (Ky.) 208 (1874); Coxe (N. J.) 133, 435 (1793); 4 Halst. (N. J.) 3 (1827); 2 Dall. (Pa.) 102 (1789), 132 (1791); 1 Desau. (S. C.) 427 (1795); 3 McC. (S. C.) 340 (1825); 20 Grat. (Va.) 124 (1870). This applies to contractual interest as well as to interest allowed as damages. 15 Wall. (U. S.) 177 (1872).

[4] 22 W. Va. 474 (1883).

[5] 37 Ga. 482 (1867); 3 H. & M'H. (Md.) 20 (1790), 140, 167 (1793); 2 Bl. Ch. (Md.) 221*n*. (1803), 645*n*. (1795); 2 Dall. (Pa.) 132 (1791); 60 Tenn. 695 (1871); 68 Tenn. 325 (1873); 3 Call (Va.) 22 (1801); 78 Va. 12 (1883), 665 (1884).

[6] 2 Dall. (Pa.) 102 (1789).

[7] 37 Ga. 482 (1867).

[8] 27 Grat. (Va.) 511, 541 (1876); 28 Grat. (Va.) 207 (1877); 29 Grat. (Va.) 379 (1877).

late rebellion;[1] that is, interest is not barred as between citizens of, and residents in, the same country.[2] As between citizens of a belligerent country and those of a neutral interest will run as though the war did not exist if a remittance can be safely made.[3]

Even then if the creditor has an agent, authorized to receive payment, living in the same jurisdiction as the debtor interest ought not to abate, if the debtor knows of his presence.[4] So, where the defendant has an agent in the plaintiff's country and payments have been made on the principal by him during the war.[5] Where a contract to pay money was made with an alien enemy before the war, and the enemy carried the contract to his own country, the obligor, not being able therefore to pay it, is relieved from paying interest on it during the war.[6] As between an agent and his principal, when the agent resides within the enemy's lines he should not be charged with interest during the war.[7] The same principle applies in cases where a surety of the enemy resides within the creditor's country.[8]

War does not disturb contractual interest, if it is not due until the war is over.[9]

This defence to the payment of interest is personal to the debtor, and is not available by a surety.[10]

[1] 32 Tex. 663 (1870).

[2] 37 Ark. 463 (1881); 32 Grat. (Va.) 613 (1880).

[3] 4 Dall. (Pa.) 286 (1803). This was the case of a debt contracted before the Revolution by citizens of Pennsylvania and Holland. The debtor was held liable for interest.

[4] 3 Wash. (U. S., C. C.) 396 (1818); 7 Wall. (U. S.) 447 (1868). The court in 2 Dall. (Pa.) 102 (1789) said that interest, even then, should not be allowed, as all intercourse with the enemy is prohibited.

[5] 1 Desau. (S. C.) 194 (1791).

[6] 3 McC. (S. C.) 340 (1825).

[7] 26 Grat. (Va.) 188 (1875).

[8] 4 H. & M'H. (Md.) 161 (1798).

[9] 15 Minn. 416 (1870).

[10] 62 Ala. 58 (1878).

CHAPTER V.

RATE OF INTEREST.

THERE are two classes of rates per cent of interest, the legal and the conventional rate.[1] The law regards a person as always bound to pay the legal rate unless there is an agreement for another.[2] Under this rule there is a diversity of opinion on this question: Where a contract is made "with interest at ten per cent" in a state where the legal rate is six per cent, will the contract carry ten per cent after maturity until it is paid, or only the legal rate? The decisions are about evenly divided. Those courts which hold that it will draw the conventional rate after maturity say that that was the presumed intention of the parties.[3] The other courts hold that the agreement of

[1] The Spanish law recognizes the same divisions. 2 Cal. 568 (1852).

[2] 9 Col. 228 (1886); 15 Col. 320 (1890); 1 Scam. (Ill.) 305 (1836); 49 Ill. 142 (1868); 57 Ill. 327 (1870); 1 Bradw. (Ill.) 555 (1878); 123 Ill. 608 (1888); 39 Kas. 73 (1888); 1 Mart. (La.) 75 (1809); 14 La. Ann. 681 (1859); 63 Md. 484 (1885).

[3] 8 Exch. (Eng.) 620 (1853); 3 C. B., N. S. (Eng.) 144 (1857); 27 L. J., C. P. (Eng.) 88 (1857); 97 U. S. 51 (1877); 103 U. S. 697 (1880); 2 Cal. 597 (1852); 29 Conn. 268 (1860); 33 Conn. 419 (1866); 20 Fla. 980 (1884); 86 Ga. 1 (1890); 14 S. E. Rep. (Ga.) 118 (1891); 28 Ill. 201 (1862); 110 Ill. 35 (1884); 17 Bradw. (Ill.) 491 (1885); 116 Ill. 391 (1886); 94 Ind. 178 (1883); 101 Ind. 1 (1884); 18 Iowa 324 (1865); 20 Iowa 490 (1866); 112 Mass. 63 (1873); 129 Mass. 82, 425, 559 (1880); 139 Mass. 360 (1885); 38 Mich. 662 (1878); 2 Minn. 350 (1858); 60 Miss. 400, 496 (1882); 64 Mo. 600 (1877); 8 Mo. App. 76 (1879); 9 Mo. App. 575, 581 (1881); 79 Mo. 226 (1883); 81 Mo. 636 (1884); 84 Mo. 66 (1884); 3 Mon. 412 (1879); 15 Neb. 256 (1883); 16 Neb. 12 (1884); 17 Neb. 491 (1885); 1 Nev. 161 (1865); 12 Vr. (N. J.)

the parties is limited to the time mentioned in the contract.[1] But if one voluntarily continues to pay the conventional rate after the maturity of the contract he cannot, in the absence of fraud, have the excess above the legal rate deducted from the principal on settlement.[2] Neither will the mere payment of the rate agreed upon after the maturity of the debt fix the rate after maturity; as, where the rate is not stated and a greater than the legal rate has

349 (1879); 4 Johns. Ch. (N. Y.) 436 (1820); 19 Hun (N. Y.) 87 (1879); 60 How. Pr. (N. Y.) 9 (1880); 25 O. St. 384, 621 (1874); 65 Tenn. 762 (1872); 7 Tex. 461 (1852); 10 Tex. 189 (1853); 16 Wis. 178 (1862); 18 Wis. 367 (1864). In Massachusetts, it is held that, after a tender of the amount due on a matured debt bearing interest at a conventional rate higher than the legal, only the legal rate can be recovered. 139 Mass 407 (1885). So, where a mortgagor's interest in land was sold on execution, the purchaser told the agent of the mortgagee that he wished to pay the mortgage, and the agent misled him. The mortgagee was held to be estopped from claiming the rate of interest named in the mortgage after the maturity of the debt, and was allowed only the legal rate. 137 Mass. 389 (1884). The court in New York, in 10 Hun (N. Y.) 173 (1877), held, that if the agreed rate was less than the legal it would continue till judgment.

[1] 22 How. (U. S.) 118 (1859); 22 Wall. (U. S.) 170 (1874); 100 U. S. 72 (1879); 108 (U. S.) 143 (1882); 7 Ala. 490 (1845); 14 Ala. 233 (1848); 4 Ark. 124 (1842); 31 Ark. 626 (1876); 32 Ark. 154, 571, 612 (1877); 36 Ark. 476 (1880); 42 Ark. 539 (1884); 54 Ark. 437 (1891); 42 Conn. 570 (1875); 68 Ind. 202 (1879); 71 Ind. 171 (1880); 72 Ind. 567 (1880); 74 Ind. 158 (1881); 2 Kas. 184 (1863); 3 Kas. 515 (1866); 7 J. J. Mar. (Ky.) 619 (1832); 13 W. P. D. Bush (Ky.) 121 (1877); 3 Mart. N. S. (La.) 185 (1824); 3 Puls. (Me.) 145, 540 (1877); 3 Haml. (Me.) 72 (1890); 15 Minn. 416 (1870); 94 N. Y. 354 (1884); 113 N. Y. 485 (1889); 15 O. St. 218 (1864); 5 W. & S. (Pa.) 51 (1842); 10 R. I. 223 (1872); 1 N. & McC. (S. C.) 67 (1818); 10 S. C. 133 (1878); 16 S. C. 469 (1881); 30 S. C. 61 (1888); 33 S. C. 210 (1890); 35 S. C. 61 (1891); 14 S. E. Rep. (S. C.) 809 (1892); 1 Utah 63 (1871); 19 Wis. 533 (1865). The court, in 43 L. J., Ch. (Eng.) 855 (1874) and 7 L. R., H. L. (Eng.) 27 (1874), says that the conventional rate in England is not allowed after the maturity of the contract, and that the court may then award what they deem just and reasonable, which is generally the agreed rate.

[2] 3 Haml. (Me.) 72 (1890).

been paid after the maturity of a note, the creditor cannot recover more than the legal rate;[1] it does not amount to an agreement to pay other than the legal rate.

A contract, bearing a conventional rate of interest, payable on demand, is a contract that stipulates what shall be paid after maturity, as the note is due as soon as made.[2] So, if payable one day after date,[3] where it specifies the rate of interest for a longer time simply.[4] If the contract says that the agreed rate shall govern "until the principal sum be paid" the contract rate must be paid accordingly, although after maturity;[5] and it matters not what the form of the contract is, the interest being regarded in such cases as agreed damages, and not technical interest.[6] The courts in Montana and Ohio hold that the words "until paid," when the time of payment is stated, are limited to the time named, after which only the legal rate is allowed.[7]

Parties may agree what per cent their contracts shall bear after maturity;[8] and the Missouri court has decided that a note bearing ten per cent interest, stipulating that if it is not paid at maturity it shall bear nine per cent for a certain length of time, shall bear the original rate after

[1] 138 Mass. 53 (1884). This may be due, partly, to a statute in Massachusetts, which provides that contracts for a greater than the legal rate shall be in writing.

[2] 4 Puls. (Me.) 80, 524 (1878); 153 Mass. 550 (1891).

[3] 31 Ark. 620 (1876); 38 Ark. 111 (1881); 40 Ark. 117 (1882); 18 S. W. Rep. (Ky.) 637 (1892); 14 S. C. 311 (1880); 22 S. C. 139 (1884).

[4] 14 S. C. 311 (1880); 22 S. C. 139 (1884).

[5] 133 U. S. 626 (1889); 4 Ark. 170, 199 (1842); 2 Col. 70 (1873); 6 Col. 587 (1883); 84 Ind. 370 (1882); 148 Mass. 231 (1889); 149 Mass. 73 (1889); 10 R. I. 299 (1872).

[6] 1 Mon. 499 (1872).

[7] 1 Mon. 612 (1872); 7 O. 1 (p. 80) (1835).

[8] 83 Ill. 226 (1876). Unless the court deems it too much. 2 Col. 70 (1873).

the specified period had expired.[1] In those cases where compound interest is allowed, the parties can agree at what rate interest payable at stated times shall bear interest after it has become due.[2] The Nebraska court holds that an agreed rate of interest after maturity is a penalty, which it will not enforce.[3]

Judgments and decrees generally bear the legal rate, and not the rate named in the contracts upon which the suits are brought.[4] Where notes bearing seven per cent interest are merged in a judgment, which bears only the legal rate, a mortgage securing the notes should be afterward reckoned in equity as bearing the judgment rate only.[5] For a fuller discussion of the rate of interest on judgments, see *judgments* in chapter three, at page 104.

A decree by the Missouri court, establishing the lien of a judgment creditor upon land fraudulently conveyed by his debtor, allowed interest upon the original judgment from its date, at the rate therein specified.[6]

Where the holder of a note which is barred by the statute of limitations agreed to take less than its face value by writing on its face, it was held to be a new contract, and henceforth to bear only the legal rate of interest.[7] But where a note thus barred is revived by a new promise, the legal conventional rate is presumed to continue.[8]

[1] 66 Mo. 453 (1877).

[2] 46 Iowa 239 (1877).

[3] 51 N. W. Rep. (Neb.) 753 (1892).

[4] 2 Beas. (N. J.) 289 (1861); 19 Hun (N. Y.) 87 (1879); 60 How. Pr. N. Y.) 9 (1880); 84 N. Y. 471 (1881); 14 O. St. 367 (1863); 16 S. C. 15, 429 (1881); 1 Wash. T. 112 (1860); *contra*, contractual interest, 14 Mo. App. 187 (1883); 25 O. St. 622 (1874); 24 W. Va. 344 (1884).

[5] 14 O. St. 367 (1863).

[6] 75 Mo. 460 (1882).

[7] 132 Ill. 627 (1890).

[8] 85 Ga. 166 (1891).

In an action on an indemnity bond given to an officer upon making a levy, the property being sold, the damages and the judgment thereon were decided by the Iowa court to bear interest at the rate of the note which the property secured.[1]

Attorney's fees stipulated for in a mortgage will bear the same rate of interest as the judgment on it.[2]

There is nothing to prevent parties to a note from allowing back interest upon the debt at the same rate that would be lawful for the future.[3] It will not be usurious.

If the holder of collateral paper, bearing eight per cent interest, collects and appropriates the same to his own use, he will be liable at only the legal rate from that time.[4]

Where interest as damages is allowed for the non-payment of contractual interest, only the legal rate will be given.[5]

In New Mexico, in an action on a note, interest at the legal rate only can be recovered on the common counts. though the note bears a higher rate by its terms.[6]

I. THE LEGAL RATE.

The terms "legal interest" and "legal rate," as used in the reports, are identical.[7] The legal rate is that rate per cent established by law, either by constitution, statute or custom, for which all parties are conclusively presumed to

[1] 66 Iowa 731 (1885).

[2] 11 Kas. 381 (1873).

[3] 39 Mich. 417 (1878).

[4] 4 Geo. (Miss.) 467 (1857).

[5] 32 N. E. Rep. (N. Y.) 129 (1892); 26 O. St. 59 (1875); *contra*, 69 N. C. 89 (1873).

[6] 3 N. M. 45 (1883).

[7] 35 Cal. 624 (1868).

have contracted in absence of an agreed rate,[1] and which is also allowed as damages.[2] In Louisiana, the early usual rate was that generally allowed at New Orleans and Bordeaux.[3] Six per cent is now the legal rate in a majority of the states, and in other places it varies from five to twelve per cent. In about one-third of the states parties can legally contract for any other rate, unless it is so high that it is unconscionable. In most of the states, however, the legislatures have fixed a maximum limit, beyond which parties cannot legally contract; and if they attempt to do so they are guilty of usury, and the contract cannot be enforced as made, if at all. See chapters on usury and the statutes, numbers ten and thirteen.

If the rate is not fixed by the parties, or by statute, it is to be regulated by the custom of the place where the contract is to be performed, found by a jury;[4] or, the jury may establish it for that case;[5] or, the court may allow a reasonable rate.[6]

Coupons do not bear the rate named in the bond unless it is so stated;[7] damages,[8] judgments for debts, decrees,[9]

[1] 9 Col. 228 (1886); 15 Col. 320 (1890); 112 Mass. 244 (1873); Pen. (N. J.) 907 (1811); 1 Halst. (N. J.) 115 (1822); 4 Halst. (N. J.) 264 (1827); 12 Vr. (N. J.) 349 (1879); 17 Stew. (N. J.) 56 (1888); 15 O. St. 40 (1864).

[2] 94 N. Y. 641 (1884); 95 N. Y. 428 (1884); 9 Ore. 266 (1881).

[3] 1 Mart. (La.) 71 (1809).

[4] 1 Wash. (U. S., C. C.) 521 (1806); 15 Wall. (U. S.) 562 (1872); Minor (Ala.) 387 (1825); 1 Stew. & Port. (Ala.) 33 (1831). The court in Arkansas says that it cannot be simply the custom of merchants. 18 Ark. 456 (1857).

[5] 1 Utah 55 (1871).

[6] 8 Port. (Ala.) 250 (1839); 1 Cal. 422 (1851). In the latter case the court allowed six per cent as a reasonable rate, because it was believed to have been the legal rate of interest of the Mexican republic at the time of the organization of the state government of California.

[7] 1 Dill. (U. S., C. C.) 529 (1870); 39 Minn. 122 (1888).

[8] 21 Iowa 326 (1866).

[9] 3 Blf. (Ind.) 457 (1834).

and judgments for interest,[1] only bear the legal rate of the *forum*, generally.[2]

How proved. Courts cannot judicially notice that another state or jurisdiction allows interest, nor what its rate per cent is; these laws must be proved as a fact is proved.[3] The finding of the jury upon the evidence is presumed to be correct.[4] If the jury have not found the rate, the court may consider evidence, in a case depending upon it.[5]

The published law of such other state is the best evidence, the testimony of a witness as to what the law is not being sufficient.[6] The interpretation of the foreign law is for the court, and not the jury.[7]

In the absence of all proof of interest in another jurisdiction it is generally presumed that no interest is allowed there, and therefore none should be allowed in the action;[8] and that if it is proved that interest is allowed in the foreign state, but its rate is not proved, or if it has no legal

[1] 1 G. Gr. (Iowa) 66 (1847); *contra*, to bear rate of contract, 5 Cal. 416 (1855).

[2] 47 Iowa 477 (1877). See judgments page 102.

[3] 2 Port. (Ala.) 239 (1835); 20 Ala. 470, 629 (1852); 81 Ala. 240 (1886); 86 Ala. 541 (1888); 4 Cal. 251 (1854); 2 Bibb (Ky.) 634 (1812); 1 Mon. (Ky.) 209 (1814); 1 J. J. Mar. (Ky.) 94, 408 (1829); 2 J. J. Mar. (Ky.) 116 (1829); 4 J. J. Mar. (Ky.) 238 (1830); 19 La. Ann. 373 (1867); 92 N. C. 266 (1885); 24 Pa. St. 435 (1855); 1 Tex. 9 (1846).

[4] Lit. Sel. Cas. (Ky.) 505 (1821); 5 S. & M. (Miss.) 573 (1845).

[5] 24 Pa. St. 435 (1855).

[6] 2 Wash. (U. S., C. C.) 253 (1808); 7 Port. (Ala.) 111 (1838); 8 Port. (Ala.) 250 (1839); 4 Cal. 251 (1854); 19 La. Ann. 373 (1867).

[7] 24 Pa. St. 435 (1855).

[8] 1 Port. (Ala.) 388 (1834); 4 Cal. 250 (1854); *contra*, 15 Gray (Mass.) 178 (1860); 2 Allen (Mass.) 236 (1861), which cases say that the *lex loci forum* governs as to interest allowed as damages. It is necessary that the foreign law be averred and proved if it would be taken advantage of. 38 Iowa 237 (1874).

rate, the general practice is to allow the legal rate of the place where the action is brought.[1]

If damages are sought to be recovered on a demand arising out of the state, and the rate of those damages is fixed by legislation, the court must allow that special rate, if it is proved.[2]

II. THE CONVENTIONAL RATE.

This is the rate per cent expressly agreed upon by the parties to a contract, be it more or less than the legal rate; and if it is not usurious or unconscionable the law will always enforce the conventional, and not the legal rate, when it is proved to exist, and what it is,[3] unless there is fraud.[4] If the rate is unconscionable the court will not be bound by it.[5] None but the legal rate is allowed, except by agreement,[6] and the language of such a contract must be clear.[7]

The law in force at the time of making the contract controls as to whether the contract is usurious or not.[8] No subsequent change in the legal rate can affect an existing conventional rate.[9]

[1] 2 Wash. (U. S., C. C.) 253 (1808); 24 Ill. 293 (1860); 26 Ill. 39 (1861); 58 Ill. 58 (1871); 38 Iowa 237 (1874); 3 Mar. (Ky.) 175 (1820); 12 La. 589 (1838); 16 La. 557 (1840); 4 Met. (Mass.) 203 (1842); 5 Gray (Mass.) 9 (1855); 7 Gray (Mass.) 566 (1856); 15 Gray (Mass.) 178 (1860); 129 Mass. 600 (1880); 4 Minn. 515 (1860); *contra*, 1 Port. (Ala.) 388 (1834).

[2] 7 Port. (Ala.) 111 (1838).

[3] 2 Cal. 568 (1852); 1 Mart. (La.) 7 (1809); 51 N. W. Rep. (Mich.) 1057 (1892).

[4] 51 N. W. Rep. (Mich.) 1057 (1892).

[5] 12 Mass. 365 (1815).

[6] 17 La. Ann. 145 (1865); 18 La. Ann. 557 (1866); 23 La. Ann. 201 (1871); 30 La. Ann. 1210, 1341 (1878); 42 La. Ann. 357 (1890).

[7] 1 Wash. T. 584 (1878).

[8] 42 Conn. 570 (1875); 44 Conn. 390 (1877); 47 Conn. 418 (1879).

[9] 14 Cal. 171 (1859); 1 Fla. 356 (1847); 5 Fla. 345 (1853).

If a contract is valid where it is made and where it is to be performed, the parties may stipulate for interest according to the law of either place.[1]

A subsequent agreement that the rate of interest shall be reduced if the debt is paid at the time when it is due is not binding, if it is not so paid, and the old rate can be recovered,[2] as there is no consideration to support the promise.

The rate may be inferred from previous dealings between the parties.[3] See chapter two, at page 20.

"Ten pr. cen." written in a note is construed to mean ten per cent interest per annum.[4]

A new promise, reviving a note that is barred by the statute of limitations, also revives the conventional rate of interest that it bore.[5]

The rate specified in a note cannot be changed by a parol agreement.[6]

A third party may contract to be substituted as debtor in place of another; and if such substitution is made, the new debtor may lawfully contract to pay the rate of interest which the debt bears, notwithstanding it may be higher than the rate then allowed by law.[7]

How proved. Generally the rate per cent agreed upon can be proved by any competent evidence,[8] unless the statutes of the state make it imperative upon parties to prove rates of interest that are larger than the legal rate

[1] 92 Ala. 164 (1890).
[2] 3 Dak. 449 (1884).
[3] 81 Ill. 15 (1875).
[4] 65 Ill. 310, 314 (1872).
[5] 79 Ga. 301 (1887).
[6] 126 Ind. 12 (1890).
[7] 4 Cush. (Miss.) 13 (1853); 2 Geo. (Miss.) 260 (1856).
[8] 42 Ill. 179 (1866).

by written evidence. Then, the statute, of course, controls, except where there are circumstances that prove an exception to the statutory requirement.[1]

If the rate per cent is included in the written contract, oral evidence cannot be admitted to change it.[2]

If the evidence of a debt made payable in another state shows on its face that it bears interest proof of the instrument is proof of that fact.[3]

A contract payable in another state at a rate higher than that permitted where the suit is brought, is governed by the rate in the contract, without pleading the law of the foreign state.[4]

[1] 28 Cal. 302 (1865).
[2] 37 Ala. 702 (1861).
[3] 13 Ala. 722 (1848), which was an action brought on a judgment.
[4] 19 Ind. 401 (1862).

CHAPTER VI.

COMPOUND INTEREST.

COMPOUND interest is interest upon interest; and, even in contracts for interest, it will generally not be allowed,[1] as it is not favored.[2] It is upon principles of justice alone that promises are ever implied or duties raised in law. Chancellor Kent said that chancery declares compound interest to be inequitable, unjust and oppressive. Interest should not become principal, except by agreement of the parties.[3] The Roman law was constant in its condemnation of compound interest;[4] and in Kentucky no agreement for compound interest will be enforced in equity.[5]

The right to compound interest, when it does exist, cannot be impaired by legislation declaring the true intent and meaning of statutes previously existing.[6]

Conversion of interest into principal by judgment or decree is not technically allowing compound interest.[7]

Compound interest is waived, where, without insisting on its payment, simple interest is accepted.[8]

[1] 13 Vt. 430 (1841).
[2] 72 Ga. 863 (1884).
[3] 8 Blf. (Ind.) 158 (1846); 16 Ind. 160 (1861).
[4] 7 Greenl. (Me.) 48 (1830).
[5] 2 Mar. (Ky.) 339 (1820).
[6] 104 U. S. 668 (1881).
[7] 2 Bland's Ch. (Md.) 306 (1830).
[8] 41 Mich. 359 (1879).

I. CONTRACTS FOR COMPOUND INTEREST.

Compound interest cannot be contracted for before the interest becomes due;[1] that is, interest must be due and payable before a contract can be made to pay interest upon that interest.[2] This principle does not arise from the usury law, but is a rule of public policy which forbids the accumulation of interest in favor of negligent creditors. It has been held not to apply where one agrees to advance money to purchase property for the benefit of himself and another, to be repaid to him, with compound interest, only out of the proceeds of sales.[3]

An agreement to pay compound interest before any interest is due on the contract does not render the contract either usurious or void; the courts will simply decline to enforce payment of the interest upon interest, and give judgment for the valid part.[4]

If an agreement is made to convert interest already due and payable into principal, or if accounts between parties are settled by rests, and therefore in effect upon the prin-

[1] 2 Salk. (Eng.) 449 (1707); Mos. (Eng.) 247 (1729); 1 Ves. jr. (Eng.) 99 (1790); 9 Ves. (Eng.) 271 (1804); 1 Ball & B. (Ire.) 428 (1810); 54 Ala. 646 (1875); 16 Col. 263 (1891); 17 Conn. 243 (1845); 24 Md. 62 (1865); 8 Mass. 455 (1812); 13 Met. (Mass.) 64 (1847); 2 Cush. (Mass.) 92 (1848); 41 Mich. 533 (1879); 2 Minn. 350 (1858); 51 Miss. 298 (1875); 1 Mon. 183 (1870); 54 N. W. Rep. (Neb.) 129 (1893); 1 Nev. 161 (1865); 1 Johns. Ch. (N. Y.) 13 (1814); 5 Paige's Ch. (N. Y.) 98 (1835); 3 Supm. Ct. (T. & C.) (N. Y. 783 (1874); 21 Ore. 333 (1891); 16 Vt. 44 (1844); 4 Rand. (Va.) 406 (1826); 20 W. Va. 148 (1882); *contra*, 54 Cal. 562 (1880); 3 Dak. 449 (1884); 84 Tex. 46 (1892); 1 Wash. 426 (1890).

[2] 16 Col. 263 (1891); 105 Ill. 540 (1883); 2 Blf. (Ind.) 43 (1827); 42 Ind. 450 (1873); 3 Gill (Md.) 408 (1845); 24 Md. 62 (1865); 41 Mich. 533 (1879); 2 Minn. 350 (1858); 51 Miss. 298 (1875); 16 Vt. 44 (1844).

[3] 9 Paige (N. Y.) 334 (1841).

[4] 16 Col. 263 (1891).

ciple of compound interest, it is allowed,[1] but it must have a consideration to support it.[2] It can be done by settling, agreeing upon a certain sum due, which will include the interest already due, or upon recovery of a judgment, which makes a new principal out of the old principal and interest combined, and this new principal will carry interest.[3] The court cannot, however, add the interest already due at the maturity of the note to the principal, and allow interest on the aggregate amount from the maturity of the note to the time the judgment is given, the interest being agreed to be paid until the note was paid.[4] If an agreement for compound interest is held valid, and no mode of reckoning is designated it must be by annual rests.[5]

It has been held that a contract to pay interest upon interest by an infant, after it has accrued, will be binding upon him if the contract is for his benefit.[6]

When coupons state that interest is to be allowed upon them, the court in Nebraska holds that the contract is good, unless it is usurious.[7]

II. WHEN ALLOWED AS DAMAGES.

A debtor is never bound to pay interest on interest un-

[1] G. Coop. Ch. (Eng.) 231 (1815); 1 Ball & B. (Ire.) 428 (1810); 23 Am. R. 99; 54 Ala. 646 (1875); 2 B. Mon. (Ky.) 335 (1842); 12 La. Ann. 20, 723 (1857); 3 Gill (Md.) 408 (1845); 23 Pick. (Mass.) 167 (1839); 1 Mon. 183 (1870); 6 Johns. Ch. (N. Y.) 313 (1822); 5 Paige's Ch. (N. Y.) 98 (1835); 17 How. Pr. (N. Y.) 255 (1859); 63 N. Y. 631 (1875); 67 N. Y. 162 (1876); 3 Ham. (O.) 18 (1827); 4 O. 363 (1831); 11 Ore. 66 (1883); 4 Yeates (Pa.) 220 (1805); 1 H. & Munf. (Va.) 4 (1806); 4 Rand. (Va.) 406 (1826).

[2] 23 Am. R. 99; 67 N. Y. 162 (1876); 57 Tenn. 490 (1870).

[3] 1 Baldw. (U. S., C. C.) 536 (1832); 34 Pa. St. 210 (1859).

[4] 3 La. 431 (1832).

[5] 58 Tenn. 46 (1870).

[6] 1 Eq. Cas. Abr. (Eng.) 287 (1699).

[7] 28 Neb. 358 (1889); 51 N. W. Rep. (Neb.) 753 (1892); 54 N. W. Rep. (Neb.) 129 (1893).

til it is due:[1] and it is not generally allowed at any time, either at law or equity,[2] to those holding simply the relation of debtor and creditor.[3] Some courts hold that interest is never a legal incident to the non-payment of interest.[4] This is the true rule, undoubtedly, where it is not due before the principal, and where no agreement, express or implied, has been made to convert interest into principal.[5] As, for instance, a mortgagee who has taken possession of the premises has no right to reckon interest on the mortgage debt to the time of taking possession, and then make the aggregate sum of principal and interest a new principal on which interest can be cast till the mortgage is redeemed.[6] Compound interest is not allowed on a mortgage,[7] preliminary to a decree in foreclosure.[8] The New York court, however,[9] holds that an assignee of a mortgagee can claim interest on the principal and interest he paid on it. In a suit on a note drawing simple interest, the court will not reckon interest to the date of the writ, and then compute interest on the aggregate of principal and interest to verdict, but only on the principal sum.[10]

There are three rules extant in the decisions of the courts relative to this subject. The

First rule is, that interest shall be allowed on interest payable at agreed times before the principal, from the

[1] 23 Ill. 377 (1860); 134 Ill. 294 (1890).

[2] 2 Bland's Ch. (Md.) 166 (1829); Conf. (N. C.) 435 (1800); 5 O. 261 (1831); 13 Tenn. 310 (1833); 43 Tenn. 582 (1866).

[3] 1 Stew. (N. J.) 403 (1877); 3 H. & M. (Va.) 89 (1808).

[4] 5 La. 33 (1832); 34 Pa. St. 210 (1859); 4 Rand. (Va.) 181 (1826).

[5] 84 Mo. 202 (1881); 34 Pa. St. 210 (1859); 1 Strob. (S. C.) 115 (1846), 426 (1847); 25 W. Va. 288 (1884).

[6] 5 Spauld. (Me.) 323 (1883).

[7] 1 Halst. Ch. (N. J.) 232, 245 (1845).

[8] 14 Ill. 1 (1852); 87 Ill. 23 (1877).

[9] 5 Wend. (N. Y.) 572 (1830).

[10] 13 N. H. 469 (1862).

time that the interest is payable.[1] This rule does not apply to any instalments of interest but those that are payable before the principal is due.[2] *Query*, as to the application of the rule where the agreement is to pay the interest at stated times until the principal shall be paid. In such a case, it seems as though the court endorsing this rule ought to allow interest on the unpaid instalments of interest.

In these cases, the terms "annual interest" and "interest annually" mean the same thing.[3]

Second rule. This is just the opposite of the foregoing rule. The reasoning of the court is that as interest can be recovered by suit at any time, the creditor's neglect may be considered a waiver of his right to compound interest.[4] The reason of the rule is very weak, however, because as a suit can be brought for the principal (unless by express agreement of the parties interest is payable at stated times before the principal) as soon as it becomes due creditors have no right to simple interest, and by not bringing a suit the right to any interest is waived.

[1] 132 U. S. 107 (1889); 46 Ala. 63 (1871); 29 Cal. 386 (1866); 23 Fla. 223 (1887); 61 Ga. 275 (1878); 65 Ga. 386 (1880); 134 Ill. 294 (1890): 9 Dana (Ky.) 331 (1840): 2 Heath (Me.) 308 (1853); 2 Mass. 568 (1803); 2 Cush. (Mass.) 92 (1848); 19 Minn. 338 (1873); 25 Minn. 314 (1879); 1 N. H. 179 (1818); 46 N. Y. 300 (1865); 1 Johns. Ch. (N. Y.) 550 (1815); 86 N. Y. 618 (1881); Conf. (N. C.) 135 (1800); Cam. & N. (N. C.) 357 (1800); 69 N. C. 89 (1873); 4 O. 373 (1831); 17 O. St. 11 (1866); 26 O. St. 59 (1875); 40 O. St. 248 (1883); 46 O. St. 345 (1889); 10 R. I. 223 (1872); 2 N. & McC. (S. C.) 38 (1819); 2 Hill (S. C.) 408 (1834); 3 Rich. (S. C.) 125 (1846); 63 Tenn. 128 (1872); 37 Tex. 315 (1872); 16 Vt. 44 (1844); 23 Vt. 286 (1851).

[2] 9 R. I. 132 (1868).

[3] 16 Vt. 44 (1844); 23 Vt. 286 (1851).

[4] 1 Ves. jr. (Eng.) 99 (1790); 54 Ala. 646 (1875); 66 Cal. 658 (1885); 17 Conn. 243 (1845); 25 Iowa 319 (1868); 7 Greenl. (Me.) 48 (1830): 3 Heath (Me.) 513 (1854): 2 Hub. (Me.) 445 (1859); 8 Mass. 455 (1812); 2 Cush. (Mass.) 92 (1848); 13 Mich. 303 (1865): 2 Minn. 350 (1858); 24 Minn. 267 (1877); 67 N. Y. 162 (1876); 1 Binn. (Pa.) 152 (1806); 35 Vt. 140 (1862); 10 Leigh (Va.) 481 (1839).

Third rule. Another rule is, that interest runs upon interest from and after a demand made for the interest; as in an action to recover the interest that was due at stated times upon a note, interest was allowed upon each instalment of interest, demand having been made therefor at each time it became due.[1]

In certain special equitable cases, compound interest is allowed in order that justice may be done to a party,[2] as in cases of default of payment on land contracts.[3] Trustees and other persons having fiduciary relations, who convert the trust money to their own use, or employ it in business or trade, or fail to invest it, are arbitrarily chargeable with compound interest,[4] generally, by annual rests.[5] This is also the rule where they will not disclose the amount of the profits they have made with the money.[6]

In reckoning interest where a judgment has been affirmed on a writ of error, care should be taken not to give interest on interest.[7] So on a suit for principal and interest of a note each should be stated separately, so that in the judgment it can be stated what part is interest, that interest be not allowed on it.[8]

Compound interest is allowed by the way of merchants accounting together, where they have charged interest on the various items, making periodical rests.[9] But not on

[1] 5 Red. (Me.) 75 (1852); 8 R. I. 47 (1864).

[2] 2 Ves. jr. (Eng.) 15 (1792); 35 Cal. 692 (1868).

[3] 44 Mich. 622 (1880).

[4] 136 Mass. 60 (1883); 1 Johns. Ch. (N. Y.) 620 (1815).

[5] 5 L. R. Ch. (Eng.) 233 (1870); 39 L. J., Ch. (Eng.) 369 (1870); 136 Mass. 60 (1883).

[6] 5 Johns. Ch. (N. Y.) 497 (at p. 517) (1821).

[7] 5 Ala. 195 (1843).

[8] Minor (Ala.) 115 (1823); 19 Cal. 97 (1861); 1 J. J. Mar. (Ky.) 166 (1829); 1 Gill (Md.) 372 (1843).

[9] 8 C. & F. (Eng.) 121 (1841); 11 Met. (Mass.) 210 (1846).

ordinary unliquidated accounts;[1] nor on the amount paid on a forged check.[2] Also, where an account, consisting of principal and interest, has been stated,[3] and a note given therefor.[4] Compound interest ceases to run when mutual dealings end.[5]

Interest is allowed on coupons, if not paid when due,[6] without demand,[7] unless a fund exists for their payment.[8] Where a mortgage is given to secure the principal and coupons given for the interest, they will draw interest after maturity the same as a note.[9]

Judgments and decrees carry interest on the aggregate of principal and interest.[10] The court in South Carolina holds, however, that as interest is stated damages on pecuniary liabilities, to find a sum with interest in an action sounding in damages is to allow damages on damages, which is an incongruity.[11]

Compound interest is allowed in an action for dividends on preferred stock,[12] by New York courts.

Where money is on deposit in the hands of a private person, who promises to pay interest on the same, and after some interest has accrued informs the owner that he

[1] 4 Cow. (N. Y.) 496 (1825); 22 O. St. 372 (1872).

[2] 91 N. Y. 74 (1884).

[3] 1 Johns. Ch. (N. Y.) 13 (1814).

[4] 88 Cal. 384 (1891).

[5] 1 Desau. (S. C.) 427 (1795).

[6] 41 Barb. (N. Y.) 9 (1863); 64 Hun (N. Y.) 120 (1892); 54 Pa. St. 94 (1867); 124 Pa. St. 58 (1889); 2 S. C. 248 (1870); 48 Tenn. 402 (1872); 32 Tex. 405 (1869); 33 Grat. (Va.) 586 (1880); 20 Wis. 50 (1865).

[7] 2 S. C. 248 (1870).

[8] 48 Tenn. 402 (1872).

[9] 70 Ill. 581 (1873).

[10] 5 Cal. 416 (1855); 13 S. E. Rep. (Va.) 438 (1891); 12 W. Va. 143 (1877); 14 W. Va. 737 (1879); 24 W. Va. 344 (1884); *contra*, 1 Nev. 613 (1865); 43 Tenn. 579 (1866).

[11] 2 Spears (S. C.) 594 (1844).

[12] 84 N. Y. 157 (1881); 85 N. Y. 272, 274 (1881).

has put that interest to his credit, it does not follow that that interest bears interest.[1] Neither can a debtor be compelled to pay compound interest on a debt by reason of an indorsement on the contract acknowledging payment of a portion of the debt, and stating an amount as due.[2]

III. IF PAID IT CANNOT BE RECOVERED.

The courts go so far as to hold that if compound interest has accrued under a prior bargain for it, and been actually paid, it cannot be recovered,[3] if it is voluntarily paid;[4] nor can the debtor have it deducted when sued for the principal debt.[5] If it is paid through error, however, it can be recovered.[6] In Montana, it is held that a note given in renewal of a note to which compound interest has been added is to that extent void.[7]

IV. COMPOUND INTEREST TABLES.

The following tables give the compound interest on one dollar for the given rates and time, one being for use when interest is compounded annually and the other semi-annually.

Multiply the amount of the principal by the compound interest on one dollar for the desired rate and time as found by the table, and the result will be the compound interest on that amount for that rate and time.

If it is desired to know what the compound interest will amount to for longer periods than those given in the

[1] 10 Hun (N. Y.) 173 (1877).

[2] 18 Hun (N. Y.) 452 (1879).

[3] 14 La. 34 (1839); 3 N. H. 40 (1824); 5 Paige's Ch. (N. Y.) 98 (1835).

[4] 15 La. 378 (1840); 3 Supm. Ct. (T. & C.) (N. Y.) 783 (1874).

[5] 14 La. 34 (1839).

[6] 14 La. Ann. 10 (1859), 3 Mon. 153 (1878); 2 Denio (N. Y.) 107 (1846).

[7] 3 Mon. 153 (1878).

tables, find out as above what the compound interest amounts to for the longest time given as above, and add it to the principal. Using this sum as a new principal, repeat the operation until the number of years desired has been covered.

COMPOUND INTEREST TABLE.

Interest compounded semi-annually.

YEARS.	4 %	5 %	6 %	7 %	8 %	9 %	10 %
1	.040400	.050625	.060900	.071225	.081600	.092025	.102500
1½	.061208	.076891	.092727	.108718	.124864	.141166	.157625
2	.082432	.103813	.125509	.147523	.169859	.192519	.215506
2½	.104081	.131408	.159274	.187686	.216653	.246182	.276282
3	.126162	.159693	.194052	.229255	.265319	.302260	.340096
3½	.148686	.188686	.229874	.272279	.315932	.360862	.407100
4	.171659	.218403	.266770	.316810	.368569	.422101	.477455
4½	.195093	.248862	.304773	.362898	.423312	.486095	.551328
5	.218994	.280084	.343916	.410600	.480244	.552969	.628895
5½	.243374	.312086	.384234	.459971	.539454	.622853	.710339
6	.268242	.344888	.425761	.511070	.601032	.695881	.795856
6½	.293607	.378510	.468534	.563957	.665073	.772196	.885649
7	.319478	.412973	.512590	.618696	.731676	.851945	.979932
7½	.345868	.448297	.557967	.675350	.800943	.935282	
8	.372786	.484504	.604706	.733987	.872981		
8½	.400241	.521617	.652848	.794676	.947900		
9	.428246	.559657	.702433	.857491			
9½	.456811	.598648	.753506	.922503			
10	.485947	.638615	.806111	.989791			
10½	.515666	.679580	.860294				
11	.545980	.721570	.916103				
11½	.576899	.764609	.973586				
12	.608437	.808724					
12½	.640606	.853942					
13	.673418	.900291					
13½	.706886	.947798					
14	.741024	.996493					
14½	.775845						
15	.811361						
15½	.847589						
16	.884540						
16½	.922231						
17	.960676						
17½	.999889						

COMPOUND INTEREST TABLE.

Interest compounded annually.

YEARS.	4 %	5 %	6 %	7 %	8 %	9 %	10 %
2	.081600	.102500	.123600	.144900	.166400	.188100	.210000
3	.124864	.157625	.191016	.225043	.259712	.295029	.331000
4	.169859	.215506	.262477	.310796	.360489	.411582	.464100
5	.216653	.276282	.338226	.402552	.469328	.538624	.610510
6	.265319	.340096	.418519	.500730	.586874	.677100	.771561
7	.315932	.407100	.503631	.605781	.713824	.828039	.948717
8	.368569	.477455	.593849	.718186	.850930	.992563	
9	.423312	.551328	.689480	.838459	.999004		
10	.480244	.628895	.790848	.967151			
11	.539454	.710339	.898300				
12	.601032	.795856					
13	.665073	.885649					
14	.731676	.979932					
15	.800943						
16	.872981						
17	.947900						

CHAPTER VII.

PARTIAL PAYMENTS.

EVERY payment on a debt is to be first applied toward the payment of interest due at the time the payment is made, or when the interest afterward becomes due under the contract, and the interest is never allowed to form a part of the principal to carry interest.[1] If the legislature should reduce the legal rate, payments made before the reduction will be first applied to the higher rate, and if made afterward to the lower rate.[2] That is, payments must first be applied to the interest on interest; second, to interest on the principal; and, third, to principal.[3] Of course, parties can agree otherwise;[4] but where no agreement is shown it is presumed that these rules were to be observed.

If part of a debt is paid before it becomes due, the debtor is not to be allowed interest on the amount he has so paid from the time he paid it to the time it became due,[5] unless by agreement, when the amount of interest, from the date of payment to the maturity of the debt is to be subtracted

[1] 2 Wash. (U. S., C. C.) 167 (1808); 17 Mass. 417 (1821); 1 Pick. (Mass.) 194 (1822); 31 N. H. 386 (1855); 43 N. H. 109 (1861); 46 N. H. 300 (1865); 2 Johns. Ch. (N. Y.) 209 (1816); 1 Dall. (Pa.) 378 (1788); 2 N. & McC. (S. C.) 395 (1820); 16 S. C. 15, 469 (1881); 4 Tex. 455 (1849).

[2] 28 O. St. 266 (1876).

[3] 17 O. St. 11 (1866).

[4] 4 Tex. 455 (1849).

[5] 7 Ala. 359 (1845).

from the amount of the interest on the whole debt to the time it became due.[1] See page 141.

The following is the approved rule in many states for casting interest on a debt where there have been partial payments. When a partial payment exceeds the amount of interest due when it is made, compute the interest to the time of such payment, add it to the principal, subtract the payment, cast interest on the remainder to the time of the second payment, add it to the remainder and subtract the second payment, and in like manner proceed from one payment to another until the time of judgment; if any payment is less than the amount of interest then due, credit it as a payment toward the interest; being always careful not to let any part of the interest become a part of the new principal, as inadvertently it may occur if the payment is less than the amount of interest due.[2]

[1] 1 Dall. (Pa.) 124 (1785).

[2] 2 Wash. (U. S., C. C.) 167 (1808); 13 Pet. (U. S.) 359 (1839); 35 Cal. 692 (1868); 72 Cal. 568 (1887); 3 Harr. (Del.) 469 (1842); 2 Fla. 445 (1849); 20 Ill. 509 (1858); 66 Ill. 351 (1872); 2 Blf. (Ind.) 43 (1827); 3 Blf. (Ind.) 18 (1832); 28 Ind. 488 (1867); 57 Ind. 248 (1877); 3 G. Gr. (Iowa) 76 (1851); 1 Mar. (Ky.) 584 (1819); 5 J. J. Mar. (Ky.) 83 (1830); 5 Dana (Ky.) 570 (1837); 7 Bush (Ky.) 197 (1871); 86 Ky. 668 (1888); 1 Mart. N. S. (La.) 571 (1823); 4 La. 239 (1832); 8 Rob. (La.) 6 (1844); 5 La. Ann. 738 (1850); 1 Heath (Me.) 265 (1853); 4 H. & M'H. (Md.) 91 (1797); 17 Mass. 417 (1821); 1 Pick. (Mass.) 194 (1822); 14 Gray (Mass.) 114 (1859); 144 Mass. 448 (1887); 146 Mass. 148 (1888); 21 Mich. 524 (1870); 57 Mich. 430 (1885); 82 Mich. 190 (1890); 8 S. & M. (Miss.) 368 (1847); 1 Geo. (Miss.) 66 (1855); 2 Geo. (Miss.) 51, 578 (1856); 54 Miss. 272 (1876); 14 Mo. 500 (1851); 10 Mon. 154 (1890); 4 Neb. 190 (1875); 7 Neb. 78 (1878); 31 N. H. 386 (1855); 43 N. H. 109 (1861); 1 Halst. (N. J.) 408 (1797); 2 Gr. Ch. (N. J.) 390 (1835); 4 Dutch. (N. J.) 13 (1859); 1 Johns. Ch. (N. Y.) 13 (1814); 6 Johns. Ch. (N. Y.) 313 (1822); 3 Cow. (N. Y.) 86a (1824); 7 Barb. (N. Y.) 452 (1849); 1 Hayw. (N. C.) 279 (1796); Bat.'s Mart. & 2d Hay'd (N. C.) 169 (1797); 5 O. 262, 263 (1831); 17 O. St. 11 (1866); 1 Dall. (Pa.) 378 (1788); 18 Tenn. 160 (1836); 29 Tex. 419 (1867); 31 Tex. 613 (1869); 1 Utah 63 (1871); 4 H. & M. (Va.) 431 (1809); 58 Wis. 56, 160 (1883).

In March, 1784, the supreme court of Connecticut "established a standing rule for computing interest on obligations, where one or more payments have been made, as follows:—Compute the interest to the time of the first payment; if that be one year or more from the time the interest commenced; add it to the principal and deduct the payment from the sum total. If there be after payments made, compute the interest on the balance due to the next payment, and then deduct the payment as above; and in like manner from one payment to another, till all the payments are absorbed; provided the time between one payment and another be one year or more.—But if any payment be made before one year's interest hath accrued, then compute the interest on the principal sum due on the obligation for one year, add it to the principal, and compute the interest on the sum paid, from the time it was paid, up to the end of the year; add it to the sum paid, and deduct that sum from the principal and interest added as above. If any payments be made of a less sum than the interest arisen at the time of such payment, no interest is to be computed but only on the principal sum for any period."[1]

These rules apply to judgments,[2] legacies,[3] where advances have been made to a firm by one of the partners,[4] and in settlement with administrators[5] and mortgagees,[6] as well as to other contracts; but they are inapplicable to accounts, with mutual credits, between merchants.[7]

Where by agreement property is applied to the payment

[1] Kirby (Conn.) 49 (1786); 14 Conn. 445 (1841).
[2] 2 N. H. 169 (1820); 8 S. & R. (Pa.) 452 (1822); 27 Vt. 20 (1854).
[3] 14 Gray (Mass.) 114 (1859); 5 Jones Eq. (N. C.) 167 (1859).
[4] 1 Geo. (Miss.) 66 (1855).
[5] 2 Geo. (Miss.) 578 (1856).
[6] 5 Pick. (Mass.) 259 (1827).
[7] 8 Fla. 214 (1858).

of a debt bearing interest, it must be applied *pro rata* to principal and interest.[1]

In Louisiana, if a payment is not sufficient to pay the interest then due, the rule is, to strike a new balance and compute interest on the balance of interest.[2]

Any payment made on a debt payable by instalments is to be treated as a partial payment of the whole debt.[3]

Upon a note, with interest annually, the computation at the end of the year should not be with rests on account of intermediate payments; but if such intermediate payments were on account of the interest accruing, but not yet due, they should be deducted at the end of the year but without interest upon them. And where a note bears simple interest and yearly payments are made of sums just equal to the interest, it is not correct to cast the interest upon such payments to the time of the final adjustment, as in process of time the whole debt would thereby be extinguished without the payment of any principal whatever, but the payments should be applied at the time they are made.[4]

Application of payments. In general, where neither the debtor nor the creditor makes an application of the payments, where there are several debts existing, the payments will first be applied to the discharge of the oldest debts, and so on till all are paid, paying interest on all the debts before any principal of the several debts is paid.[5] Receiving the interest and part of the principal as so much paid generally, and not as payment of the principal itself,

[1] 1 La. Ann. 265 (1846).
[2] 10 La. Ann. 159 (1855).
[3] 3 Cow. (N. Y.) 86 (1824); 7 Barb. (N. Y.) 452 (1849).
[4] 46 N. H. 300 (1865).
[5] 11 W. Va. 519 (1877).

does not preclude the recovery of the remainder of the interest.[1]

The fact that the sum sued for is precisely the amount of the interest does not show that the principal, as such, has been paid.[2]

[1] 13 Wend. (N. Y.) 639 (1835).
[2] 5 Cow. (N. Y.) 331 (1826).

CHAPTER VIII.

PLEADING AND PRACTICE.

INTEREST follows the principal as an incident to it, so long as it remains an incident; but when it is separated and set apart from the principal by actual payment, or by being carried, when due, to the credit of the owner of the principal, in his account with the debtor, and this in pursuance of a promise in the contract creating and defining the principal debt, it is so separated and disjoined from the principal as to cease to be an incident to it, and does not follow it.[1]

It is optional with a party whether he will claim interest or not, — a part, the whole or none, that is,[2] if the law allows it; and on a suit for it, it must rise or fall with the principal debt.[3]

A suit cannot be brought for interest alone when it is due as damages,[4] nor after the principal has been paid.[5] If the principal has been paid, and contractual interest due has not been paid, the interest will remain due, and

[1] 6 O. 159 (1856).

[2] 2 Gilm. (Ill.) 389 (1845); Spen. (N. J.) 265 (1844); 45 Pa. St. 235 (1863); 28 Vt. 565 (1856).

[3] 3 Spauld. (Me.) 140 (1882).

[4] 12 La. Ann. 95 (1857). See 56 Ind. 288 (1877).

[5] 19 Conn. 529 (1849); 2 Mart. (La.) 83 (1841); 2 La. 518 (1831); 4 La. Ann. 29 (1849); 12 La. Ann. 95 (1857); 4 Hubb. (Me.) 481 (1861); 4 Puls. (Me.) 572 (1878); 11 Mass. 217 (1814); 3 Johns. (N. Y.) 229 (1808); 15 Wend. (N. Y.) 76 (1835); 119 N. Y. 1 (1890); 22 Vt. 437 (1850); 56 Vt. 609 (1884).

an action may be maintained for its recovery, if it was agreed to let the interest remain unpaid awhile, or something is said or done amounting to such an agreement.[1] Interest under a contract for it, not due before the principal, cannot be sued for, therefore, before the principal is due,[2] and even then it must be included in the suit brought to recover the principal.[3] If it is interest that is due before the principal, as where interest has been agreed to be paid semi-annually or annually it can be recovered by a suit brought before the principal of the debt is due.[4] If the contract stipulates, however, that the interest shall be due and payable annually, not simply till the principal is due, but till it is paid, then a suit can be brought for the interest alone after the principal is due.[5]

If a plaintiff commences an action of debt on a judgment, and the amount of the principal is then paid to him, he may continue the action for the recovery of the interest. To stop interest on a debt after suit is brought thereon, a rule to pay the money into court should be obtained, and complied with.[6]

I. PLEADING.

Interest must be pleaded for, either in a count or in a bill of particulars,[7] but the plea need not state that it has

[1] 10 Leigh (Va.) 481 (1839).

[2] 2 Mass. 568 (1803); 3 Mass. 221 (1807); 7 Barb. (N. Y.) 560 (1849); 16 Vt. 44 (1844).

[3] 1 Espi. (Eng.) 110 (1794); 1 Appl. (Me.) 31 (1841).

[4] 21 Conn. 388 (1851); 5 Red. (Me.) 75 (1852); 38 Mo. 461 (1866); 11 Mo. App. 251 (1881); 15 Wend. (N. Y.) 76 (1835); 110 N. C. 311 (1892); 4 O. 373 (1831); 1 Binn. (Pa.) 152 (1806); 1 R. I. 298 (1850). See 32 Ind. 328 (1869).

[5] 3 Conn. 415 (1820).

[6] 1 N. & McC. (S. C.) 242 (1818).

[7] 1 Bradw. (Ill.) 94 (1878); 11 La. 224 (1837); 20 La. Ann. 217 (1868); 30 La. Ann. 734 (1878); 7 Rich. (S. C.) 118 (1854); 14 Tex. 351 (1855); *contra*, on an award, 69 Ill. 179 (1873).

not been paid.[1] Generally, the claim for interest must be made at the time of claiming the principal.[2] The contract itself may set out the fact that interest has been agreed to be paid, and the pleading of a copy of the contract will be sufficient, the production of the instrument being generally competent evidence of the agreement to pay interest. But if the interest is claimed simply as damages, there having been no agreement to pay interest, it must be expressly claimed in the declaration.[3] Thus much depends upon whether the interest is contractual interest, or interest allowed as damages.[4]

In a declaration in debt on a judgment the usual *ad damnum* clause, say the Alabama and Vermont courts, is a sufficient allegation of damages to entitle the plaintiff to recover interest.[5]

In Alabama a court will not decree interest on a balance unless it is specially asked for in the bill; but this rule applies only to interest due at the time the bill is filed. When the interest accrues subsequently, it is the practice of the court, upon further directions to order that the interest be computed, although there is no prayer in the bill to that effect.[6]

Interest as damages can be recovered in an action of *assumpsit* as well as on account;[7] and for money had and received, if the demand bears interest.[8]

[1] 3 Blf. (Ind.) 401 (1834).

[2] 14 Cal. 171 (1859).

[3] Kirby (Conn.) 35 (1786); 1 G. Gr. (Iowa) 336 (1848); 5 Kas. 254 (1869); 16 Kas. 209 (1876); 20 La. Ann. 217 (1868); 30 La. Ann. 734 (1878). The courts say, in the cases cited 1 How. (Miss.) 230 (1835) and 7 Rich. (S. C.) 23 (1853), that a count is unnecessary where the law gives interest as a matter of course.

[4] 14 Tex. 351 (1855).

[5] 2 Port. (Ala.) 519 (1835); 27 Vt. 20 (1854).

[6] 19 Ala. 468 (1851).

[7] Quincy (Mass.) 5 (1762).

[8] Cheves (S. C.) 61 (1840).

Where a petition prays judgment for "interest and costs," interest is allowed only from the commencement of the action.[1]

Interest cannot be recovered prior to the time it is claimed in the plea or petition.[2] Neither can the jury allow it prior to the date claimed in the pleadings.[3]

Interest will be allowed against a trustee, even if it is not prayed for, if the facts disclosed show that equitable interest should be given.[4]

In those cases where the allowance of interest as damages is in the discretion of the jury, interest need not be expressly claimed.[5]

In an action of debt on a decree for money which did not give running interest thereon, the declaration demanded interest from the date of the decree, as part of the debt, and the declaration was held bad on general demurrer by the Virginia court, for demanding interest as part of the debt.[6]

A suit for an instalment of interest before the principal is due cannot be brought on a general *indebitatus* count in *assumpsit* for money had and received without stating the nature of the indebtedness.[7] So it is recoverable in an action of debt,[8] and if this is the form interest need not be demanded.[9]

Foreign contracts. See chapter nine, pages 190 and 193.

[1] 5 Iowa 503 (1857); 6 Iowa 235 (1858); 7 Iowa 85, 320 (1858); 10 Iowa 124, 233, 236 (1859); 40 Iowa 49 (1874).

[2] 45 Kas. 751 (1891).

[3] 2 Mo. App. 235 (1876).

[4] 16 Md. 416 (1860).

[5] 61 Ga. 482 (1878).

[6] 7 Leigh (Va.) 175 (1836).

[7] 21 Conn. 388 (1851).

[8] 5 T. R. (Eng.) 553 (1794); 2 Chit. (Eng.) 234 (1817).

[9] 3 McC. (S. C.) 201 (1825).

II. PRACTICE.

(*a*) *Province of the court.* A justice has no authority to render a judgment bearing more than legal interest, even by the consent of parties.[1]

An appellate court cannot change the amount of interest erroneously found due by a jury in the lower court; a new trial should be granted.[2] But a charge allowing improper interest can be corrected by writing off the excess, instead of having a new trial.[3] Errors in computation of interest should be corrected by motion in the court where the mistake was made.[4] And a motion for a new trial is a proper remedy to correct errors in the allowance of interest generally.[5] A slight mistake in the calculation, as of a few cents, will not cause the judgment to be set aside, and a new trial granted.[6] Neither is such a mistake, where the dates are given, evidence of fraud.[7] Where interest is improperly allowed by a referee on a running account, and no objection is made for that reason, the judgment will not be reversed.[8]

There are cases, of pure damages, where the question of allowance of interest is left to the discretion of the tribunal, whether the jury or court.[9]

[1] 3 Ind. 154 (1851).

[2] Minor (Ala.) 180 (1823).

[3] 67 Ga. 600 (1881).

[4] 13 Cal. 536 (1859); 61 Mich. 28 (1886). Where the verdict shows how much of it is principal, the court in Tennessee will enter judgment for the principal, if the plaintiff consents, rather than order a new trial. 91 Tenn. 35 (1891).

[5] 1 Speer (S. C.) 209 (1843); 16 S. C. 587 (1881); *contra*, error in rebate, 96 Ind. 510 (1884).

[6] 12 Cal. 479 (1859); 36 Mich. 149 (1877).

[7] 13 Cal. 76 (1859).

[8] 17 Cal. 407 (1861).

[9] 118 U. S. 507 (1886); 1 Cal. 422 (1851).

A judgment modified by the supreme court does not prevent its drawing interest from the time of rendering judgment in the court below;[1] but the court below cannot change the interest unless so directed.[2]

The allowance of interest and costs in a cause in admiralty rests in the discretion of the court below, and its action will not be disturbed on appeal.[3]

Where the allowance of interest is in the court's discretion, the supreme court will not revise the allowance unless there is a manifest abuse of their discretion.[4]

The court can instruct a jury to allow interest without naming the rate.[5]

The court cannot render judgment for interest as damages without the intervention of a jury;[6] but it can award and render judgment for contractual interest, on default, without a jury.[7]

The court can ask the jury if they have included interest in their verdict, and if they have not done so, can send them out again to ascertain it.[8] If they have returned a verdict for a certain sum and "interest thereon," the court can direct them to retire and reckon the interest.[9]

If a decree states the wrong date from which interest is to run, the supreme court can correct it.[10]

When interest upon account is charged upon a wrong principle, if no substantial damage is done to either party

[1] 46 Cal. 204 (1873).
[2] 33 Cal. 484 (1867).
[3] 123 U. S. 349 (1887).
[4] 91 Tenn. 525 (1892).
[5] 70 Iowa 465 (1886).
[6] Sneed (Ky.) 2 (1801).
[7] Sneed (Ky.) 135 (1802).
[8] 78 Mich. 195 (1889).
[9] 79 Mich. 307 (1890).
[10] 52 N. W. Rep. (Mich.) 73 (1892)

the court will not disturb it.[1] So, if interest has erroneously been included in a judgment, and it can be separated from the principal, the supreme court will not direct a new trial, but order the proper correction to be made.[2] But if the principal cannot be separated, a new trial will be granted.[3] Where a judgment is made to cover interest and there are no data to show how much is due, the finding of the jury is treated on error as a mistrial.[4]

A mistake in the calculation of interest in a settlement will be relieved in equity;[5] but a party cannot complain of a mistake in the amount of interest due in his own favor.[6]

It is held in Tennessee that the court may calculate the interest if there is no objection.[7]

Whether interest should be allowed in a given case is generally a matter of law for the court,[8] to be given to the jury in the charge.

In Texas, it is held that the court cannot add interest to a verdict found by the jury, unless it follows as an incident, as on a note, and not where the amount is uncertain.[9]

A verdict "in full of all claims" excludes the addition of interest on it to the day of trial.[10]

(*b*) *Province of the jury.* In absence of contrary proof, it is presumed that the jury, or those who award the verdict, reckoned the interest into the amount of damages they

[1] Phil. Eq. (N. C.) 116 (1867).
[2] 98 N. C. 550 (1881).
[3] 1 Brev. (S. C.) 103 (1804).
[4] 38 Mich. 609 (1878).
[5] 16 Mo. 457 (1852).
[6] 15 Nev. 452 (1880).
[7] 80 Tenn. 323 (1883).
[8] 3 Strob. (S. C.) 439 (1849).
[9] 17 Tex. 408 (1856); 65 Tex. 137 (1885).
[10] 35 Tex. 427 (1871).

find, it being an element of damage;[1] which they can do if they wish.[2] The affidavits of jurors are receivable to show whether or not interest is included in their verdict.[3] If the jury fails to fix the rate of interest, the court cannot enter judgment for it.[4] If they give the rate it should be included in the judgment.[5]

A verdict for a specified sum, "with interest thereon from 16th Feb., 1836," is not void for uncertainty, either as to principal or interest.[6]

Though, upon a liquidated claim interest can be recovered from the time when the cause of action accrued, upon an unliquidated counter-claim thereto, accruing at the same time, interest is recoverable only from the date of service of the answer.[7]

When a suit is brought on a demand bearing interest, and the defendant pleads in set-off a note not bearing interest, the plaintiff is entitled to calculate interest on the whole demand up to verdict.[8] Where the demand does not bear interest, and the defendant pleads a note bearing interest in set-off, the jury must give interest on the note in set-off up to the time of the verdict,[9] although the subject of the suit does not bear interest.

In an appeal from an award of commissioners allowing damages for land taken for a park, it is not error for the

[1] 22 Iowa 49 (1867); 36 Iowa 121 (1872); 4 Kas. 36 (1866); 28 Kas. 390 (1882); 5 Mart. N. S. (La.) 448, 457 (1827); 7 Mart. N. S. (La.) 224, 263 (1828); 3 La. 486 (1832); 4 La. Ann. 6 (1849); *contra*, 16 S. C. 587 (1881).

[2] 33 Iowa 422, 502 (1871).

[3] 61 Iowa 693 (1883).

[4] 25 Kas. 83 (1881).

[5] 25 Kas. 117 (1881).

[6] 1 McM. (S. C.) 429 (1840).

[7] 77 Wis. 548 (1890).

[8] 1 N. & McC. (S. C.) 24 (1817).

[9] 4 Rich. (S. C.) 600 (1851).

jury to add interest to the value of the land from the time of the assessment.[1] It is in their discretion. If the jury does not bring in more damages than the award gives, no interest should be allowed on the award, the owner being the cause of the delay.[2] But, otherwise, if the county appeals, either alone or with the owner.[3] If the county pays before the verdict interest to that time only should be allowed.[4]

A jury may in their discretion allow interest on a partial loss under a policy of insurance.[5] So, in an action of trespass to real property.[6] So, on wages, without its being expressly claimed.[7] The question of allowance of interest should be left to the jury when there is no usage, no precise time of payment fixed, no account rendered, or demand made, says the court in Pennsylvania.[8]

In an action of debt on a single bill for a certain sum, the jury may be charged to add interest;[9] and in their discretion they may give interest, from the begining of the action, on damages for injuries to person and property,[10] and the court may so charge the jury. In such cases the court should not charge the jury to give interest, says the Iowa court.[11] The court in California has recently decided that the jury cannot give interest on damages that are unliquidated and uncertain.[12]

[1] 4 Zab. (N. J.) 47 (1853).
[2] 8 Vr. (N. J.) 222 (1874).
[3] 8 Vr. (N. J.) 222 (1874).
[4] 1 Harr. (N. J.) 265 (1837).
[5] 1 Johns. (N. Y.) 315 (1806).
[6] 96 N. Y. 477 (1884).
[7] 61 Ga. 482 (1878).
[8] 12 S. & R. (Pa.) 393 (1825).
[9] 2 Mill (S. C.) 68 (1818).
[10] 10 Rich. (S. C.) 382 (1857): 34 Wis. 139 (1874).
[11] 53 N. W. Rep. (Iowa) 421 (1892).
[12] 32 Pac. Rep. (Cal.) 511 (1893).

Where a jury does not give interest on a bond, which they ought to have done, the plaintiff's remedy is by appeal, says the South Carolina court.[1]

In cases where damages are not capable of exact measurement, the jury may resort to the calculation of interest in the jury room, but the verdict must be for a fixed sum.[2]

(c) *Province of the clerk.* The clerk of the court must include interest in the judgment from the time of the verdict;[3] notwithstanding the fact that the jury may have included it in their verdict in an action for personal injuries causing death, says the New York court.[4] Interest on the debt must be included in the judgment when rendered to be collected.[5] In entering judgment on notes, interest should be added to the principal to the time of the judgment, and then entered for the gross sum.[6] When a verdict is rendered for a certain sum and interest thereon, the interest is to be computed from the maturity of the contract.[7]

A statutory provision that judgments shall draw interest from the day of their entry until they are satisfied includes a judgment for costs.[8]

(d) *Evidence.* If a promise to pay interest is stated in the declaration, an express promise must be proved,[9] in an action of *indebitatus assumpsit;* and if a written con-

[1] 10 Rich. (S. C.) 217 (1857).

[2] 3 Strob. (S. C.) 439 (1849).

[3] 82 Cal. 184 (1889); 91 N. Y. 661 (1883). From verdict to time of actual entry of judgment, 62 Iowa 433 (1883); if the verdict does not give it, 87 Va. 269 (1891).

[4] 91 N. Y. 661 (1883).

[5] 30 Cal. 78 (1866).

[6] 5 Cal. 416 (1855); 12 W. Va. 143 (1877); 14 W. Va. 737 (1879).

[7] 81 (Ga.) 93 (1888).

[8] 32 Pac. Rep. (Col.) 615 (1893).

[9] 1 Mass. 31 (1804).

tract does not call for interest, it cannot be claimed by parol evidence.[1]

If an instrument set out in the pleadings does not mention interest, while the instrument introduced in the evidence does at a certain rate, it is held to be no material variance.[2]

It can be shown by oral testimony that a note due at a specified time was not to bear interest after it was due.[3] So, an oral contract to change the rate of interest after the mortgage matures and to pay it semi-annually instead of annually is valid.[4] Parol evidence is also admissible to rebut an equity against an execution arising out of an obligation to invest funds so as to make interest.[5]

In England, interest is not recoverable on a bill of exchange unless the instrument is produced, that is, after maturity.[6]

(e) *Foreign law and contracts.* The court cannot judicially know the rate of interest of another country, it must be alleged[7] and proved as a fact by the best evidence.[8] A judgment, therefore, for interest on a note made in another state is erroneous, unless the rate of interest of the place is proved;[9] so the court of Texas decided in 1846. But the same court in later times holds, that, if the foreign law is not averred and proved, the

[1] 2 Mart. (La.) 78 (1811).

[2] Mor. (Iowa) 106 (1840).

[3] 79 Ky. 277 (1881).

[4] 12 Stew. (N. J.) 376 (1885).

[5] 2 Hill Ch. (S. C.) 146 (1835).

[6] Ry. & M. (Eng.) 145 (1824); 15 Q. B. (Eng.) 26 (1850); 14 Jur. Eng. 372 (1850); 19 L. J., Q. B. (Eng.) 293 (1850).

[7] 2 Tex. 189 (1847); 5 Tex. 87, 262 (1849); 10 Tex. 350 (1853); 14 Tex. 351 (1855).

[8] 1 Tex. 93 (1846).

[9] 1 Tex. 9 (1846).

court will presume it to be the same as that of the *forum* and give interest accordingly.[1] See page 190.

(f) Miscellaneous decisions. A judgment debtor is not liable for interest on costs where payment is delayed by error proceedings.[2]

In excepting to the rate of interest allowed by a master, it must be done particularly and not under a general exception to the allowance of interest.[3]

Judgment *nunc pro tunc* should be given with interest from the time judgment ought to have been entered.[4]

Interest given by a judgment forms a part of it, and must be secured in an appeal bond, which together form the judgment of the court appealed from.[5]

The rate to be recovered by the plaintiff should be stated in the judgment,[6] says the Kentucky court.

Interest runs during an appeal.[7]

Where a defendant (in an action before a justice of the peace) offers a certain sum and costs, it is presumed to carry interest;[8] that is, that it may equal a subsequent judgment bearing interest from at least the time of the offer.

Where an action of debt is brought on a judgment, interest thereon is recoverable on the accumulated sum of the original principal and interest and costs.[9]

Interest cannot be recovered on judgments on *scire facias*.[10]

Interest on judgments can only be collected where the

[1] 31 Tex. 61 (1868); 52 Tex. 396 (1880).
[2] 31 Neb. 816 (1891).
[3] 129 Mass. 517 (1880).
[4] 20 Iowa 41 (1865).
[5] 2 La. 85 (1830).
[6] 2 Bibb (Ky.) 99 (1810).
[7] 24 Pa. St. 391 (1855).
[8] 39 Pa. St. 111 (1861).
[9] 2 Brev. (S. C.) 99 (1806); 7 Leigh (Va.) 346 (1836).
[10] 2 Mill (S. C.) 146 (1818); 1 McC. (S. C.) 171 (1821).

original cause of action bore interest, says the South Carolina court.[1] But, in an action of debt on a judgment, interest is recoverable thereon, whether the original cause of action bore interest or not.[2] See chapter three, page 102, for a fuller statement of the law. Where interest is rendered on a previous judgment which bore interest, interest must be calculated on the principal sum of the first judgment.[3]

Where interest is due from certain dates which are not shown in the evidence, it will be allowed from the date of the writ only.[4]

Where a note is payable on time, with interest from date if not punctually paid, the back interest is recoverable as stipulated damages; and if, in entering up judgment, such interest is not computed, the judgment may be amended, though the original execution had issued and been returned satisfied.[5]

In computing the days of grace allowed on a bond for the payment of interest, the day when the interest became payable will be excluded.[6]

Although the discount claimed by the defendant in a building contract may reduce the amount covenanted to be paid, yet it does not impair the claim for interest on the balance, when adjusted by the verdict of the jury.[7]

Nothing is left on a judgment obtained by default, but to compute interest in order to entitle the plaintiff to his judgment.[8]

An action of *special assumpsit*, on a warranty of sound-

[1] 3 McC. (S. C.) 166 (1825); Rice (S. C.) 21 (1838).
[2] 1 Hill (S. C.) 79 (1833).
[3] 2 Hill (S. C.) 313 (1834).
[4] 76 Iowa 707 (1888).
[5] 1 Kelley (Ga.) 467 (1846).
[6] 24 Atl. Rep. (N. J.) 369 (1892).
[7] 2 Speer (S. C.) 536 (1844).
[8] 2 Speer (S. C.) 573 (1844).

ness, for damages, says the South Carolina court, is subject to the rule governing actions sounding in damages that interest is not recoverable *eo nomine*,[1] but must be given as *damages*.

In equity, interest is not carried beyond the date of the final decree.[2]

When the clerk, on assessing the plaintiff's damages, over-calculates the amount of interest, the plaintiff may without notice or rule, obtain leave to enter a remittitur for the excess, or may himself, without an order, enter such remittitur on the judgment and execution.[3]

Where, on appeal from a judgment for personal injuries, the only error is in the allowance of interest on the amount recovered for the time prior to the judgment, the supreme court will affirm the judgment on condition that the appellee remit the amount allowed as interest, says the Tennessee court.[4]

Where a plaintiff is entitled to interest on an amount due him from the commencement of the action, he may include such interest in a judgment taken by default, although the damages were unliquidated and the interest was not specifically demanded in the complaint.[5]

III. EFFECT OF INTEREST ON JURISDICTION OF COURT.

The jurisdiction of a court having original jurisdiction is determined by the amount claimed, whether it is principal alone or principal and interest combined.[6] It is op-

[1] 2 Speer (S. C.) 594 (1844).
[2] 3 Call (Va.) 22 (1801).
[3] 14 Rich. (S. C.) 63 (1866).
[4] 91 Tenn. 35 (1891); 17 S. W. Rep. (Tenn.) 882 (1891).
[5] 68 Wis. 61 (1887).
[6] 45 Pa. St. 235 (1863); 2 N. & McC. (S. C.) 487 (1820); *contra*, 60 Cal. 653 (1882); 28 Vt. 565 (1856).

tional with the plaintiff, whether or not to claim interest, either the whole or a part.[1]

The test of the appellate jurisdiction of the United States supreme court is the principal and interest computed to the time of the judgment in the court below, added together.[2]

If the claim is not, at the time of the appeal, large enough to give jurisdiction to the appellate court, the subsequent accruing of interest will not aid it.[3]

IV. RECOVERY OF INTEREST PAID BY MISTAKE.

Excess of interest paid by mistake cannot be recovered;[4] but, if it is paid when none is due it can be.[5]

Interest paid under a mistake of fact may be recovered;[6] but usury cannot be, in absence of statute,[7] as it is usually a mistake of law, if a mistake at all.[8]

Compound interest paid through error of fact can also be recovered;[9] whether the error be made by the one paying the interest or by some other person whom he trusted to make the calculation.[10]

[1] 45 Pa. St. 235 (1863); *contra*, 2 N. & McC. (S. C.) 487 (1820).
[2] 133 U. S. 610 (1889); 137 U. S. 689 (1891).
[3] 16 Conn. 34 (1843).
[4] 46 Ark. 167 (1885); 59 Vt. 75 (1886).
[5] 59 Vt. 75 (1886).
[6] 84 Ky. 306 (1886).
[7] 102 N. C. 137 (1889).
[8] 16 O. St. 418 (1865).
[9] 14 La. Ann. 10 (1859).
[10] 2 Denio (N. Y.) 107 (1846).

CHAPTER IX.

CONFLICT OF LAWS.

WHEN laws of different places and dates conflict it is often difficult, especially in interest, to decide which should govern.

I. LAW OF WHAT PLACE GOVERNS.

(*a*) *Generally.* Interest will be allowed upon debts contracted abroad, if the *lex loci contractus* authorizes it, as well as upon those contracts made in the state where the suit is brought.[1] Contractual interest and the legal rate per cent are governed by the law of the place of performance of the contract.[2]

[1] 7 Port. (Ala.) 110 (1838).

[2] 2 Burr. (Eng.) 1094 (1760); 1 W. Bl. (Eng.) 267 (1760); 2 Sim. (Eng.) 194 (1828); 2 Beav. (Eng.) 282 (1840); 9 Exch. (Eng.) 25 (1853); 17 Jur. (Eng.) 820 (1853); 1 Wash. (U. S., C. C.) 521 (1806); 2 Wash. (U. S., C. C.) 253 (1808); 3 Wheat. (U. S.) 101 (1818); 4 Wash. (U. S., C. C.) 296 (1822); 10 Wheat. (U. S.) 367 (1825); 13 Pet. (U. S.) 65 (1839); 3 McLean (U. S., C. C.) 268 (1843); 1 Wall. (U. S.) 298 (1863); 93 U. S. 344 (1876); 96 U. S. 51 (1877); Minor (Ala.) 387 (1825); 4 Port. (Ala.) 128 (1836); 7 Port. (Ala.) 111 (1838); 8 Port. (Ala.) 250 (1839); 9 Port. (Ala.) 9 (1839); 10 Ala. 773 (1846); 12 Ala. 54 (1847); 18 Ala. 209 (1850); 37 Ala. 702 (1861); 62 Ala. 518 (1878); 81 Ala. 240 (1886); 33 Conn. 419, 570 (1866); 21 Ga. 135 (1857); 17 Ind. 77 (1861); 18 Ind. 246 (1862); 19 Ind. 223 (1862); 72 Ind. 567 (1880); 112 Ind. 435 (1887); 11 Iowa 1 (1860); 1 Mar. (Ky.) 254, 397 (1818); Lit. Sel. Cas. (Ky.) 507 (1821); 4 J. J. Mar. (Ky.) 238 (1830);

Some courts hold that, whether or not interest as damages shall be allowed, and also the rate, the *lex fori*, or law of the place where the contract is sought to be enforced governs.[1]

If no place of performance is shown to the court it will be presumed that the contract is payable in the jurisdiction where it was made;[2] and if a note states on its face that it is payable in A. it will be presumed that A is in the state where the suit is brought.[3] These presumptions are

1 B. Mon. (Ky.) 29 (1840); 6 Bush (Ky.) 690 (1869); 13 La. 91 (1839); 3 La. Ann. 88, 401 (1848); 12 La. Ann. 815, 817 (1857); 12 Mass. 4 (1815); 2 Met. (Mass.) 8 (1840); 11 Met. (Mass.) 210 (1846); 11 Gray (Mass.) 38 (1858); 126 Mass. 360 (1879); 12 Miss. (4 S. & M.) 667 (1845); 57 Miss. 308 (1879); 19 Nev. 121 (1885); 43 N. H. 109 (1861); 47 N. H. 405 (1867); 15 N. J. L. (3 Green) 328 (1836); 17 N. J. L. (2 Har.) 185 (1839); 4 Johns. (N. Y.) 183 (1809); 3 Johns. Ch. (N. Y.) 587 (1818); 17 Johns. (N. Y.) 511 (1820); 2 Paige (N. Y.) 604 (1831); 6 Paige's Ch. (N. Y.) 627 (1837); 22 Barb. (N. Y.) 118 (1856); 62 N. Y. 151 (1875); 79 N. Y. 136 (1879); Bat.'s Mart. & 2d Hay'd (N. C.) 149 (1797); 5 Ired. L. (N. C.) 590 (1845); 7 Ired. L. (N. C.) 424 (1847); 11 Ired. L. (N. C.) 303 (1850); 7 Jones L. (N. C.) 506 (1860); 94 N. C. 286 (1886); 2 W. & S. (Pa.) 327 (1841); 2 Pa. St. 85 (1845); 2 Grant's Cas. (Pa.) 73 (1853); 1 N. & McC. (S. C.) 67 (1818); 10 Tex. 350 (1853); 21 Tex. 77 (1858); 22 Tex. 109 (1858); 23 Vt. 286 (1851).

[1] 2 Beav. (Eng.) 282 (1840); 3 Wheat. (U. S.) 101 (1818); 17 Wall. (U. S.) 123 (1872); 137 U. S. 689 (1891); 1 Cal. 422 (1851); 1 Root (Conn.) 314 (1791); 112 Ind. 435 (1887); 15 Gray (Mass.) 178 (1860); 105 N. Y. 670 (1887); *contra*, 16 La. 58 (1840); 19 Nev. 121 (1885). The court in 13 La. 91 (1839) says that the place of performance governs the rate of interest after maturity. Indian interest was allowed on a tort committed in India. 1 P. Wm. (Eng.) 395 (1717).

[2] 11 Ves. (Eng.) 314 (1805); 1 Wash. (U. S., C. C.) 521 (1806); 2 Wash. (U. S., C. C.) 253 (1808); 3 Wheat. (U. S.) 101 (1818); 3 Conn. 253 (1830); 1 B. Mon. (Ky.) 29 (1840); 12 Mass. 4 (1815); 11 Met. (Mass.) 210 (1846); 47 N. H. 405 (1867); 2 Harr. (N. J.) 185 (1839); 1 Paige's Ch. (N. Y.) 220 (1828); 2 Paige (N. Y.) 604 (1831); 22 Barb. (N. Y.) 118 (1856); 92 N. C. 266 (1885); 14 Vt. 33 (1842); 32 Vt. 93 (1859).

[3] Minor (Ala.) 167 (1823); 11 Ala. 270 (1847); 4 Tex. 420 (1849).

only *prima facie*,[1] however, and parol evidence is admissible to show that the contracts are payable elsewhere.[2]

The location of property given to secure notes, etc., has no effect upon the question of what place governs in case of a conflict of law, as regards the allowance of interest, it being decided as though there were no security.[3]

If the rate is good and legal where the interest is stipulated to be paid, it is good and valid everywhere; and if it is illegal there it is illegal everywhere.[4]

The parties to a contract made in one state and payable in another, may, however, stipulate for the rate of interest of either place, if it is done in good faith, and not as a cover for usury,[5] although in the place other than the one whose rate is agreed upon it may be an illegal rate.[6]

In a certain case, where an agent in California retained the proceeds of sales of goods, which he was to send to his principal in New York, it was decided by the New

[1] 2 Atk. (Eng.) 382 (1742); 18 Ala. 209 (1850); 14 Vt. 33 (1842); *contra*, 5 Ired. L. (N. C.) 590 (1845); 7 Jones L. (N. C.) 506 (1860).

[2] 18 Ala. 209 (1850); 14 Vt. 33 (1842); 23 Vt. 286 (1853); *contra* 5 Ired. L. (N. C.) 590 (1845); 7 Jones L. (N. C.) 506 (1860), which decide that the parties must be presumed to have had the place of payment in view when the contract was made.

[3] 36 Ark. 569 (1880); 2 Day (Conn.) 280 (1806); 11 Ind. 117 (1858); Quincy (Mass.) 9 (1762); 1 Halst. Ch. (N. J.) 17 (1845), 631 (1847); 2 Beas. (N. J.) 253 (1861); 1 McCart. (N. J.) 56 (1861), 355 (1862); 5 C. E. Gr. (N. J.) 288 (1869); 1 Keyes (N. Y.) 347 (1864); 53 Barb. (N. Y.) 350 (1867); 37 How. Pr. (N. Y.) 181 (1867); 37 N. Y. 444 (1868); 64 How. Pr. (N. Y.) 503 (1881); 7 O. St. 387 (1851); 10 R. I. 393 (1873); *contra*, 2 Atk. (Eng.) 382 (1742).

[4] 16 Ind. 475 (1861).

[5] 10 Wheat. (U. S.) 367 (1825); 13 Pet. (U. S.) 65 (1839); 1 Wall. (U. S.) 298 (1863); 96 U. S. 51 (1877); 85 Mich. 561 (1891); 46 N. H. 300 (1865); 60 N. H. 452 (1881); 26 Barb. (N. Y.) 208 (1857); 2 Pa. St. 85 (1845); 14 Vt. 33 (1842); 12 Wis. 692 (1860); 13 Wis. 198 (1860). See 2 Johns. Cas. (N. Y.) 355 (1801) and the citations under usury, page 191.

[6] 60 N. H. 452 (1881).

York court that California law should govern as to the rate per cent of the interest.[1]

Practice. Upon foreign contracts interest according to the law of the *forum* will be decreed if the foreign law is not pleaded and proved, and there is no agreement as to interest.[2] The court cannot judicially know the foreign rate of interest.[3]

Interest cannot be allowed on a contract made abroad on proof that it is customary there, without showing that it is legal also.[4]

The court in Mississippi decided that in absence of proof of the rate per cent of another state, the finding of the jury should be presumed to be correct.[5]

The place named with the date of a contract is evidence of the place where it was made.[6]

Legacies. The law of the place where the estate is being settled governs in legacies.[7]

(*b*) *Usury.* When a contract is usurious, but the law of the state where it is made does not avoid it on that ground, but only affects the remedy upon it, the courts of other states can enforce the contract, but only by those remedies afforded by their own law.[8]

[1] 47 Barb. (N. Y.) 9 (1866).

[2] 18 Ind. 246 (1862); 13 Mo. 462 (1850); 16 N. H. 134 (1841); 31 Tex. 61 (1868); 52 Tex. 396 (1880). The earlier Texas cases decided that unless the foreign law of interest was averred and proved the court should not allow any interest, notwithstanding a verdict for interest had been returned. 1 Tex. 9 (1846); 2 Tex. 189 (1847); 5 Tex. 87, 262 (1849); 10 Tex. 250 (1853); 14 Tex. 351 (1855). The Louisiana court also allows no interest. 6 Mart. N. S. (La.) 606 (1828).

[3] 1 Tex. 9 (1846).

[4] 6 Mart. N. S. (La.) 567 (1828).

[5] 5 S. & M. (Miss.) 573 (1845).

[6] 16 N. H. 134 (1844).

[7] 38 L. T., N. S. (Eng.) 215 (1878).

[8] 10 Mich. 283 (1862).

In absence of other stipulations the place of performing the contract will govern; and if it is not usurious there it will not be usurious anywhere,[1] unless the place of payment was inserted as a device to evade the usury law,[2] which may be shown in evidence.[3] Parties may stipulate for interest at the place of making the contract, or the place of its performance, if it is not done as a cover for usury.[4] The Mississippi court holds that if the rate named is prohibited by the law of the place of performance, then the place of making the contract will govern.[5] If no place of payment is named, then the place where it was made governs.[6] Where a loan is made by a party in one state

[1] 12 Wall. (U. S.) 226 (1870); 11 Ind. 117 (1858); 79 Ind. 172 (1881); 3 Dana (Ky.) 497 (1835); 2 La. 114 (1830); 22 La. Ann. 418 (1870); 1 S. & M. (Miss.) 176 (1843); 11 S. & M. (Miss.) 140 (1848); 1 Halst. Ch. (N.J.) 17 (1845), 631 (1847); 5 C. E. Gr. (N. J.) 288 (1869); 12 C. E. Gr. (N. J.) 360 (1876); 1 Paige (N. Y.) 220 (1828); 7 Paige (N. Y.) 615 (1839); 3 Sandf. Ch. (N. Y.) 313 (1846); 5 N. Y. (1 Seld.) 178 (1851); 6 N. Y. (2 Seld.) 124 (1851); 26 Barb. (N. Y.) 208 (1857); 1 Keyes (N. Y.) 317 (1864); 53 Barb. (N. Y.) 350 (1867); 37 N. Y. 444 (1868); 19 S. C. 583 (1883); 87 Tenn. 731 (1889); 55 Tex. 167 (1881); 14 Vt. 33 (1842).

[2] 12 Wall. (U. S.) 226 (1870); 40 Tenn. 249 (1859); 43 Tenn. 31 (1866).

[3] 56 Tenn. 242 (1877).

[4] 13 Pet. (U. S.) 65 (1839); 1 Wall. (U. S.) 298 (1863); 96 U. S. 51 (1877); 2 McArt. (D. C.) 371 (1876); 88 Ga. 756 (1891); 15 S. E. Rep. (Ga.) 812 (1892); 22 Iowa 194 (1867); 8 Mart. N. S. (La.) 1 (1829); 85 Mich. 561 (1891); 46 N. H. 300 (1865); 38 Barb. (N. Y.) 352 (1862); 45 Barb. (N. Y.) 340 (1865); 25 O. St. 413) 1874); 39 O. St. 63 (1883); 19 S. C. 583 (1883); 40 Tenn. 249 (1859); 43 Tenn. 31 (1866); 45 Tenn. 497 (1868); 51 Tenn. 607 (1874); 79 Tex. 246 (1891). The Wisconsin court holds that this cannot be done if the rate of interest of the place where the contract is to be performed is greater than that of the place of making the contract. 3 P. 78 (3 C. 83) (Wis.) (1850); 21 Wis. 340 (1867). Where land held for security lies in the borrower's state. 15 S. E. Rep. (Ga.) 812 (1892).

[5] 5 Geo. (Miss.) 181 (1875).

[6] 18 Ark. 462 (1857); 26 Ark. 357 (1870); 33 Ark. 645 (1878); 2 McArt. (D. C.) 371 (1876); 5 Geo. (Miss.) 528 (1857); 37 How. Pr. (N. Y.) 181 (1867); 88 Pa. St. 118 (1878); 11 W. Va. 523 (1877); 20 W. Va. 140 (1882); 3 P. 78 (3 C. 83) (Wis.) (1850); 21 Wis. 340 (1867).

to a party in another state, to be used in the other state, which is also the *forum*, the law of the latter place governs.[1]

If a note stipulates, that if the contract is usurious in one state, the interest shall be reckoned by the law of another state it is usurious.[2]

A deed of even date with the note and a part of the same transaction is admissible to show the real situs of the contract.[3]

While the courts of one state will not enforce the penal statutes of another state, yet when a contract is made with reference to the laws of another state, and is usurious there, the forfeiture provided by such laws will be enforced.[4] The court in North Carolina holds that where an usurious agreement is made there, but illegal interest received on it in South Carolina, an action will not lie to recover the penalty in North Carolina.[5]

A foreign corporation may make a valid loan in New York at seven per cent interest, although its charter is granted by a state wherein interest is restricted to a lower rate, and forbids it to make any contract which, by the existing laws, amounts to usury.[6]

It is the intention of the parties that rules as to place;[7] the mere signing a note in a certain state not necessarily making it payable there, if no place of payment is named.[8] A resident of Texas, being in New York, signed notes there, dating them "Texas," no place of performance being designated; and it was held that Texas was the place of making, and of payment,—principally because the rate

[1] 93 U. S. 344 (1876).

[2] 69 Miss. 770 (1892).

[3] 88 Ga. 756 (1891).

[4] 22 Iowa 194 (1867).

[5] Tay. Term (N. C.) 622 (1816).

[6] 12 N. Y. (2 Kern.) 495 (1855).

[7] 10 Wis. 333 (1860).

[8] 12 Wis. 692 (1860); 13 Wis. 198 (1860).

of the notes was lawful in Texas and not in New York,[1] suit upon them being brought in Texas.

All renewals[2] and discounts[3] have the domicile of the original contract. But where a draft is drawn in Connecticut, and made payable in New York, where it is also accepted for the accommodation of the drawer, who negotiated it in Connecticut, it is governed by the laws of Connecticut.[4] An agreement for the forbearance of a debt already due, made in another state, is governed by the laws of that other state.[5]

While the law of the place of the contract interprets and construes it, the law of a place where it is put in suit determines all questions as to the manner in which the same may be enforced.[6]

Practice. The foreign law of usury must be pleaded and proved if suit is brought on a foreign contract, as the court cannot judicially know what it is.[7] It will not be presumed to be the same as the law of the *forum*.[8] The plea must state the law of the foreign state.[9]

II. LAW OF WHAT TIME GOVERNS.

The law in force at the time of making a contract governs as to contractual interest and its conventional rate;[10]

[1] 35 Tex. 313 (1871).
[2] 12 O. St. 610 (1861).
[3] 6 Lans. (N. Y.) 455 (1872); 4 Hun (N. Y.) 231 (1875).
[4] 13 Hun (N. Y.) 40 (1878).
[5] 87 N. Y. 130 (1882).
[6] 26 Ark. 356 (1870).
[7] 4 W. Va. 4 (1870).
[8] 23 Wis. 383 (1868).
[9] 17 Grat. (Va.) 47 (1861).
[10] 42 Conn. 570 (1875); 44 Conn. 300 (1877); 47 Conn. 118 (1879); 61 Ga. 458 (1878); 62 Ga. 86 (1878); 1 Mar. (Ky.) 254, 397 (1818); Lit. Sel. Cas. (Ky.) 507 (1821); 4 J. J. Mar. (Ky.) 238 (1830); 6 Bush (Ky.) 690 (1869); 4 La. 87 (1832); 12 La. 530 (1838); 3 Vr. (N. J.) 423 (1868); 7 C. E. Gr. (N. J.) 441 (1871); 11 C. E. Gr. (N. J.) 456 (1875); 25 Hun (N. Y.) 159 (1881); 84 N. Y. 471 (1881).

so the passing of a usury law does not affect existing contracts;[1] but an agreement fixing the rate of interest on future dealings between the parties, terminates by the passage of a law making that rate usurious.[2] If the rate is given as "lawful interest for the time," the rate will vary with the statute.[3] If it is interest that is allowed as damages, or contractual interest, and no rate has been agreed upon, it will vary with the statutory rate, if changes occur in that.[4] In actions for causing death by a wrongful act, negligence or default, two cases decided in New York in the same year are apparently contrary to each other. The court in one of them, decided in the court of appeals, held that the damages should bear interest from the time of the injuries to verdict at the rate according to the law in force at the time of the verdict;[5] and, in the other, the supreme court held that the rate should follow the statute from the time of the death to the verdict, as in other cases.[6]

Although the passage of a usury law does not affect existing contracts, yet a new statute, repealing an existing usury law, does affect them, and precludes the defence in a suit then pending.[7] So, a forfeiture, being in the nature of a penalty, falls with the repeal of the law creating it.[8] So a void contract may be cured by subsequent legisla-

[1] 64 Ga. 137 (1879); 76 Ga. 322 (1886); 20 Bradw. (Ill.) 536 (1886); 7 Allen (Mass.) 139 (1863).

[2] 4 Geo. (Miss.) 299 (1857).

[3] 3 Vr. (N. J.) 423 (1868).

[4] 42 Cal. 279 (1871); 44 Cal. 366 (1872); 46 Cal. 323 (1873); 50 Cal. 244 (1875); 63 Cal. 503 (1883); 49 Conn. 519 (1882). See 47 Cal. 9 (1873).

[5] 86 N. Y. 401 (1881).

[6] 23 Hun (N. Y.) 578 (1881).

[7] 30 Ark. 135 (1875).

[8] 99 Ill. 188 (1881); 81 Ky. 129 (1883).

tion;[1] that is, it may be given force and obligation,—it does not impair the obligation of a contract; but it does not strictly give validity to an usurious contract void under the statute existing when the contract was made.[2] The Wisconsin court holds that a new statute cannot validate a contract even for the principal when the former statute avoided it wholly.[3]

The change in the statute, properly, only affects the remedy, and the law in force at the time the remedy is sought governs in usury,[4] that is, the defendant can or cannot set up the remedy.

Usury paid is governed by the law then in force, if the statute is directed toward the receipt of usurious interest.[5] And a contract for forbearance is governed by the law in force when it was made.[6]

When a contract was made, a usury law existed; the law was afterward repealed, and then reënacted before the contract was sued on. It was held that the defendant could not offset usury paid while the statute was repealed.[7] So, interest paid while the statute was in force, if it continues in force till the suit is brought, may be offset.[8]

Money paid as usury when the law does not allow recoupment can be recouped if a statute is afterward passed giving that right.[9]

[1] 99 Ill. 188 (1881); 7 Blf. (Ind.) 474 (1845); 8 Blf. (Ind.) 67 (1846), 371 (1847); 1 Ind. 32 (1848); 30 Ind. 204 (1868); 33 Ind. 87 (1870); *contra*, 12 La. Ann. 221 (1857).

[2] 36 Wis. 186 (1874).

[3] 18 Wis. 298 (1864).

[4] 7 Blf. (Ind.) 474 (1845); 19 Ind. 68, 121 (1862); 26 Ind. 338 (1866); 31 Ind. 389 (1869); 32 Ind. 16 (1869); 39 Ind. 270 (1872); 52 Tenn. 695 (1875); *contra*, 39 Tex. 365 (1873). See 19 Ill. 121 (1857).

[5] 15 O. St. 218 (1864).

[6] 3 C. E. Gr. (N. J.) 451, 452, 482 (1867).

[7] 64 Ga. 510 (1880).

[8] 5 Ind. 308 (1854).

[9] 19 Ind. 68 (1862); 20 Ind. 108 (1863); 55 Ind. 226 (1876); 83 Ind. 204 (1882).

The repeal of a usury statute does not revive a former one.[1]

Novation. A third party may contract to be substituted as debtor in the place of another; and if such substitution is made, the new debtor may lawfully contract to pay the rate of interest which the debt bears, notwithstanding it may be higher than the rate then allowed by law.[2] So bills of exchange given after the usury statute was repealed, in renewal of usurious bills, given before the usury law was in force, are valid.[3]

[1] 3 N. M. 327, 344 (1886).

[2] 4 Cush. (Miss.) 13 (1853); 2 Geo. (Miss.) 260 (1856).

[3] 1 H. & C. (Eng.) 703 (1863); 9 Jur., N. S. (Eng.) 1016 (1863); 32 L. J., Exch. (Eng.) 265 (1863); 11 W. R. (Eng.) 1019; 8 L. T., N. S. (Eng.) 638 (1863).

CHAPTER X.

USURY.

EVERY state has a fixed rate per cent at which interest, whether it is contractual interest, or interest allowed as damages, shall be reckoned, provided no other rate has been agreed upon; and, the majority of the states have passed laws fixing the maximum limit of the rate per cent for which interest can be contracted; and interest contracted for or paid above that amount is called usury. In this chapter, the term "legal rate" generally means the maximum legal rate.

In very early times it was found necessary to curb the weakness of men for gain, and from the accumulated experience of centuries it was deemed best for the public's interest to limit the amount that men should pay for the use of money.[1] The industrious, enterprising and producing classes of men are to be protected from the greed of those who hold the money. All kinds of business require capital in their prosecution, and if left free to charge what they would for the use of money, the holders of it would discourage all enterprise. This is the view that Lord Bacon took of the matter, and there is scarcely a nation that has not regarded it in a similar light. The Romans found that the extremes the law could reach respecting interest, that is, no interest and unlimited inter-

[1] 3 Gilm. (Ill.) 547 (1846).

est, were alike harmful, the first leading to the stagnation of business, and the other to merciless extortion. Usury laws have also been passed in China and other heathen countries.[1]

In early times it was generally a criminal offence to take usurious interest; but now it is only a civil offence, except in a few of the states where it is a misdemeanor.

If a contract is made for the payment of a larger rate per cent than the law allows (not a smaller rate[2]) or for a certain sum of money which amounts to more than the legal maximum rate,[3] it is termed an usurious contract,[4] and the amount above the legal maximum limit is usury. It is clear then that unless there is a fixed maximum rate, there can be no usury.[5] The usury law applies to the loan or use of property as well as money, if the statute so declares.[6]

The usury laws in the various states that have them are very unlike. In some states the statute,—for the usury law is always a creature of legislation,[7]—has made the entire contract void, in others voidable; in some states the creditor forfeits all the interest, in others the interest above the legal maximum rate; or, if the usurious interest has been paid the creditor can be compelled to pay back, in some states twice, and in others three times the amount that he has received in excess of the maximum legal rate.[8]

[1] 3 Johns. Ch. (N. Y.) 395 (1818); 16 Johns. (N. Y.) 367 (1819); 5 Hill (N. Y.) 523 (1843); 14 Barb. (N. Y.) 131 (1852).

[2] 16 Pa. St. 269 (1851); 19 Pa. St. 117 (1852).

[3] 9 Wis. 361 (1859).

[4] 7 B. Mon. (Ky.) 542 (1847); 4 Md. 455 (1877).

[5] 25 Ark. 625 (1869); 31 Ark. 484 (1876).

[6] 1 Bibb (Ky.) 333 (1809).

[7] 77 Cal. 518 (1888).

[8] See the statutes of the various jurisdictions in chapter thirteen

Of course, a special rate of interest ordered by the legislature at any time cannot be usurious.[1]

Usury is not necessarily fraudulent, and must be governed by other rules.[2]

If the statute declares that usurious contracts are void (and they cannot be void in any other way[3]), they cannot be ratified or confirmed by the parties,[4] nor be set up anywhere or at any time, whether usury laws prevail in the place where the suit is brought or not; being simply null,[5] even in the hands of an innocent purchaser.[6] To have this result they must be void in themselves.[7] But if the statute merely says that "it shall not be lawful" to contract for more than the authorized rate, the contract is void for the entire interest, and recovery could be had only of the principal.[8] The courts say continually that an usurious contract is void, when they mean that it is voidable.

Even if the statute says that no interest shall be collected the court may allow interest as damages from the time the debt should have been paid at the legal rate.[9] What is called interest may not always be interest, technically.[10]

Usury avoids a contract in equity as well as at law.[11]

[1] 69 Ala. 413, 456 (1881).

[2] 93 Ala. 59 (1890); 76 Pa. St. 52 (1874); 81 Pa. St. 309 (1876).

[3] 11 South. Rep. (Miss.) 531 (1892).

[4] 4 Bibb (Ky.) 319 (1816); 3 Brev. (S. C.) 54 (1812).

[5] 1 Port. (Ala.) 57 (1834); 5 Day (Conn.) 128 (1811); 2 Shepl. (Me.) 240 (1837); 2 N. H. 42 (1819).

[6] 1 Port. (Ala.) 57 (1834); 5 Tex. 171 (1849); 79 Tex. 120 (1890).

[7] 2 Puis. (Me.) 212 (1876).

[8] 73 Ala. 111 (1882).

[9] 27 Conn. 363 (1858); 33 Conn. 81 (1865).

[10] 10 Allen (Mass.) 82 (1865).

[11] 5 Vt. 279 (1833).

Merchants or other customs will not be permitted to modify or affect usury laws.[1]

United States banks,[2] and other banking companies,[3] and corporations are within the provisions of usury laws, and are affected by them the same as individuals,[4] national banks being under the exclusive control of the United States laws.[5] The taking of usurious interest is liable to cause the loss of their charter.[6]

There must be an agreement to pay usury at least.[7] A stipulation in arbitration articles that illegal interest shall be allowed, is valid, as it is not a contract.[8]

It is not necessary to constitute it usury that the contract be payable in money alone; it may be payable in chattels.[9]

More than legal interest contracted for or received through a mistake in calculation, or otherwise, either by the parties themselves, or by one of their clerks,[10] is not usury,[11] and no penalty attaches.[12] But it must be a mistake of fact and not of law.[13] So if an executor igno-

[1] 109 N. C. 539 (1891); 39 Pa. St. 361 (1861).

[2] 5 Heath (Me.) 109 (1855).

[3] 24 Conn. 147 (1855); 9 Mass. 49 (1812).

[4] 7 How. (Miss.) 508 (1843); 33 Vt. 346 (1860). 621 (1861).

[5] 44 Ind. 298 (1873); 115 Mass. 539, 547 (1874).

[6] 4 Geo. (Miss.) 474 (1857).

[7] 3 Gr. Ch. (N. J.) 128 (1837); 1 Gr. Ch. (N. J.) 44 (1838); 29 N. Y. 337 (1864); 81 N. Y. 293 (1881); 85 N. Y. 550 (1881).

[8] 45 O. St. 377 (1877).

[9] 10 Ired. L. (N. C.) 315 (1849).

[10] 4 Rand. (Va.) 406 (1826).

[11] 4 Pet. (U. S.) 205 (1830); 4 Hous. (Del.) 315 (1872); 53 N. W. Rep. (Iowa) 410 (1892); 7 La. 198 (1834); 3 N. H. 185 (1825); 2 Cow. (N. Y.) 678 (1824); 12 N. Y. (2 Kern.) 223 (1855); 87 N. Y. 50 (1881); 101 N. C. 99 (1888); 1 O. St. 409 (1853).

[12] 4 Pet. (U. S.) 205 (1830); 9 Ark. 22 (1848); 25 Ark. 191, 258 (1868).

[13] 2 Cow. (N. Y.) 678 (1824); 31 N. Y. 472 (1865); 1 O. St. 409 (1853).

rantly receives unlawful interest reserved in a note payable to his testator, he is not responsible, either personally or as executor.[1] Though a note given in payment of a preëxisting debt exceeds the amount of such debt, the payee is not guilty of a violation of the usury laws, says the Texas court, when it appears that, being very ill, he intrusted the computation of the interest on the old debt to a third person, who drew the note, and that he protested against the excessive interest, and gave positive instructions that the maker should not be held liable for it, since the intent to take usury constitutes the offence.[2]

The offence against the statute of usury is complete when more than legal interest is reserved or taken when the loan is made, whether the principal sum is ever repaid or not.[3] The language of the statute governs.

Most of the decisions of the highest courts of the country pertaining to usury have principally concerned the construction of the statutes of the various states. The principles here given are not local in their application, but have a general bearing upon usury in all states whether usury laws prevail there or not.

I. WHAT CONTRACTS ARE USURIOUS.

To make a contract usurious it must be for a loan,[4] to be returned at all events,[5] and not a sale.

Each and every instance of the receipt of usury is an offence.[6]

The contract must be usurious in itself,[7] and at the time

[1] 7 Allen (Mass.) 59 (1863).

[2] 21 S. W. Rep. (Tex.) 69 (1893).

[3] 5 Mass. 53 (1809).

[4] 1 Black (U. S.) 115 (1861); 4 Ind. 283 (1853); 11 La. 491 (1838); 15 La. Ann. 457 (1860); 14 Ore. 47 (1886); 85 Va. 621 (1889).

[5] 10 Md. 57 (1856).

[6] 4 W. & S. (Pa.) 449 (1842).

[7] 1 Root (Conn.) 110 (1789); 5 Fla. 504 (1854); 2 Shepl. (Me.) 240 (1837); 2 Puls. (Me.) 212 (1876); 23 Vt. 215 (1851); 37 Vt. 608 (1865).

when it is made,[1] and if the statute requires that there be a corrupt agreement, then the minds of the contracting parties must meet as to its usurious nature, that is, both must really know they are committing usury.[2] An inadvertent violation of the usury law is not usurious.[3] Where there is an agreement for usury, the corrupt nature of it is presumed.[4] In New Jersey, if notes stipulate for interest at a lawful rate, and more is taken, a corrupt original agreement is presumed, unless it is taken by an executor of the creditor.[5]

In construing usury statutes, it is the practice both in England and America to allow no contract to be good if usury will be its ultimate effect.[6] It is the intention of the parties in making a contract, and not the form or language used that determines whether it is usurious or not,[7] all devices, shifts and subterfuges to cover usury

[1] 8 Mass. 101, 256 (1811); 9 Mass. 45 (1812); 2 N. H. 42 (1819); 10 R. I. 503 (1873); 17 Vt. 231 (1845); 19 Vt. 540 (1847). A renewal of a note, payable in Confederate money, for the same amount for which it was originally drawn, without scaling, after the purchasing power of Confederate money had greatly depreciated, is not usury. 9 W. Va. 333, 345 (1876).

[2] 3 Day (Conn.) 268 (1808); 4 Day (Conn.) 96 (1809); 32 Barb. (N. Y.) 557 (1860); 33 Barb. (N. Y.) 229 (1860); 44 Barb. (N. Y.) 521 (1865).

[3] 67 Miss. 146 (1889).

[4] 2 Harr. (N. J.) 487 (1840); 2 Beas. (N. J.) 351, 357 (1861).

[5] 3 Gr. Ch. (N. J.) 128 (1837).

[6] 5 B. Mon. (Ky.) 150 (1844); 6 B. Mon. (Ky.) 530 (1846); 44 Pa. St. 32 (1862).

[7] 4 Port. (Ala.) 128 (1836); 11 Ala. 236 (1847); 46 Ga. 166 (1872); 49 Ga. 133, 514 (1873); 78 Ga. 635 (1887); 3 Gilm. (Ill.) 547 (1846); 19 Ill. 623 (1858); 27 Ill. 301 (1862); 35 Ill. 186 (1864); 57 Ill. 500 (1870); 62 Ill. 461 (1872); 89 Ill. 123 (1878); 106 Ill. 99 (1883); 108 Ill. 633 (1884); 7 Ind. 680 (1856); 9 Ind. 140 (1857); 7 G. & J. (Md.) 20 (1835); 2 Md. Ch. 201 (1850); 6 Neb. 151 (1877); 8 Neb. 423 (1879); 3 Gr. (N. J.) 255, 258 (1836); 2 Halst. Ch. (N. J.) 253 (1847); 1 C. E. Gr. (N. J.) 537 (1863); 10 C. E. Gr. (N. J.) 491 (1875); 9 Cow. (N. Y.) 65 (1828); 1 Denio (N. Y.) 133 (1845); 62 N. Y. 341 (1875); 6 O. St.

being ineffectual,[1] no matter how complicated a contract may be;[2] and oral evidence is admissible to show usury in a written contract.[3] A note cannot be made larger than the amount really loaned, and then a legal rate of interest be written in;[4] and although a partial payment is made on such a note and a new one given for the balance it is still usurious.[5] So notes cannot be antedated for the purpose of getting more than legal interest.[6] So, if at the making of a note, bearing the full amount of legal interest from its date, an extra premium or bonus,[7] either in chattels or money,[8] is paid by the borrower to the lender,[9] it is usurious; but it is legal if it is paid by or to a third

19 (1856); 44 Pa. St. 32 (1862); 1 R. I. 151 (1840): 24 Tenn. 406 (1844): 26 Tenn. 35 (1846); 41 Tenn. 180 (1860): 2 Call (Va.) 421 (1800); 4 Rand. (Va.) 406 (1826); 58 Wis. 56 (1883).

[1] 79 Ala. 76 (1885); 4 Hous. (Del.) 289 (1871); 78 Ga. 251 (1886); 9 Rob. (La.) 125 (1844); 12 Rob. (La.) 273 (1845): 11 La. Ann. 638 (1856); 16 Md. 11 (1859); 67 Md. 18 (1887); 68 Miss. 310 (1890): 1 McCart. (N. J.) 229 (1862): 2 McCart. (N. J.) 476 (1863); 1 C. E. Gr. (N. J.) 537 (1863); 78 N. Y. 137 (1879); 1 Hayw. (N. C.) 336 (1796); 12 O. 544 (1841); 25 O. St. 420 (1874); 24 Tenn. 373 (1844); 43 Tenn. 31 (1846); 2 Call (Va.) 421 (1800); 17 Wis. 383 (1863).

[2] Hill & D. Supp. (N. Y.) 65 (1843).

[3] 5 Lit. (Ky.) 84 (1824); 7 Mon. (Ky.) 252 (1828); 7 Dana (Ky.) 300 (1838); 7 Bush (Ky.) 79 (1869); 43 Minn. 307 (1890).

[4] 65 Iowa 403 (1884); 12 Kas. 500 (1874); 3 Mart. N. S. (La.) 622 (1825); 19 La. 185 (1841); 46 Minn. 400 (1891); 4 Cush. (Miss.) 468 (1853); 1 C. E. Gr. (N. J.) 445 (1863); Harp. (S. C.) 81 (1823), 372 (1824); 2 Rich. (S. C.) 73 (1845); 21 S. W. Rep. (Tex.) 930 (1893); 2 Wms. (Vt.) 130 (1855); 30 Vt. 628 (1858).

[5] 1 Dall. (U. S.) 216 (1787).

[6] 68 Iowa 255 (1885).

[7] 50 Iowa 596 (1879); 12 W. P. D. Bush (Ky.) 110 (1876); 3 La. 387 (1832); 19 La. 185 (1841); 11 La. Ann. 511 (1856); 12 La. Ann. 660 (1857); 16 La. Ann. 239 (1861); 34 La. Ann. 893 (1882); 52 Md. 148 (1879): 8 Mass. 135 (1811); 34 Barb. (N. Y.) 157 (1860); 35 Barb. (N. Y.) 44 (1860): 10 O. 378 (1842). See 3 Ch. Sent. (N. Y.) 4 (1843); 1 How. Pr. (N. Y.) 44 (1844).

[8] 2 Halst. Ch. (N. J.) 73 (1846).

[9] 21 S. W. Rep. (Ark.) 432 (1893). See page 241.

person.[1] The bonus or premium received must be large enough to make the amount of interest contracted for and the bonus together amount to more than legal interest to make it usurious.[2] It is usurious if the note is written for the full amount and some privilege is given beside.[3] The premium or bonus must be certain.[4] Where an insurance company made a loan, and for its own security the owner had the property insured in that company, which received the premium, it was not usurious;[5] but if no policy had been issued it would have been held otherwise.[6] It is not usurious, in getting a loan, for the borrower to do what he is already legally bound to do as a condition for the loan.[7] A gift from the borrower to the lender, made immediately after a loan, is not usurious;[8] but where the borrower receives in his hand the full amount of the principal named in the note, and then passes back part of it, with the intention of making the amount actually loaned less than the face of the note, it is usurious.[9]

An actual loan cannot be made in the form of a sale;[10]

[1] 25 Hun (N. Y.) 490 (1884). A maker of a note can pay an accommodation indorser for his indorsement and for procuring its discount at a bank, and it will not affect the bank discounting it in good faith. 37 N. Y. 356 (1867).

[2] 1 Doug. (Eng.) 235 (1779).

[3] 5 C. E. Gr. (N. J.) 300 (1869); 7 Paige (N. Y.) 557 (1839).

[4] Add. (Pa.) 124 (1793).

[5] 3 Wend. (N. Y.) 296 (1829); 3 Edw. (N. Y.) 199 (1838).

[6] 1 Hall (N. Y.) 480 (1829).

[7] 36 Barb. (N. Y.) 619 (1862); 69 N. Y. 339 (1877).

[8] 32 Barb. (N. Y.) 557 (1860). See 56 N. Y. 640 (1874).

[9] 2 Ind. 546 (1851); 81 Iowa 569 (1890); 30 Md. 485 (1869); 60 Vt. 209 (1887).

[10] 5 Day (Conn.) 166 (1811); 1 McArt. (D. C.) 144 (1873); 49 Ga. 133 (1873); 81 Ga. 81 (1888); 1 Gilm. (Ill.) 690 (1844); 3 Gilm. (Ill.) 547 (1846); 15 Ill. 519 (1854); 18 Ill. 101 (1856); 5 Mon. (Ky.) 469 (1827); 3 Dana (Ky.) 567 (1835); 1 Gr. Ch. (N. J.) 453 (1841); 1 C. E. Gr. (N. J.) 210 (1863); 62 N. Y. 344 (1875); 30 Tex. 400 (1867); 2 Call (Va.) 421 (1800); 7 Leigh (Va.) 26 (1836).

and the value of the property can be shown to prove it a loan.[1] So if the price of goods sold is agreed to be much higher than the real value, and credit is given with interest on the sum due in the meantime.[2] So a note given for goods sold on credit at higher price stipulating that if not paid at maturity of credit it is to bear the highest conventional rate from the date of sale till paid, is usurious.[3] So if cash price is fixed, and more than legal interest is charged on deferred payments,[4] it is usurious though not called a loan.[5] So if a mortgagee buys a chattel of his mortgagor, for an agreed cash price, and charges its value in his account for advances, as a much larger sum; that, too, is usurious.[6] It is also usurious to make contracts part of the consideration of another contract[7] at their face value, when they are really worth much[8] less,[9] unless the borrower claims them to be worth as much to him;[10] and, also, making a note payable in a specific commodity, which is agreed to be at a lower rate than its current value;[11] or, where a purchase of property is made by the lender, at a high price, on condition of a loan;[12] or a loan of depreci-

[1] 78 Ga. 635 (1887); 1 C. E. Gr. (N. J.) 537 (1863).

[2] 36 Ark. 248 (1880); 9 Rob. (La.) 194 (1844); 62 N. Y. 344 (1875); 2 Spear (S. C.) 238 (1843).

[3] 9 Rob. (La.) 194 (1844).

[4] 75 Ga. 739 (1885).

[5] 1 Stew. (Ala.) 391 (1828).

[6] 85 Ala. 394, 417 (1888).

[7] 2 Rand. (Va.) 109 (1823).

[8] Must be worth considerably less. 1 Barb. (N. Y.) 432 (1847); 19 N. Y. (5 Smith) 37 (1859).

[9] 1 Johns. Ch. (N. Y.) 536 (1815); 19 Johns. (N. Y.) 496 (1822); 7 Paige (N. Y.) 557, 615 (1839); 2 Hill (N. Y.) 499 (1842); 5 Barb. (N. Y.) 613 (1849); 7 N. Y. (3 Seld.) 328 (1852); 5 Ired. L. (N. C.) 692 (1845); 11 Vt. 300 (1839); 3 Grat. (Va.) 148 (1846); *contra*, in New York, 31 Vt. 653 (1859). See 3 Conn. 266 (1820).

[10] 2 Hill (N. Y.) 499 (1842).

[11] 8 Mass. 266 (1811).

[12] 7 Ind. 250 (1855); 17 N. H. 43 (1845); 100 Pa. St. 551 (1882); 5 Rand. (Va.) 132 (1827).

ated currency or notes, to be repaid in bankable bills,[1] if usury is intended. Each of these cases is usurious. Neither can usury be covered up by a purchase of an annuity.[2] But it is not usurious where the property is agreed to be at the value it will be sold for six months hence.[3] Nor is a note usurious if its interest is to be paid "in gold or its equivalent."[4]

As already stated, if a loan of property is estimated above its specific value at the time the contract is made it is usurious;[5] and proof that the property subsequently sold at the estimated amount in payment of the debt does not make it legal.[6] So, reckoning depreciated bank notes of other banks at par is usurious, even if they afterward reach par.[7] Also, if bank shares are given by the lender at a higher than the market price.[8]

An actual loan cannot be made in the form of rent;[9] nor for the use of a chattel if the use is worth much more than the legal interest on the loan;[10] or, for an article which is worth more than the legal rate;[11] or, as damages

[1] 9 Tenn. 243 (1829), 444 (1830); 15 Tenn. 545 (1835); 19 Tenn. 585 (1838); 24 Tenn. 406 (1844).

[2] 1 Pet. (U. S.) 205 (1830).

[3] 7 N. Y. (3 Seld.) 328 (1852).

[4] 101 Pa. St. 32 (1882).

[5] 12 Rob. (La.) 273 (1845); 34 Barb. (N. Y.) 157 (1860).

[6] 12 Rob. (La.) 273 (1845).

[7] 6 Mon. (Ky.) 376 (1827); 7 Mon. (Ky.) 336, 354 (1828); 4 J. J. Mar. (Ky.) 48 (1830); 2 Dana (Ky.) 225 (1834); 3 Dana (Ky.) 369 (1835); 8 S. & M. (Miss.) 533, 543 (1847); 11 S. & M. (Miss.) 140 (1848); 14 S. & M. (Miss.) 18 (1850); 5 Cush. (Miss.) 801 (1854).

[8] 7 Mart. N. S. (La.) 408 (1829).

[9] 65 Ala. 382 (1880); 5 Day (Conn.) 100 (1811); 19 Ga. 551 (1856); 52 Ga. 69 (1874); 59 Ga. 584 (1877); 77 Ga. 369 (1886); 7 Ind. 359 (1855); 6 Mon. (Ky.) 160 (1827); 1 J. J. Mar. (Ky.) 557 (1829); 13 S. & R. (Pa.) 218 (1825); 53 Vt. 539 (1881).

[10] 2 Stew. & Port. (Ala.) 323 (1832); 3 Bibb (Ky.) 207 (1813); 4 Bibb (Ky.) 328 (1816); 4 Mart. N. S. (La.) 167 (1826); 13 La. Ann. 364 (1858).

[11] 8 Leigh (Va.) 330 (1837).

to hired property.[1] A contract for purchasing a chattel at half price, and at the same time loaning the vendor another sum of money, on the condition that if a sum larger than the purchase price and the loan with the interest combined, shall be secured, that the chattel shall be restored, and the money lent considered as paid, is usurious.[2]

A mortgage given to secure a part of the purchase money, though not a technical loan, comes under the usury law.[3]

A loan of chattels is not within the usury law, unless the statute expressly says so, or it is a disguise for an usurious loan of money; and, therefore, on a *bona fide* loan of chattels it is immaterial what compensation is received.[4] In New York, it is held to apply to a loan of notes;[5] and in North Carolina the acceptance of chattels as well as money brings them under the usury law.[6]

Where, in lieu of policies of life insurance on which notes have been given, paid up policies are issued, containing a provision that in case interest on the notes is not paid as agreed, the policy shall become void, and the provision will not be relieved against as being unconscionable or oppressive, and is not void on the ground of usury as it is not a contract for the borrowing or loaning of money.[7]

Commissions charged on an exchange of notes, are usurious if more than legal interest is thus taken.[8]

[1] 59 Vt. 75 (1886).

[2] 1 Mar. (Ky.) 65 (1817).

[3] 1 C. E. Gr. (N. J.) 210 (1863).

[4] 5 Cow. (N. Y.) 144 (1825); 4 Wend. (N. Y.) 679 (1830); 17 Wend. (N. Y.) 280 (1837); 5 N. Y. (1 Seld.) 315 (1851).

[5] 13 Johns. (N. Y.) 40 (1816); 16 Johns. (N. Y.) 367 (1819); 22 How. Pr. (N. Y.) 4 (1861).

[6] 98 N. C. 244 (1887).

[7] 82 N. Y. 172 (1880).

[8] 2 Johns. Ch. (N. Y.) 182 (1816); 5 Johns. Ch. (N. Y.) 122 (1821).

Notes exchanged have a good consideration and may be enforced against each other;[1] but an exchange to carry an usurious contract into effect will be usurious,[2] in spite of their sale nature.

An advance, by an auctioneer, upon goods left for sale, for five per cent beyond commission is usurious.[3]

It is also usurious to give in exchange for a security, for the payment of a sum with interest, a check for the same amount, payable at a future day without interest.[4]

An agreement to pay seven per cent for the loan of a five per cent security is usurious.[5]

A mortgage founded on an usurious consideration can be avoided by all parties having liens upon the property, says the New York court of appeals.[6]

One who takes a note at its inception at a greater discount than the legal rate must be conclusively presumed to have intended to loan, as the transaction can have no other character. His want of knowledge that the note takes its inception in his hands makes no difference in the rule.[7]

It is immaterial says the Tennessee court whether usury is agreed to be paid before or after the maturity of the principal.[8]

An agreement, whereby, upon the non-happening of a certain contingency, a lender is to receive usurious inter-

[1] 3 Wend. (N. Y.) 62 (1829); 2 Denio (N. Y.) 621 (1846); 13 Barb. (N. Y.) 15 (1852); 10 N. Y. (6 Seld.) 198 (1851).

[2] 11 Paige (N. Y.) 660 (1845).

[3] 12 La. Ann. 20, 723 (1857); 16 Wend. (N. Y.) 574 (1837).

[4] 2 Barb. (N. Y.) 56 (1847).

[5] 5 Barb. (N. Y.) 613 (1849); 14 N. Y. (4 Kern.) 93 (1856); *contra*, 4 N. Y. (4 Comst.) 463 (1851).

[6] 27 N. Y. 568 (1863).

[7] 65 N. Y. 522 (1875).

[8] 56 Tenn. 242 (1877).

est, but upon its happening he may collect the loan with legal interest only, is usurious notwithstanding the contingency, says the court in Wisconsin. This was a case where interest was to be paid from the profits of a firm, but not under a certain per cent,[1] no matter what the profits amounted to. If a lender is to have a share of the profits of a firm for the interest on his money used in its business it is not usurious;[2] but if he is to receive such share beside the legal interest it is.[3]

The renewal of a valid note by one of a larger amount is also usurious.[4]

Where a note bears a legal rate, but in a separate writing the borrower agrees to pay five per cent more interest on it, it is usurious.[5] The two contracts must be construed together as forming one transaction.[6] And the law is the same if the contract for the usurious interest is oral.[7] Though separate notes are given for the amount of the excess of the legal rate, if paid, the debtor shall have credit on the principal for the amount.[8]

A loan at the highest rate of interest, and a slave pledged, with an agreement not to account for the hire of the slave, is an usurious contract.[9]

It is usurious for a mortgagee to exact as part consideration for his loan, his employment at an exorbitant price, when his services are not needed.[10]

[1] 9 Wis. 361 (1859).
[2] 108 N. Y. 187 (1888).
[3] 19 La. 185 (1841).
[4] 8 Tenn. 392 (1828).
[5] 2 McC. (S. C.) 369 (1823).
[6] 15 O. St. 218 (1864).
[7] 18 Wis. 298 (1864).
[8] 11 Ind. 258 (1858).
[9] 3 J. J. Mar. (Ky.) 108 (1829).
[10] 3 Stock. (N. J.) 49 (1855).

(*a*) *Usury in original contract.* To avoid a contract on the ground of usury, the usury must have been in it from the beginning.[1]

A deed tainted with usury is void for title,[2] if made directly from debtor to creditor; or, if the debtor, holding the equitable title, causes the third party holding the legal title to convey it to the creditor;[3] but it is good as an equitable mortgage to secure the principal only.[4] If the holder of such a deed, by notice given at the sale of the amount of the debt due to him, including the usurious interest, causes property to bring less than its full value, he becoming the purchaser, he is liable to the grantor for the difference.[5]

Usury taints the whole of a contract.[6] If two notes are a part of one transaction, one of them only being usurious, the whole transaction is usurious, so both notes become so.[7] Also, if the contract and security for it form one entire transaction, and the security is usurious, the whole transaction is.[8] If the entire consideration of a contract is usury it is invalid.[9]

Where an usurious chattel mortgage authorized the mortgagee to take possession before default, a taking and sale by the mortgagee is held to be a wrongful conversion.[10]

Where, in the obligation for the mortgage debt, any

[1] 88 N. C. 344 (1883).

[2] 54 Ga. 554 (1875); 55 Ga. 412 (1875), 691 (1876); 56 Ga. 33 (1876); 75 Ga. 159 (1885); 78 Ga. 220 (1886).

[3] 66 Ga. 398 (1881).

[4] 64 Ga. 71 (1879); 68 Ga. 821 (1882); *contra*, 80 Ga. 423 (1888).

[5] 64 Ga. 71 (1879).

[6] 3 Dak. 328 (1884); 40 Tenn. 723 (1859).

[7] Cro. Jac. (Eng.) 508 (1641); 11 Mass. 74 (1814).

[8] 13 Conn. 219 (1839).

[9] 71 Ga. 549 (1883).

[10] 35 Minn. 196 (1886).

illegal interest has been incorporated, it will be deducted from the amount.[1]

A note has no legal inception until it is delivered to some person as evidence of an existing contract. Therefore a note payable to A, or bearer, which is never delivered to A, but which is first delivered to one who lends money on it on usurious terms, is usurious in its inception.[2] So with a stolen note.[3]

The Georgia court says that the taint of usury results not from payment, but from agreement whether it is performed or not;[4] so a breach of an usurious contract to lend money is not actionable.[5]

(*b*) *Discounting.* Discounting a note at an illegal rate is usury.[6] Discounting a note is different from a purchase of it; it is a loan,[7] and therefore comes under the usury law, whereas a sale of it would not.[8]

What constitutes a discount and what a sale is a nice question. It seems to the writer that discounts of business paper should be *prima facie* deemed sales,[9] while those of accommodation paper should be held to be loans.[10] Generally, it depends upon the terms of the agreement, as to whether or not it is to be repaid.[11]

If a bank discounts a note for the legal rate, and in addition makes a charge for collecting in the place where

[1] 17 O. 336 (1848).

[2] 20 Johns. (N. Y.) 288 (1822).

[3] 16 Wend. (N. Y.) 574 (1837); 2 Sandf. (N. Y.) 60 (1848); 16 Barb. (N. Y.) 548 (1853).

[4] 84 Ga. 181 (1889).

[5] 79 Ga. 347 (1887).

[6] 28 Ala. 580 (1856).

[7] 15 O. St. 68 (1864).

[8] 2 Harr. (N. J.) 191 (1839).

[9] 2 Conn. 175 (1817).

[10] 15 O. St. 68 (1864).

[11] See 2 Harr. (N. J.) 191 (1839).

the paper is payable, when the bank is, at the very time, selling drafts upon that place at a premium, it is usury.[1] So, where a bank as a condition of the discount of a note, requires the applicant to have another note discounted, and to leave the proceeds with it, with a check drawn against the deposit, bearing date the day the note is payable, it is usurious.[2] So, if a bank requires one applying for discount to keep a deposit with it, it makes the discount usurious.[3] So, if a bank discounts a note for legal interest but gives therefor its own paper for its face value, which is worth only about one-half of its face, it is usury:[4] or, if the bank notes are at a discount and payable at a future day without interest.[5] Where a bank discounts a note at the highest rate of interest, and gives the holder as cash notes due two or three months later, it is also usurious.[6]

If a bank is chartered to make loans and not to buy paper, all discounts must be deemed to be loans.[7]

(c) *Forbearance to sue.* A promise to pay usurious interest for forbearance is usurious, as it is essentially for a loan.[8] It is no bar to the foreclosure of a mortgage security.[9] A simple sum of money given for forbearance

[1] 2 Hill (N. Y.) 451 (1842).

[2] 22 How. Pr. (N. Y.) 478 (1862).

[3] 32 N. Y. 119 (1865).

[4] 2 Pet. (U. S.) 527 (1829).

[5] 1 Pet. (U. S.) 37 (1828).

[6] 3 Halst. (N. J.) 125 (1825).

[7] 15 O. St. 68 (1864).

[8] 3 Fla. 110 (1850): 19 Ill. 623 (1858): 66 Ill. 532 (1873); 11 Ind. 258 (1858); 14 Ind. 401 (1860); 15 Ind. 50 (1860); 21 Ind. 129 (1863); 17 Iowa 578 (1864); 47 Iowa 62 (1877): 7 B. Mon. (Ky.) 176 (1847); 3 Geo. (Miss.) 142 (1856): 1 C. E. Gr. (N. J.) 210 (1863): 70 N. Y. 63 (1877); Tay. & Conf. (N. C.) 167 (1800): 1 Strob. (S. C.) 461 (1847); 5 Strob. (S. C.) 151 (1850); 28 S. C. 504 (1887); 76 Va. 419 (1882): 85 Va. 621 (1889).

[9] 14 Ind. 401 (1860).

may be regarded as interest, and be usurious.[1] The note itself is not tainted, but the excess can be offset.[2] A note given for past forbearance is without consideration;[3] and the same is true in regard to indulgence on an execution.[4] Such interest is not a penalty.[5] A contract to grant indulgence on an execution on payment of costs, attorney's fees and commission for collecting the claim, amounting to more than the legal rate is usurious.[6]

(*d*) *Lender must receive the usury.* The illegal interest must be paid to the lender,[7] or to his agent,[8] and not to any one else, unless it is so agreed, and so paid to the lender's knowledge,[9] to make it usury. So, if commissions are paid to a stranger, it is not usury;[10] but if paid to the lender it is.[11]

(*e*) *Receipt of usurious interest.* Neither a legal contract nor its security is affected by the subsequent receipt of usurious interest; the usury must be in the contract originally to affect it.[12] An executor is responsible for usurious interest received by himself, and also by his testator.[13] An administrator is also accountable to the borrower for usury he has received, though he has settled with the estate.[14]

[1] 15 Ind. 428 (1860); 32 O. St. 107 (1878).

[2] 17 Ind. 209 (1861); 17 Iowa 64 (1864).

[3] 39 Ill. 539 (1864).

[4] 1 Rich. Eq. (S. C.) 414 (1845).

[5] 28 S. C. 504 (1887).

[6] 4 Leigh (Va.) 581 (1833).

[7] 25 Amer. Rep. 253; 66 Ga. 638 (1881); 2 Mar. (Ky.) 300 (1820); 2 Hill (N. Y.) 635 (1842); 5 Denio (N. Y.) 85 (1847).

[8] 1 Stew. (N. J.) 345 (1877). See page 239.

[9] 13 Stew. (N. J.) 502 (1885).

[10] 121 U. S. 105 (1887).

[11] 10 O. 378 (1842).

[12] 1 Madd. (Eng.) 331 (1816); 1 Root (Conn.) 70 (1789); 8 Mass. 101. 256 (1811); 9 Mass. 45 (1812).

[13] 8 B. Mon. (Ky.) 432 (1848).

[14] 5 B. Mon. (Ky.) 145 (1844).

The use of the proceeds of collateral security paid before the debt is due will not affect the original contract, unless it was stipulated at the time the contract was made that the lender was to have such use.[1]

When the payee of an usurious note sells it for the amount actually loaned thereon with legal interest only, he is not regarded as a recipient of illegal interest, although the maker afterward paid the full amount including the usurious interest to the indorsee.[2]

Neither is it usurious if the defendant in order to induce the plaintiff to purchase a note adds upon the face of it his own name as security.[3]

Where a mortgage is executed upon a sufficient consideration, it is not rendered usurious by a previous understanding with a third person that he will purchase it at a sum less than its face.[4]

Receiving a note for usurious interest is payment of it (as far as receipt is concerned).[5]

Taking a partial payment on an usurious note is also deemed to be a receipt of usury.[6]

II. WHAT CONTRACTS ARE NOT USURIOUS.

There can be no usury in a contract which expressly stipulates that the borrower shall not pay more than the legal rate of interest.[7]

It is legal to loan coin to be paid in kind.[8]

A note payable on time, with interest from its date, is not usurious.[9] Neither is a bond conditioned to pay a

[1] 19 Barb. (N. Y.) 584 (1855).
[2] 3 Virg. (Me.) 358 (1867).
[3] 13 Barb. (N. Y.) 45 (1852); 10 N. Y. (6 Seld.) 198 (1854).
[4] 94 N. Y. 129 (1883).
[5] 1 Dall. (Pa.) 216 (1787).
[6] 1 Dall. (Pa.) 216 (1787); 4 W. & S. (Pa.) 115 (1842).
[7] 19 S. W. Rep. (Ark.) 918 (1892); 28 S. C. 534 (1887).
[8] 62 Tenn. 392 (1871).
[9] 9 Tenn. 502 (1831).

thousand pounds or such further sum as shall be equal to it at a certain date.[1]

It is proper to include days of grace;[2] and, says the North Carolina court, it is not usurious if one is not entitled to them, even.[3] It seems to the writer very doubtful if other courts follow this latter decision, as the mistake appears to have been one of law rather than of fact, and upon that ground there can be no excuse for it.

(*a*) *Usury must be paid for the use of money, etc.* The contract must be for a loan, and not a sale,—usury not existing in a sale,[4] no matter what the price, or other inducement, unless it is a cover for usury.[5] So a man may sell his credit;[6] and it will not be usurious unless it

[1] 2 H. & M. (Va.) 550 (1808).

[2] 2 Conn. (N. Y.) 712 (1824).

[3] 1 Dev. L. (N. C.) 100 (1826).

[4] 9 Pet. (U. S.) 418 (1835); 12 Wall. (U. S.) 226 (1870); 54 Ala. 39 (1875); 55 Ark. 265 (1891); 1 Root (Conn.) 393 (1792); 24 Ill. 345 (1860); 68 Ill. 530 (1873); 83 Ill. 519 (1876); 90 Ill. 152 (1878); 11 Ind. 117 (1858); 14 Ind. 607 (1860); 15 Iowa 93, 362 (1863); 31 Iowa 444 (1871); Hardin (Ky.) 186 (1807); 3 Mar. (Ky.) 390 (1821); 4 Lit. (Ky.) 125 (1823); 5 Mon. (Ky.) 69 (1827); 1 J. J. Mar. (Ky.) 497 (1829); 3 B. Mon. (Ky.) 68 (1842); 6 B. Mon. (Ky.) 530 (1846); 7 B. Mon. (Ky.) 541, 549 (1847); 11 La. 491 (1838); 15 La. 306 (1840); 9 Neb. 11 (1879); 14 Neb. 378 (1883); 3 Stock. (N. J.) 362 (1857); 9 C. E. Gr. (N. J.) 120 (1873), 358 (1874); 15 Johns. (N. Y.) 44 (1818); 8 Cow. (N. Y.) 669 (1826); 2 Wend. (N. Y.) 256, 569 (1831); 9 Paige (N. Y.) 478 (1842); 4 Hill (N. Y.) 472 (1842); 4 N. Y. (4 Comst.) 225 (1850); 13 Barb. (N. Y.) 45 (1852); 10 N. Y. (6 Seld.) 198 (1854); 33 N. Y. 53 (1865); 35 N. Y. 494 (1866); 6 O. St. 256 (1856); 14 O. St. 396 (1863); 1 Dall. (Pa.) 216 (1787); 2 Dall. (Pa.) 92 (1785); 3 McC. (S. C.) 365 (1827); 4 McC. (S. C.) 402 (1827); 40 Tenn. 723 (1859); 4 H. & M. (Va.) 490 (1810); 2 Munf. (Va.) 36 (1811); 4 Munf. (Va.) 303 (1814); 6 Munf. (Va.) 472 (1820); 9 Leigh (Va.) 556 (1838); 16 S. E. Rep. (W. Va.) 512 (1892); 3 Wis. 725 (1854); 16 Wis. 22 (1862). See 21 Wend. (N. Y.) 285 (1839); Hill & D. Supp. (N. Y.) 252 (1843).

[5] 10 S. & M. (Miss.) 89 (1848); 12 S. & M. (Miss.) 286 (1849); 3 Stock. (N. J.) 362 (1857); 9 C. E. Gr. (N. J.) 120 (1873); 40 Tenn. 723 (1859).

[6] 4 Denio (N. Y.) 264 (1847); 3 N. Y. (3 Comst.) 344 (1850); 4 N. Y. (4 Comst.) 363 (1850).

is in fact a loan.[1] An exchange of credits, securities, or commodities, which the parties *bona fide* estimate at equivalent values, is not illegal, unless it is a mere device to cover usury.[2] A sale with a right to repurchase may be a device to evade the usury law, if the property is of greater value;[3] but is not on its face usurious although, if not paid at maturity of a loan, it is to bear a large rate of interest.[4]

Negotiable paper and securities may also be sold for what they will bring, the same as chattels.[5] There is a distinction, however, between business and accommodation paper. If it is business paper, a note or bill may be sold at an usurious discount,[6] and yet not be illegal, although it is indorsed by the party making the sale.[7] But if it is accommodation paper, which does not become effective until negotiated, and is made simply to raise money on, it is treated as a loan by the indorsee, and is *prima facie* usurious.[8] The drawer of a bill may sell it after acceptance.[9] The test is whether or not it was a perfect and available instrument in the hands of the payee at the time of the transfer, upon which, when due, he could have

[1] 3 N. Y. (3 Comst.) 344 (1850).

[2] 9 Pet. (U. S.) 378 (1835); 5 Mon. (Ky.) 469 (1827); 3 La. Ann. 157 (1848); 14 N. Y. (4 Kern.) 93 (1856).

[3] 3 Dana (Ky.) 173 (1835).

[4] 54 Iowa 243 (1880); or, interest on a larger time price, 32 S. C. 594 (1890).

[5] 3 Dutch. (N. J.) 624 (1858); 79 N. Y. 224 (1879); 91 N. Y. 199, 324 (1883); 29 Hun (N. Y.) 129 (1883).

[6] 2 Scam. (Ill.) 561 (1840); 11 Ind. 117 (1858); 31 Iowa 444 (1871); 26 Tenn. 451 (1846).

[7] 17 Ala. 761 (1851); 14 Ind. 607 (1860); 3 Shepl. (Me.) 163 (1838); 4 Shepl. (Me.) 456 (1840); 20 Me. (2 Appl., 7 Shepl.) 98 (1841). Judge Parsons held such a note usurious in 4 Mass. 156, but Chief-justice Weston, of the Maine court, thought that the Massachusetts case turned on another point.

[8] 12 Wall. (U. S.) 226 (1870); 17 Conn. 441 (1846); 1 H. & G. (Md.) 477 (1827); 44 Barb. (N. Y.) 87 (1865).

[9] 21 Wend. (N. Y.) 94 (1840).

maintained an action against the maker.[1] It is a question for the jury.[2]

Interest payable on a debt after its maturity at more than the legal rate, none being payable before maturity, is not usurious, but is to be regarded as a penalty for non-payment according to contract.[3]

The usury must always be paid either directly or indirectly, expressly or essentially, for the *use* of money, etc.,[4] and paid to the lender,[5] in order to bring it under the usury statutes. Therefore, when the full legal amount has already been agreed to be paid for the loan, it is not usurious to make, *bona fide*,[6] an agreement to pay in addition to that, the attorney's fee and costs,[7] in case it is necessary to bring suit on the claim, and a suit should be brought.

Neither is it usurious to pay commission, etc.,[8] to a

[1] 6 Ind. 232 (1855); 10 Md. 57 (1856).

[2] 10 Md. 57 (1856).

[3] 32 N. E. Rep. (Ill.) 495 (1892); 3 Pinn. 78 (3 Chand. 83) (Wis.) (1850).

[4] 52 Fed. Rep. (Ark.) 618 (1892); 1 Root (Conn.) 393 (1792).

[5] 120 Ill. 390 (1887); 121 Ill. 119 (1887); 132 Ill. 550 (1890); 133 Ill. 199 (1890); 2 Stew. (N. J.) 454 (1878).

[6] 2 Paige (N. Y.) 267 (1830).

[7] 11 South. Rep. (Ala.) 836 (1892); 120 Ill. 390 (1887); 122 Ill. 352 (1887); 53 Ind. 258 (1876); 54 Ind. 380 (1876); 29 Iowa 184 (1887); 30 Iowa 131 (1870); 11 La. Ann. 34 (1856); 4 How. (Miss.) 573 (1840); 3 S. & M. (Miss.) 781 (1844); 1 O. St. 409 (1853); 3 Ore. 389 (1872); 7 Watts (Pa.) 126 (1838); 12 Wis. 453 (1863); *contra*, 49 Iowa 234 (1878); 10 Bush (Ky.) 115 (1873); 69 Miss. 770 (1892); 16 S. E. Rep. (N. C.) 325 (1892).

[8] 15 Ves. (Eng.) 120 (1808); 2 Dea. & Ch. (Eng.) 12 (1832); 1 L. J., N. S., Bky. (Eng.) 73 (1832); 8 Moore P. C. (Eng.) 227 (1853); 30 L. J., C. P. (Eng.) 193 (1861); 25 Amer. Rep. 253; 26 Amer. Rep. 583 (1877); 61 Ala. 507 (1878); 18 Ark. 456 (1857); 47 Ga. 82 (1872); 79 Ga. 356 (1887); 87 Ill. 513 (1877); 90 Ill. 492 (1878); 100 Ill. 611 (1881); 110 Ill. 390 (1884); 17 Bradw. (Ill.) 539 (1885); 113 Ill. 382 (1885); 120 Ill. 390 (1887); 121 Ill. 119 (1887); 132 Ill. 550 (1890);

broker for making the loan, or to any one other than the lender.[1] Commissions may be a cover for usury.[2] In this matter of commissions, as well as in similar circumstances, the intent of the parties must govern, and that intent is a matter of fact to be found by a jury, as to whether it is an adequate compensation, or usurious interest under the name of commission, etc.[3] Such contracts are viewed with great jealousy, as they are liable to be perverted to usurious purposes. It is not usurious for the agent of the lender to divide commissions with the agent of the borrower.[4] And the agent of the lender, even with the lender's knowledge, may be paid a proper commission, and it will not be usurious.[5] But if the lender negotiates the loan himself, and retains commission, it is usurious.[6]

It will not be usurious, however, if a broker gives a portion of his commission to the lender.[7]

133 Ill. 199 (1890); 46 Iowa 32 (1876); 46 Iowa 319 (1877); 51 Iowa 297 (1879); 7 Paige (N. Y.) 413 (1839); 10 Paige (N. Y.) 94 (1843); 3 Sandf. Ch. (N. Y.) 564 (1846); 11 Barb. (N. Y.) 80 (1851); 20 How. Pr. (N. Y.) 519 (1861); 21 How. Pr. (N. Y.) 404 (1861); 69 N. Y. 597 (1877); 70 N. Y. 239 (1877); 7 Watts (Pa.) 126 (1838); 45 Tenn. 497 (1868); 85 Va. 390 (1888). See 92 N. C. 450 (1885).

[1] 21 How. (U. S.) 414 (1858); 90 Ill. 492 (1878); 6 Bradw. (Ill.) 523 (1880); 66 Miss. 365 (1889); 4 Stew. (N. J.) 40 (1879); 1 Johns. Ch. (N. Y.) 6 (1814); 7 Johns. Ch. (N. Y.) 69 (1823); 20 How. Pr. (N. Y.) 519 (1861); 21 How. Pr. (N. Y.) 404 (1861); 76 N. Y. 614 (1879).

[2] 50 Iowa 596 (1879); 35 Minn. 513 (1886).

[3] 4 M. & S. (Eng.) 92 (1815); Holt (Eng.) 256 (1816); 17 Ala. 774 (1850); 18 Ala. 552 (1851); 2 Day (Conn.) 483 (1807); 2 Conn. 341 (1817); 8 Conn. 513 (1831); 14 Conn. 591 (1842); 30 Conn. 175 (1861); 46 Iowa 46 (1877); 1 Pick. (Mass.) 288 (1823); 59 Vt. 569 (1887). See 1 Hill (N. Y.) 224 (1843).

[4] 56 Iowa 426 (1881).

[5] 89 Mo. 375 (1886).

[6] 50 Iowa 596 (1879).

[7] 53 How. Pr. (N. Y.) 319 (1877).

Neither is it usurious for a lender to retain what he has been obliged to pay for the cost of exchange[1] in making the loan. It is usurious if the taker makes a profit from it,[2] or it is done to evade the usury law.[3] But a loan is not rendered usurious by the general advantage obtained by the lender by means of the difference of exchange between the place of the loan and the place of payment, both of which are within the state;[4] even though it is made to be discounted in the particular place for the purpose of enabling the person discounting it to make a profit by the rate of exchange.[5]

Neither is it usurious to contract for premiums;[6] nor to retain the amount paid, or to be paid, for taxes[7] generally, state tax on loan,[8] travelling expenses to see security,[9] attorney's fee for examining title,[10] etc.,[11] and other expenses;[12]

[1] 48 Ga. 9 (1873); 82 Ga. 312 (1889); 52 Ill. 130 (1869); 10 Wend. (N. Y.) 116 (1833); 10 Paige (N. Y.) 109 (1843); 12 N. Y. (2 Kern.) 223 (1855); 19 N. Y. (5 Smith) 245 (1859); 34 Barb. (N. Y.) 336 (1861); 46 Barb. (N. Y.) 98 (1866); 52 N. Y. 649 (1873); 25 O. St. 413 (1874); 17 Wis. 157 (1863); 26 Wis. 473 (1870); *contra*, 7 Blf. (Ind.) 105 (1844); 17 Iowa 436 (1864).

[2] 34 Barb. (N. Y.) 336 (1861).

[3] 13 O. 1 (1844); 12 Wis. 480 (1860); 13 Wis. 216 (1860); 16 Wis. 22 (1862).

[4] 33 N. Y. 613 (1865).

[5] 13 Barb. (N. Y.) 339 (1851); 19 N. Y. (5 Smith) 134, 245 (1859).

[6] 3 Mar. (Ky.) 174 (1820); 7 Mass. 433 (1811).

[7] 114 Ill. 133 (1885); 24 Md. 62 (1865); 33 Hun (N. Y.) 415 (1884).

[8] 13 Ala. 779 (1848).

[9] 55 Iowa 555 (1881).

[10] 43 Minn. 517 (1890); 3 Stew. (N. J.) 543 (1879); 4 Stew. (N. J.) 40, 375 (1879); 85 Va. 390 (1888).

[11] 21 S. W. Rep. (Tex.) 946 (1892).

[12] 21 S. W. Rep. (Ark.) 478 (1893); 103 Ill. 362 (1882); 46 Iowa 46 (1877); 21 Denio (N. Y.) 119 (1846); 2 Keyes (N. Y.) 41 (1865); 38 N. Y. 281 (1868); 76 N. Y. 614 (1879); 7 Watts (Pa.) 126 (1838). Paying another's commission. 51 Ala. 336 (1874).

and the amount of brokerage, even if the lender is a stockholder of the debtor corporation.[1]

It is not usurious to contract for a large rate of interest where the lender runs an extraordinary risk;[2] as it is then not interest.[3] The risk must be a real one,[4] something greater than the common risk of death or insolvency of the borrower; and in determining whether or not it is such the transaction will be subjected to the most searching scrutiny,[5] as there are circumstances under which it would be usurious.[6] In consequence of this exception to the law of usury, bottomry is not generally affected by the usury statute,[7] because there is a real risk there.

Upon a loan of money, the retaining by the lender, with the assent of the borrower, of a sum out of the amount loaned for services rendered by the lender to the borrower, and not for the use of the money, does not make the transaction usurious.[8]

To pay the lender the discount that he loses in selling a former note to raise money for the borrower is not usury.[9]

In rebuttal of the defence of usury the fact that some interest was lost on the money loaned by withdrawing it from the savings bank, however, is of no force when the loan is made for no defined term of credit, but is payable pres-

[1] 85 Va. 390 (1888).

[2] 2 Jur. (Eng.) 98 (1838); 51 Ala. 336 (1874); 64 Ala. 527 (1879); 65 Ala. 511 (1880); 82 Ala. 315 (1886); 85 Ala. 379 (1888); 92 Ala. 135, 161 (1890); 4 Del. Ch. 198 (1871); 101 Ill. 523 (1882); 15 Bradw. (Ill.) 369 (1884); 9 Dana (Ky.) 313 (1840); 25 Hun (N. Y.) 121 (1881).

[3] 8 Conn. 513 (1831); 48 Ga. 9 (1873).

[4] 7 How. (Miss.) 508 (1843); 2 Paige (N. Y.) 267 (1830).

[5] 4 Del. Ch. 198 (1871); 14 Ill. 103 (1852); 6 Mon. (Ky.) 554 (1828).

[6] 85 Ala. 379, 394 (1888).

[7] 1 Atk. (Eng.) 341 (1750); 2 Ves. sr. (Eng.) 143 (1751); 32 N. Y. 571 (1865).

[8] 53 N. W. Rep. (Minn.) 648 (1892).

[9] 61 Iowa 271 (1883).

ently, and might be demanded at once, or suffered to run for years, drawing all the time the usurious rate.[1]

Neither is it usurious to agree to have certain profits of the business in which the loan is used for the use of it;[2] unless the agreement is to receive a share of the profits beside the legal interest on the loan, when it is usurious.[3]

(*b*) *Frequent payments of interest.* A contract is not made usurious by the interest on it being payable quarterly, semi-annually, or for any period less than a year.[4]

(*c*) *Compound interest.* An agreement to make interest principal after it has become due, either expressly or impliedly, or the taking of compound interest, is not usury.[5] If the interest is not due (where a contract for compound interest is allowed) it is usurious, whether the contract for the compound interest was made at the same time as

[1] 32 N. E. Rep. (N. Y.) 635 (1892).

[2] 12 South. Rep. (Miss.) 145 (1892); 9 Paige (N. Y.) 334 (1841); 22 Barb. (N. Y.) 118 (1856); 108 N. Y. 187 (1888).

[3] 19 La. 185 (1841); 32 N. E. Rep. (N. Y.) 13 (1892).

[4] 44 Conn. 493 (1877); 31 Ill. 490 (1863); 8 Blf. (Ind.) 67 (1846); 2 Ind. 631 (1851); 34 Ind. 115 (1870); 1 Met. (Ky.) 664 (1858); 5 Paige (N. Y.) 98 (1835); 24 Wend. (N. Y.) 164 (1840); 25 O. St. 622 (1874); 3 Wis. 443 (1854).

[5] 14 Amer. Rep. 352 (1874); 6 Ark. 463 (1846); 18 Ark. 9 (1856); 46 Ark. 50 (1885); 11 Conn. 487 (1834); 48 Conn. 116 (1880); 13 Fla. 451, 482 (1871); 37 Ga. 384 (1867); 79 Ga. 213 (1887); 109 Ill. 151 (1883); 124 Ill. 488 (1888); 132 Ill. 550 (1890); 92 Ind. 96 (1883); 60 Iowa 79 (1882); 2 B. Mon. (Ky.) 336 (1842); 5 La. Ann. 615 (1850); 12 La. Ann. 20, 723 (1857); 1 Fairf. (Me.) 315 (1833); 16 Neb. 12 (1884); 54 N. W. Rep. (Neb.) 129 (1893); 3 N. H. 40 (1824); 1 Wend. (N. Y.) 521 (1828); 1 Barb. (N. Y.) 627 (1847); 3 Barb. (N. Y.) 222 (1848); 55 N. Y. 621 (1874); 6 Jones L. (N. C.) 582 (1859); 3 O. 17 (1827); 4 O. 363 (1831); 17 O. 336 (1848); 46 O. St. 345 (1889); 4 Yeates (Pa.) 220 (1805); 3 Brev. (S. C.) 417 (1814); 41 Tenn. 233 (1860); 45 Tenn. 497, 584 (1868); 57 Tenn. 490 (1870); 58 Tenn. 46 (1870); 5 Tex. 171 (1849); 23 Tex. 308 (1859); 53 Tex. 559 (1880); 43 Vt. 249 (1870); 24 W. Va. 634 (1884); 31 W. Va. 410 (1888); 3 Wis. 443 (1854); 12 Wis. 453 (1863); 28 Wis. 416 (1871); *contra*, 68 Ind. 181 (1879); 70 Ind. 373 (1880); 76 N. C. 314 (1877).

the original agreement or at any time before the interest became due.[1] In such cases, to determine whether or not the interest exceeds the legal rate both the simple and compound interest are added together.[2] Neither are quarterly rests usurious.[3] Simple interest paid for the forbearance of usury is not therefore usury.[4] The court in West Virginia holds that compound interest paid for forbearance is usury.[5]

(*d*) *Interest on condition, etc.* If it is uncertain at the time of making the contract what the interest will amount to, whether more or less than the legal rate, it is not usurious.[6] Where interest is payable on a contingency,[7] or, by the terms of the contract, payment by a day certain may avoid any stipulated usury, the contract is not usurious,[8] the interest in the latter case being regarded as a penalty for the default, and not as interest.[9] But when the debt cannot be discharged by payment of the debt and lawful interest thereon it is usurious.[10] Upon the same principle an illegal rate of interest after maturity is not

[1] 35 Ark. 52 (1879); 85 Ill. 102 (1877); 108 Ill. 633 (1884); 134 Ill. 294 (1890); 28 Neb. 358 (1889); 51 N. W. Rep. (Neb.) 753 (1892).

[2] 51 N. W. Rep. (Neb.) 753 (1892).

[3] 2 Halst. Ch. (N. J.) 625 (1848); 4 Halst. Ch. (N. J.) 795 (1853).

[4] 15 N. H. 52 (1844).

[5] 24 W. Va. 634 (1884).

[6] 6 Cow. (N. Y.) 653 (1827).

[7] 1 Wall. (U. S.) 604 (1863); 10 Mass. 284 (1813); 3 Gray (Mass.) 225 (1855); 106 Mass. 413 (1871); 118 Pa. St. 89 (1888).

[8] 4 Pet. (U. S.) 205 (1830); 2 Stew. (Ala.) 426 (1830); 4 Ark. 44 (1842); 1 Root (Conn.) 393 (1792); 13 Ill. 577 (1852); 26 Ill. 54 (1861); 35 Ill. 324 (1864); 39 Ill. 521 (1866); 53 Ill. 416 (1870); 78 Ill. 53 (1875); 91 Ill. 575 (1879); 4 Bradw. (Ill.) 338 (1879); 108 Ill. 633 (1884); 7 Ind. 416 (1856); 11 Bush (Ky.) 189 (1874); 5 La. Ann. 505 (1850); 8 Mass. 257 (1811); 1 Dev. Eq. (N. C.) 433 (1830).

[9] 11 Bush (Ky.) 189 (1874); 1 Dev. Eq. (N. C.) 433 (1830); 6 Munf. (Va.) 433 (1819).

[10] 11 Bush (Ky.) 189 (1874).

usurious,[1] even if the conditional interest should then run from the date of the contract,[2] but the Iowa court will not allow more than the legal rate.[3] Parties cannot take advantage of this rule and make their notes payable only one day after date, and stipulate therein that if they are not then paid they shall draw interest at an usurious rate, it being so plainly the intention of the parties that such notes are not to be paid at maturity, and that it is a cover for usury, that they are deemed to be usurious.[4]

(*e*) *Made payable in another state.* Parties can agree to make a contract payable in another state from that in which either of them resides, even for the purpose of reserving the interest of that state, the laws of which allow a larger rate.[5]

(*f*) *Ante-date interest.* A note bearing interest from a time prior to its date is not usurious on its face;[6] and it is not usurious if the borrower is responsible for interest on the loan before the date of the note.[7]

(*g*) *Ante-dated notes.* Notes dated, to evade the usury law, before the loans are made are usurious.[8] The court in Wisconsin has decided that it is not usurious to give in payment for several claims for interest which fell due at various times a single note bearing interest from the average of those times.[9]

[1] Mor. (Iowa) 425 (1844); 1 G. Gr. (Iowa) 128 (1848); 3 Iowa 244 (1856); 10 Iowa 432 (1860); 29 Iowa 120 (1870); *contra*, 12 Rob. (La.) 178 (1845).

[2] 25 Iowa 28 (1868).

[3] 3 Iowa 244 (1856); 21 Iowa 326 (1866).

[4] 25 Ill. 218 (1861); 35 Ill. 324 (1864); 53 Ill. 416 (1870).

[5] 35 Ala. 580 (1860); 29 Ind. 158 (1867).

[6] 7 Wall. (U. S.) 499 (1868); 4 Pick. (Mass.) 173 (1826); 28 Tex. 322 (1866); 17 Wis. 297 (1863).

[7] 87 N. Y. 50 (1881); 1 McC. (S. C.) 145 (1821).

[8] 68 Iowa 255 (1885); 3 Gr. (N. J.) 255, 258 (1836); 14 Wis. 648 (1861).

[9] 20 Wis. 275 (1866).

(*h*) *Reckoning time.* Calling thirty days a month is not usurious, if done in good faith.[1]

(*i*) *Trifling amount of usury.* Where the amount of usury received is insignificant, as, for instance, only two cents over the legal amount, the court should not let the case go to the jury, as it is too trifling,[2] but presume it to be an error in calculation.[3]

The long-continued practice of banks taking interest according to printed tables not exactly correct, without objection, may be conclusive of good faith in taking interest.[4]

(*j*) *Interest in advance.* Taking or reserving interest at the time of making the loan, or at any time before it becomes due is not usury.[5] This rule exists rather from necessity than principle.[6] Reserving is the same as taking, except when penalties are to be inflicted upon the lender when they may be different, as where the statute applies to the *taking* and not to the *reserving* of interest.[7]

[1] 12 Pick. (Mass.) 586 (1832); 2 Harr. (N. J.) 487 (1840).

[2] 10 G. & J. (Md.) 299 (1838).

[3] 2 Cow. (N. Y.) 664, 678 (1824).

[4] 1 Vt. 399, 426, 430 (1829).

[5] 8 Wheat. (U. S.) 339 (1823); 3 Pet. (U. S.) 36 (1830); 3 How. (U. S.) 62 (1845); 141 U. S. 384 (1891); 1 Stew. (Ala.) 442 (1828); 51 Ark. 548 (1889); 2 MacArt. (D. C.) 371 (1876); 16 S. E. Rep. (Ga.) 710 (1892); 4 Scam. (Ill.) 21 (1842); 31 Ill. 490 (1863); 77 Ill. 525 (1875); 110 Ill. 235, 390 (1884); 132 Ill. 550 (1890); 8 Blf. (Ind.) 67 (1846); 2 Ind. 631 (1851); 14 Ind. 401 (1860); 34 Ind. 115 (1870); 53 N. W. Rep. (Iowa) 410 (1892); 7 Kas. 405 (1871); 12 W. P. D. Bush (Ky.) 57 (1876); 7 Rob. (La.) 539 (1844); 12 Pick. (Mass.) 586 (1832); 54 N. W. Rep. (Neb.) 129 (1893); 15 Johns. (N. Y.) 162 (1818); 2 Cow. (N. Y.) 664, 678, 712, 766 (1824); 4 Wend. (N. Y.) 652 (1830); 12 N. Y. (2 Kern.) 223 (1855); 19 N. Y. (5 Smith) 245 (1859); 30 Hun (N. Y.) 201 (1883); 1 Dev. L. (N. C.) 100 (1826); 30 S. C. 61 (1888); 40 Tenn. 723 (1859); 2 Grat. (Va.) 372 (1845); *contra*, 8 Allen (Mass.) 78 (1864).

[6] 40 Tenn. 723 (1859).

[7] 9 Pet. (U. S.) 378 (1835), overruling 2 Pet. (U. S.) 527 (1829).

It is, however, usurious to deduct in advance interest on interest payable at a future day.[1]

(*k*) *Charging market rates on time bills.* Banks can charge market rates on time bills.[2]

(*l*) *Time price higher than cash price.* If the time price of goods is higher than the cash price, with lawful interest thereon,[3] it is not usurious,[4] unless it is a device to cover usury.[5]

(*m*) *Fluctuating values.* A contract to return in autumn a certain quantity of corn, usurious in amount, is not illegal, because corn fluctuates in value, and it cannot be reckoned in advance.[6] So, a "note" payable "in Baltimore bank notes with twelve and a half per cent. interest" is not usurious.[7] Where a bank's notes are payable in bills of another state, upon a renewal of the loan it is not usurious to take a premium equal to the difference between those bills and other bills current at the place of the bank.[8] If it is payable in money, or in United States notes, or gold coin, it is usurious.[9] If the value of the bills is uncertain, there is no usury;[10] and so, if for the loan of five thousand dollars and labor, the debtor promises to board and lodge the lender's family it is not usurious.[11]

[1] 30 S. C. 61 (1888).

[2] 13 How. (U. S.) 151 (1851).

[3] 15 Ind. 50 (1860); 23 Iowa 185 (1867); 28 Iowa 220 (1869).

[4] 1 Black (U. S.) 115 (1861); 75 Ga. 739 (1885); 1 Duv. (Ky.) 359 (1864); 4 N. Y. (4 Comst.) 225 (1850); 72 Tenn. 145 (1879). See page 205.

[5] 9 Paige (N. Y.) 211 (1841).

[6] 12 Fla. 532 (1869); 59 Ga. 292 (1877); 19 Ill. 132 (1857).

[7] 14 Ill. 103 (1852).

[8] 7 Mass. 433 (1811).

[9] 57 Ill. 534 (1871).

[10] 1 J. J. Mar. (Ky.) 494 (1829); 7 J. J. Mar. (Ky.) 37 (1831).

[11] 10 C. E. Gr. (N. J.) 491 (1875); 12 C. E. Gr. (N. J.) 489 (1875).

(n) *Security for first loan when making second.* Insisting upon security for a former loan, as a condition for a subsequent one does not render either loan usurious, unless the object is to obtain a larger premium or compensation for either of the loans than the law allows.[1]

(o) *Payment of usurious interest by stranger at debtor's request.* Where a debtor borrows money with which to pay a usurious debt, there is no usurious taint in the new contract because of the usury in the old, even if the second lender knows the purpose for which it is to be used:[2] and it is the same if the original claim is void for usury.[3] So, if a third party gives, instead of money, his note to the original creditor in payment of the usurious loan there is no usury in the new note.[4] An administrator has been held to be such a third party, in a case where he gave his personal note for a debt due from his intestate, which included usurious interest, he not being allowed to set up the usury in the original contract.[5] If a surety pays an usurious debt at the debtor's request, by giving his own note therefor, there is no usury in the new contract between the surety and the debtor.[6]

So a promise made by A to pay B money if B will forbear suing C is not usurious as it is not between the parties to the subject matter.[7]

If, however, money, with which to pay a valid debt,

[1] 27 Conn. 432 (1858).

[2] 116 U. S. 98 (1885); 15 Ind. 257 (1860); 17 Iowa 436 (1864); 18 Iowa 546 (1865); 56 Iowa 532 (1881); 53 N. W. Rep. (Iowa) 410 (1892); 54 N. W. Rep. (Iowa) 266 (1893); 4 Lans. (N. Y.) 507 (1871); 83 Va. 659 (1887).

[3] 17 Ind. 77 (1861).

[4] 5 Allen (Mass.) 165 (1862); 61 N. H. 121 (1881).

[5] 8 N. H. 276 (1836).

[6] 90 Ill. 283 (1878); 25 Kas. 479 (1881); 18 S. W. Rep. (Ky.) 1034 (1892).

[7] 52 Vt. 421 (1880).

is borrowed at an usurious rate, and the collateral of the valid debt is assigned to the second lender, the latter will not be secure from the effect of the usury on the collateral.[1]

If C borrows money of B, at an usurious rate of interest to loan A, at A's request, C cannot recover of A the usury paid by him to B.[2]

(*p*) *Oppressive contracts.* There is a well settled distinction between usurious and oppressive contracts at both law and equity.[3] A contract is not fraudulent for usury unless the usury is so excessive as to render the debt a simulated one.[4]

III. CONTRACTS TO EFFECT USURIOUS CONTRACTS.

Usury affects a contract,[5] and can be recovered,[6] as long as it can be traced; that is, it affects all subsequent contracts of which it is the basis.[7]

A note given by an indorser to an indorsee to take up the indorsed paper does not make a new contract, or wipe out the usury in the prior note; and on the subsequent discovery of the usury the maker of the second note can avoid it.[8]

Although a judgment cannot generally be impeached for usury, yet the consideration of a recognizance or statute acknowledgment of a debt may.[9] So a bill of sale in a trover suit may be attacked by the defendant by showing usury.[10]

[1] 41 Ill. 31 (1866).
[2] 70 Tenn. 137 (1878).
[3] 11 Conn. 487 (1836).
[4] 45 Ala. 582 (1871).
[5] 62 Pa. St. 481 (1869); 109 Pa. St. 625 (1885).
[6] 81 Ky. 129 (1883).
[7] 78 Tex. 478 (1890).
[8] 27 Wis. 177 (1870).
[9] 5 Greenl. (Me.) 374 (1828).
[10] 81 Ga. 81 (1888).

(*a*) *Subsequent security.* Where the original contract is usurious, any subsequent one made to carry it into effect and obtain the fruits of it,[1] or given in payment and discharge thereof,[2] is also usurious; including securities subsequently given[3] in renewal to the same extent as the debt itself;[4] and it makes no difference whether the party in whose name the substituted security is given was privy to, or ignorant of the original corrupt agreement or not;[5] nor whether it be given by the debtor or a third person,[6] or to the administrator of the original lender;[7] there being in each case no new consideration.[8] So a mere change of securities to the same person who reserved the usury does not purge the original consideration of it,[9] whether in renewal or payment of the loan.[10]

(*b*) *Renewal.* A new contract substituted for an usurious one is affected by the usury[11] to the same extent as

[1] 1 Campb. (Eng.) 165 (1807); 13 Pet. (U. S.) 345 (1839); 2 Conn. 276 (1817); 4 Hous. (Del.) 475 (1873); 1 Kelley (Ga.) 392. 416 (1846); 2 Shepl. (Me.) 240 (1837); 9 Shepl. (Me.) 184 (1842); 122 Mass. 495 (1877); 20 Johns. (N. Y.) 285 (1822); 9 Cow. (N. Y.) 647 (1823); 13 Wend. (N. Y.) 505 (1835); 2 Denio (N. Y.) 621 (1846); 3 Sandf. Ch. (N. Y.) 313 (1846); 5 N. Y. (1 Seld.) 178 (1851). The security of a judgment is not affected by usury in the debt on which the judgment was obtained, says the court in 2 Cai. (N. Y.) 150 (1804).

[2] 62 Pa. St. 481 (1869). See pages 226 and 248.

[3] 3 How. (U. S.) 62 (1845); 72 Ga. 807 (1884); 11 Neb. 465 (1881); 24 Neb. 630 (1888); 33 N. Y. 55 (1865). Payments are to be applied *pro tanto* to debt and security. 11 Neb. 465 (1881); 24 Neb. 630 (1888).

[4] 59 Ga. 546 (1877); 72 Ga. 807 (1884). See page 225.

[5] 5 Conn. 154 (1823).

[6] 35 Barb. (N. Y.) 96 (1861).

[7] 5 Strob. (S. C.) 154 (1850).

[8] 35 Barb. (N. Y.) 96 (1861).

[9] 57 Ala. 108 (1876).

[10] 61 Ala. 507 (1878).

[11] 11 Bush (Ky.) 393, 399 (1875); 5 G. & J. (Md.) 23 (1832); 2 Md. Ch. 201 (1850); 37 Minn. 441 (1887); 62 Pa. St. 481 (1869).

the old one;[1] as where new notes are given for old ones. There must be the same promisor,[2] though the promisee may be the personal representative of the original payee.[3] But usury is not a defence to a suit on a note, when the maker renewed it in the hands of a subsequent holder, who gave full value for it, and who had no knowledge of the usury.[4]

If any part of the original usury is carried into the new note it is usurious.[5]

Where two or more notes are given in payment of a note and usurious interest upon it, it is presumed that the usurious interest entered into the consideration of each of the notes in proportion to their relative amounts.[6] So, if the two notes are given, one for the principal and the other for the interest, and the latter is renewed annually.[7]

If a note is given in payment of a balance due on an usurious note, it is usurious;[8] even in the hands of a party to whom it was given as security, which usury an indorser can plead in defence of an action against him.[9]

[1] 23 Ala. 537 (1853); 5 Conn. 154 (1823); 45 Ill. 178 (1867); 60 Ill. 367 (1871); 3 Mar. (Ky.) 419 (1821); 1 Duv. (Ky.) 239 (1864); 78 Ky. 513 (1880); 10 S. & M. (Miss.) 89 (1848); 9 Stew. (N. J.) 612 (1883); 20 Johns. (N. Y.) 285 (1822); 9 Cow. (N. Y.) 647 (1823); 13 Wend. (N. Y.) 505 (1835); 2 Denio (N. Y.) 621 (1846); 2 Sandf. Ch. (N. Y.) 313 (1846); 5 N. Y. (1 Seld.) 178 (1851); 51 N. Y. 43 (1872); 12 O. 153 (1843); 1 Dall. (Pa.) 216 (1787); 85 Pa. St. 376 (1877); 2 Desau. (S. C.) 333 (1806); 2 Speer (S. C.) 83 (1843); 81 Tex. 57 (1891); 53 Vt. 501 (1881); 16 Wis. 22 (1862).

[2] 89 Pa. St. 328 (1879).

[3] 5 N. H. 376 (1831); 60 N. H. 452 (1881); 5 Strob (S. C.) 151 (1850).

[4] 59 Ala. 179 (1877); 2 Conn. 132, 134 (1816); 1 Barb. Ch. (N. Y.) 43 (1845); 14 Hun (N. Y.) 414 (1878); 21 Vt. 123 (1849). See page 248.

[5] 13 Ala. 121 (1848).

[6] 3 Mon. (Ky.) 347 (1824); 12 Shepl. (Me.) 33 (1845); 1 Red. (Me.) 414 (1850).

[7] 22 Ala. 262 (1853).

[8] 12 Iowa 364 (1861); 24 Iowa 441 (1868); 52 Iowa 114 (1879); 19 S. W. Rep. (Ky.) 171 (1892); 1 Greenl. (Me.) 167 (1821); 12 Shepl. (Me.) 33 (1845); *contra*, 2 Halst. (N. J.) 130 (1824).

[9] 1 Greenl. (Me.) 167 (1821); 12 Shepl. (Me.) 33 (1845).

If the usury in the original note is first deducted, and the new note is then given for the principal and legal interest only it is valid.[1]

If a note tainted with usury is renewed by a series of subsequent notes, each renewal being accompanied by a new payment of usury, the forfeiture therefor is for all the usurious interest paid and it will be deducted[2] against an indorsee for value and before maturity of the last note.[3]

The Illinois court holds that a subsequent promise to pay the usurious interest in a contract is invalid.[4]

If usurious notes in a running account are renewed, the usury affects all the items.[5]

Usury does not vitiate a note given by the party on whom the usury is practised to a creditor of the usurer, in discharge of a lawful debt due by such usurer, the creditor having no knowledge of the usury.[6]

Where an usurious indebtedness has been paid in full and discharged, notes subsequently given in partial revival of such indebtedness are not usurious.[7] In a Kentucky case, decided some years ago, A enjoined a judgment obtained against him by B on the ground that it was for usurious interest which had been reserved in various transactions between them, C proposed to A to lend him money at an usurious rate of interest and pay the cost of the injunction, if A would discontinue his proceedings for an

[1] 13 Ala. 121 (1848); 3 Day (Conn.) 356 (1809); 3 Mon. (Ky.) 347 (1824). See page 247.

[2] 83 Ind. 436 (1882); 21 S. W. Rep. (Ky.) 1050 (1893); 2 Allen (Mass.) 551 (1861); *contra*, 98 U. S. 555 (1878); 104 U. S. 52 (1881); 10 Mass. 121 (1813).

[3] 2 Allen (Mass.) 551 (1861).

[4] 106 Ill. 99 (1883); 108 Ill. 633 (1884).

[5] 63 Miss. 231 (1885).

[6] 3 Lit. (Ky.) 5 (1823).

[7] 57 Iowa 39 (1881).

injunction. A agreed to the proposition, and executed a note to C for the money, which was then advanced, and the agreed interest, and also gave him an order to his counsel directing the dismission of the suit, "as B had satisfied him in full." Within five days thereafter C assigned the note, without recourse, to B, who says he then paid him the said sum of money. Suit was afterward brought, and judgment obtained, upon the note by B, and A filed a bill for an injunction against the suit, on the ground of usury, and it was held that he could set up usury in the last judgment.[1] The Kentucky court holds generally that usury may be pleaded in defence to notes given for judgments obtained on usurious consideration.[2]

Sureties have the same right on renewal notes as on the originals.[3]

Where a principal becomes insolvent, and his sureties obtain indulgence from the creditor by agreeing to pay ten per cent interest per annum, which they do, and then take a note of their principal for payment, including the ten per cent interest paid by them, the Kentucky court holds that the last note is usurious.[4]

Additional security. A legal note given in renewal of a prior note infected with usury, with different or additional parties as securities, is legal.[5] So, if the unlawful interest has been paid, and a new note is afterward given for the principal and legal interest, endorsed by a stranger as security. And if they afterward take up the note, giving their own therefor, the makers of the last note cannot have the usurious interest originally paid deducted when suit is

[1] 5 B. Mon. (Ky.) 18 (1844).

[2] 1 Mon. (Ky.) 266 (1824); 7 Mon. (Ky.) 353 (1828).

[3] 39 Ind. 106 (1872).

[4] 2 Lit. (Ky.) 326 (1822).

[5] 77 Ill. 525 (1875); 5 G. & J. (Md.) 23 (1832); 2 Md. Ch. 201 (1850); 11 Paige (N.Y.) 635 (1845); 79 Va. 458 (1884).

brought on the last note.[1] If, however, any part of the unlawful interest is included in the new security, it is to that extent without consideration.[2]

(c) *Absolute deed.* If a transaction is a loan, an absolute deed given for its security will be construed to be a mortgage, and affected by the usury in the loan.[3]

As between the parties to such a deed, it may be avoided[4] by parol proof of the usury;[5] and the rule is the same if the grantee quitclaims the property to a third party, who knows of the usury.[6] So, it may be shown as a defence to a bill of foreclosure.[7]

(d) *Forbearance.* When unlawful interest has been reserved or received for forbearance of an originally valid debt, the original agreement or security, is not avoided by the subsequent usurious agreement for forbearance,[8] notwithstanding the security may have been changed;[9] and it is only affected as a payment upon it of the amount paid for the forbearance.[10]

(e) *Novation.* In the novation of a debt, the rate of interest of the old contract may be agreed upon, notwithstanding the legal rate may have been reduced below the contract rate before the novation took place.[11]

[1] 9 Mich. 21 (1860); 10 Mich. 148 (1862).

[2] 10 Mich. 148 (1862).

[3] 50 N. Y. 437 (1872); 84 N. Y. 627 (1881). See 59 Barb. (N. Y.) 651 (1870) and 14 Hun (N. Y.) 537 (1878).

[4] 67 Ga. 713 (1881); 70 Ga. 831 (1883).

[5] 7 Conn. 409 (1829); 39 Iowa 519 (1874).

[6] 53 Vt. 202 (1880).

[7] 8 Conn. 35 (1830); 53 Vt. 202 (1880).

[8] 3 La. 401 (1832); 5 La. Ann. 505 (1850); 35 Minn. 513 (1886); 44 Minn. 218 (1890); 3 N. H. 185 (1825); 7 Paige (N. Y.) 413 (1839); 8 Paige (N. Y.) 518 (1841).

[9] 3 N. H. 185 (1825).

[10] 17 Iowa 64, 578 (1864).

[11] 2 Geo. (Miss.) 260 (1856).

Where a novation is by a new party being introduced for a year, and then released by consent of all, and the old contract resumed, it is still affected by the original usury.[1]

So usury on an old debt, if included in a new, on a novation, entitles the debtor to a deduction for such usury, in a suit on the new contract,[2] in a case where only a part of the makers signed the new note.

(*f*) *Awards, decrees and judgments.* Unless statutes give the right, borrowers cannot generally set up usury in judgments, etc., obtained on usurious contracts. For a full discussion of the law on this subject, see page 295.

IV. SUBSEQUENT CONTRACTS FOR USURY.

(*a*) *To pay.* A contract which, in its inception, is unaffected by usury cannot be invalidated by any subsequent usurious transaction or security.[3] So, such a contract is not affected by a subsequent agreement to pay usury in consideration of forbearance;[4] and where a valid note is discounted at an usurious rate of interest, and the defendant afterward pays the interest and a part of the principal, and gives a new valid note for the residue, the new note is not infected with the usury.[5]

Where a purchase-money mortgage is set aside for usury

[1] 59 Ga. 546 (1877).

[2] 11 Bush (Ky.) 393 (1875).

[3] 1 Pet. (U. S.) 37 (1828); 7 Pet. (U. S.) 103 (1833); 19 S. W. Rep. (Ark.) 968 (1892); 3 Gr. (N. J.) 255, 258 (1836), 509 (1834); 3 Gr. Ch. (N. J.) 128 (1837); 2 Beas. (N. J.) 66 (1860); 1 McCart. (N. J.) 153 (1861); 1 C. E. Gr. (N. J.) 445 (1863); 2 Cai. Cas. (N. Y.) 66 (1805); 19 Johns. (N. Y.) 294 (1822); 13 Wend. (N. Y.) 505 (1835); 4 Sandf. Ch. (N. Y.) 312 (1846); 13 Barb. (N. Y.) 561 (1852); 33 Barb. (N. Y.) 657 (1861); 41 Barb. (N. Y.) 359 (1864); 44 Barb. (N. Y.) 87, 321 (1865); 39 N. Y. 28, 325 (1868); 55 N. Y. 643 (1873); 4 Daly (N. Y.) 418 (1873); 2 Bail. (S. C.) 574 (1832); 3 Wis. 725 (1854).

[4] 79 Ala. 76 (1885); 83 Ala. 323 (1887); 9 Ga. 30 (1850).

[5] 2 Halst. (N. J.) 130 (1824).

the original debt is not invalidated, and remains an equitable lien upon the property.[1]

The subsequent contract is of course usurious so far as itself is concerned; as, for example, an agreement to pay usurious interest for further forbearance of an existing debt,[2] or for past forbearance.[3] Such subsequent agreement for forbearance will not discharge a surety on the original valid contract, however.[4] An usurious security given for a legal one is also usurious,[5] but the claim is valid.[6]

Subsequent payments of usurious interest are regarded as partial payments on the debt and legal interest.[7]

The indorsement of a note for an usurious consideration does not vitiate the note itself, and is valid to pass title to the indorsee, who can collect it of the maker, says the court of Wisconsin.[8]

(*b*) *To receive.* If there was originally a legal consideration the subsequent taking of an usurious instrument as security does not impair the original contract.[9] It is the same with the subsequent receipt of usurious interest.[10]

Where a promisor in an usurious contract makes it the consideration of a new contract with a third person, not a party to the original contract, or to the usury paid or reserved in it, and the new contract is not a contrivance to evade the statute, the latter is not usurious.[11]

[1] 9 Paige (N. Y.) 211 (1841).
[2] 59 Vt. 75 (1886).
[3] 2 N. H. 333 (1821); 15 N. H. 91 (1844).
[4] 50 Ill. 54 (1869).
[5] 2 Grat. (Va.) 372 (1845). See page 238.
[6] 35 Vt. 503 (1863). See sureties, page 244.
[7] 79 Ala. 76 (1885).
[8] 3 Wis. 725 (1854).
[9] 13 Conn. 219 (1839).
[10] 36 Iowa 516 (1873).
[11] 116 U. S. 98 (1885).

An usurious note given in payment of a legal claim can be recovered only to the extent of the original valid principal and interest thereon up to the time of taking the illegal interest under the Florida statute which declares the interest included in an usurious contract void.[1]

If the usurious interest is taken by the original obligee it furnishes *prima facie* evidence that the agreement was corrupt.[2]

Judgment being obtained on a debt secured by deed, the creditor subsequently made a deed back to the debtor, and on execution levied, the debtor was not allowed, by the Georgia court, to then set up usury in the original deed.[3]

If a renewal note is invalid, the original contract, or what remains of the amount due upon it, if a part has been paid, continues to be valid;[4] but the holder can recover thereon only what he could on the second note.[5]

V. LEGAL CONSIDERATION OF USURIOUS CONTRACTS.

A legal instrument, debt or demand is affected only in the interest part of it, and not destroyed by being mingled with an usurious transaction as a part or the whole of its consideration;[6] and were it otherwise its redemption would purge the taint of usury.[7] Principal and legal interest of such consideration can be recovered.[8]

[1] 1 Fla. 356 (1847).

[2] 3 Gr. Ch. (N. J.) 128 (1837).

[3] 66 Ga. 102 (1880). See page 295.

[4] 21 Amer. Rep. 609 (1876); 64 N. Y. 294 (1876); 6 Hun (N. Y.) 632 (1876); 79 Va. 597 (1884).

[5] 1 Cart. (Ind.) 32 (1848); 79 Va. 597 (1884).

[6] 1 H. Bl. (Eng.) 462 (1790); 88 Ga. 209, 479 (1891); 12 Pick. (Mass.) 126 (1831); 1 Barb. (N. Y.) 36 (1847); 96 N. C. 214 (1887); 3 Grat. (Va.) 148 (1846); 6 Vt. 551 (1834).

[7] 1 Barb. (N. Y.) 36 (1847).

[8] 4 Wall. (U. S.) 572 (1866); 88 Ga. 209 (1891); 79 Va. 597 (1884).

An usurer gets no title to securities if the original contract is void in his hands, says the Ohio court;[1] and the supreme court of the United States holds that the indorsement of the note of a stranger and its delivery to a bank as collateral security for an usurious loan passes no title thereto.[2]

VI. USURIOUS INTEREST AS A CONSIDERATION.

The payment of usurious interest is sufficient to support a promise of forbearance.[3]

But a promise to pay such interest in the future is to that extent without consideration.[4]

A promise by the maker to pay usurious interest to an innocent holder of an usurious note, if he will forbear to sue, is binding, and may be enforced if the delay is given.[5]

If new notes are given by the maker to third parties, and they are assigned to the holders of the original usurious notes, they are usurious also;[6] but if new notes are given to a *bona fide* holder, usury paid to the original payee cannot be deducted from the new notes, they being deemed a payment and discharge of the old ones.[7]

Where a vendor accepts his own usurious note as part of the consideration of a contract, he does not thereby sanction the usury; and a stipulation that the price of the property which the note was given to secure shall be re-

[1] 6 O. St. 19 (1856).

[2] 1 Pet. (U. S.) 37 (1828).

[3] 71 Tex. 241 (1888); 21 Vt. 38 (1848); *contra*, a mortgage may be foreclosed before such period of forbearance is out. 8 C. E. Gr. (N. J.) 554 (1872); 12 C. E. Gr. (N. J.) 80 (1876); 90 Pa. St. 94 (1879).

[4] 23 Ind. 4 (1864).

[5] 8 Ala. 53 (1845).

[6] 1 Duv. (Ky.) 237 (1864).

[7] 1 Duv. (Ky.) 51 (1863).

duced if the usury is not allowed is not binding on the vendor.[1]

Where a surety in an execution signs a replevin bond upon an arrangement with his principal, by which the latter gives him a note binding himself to pay an increase of three per cent upon the sum replevied, in case the surety shall pay it, the transaction is usurious.[2] Where an assignor agrees with his assignee that in the event of the insolvency of the obligor in the assigned note, he will refund more than the consideration and legal interest, it is usurious.[3]

VII. SUBROGATION.

No equitable right of subrogation to securities can arise where in order to establish it resort must be had to an agreement which is void by reason of usury. For example, where A borrows money of B, and gives his absolute deed. A afterward borrows money at usurious interest of C to pay the loan, and gets B to convey the land to C. It is held that C will not be subrogated to the rights of B.[4]

VIII. PARTIES.

(*a*) *Agents.* If a person knows that he is dealing with an agent of another the law deems him to be dealing with the principal.[5]

If an agent, without authority from, knowledge of, or subsequent ratification of his principal, makes an usurious contract, the principal is not bound by it,[6] as where an

[1] 9 B. Mon. (Ky.) 468, 469 (1849).

[2] 3 Dana (Ky.) 362 (1835).

[3] 4 J. J. Mar. (Ky.) 276 (1830).

[4] 53 Ark. 273 (1890).

[5] 25 Mich. 447 (1872).

[6] 116 U. S. 98 (1885); 51 Ark. 534, 548 (1889); 54 Ark. 40 (1890); 90 Ill. 281 (1878); 51 Iowa 398 (1879); 3 Lans. (N. Y.) 34 (1870); 54 N. Y. 360 (1873); 55 Hun (N. Y.) 171 (1889); 10 Vt. 548 (1838); 16 Wis. 259 (1862); 36 Wis. 390 (1874).

agent takes two notes for the loan, one to the principal with legal interest, or with none, and the other to himself for the excess above the legal interest.[1]

When a principal learns of his agent's usurious contract he must return the excess of interest, or annul the contract.[2] The Minnesota court holds that the principal will be bound by the agent's contract if he sanction it, even when the usury is taken for the agent's own benefit.[3]

Where an usurious security, including the usury, is for a larger sum than the principal knows he ought to have, and without an explanation he accepts and has the benefit of it, it is an adoption and ratification by him.[4] But if the agent takes an absolute deed as a security it will be deemed a mortgage, and the principal by accepting the deed for the principal and legal interest does not thereby ratify the act of the agent in exacting the usury.[5] Taking a mortgage and enforcing it for the amount loaned and lawful interest, does not constitute a ratification of the agent's illegal act.[6]

The written authority of a principal to his agent to make loans does not exclude oral evidence of advice, etc.[7]

There is no presumption that an agent has authority from his principal to violate the law,[8] nor that the principal knew of the agent's act.[9] The Connecticut and Massachusetts courts hold, however, that authority to make an usurious loan is not presumed when the agency is specified and limited to a single transaction, but that it

[1] 116 U. S. 98 (1885); 33 Conn. 81 (1865).
[2] 92 N. Y. 31 (1883).
[3] 46 Minn. 360 (1891).
[4] 130 N. Y. 102 (1891).
[5] 52 N. W. Rep. (Minn.) 39 (1892).
[6] 31 Minn. 495 (1884).
[7] 46 Minn. 360 (1891).
[8] 53 Fed. Rep. (Ark.) 410 (1892).
[9] 3 Lans. (N. Y.) 34 (1870).

may be presumed when the agency is general, and the business that of making, managing and collecting the loans of a principal.[1] But, being a presumption of fact, it may be rebutted.[2]

If an agent, authorized to purchase securities, buys a note and mortgage for his principal, knowledge of the usury by the agent does not affect the principal.[3]

Liability. An agent is not excused from personal liability on an usurious contract, if he does not disclose his agency at the time the transaction occurs,[4] even though he intends the note for his principal.[5] Where a note for borrowed money is given to an agent without the borrower's knowledge of the agency, supposing the agent to be the actual lender, it is usurious, if it includes illegal interest, although it might not have been usurious between the borrower and the principal, had the principal been disclosed.[6]

An agent who has received usurious interest for his principal, and has been notified before he paid it over that he will be held personally accountable for it to the party paying it, cannot shield himself by claiming that the suit should have been brought against the principal.[7]

Bonus, etc. The decisions regarding the right of an agent to receive a bonus, etc., are not in harmony, but the following statement is believed by the writer to be correct in principle. The borrower's agent has the right to receive a bonus from him,[8] and the lender's agent has also

[1] 33 Conn. 81 (1865); 7 Gray (Mass.) 287 (1856).

[2] 33 Conn. 81 (1865).

[3] 18 Kas. 529 (1877).

[4] 23 Ala. 537 (1853); 5 Mass. 53 (1809); 43 Vt. 249 (1870).

[5] 23 Ala. 537 (1853); 3 Hawks (N. C.) 28 (1824); 3 Dev. (N. C.) 43 (1831); 43 Vt. 249 (1870).

[6] 53 Iowa 627 (1880).

[7] 60 Miss. 349 (1882).

[8] 53 Fed. Rep. (Ark.) 410 (1892).

the right to receive a bonus or compensation from the borrower, and it does not make the loan usurious to the lender,[1] even when there is an agreement between the principal and his agent that the latter may receive such bonus and nothing more for his services from his principal;[2] and it makes no difference whether the brokerage is secured separately or taken from the loan.[3] So, on forbearance.[4]

Neither is it usurious when the lender's agent is paid by the borrower for legal services, drawing papers, etc., without the knowledge of the lender.[5]

In all these cases, however, the jury have a right to consider the amount of the bonus, etc., received in the light of the value of the service performed by the agent, and if it is grossly unreasonable they can legally assume that it is for the use of the lender and therefore an usurious transaction.[6]

The fact that the lender's agent uses his power with regard to making a loan to induce the borrower to subscribe and pay for some stock in a corporation in which the agent, and not the lender, is interested, and which afterward proves worthless, does not constitute usury.[7]

[1] 28 Minn. 211 (1881); 31 Minn. 495 (1884); 33 Minn. 194 (1885); 35 Minn. 513 (1886); *contra*, 46 Minn. 360 (1891); 5 Neb. 261 (1876); 6 Neb. 151 (1877). If the principal does not know it. 1 Stew. (N. J.) 508 (1877); 2 Stew. (N. J.) 454 (1878); 14 Stew. (N. J.) 63, 92 (1886); 16 Stew. (N. J.) 15 (1887); 21 Barb. (N. Y.) 181 (1855); 21 N. Y. 219 (1860); 32 N. Y. 165 (1865); 45 Barb. (N. Y.) 422 (1865); 81 N. Y. 552 (1880); 92 N. Y. 34 (1883); 68 Tex. 593 (1887).

[2] 28 Minn. 211 (1881); 31 Minn. 495 (1884); 33 Minn. 194 (1885); 35 Minn. 513 (1886); 3 C. E. Gr. (N. J.) 481 (1867).

[3] 7 Paige (N. Y.) 413 (1839); 3 Sandf. Ch. (N. Y.) 564 (1846).

[4] 4 Stew. (N. J.) 381 (1879); *contra*, it will be usurious, 2 Va. Cas. 471 (1825).

[5] 19 Hun (N. Y.) 227 (1879).

[6] 54 N. W. Rep. (Minn.) 591 (1893).

[7] 26 Wis. 473 (1870).

The president of a bank compelled a borrower from the bank to pay him a commission in addition to the interest paid to the bank, and also to buy from him some worthless stocks, as a condition to obtaining the loan; but it did not appear that the bank received the commission or was benefited by the sale of the stock, and it was held, that, under those facts, the transactions did not render the loan usurious.[1]

Where an agent has an agreement with his principal that all commissions on loans and all bonuses payable by borrowers shall belong to the principal, he is presumed to be acting for the principal in collecting usurious interest when the principal knows of it, though the agent actually receives all such benefits.[2]

Where one trustee receives an usurious bonus for loaning money of the estate, and the other trustees know nothing of it, it does not affect the mortgage they hold.[3]

An agent cannot receive a bonus for a loan, and then loan his own money, as it is usurious.[4] Neither can he borrow the money he is lending from a third person, and be free from usury.[5]

A borrower's agent may exact a bonus, and it will not have an usurious effect upon the loan,[6] if the lender receives none of it.

An agent with whom money is deposited by his princi-

[1] 32 N. E. Rep. (Ill.) 534 (1892).

[2] 30 Pac. Rep. (N. M.) 859 (1892).

[3] 12 Hun (N. Y.) 574 (1878); 16 Hun (N. Y.) 209 (1878).

[4] 8 C. E. Gr. (N. J.) 174 (1872); 11 C. E. Gr. (N. J.) 218 (1875); 8 Cow. (N. Y.) 299 (1828); 5 Wend. (N. Y.) 181 (1830); 1 N. Y. Leg. Obs. 107 (1842); 3 N. Y. (3 Comst.) 470 (1850); 21 Barb. (N. Y.) 181 (1855).

[5] 9 Cow. (N. Y.) 647 (1823).

[6] 3 Neb. 256 (1874); 13 Neb. 157 (1882); 27 Neb. 880 (1889); 20 Wis. 407 (1866); 33 Wis. 252 (1873); 34 Wis. 550 (1874).

pal to be loaned on usurious terms cannot set up usury by way of defence in an action by his principal for the balance in his hands.[1]

A factor cannot charge a commission for advancing money, and full legal rate of interest on the money advanced, as it is then usurious.[2]

(*b*) *Banks.* Usury laws affect banks, being applicable to them generally as to individuals,[3] unless otherwise affected by statute.[4]

A clause in the charter of a bank, limiting interest on discounts, does not apply after the breach of a contract.[5]

(*c*) *Indorsers and guarantors.* If an indorsee of an usurious note fails to recover of the maker because of usury, he can collect the amount due by the note (except the costs of his action against the maker) of his indorser, who was the payee,[6] that is, the indorser cannot set up usury originally in the note;[7] but if the usury is between the indorser and indorsee he can do so.[8]

In New Jersey, where the statute declared that every usurious contract was void, it was held that if the contract between the indorser and indorsee were usurious, the latter could maintain no action against the maker or any party prior to the indorsement, although the instrument was good in its creation, because he can get no title to it by the indorsement.[9]

[1] 14 Iowa 251 (1862).

[2] 5 La. Ann. 505, 547 (1850); 12 La. Ann. 20, 723 (1857); 47 Pa. St. 485 (1864).

[3] 49 Tenn. 173 (1872); 63 Tenn. 499 (1872); 5 Rand. (Va.) 132 (1827); 10 Wis. 230 (1860); 13 Wis. 216 (1860); 18 Wis. 102 (1864).

[4] 63 Tenn. 499 (1872).

[5] 9 Wend. (N. Y.) 471 (1833).

[6] 9 Mass. 1 (1812).

[7] 6 Hill (N. Y.) 492 (1844).

[8] 2 Brev. (S. C.) 199 (1807).

[9] 2 Harr. (N. J.) 191 (1839).

Though an indorser cannot be compelled to pay more than the amount he received, with interest, yet, if he pay voluntarily, equity will not relieve.[1]

If a note stipulates for interest anterior to its date, it does not put the indorsee upon inquiry about usury.[2]

Accommodation indorsers. A stranger may legally take a bonus for his indorsement.[3]

Notes are not affected by an agreement of the maker which estops him from interposing the defence of usury.[4]

A discount greater than the legal rate is not such fraud on accommodation indorsers as to discharge them.[5]

An accommodation indorser of a note who takes it up at maturity, in ignorance of the fact that it has been discounted at an usurious rate, may maintain an action against the maker for reimbursement.[6]

Guarantors. If a note is usurious to the maker it is also usurious to a guarantor.[7]

Where a note is sold and transferred, and a guaranty of its payment given in consideration of a sum less than the amount due on the note, it is not usurious.[8]

Indorsers and guarantors of notes usuriously discounted for them by third persons are liable thereon to the holder, notwithstanding the usury.[9]

Where a person, innocent of usury, indorses an usurious note, the indorsement is void, the statute making usurious contracts void.[10]

[1] 26 Tenn. 451 (1846).
[2] 5 Tex. 171 (1849).
[3] 29 N. Y. 515 (1864).
[4] 2 Weekly Dig. (N. Y.) 441 (1876).
[5] 49 Tenn. 173 (1872).
[6] 11 Hun (N. Y.) 119 (1877).
[7] 28 S. C. 504 (1887).
[8] 21 Wend. (N. Y.) 285 (1839); Hill & D. Supp. (N. Y.) 252 (1843); 13 Barb. (N. Y.) 45 (1852); 10 N. Y. (6 Seld.) 198 (1854).
[9] 52 Md. 78 (1879); 28 Wis. 198 (1871).
[10] 2 McC. (S. C.) 178 (1822).

(*d*) *Partners.* A lender can recover of a firm the principal and legal interest of a note signed by one of the partners in the firm's name;[1] but one partner individually cannot sue when the borrower is his firm.[2] And in an action alleging partnership, and asking dissolution and an accounting, the plaintiff cannot recover on proof of a loan bearing legal interest besides a share of the profits, as it is usurious.[3]

When one of two partners, without the knowledge of the other, borrows money at usurious interest, and executes a note in the firm-name, afterward paying the interest, and the other partner, ignorant of the payment of the usury, executes his own note in lieu of the other's, he cannot set up in defence the plea of usury by his partner when sued.[4]

Where one partner sold out to another calling the value of the property ten per cent more than it was worth, by agreement, and notes then being made for that amount to run for several years at the highest legal rate of interest it was held to be usury.[5]

If one partner tells another not to pay certain debts because they are usurious, and the other partner then pays them, the first can recover his share of the usury from the other partner on accounting.[6]

A loan at usurious interest of money to be employed in the borrower's business does not make the lender a partner.[7]

(*e*) *Sureties.* An usurious contract for an extension of the time of payment of a note, will not discharge a surety

[1] 40 Ga. 167 (1869).
[2] 50 Tenn. 242 (1873).
[3] 62 N. Y. 508 (1875).
[4] 14 Ala. 186 (1848).
[5] 2 Spear (S. C.) 238 (1843).
[6] 50 N. W. Rep. (Iowa) 66 (1891); 57 Mo. 399. 503 (1874).
[7] 72 Pa. St. 241 (1872).

thereon;[1] but the payment of usurious interest is sufficient to support a promise of forbearance and will discharge a surety.[2] The court in Georgia holds, however, that a surety is discharged when the creditor agreed to take a mortgage with waiver of homestead right, and took one that was void for usury.[3]

A surety may set up usury as a defence to a note, given in renewal of others, when the usurious interest was paid on the original note.[4] A surety may set up usury even though his principal has waived it.[5]

Sureties are usually held for the principal and legal interest, whether they knew of the usury in the note or not.[6]

If a surety on a note, by request of the maker, who agrees to be jointly responsible with him, pays, after maturity, usurious interest thereon, he may recover what he has paid of the maker,[7] it being paid as between him and the maker, at the request of and for the use of the principal; and it makes no difference that a part thereof was usurious interest and not collectible of the surety, nor that part of it had accrued after maturity.[8] But if the surety knows of the usury and voluntarily pays it, he cannot afterward recover it of his principal.[9]

A deed to indemnify a surety is not void for usury in the original debt[10] reduced to judgment; and such usury does not affect a surety who pays the judgment.[11]

[1] 16 Ind. 218 (1861); 12 Kas. 500 (1874); 95 Pa. St. 65 (1880); 14 Tex. 600 (1855); *contra*, 108 N. C. 245 (1891).

[2] 71 Tex. 211 (1888); 21 Vt. 38 (1848).

[3] 81 Ga. 691 (1888).

[4] 39 Ind. 106 (1872).

[5] 15 S. E. Rep. (Ga.) 483 (1892).

[6] 3 O. St. 302 (1854).

[7] 25 Iowa 555 (1868); 48 Iowa 26 (1878); 7 B. Mon. (Ky.) 388 (1847).

[8] 1 Kelly (Ga.) 140 (1846); 51 Vt. 253 (1878).

[9] 3 Kelly (Ga.) 162 (1847); 8 Ga. 562 (1850).

[10] 76 Ga. 669 (1886).

[11] 74 Ga. 701 (1885); 22 Tenn. 547 (1842).

If one of several sureties has been compelled to pay usury, he may recover a proportionate part of what he has paid of his co-sureties.[1]

If a surety gives his own note for the usury, he cannot set up usury in a suit upon it, it being deemed a payment or purchase, and not a renewal.[2]

IX. PURGING CONTRACTS OF USURY.

(*a*) *By agreement.* A borrower, by a contemporaneous agreement, cannot waive the right to retain or recover usurious interest paid,[3] or waive the right to set up the defence of usury.[4]

A usurious contract that is void by statute cannot be afterward so confirmed as to make it available to either party.[5]

Contracts may be purged of the usury contained in them by an accounting and taking out the usury, new security being given for the balance.[6] A *bona fide* agreement to free it will be sufficient,[7] and it will afterward stand as a legal contract. If the maker of a note promises to give a new note less the usurious excess of interest, on the promise of the holder to cancel the original note, it will be enforced in law.[8]

A renewal does not purge the original usury, unless the agreement is discharged, or it combines new parties and has a new consideration, and not then if it is done to

[1] 25 Iowa 555 (1868).

[2] 48 Iowa 26 (1878).

[3] 72 Pa. St. 54 (1872).

[4] 22 Hun (N. Y.) 264 (1880).

[5] 8 W. & S. (Pa.) 31 (1844).

[6] 1 Kelley (Ga.) 410 (1846); 6 Ga. 253 (1849).

[7] 10 Wheat. (U. S.) 367 (1825); 28 Ind. 435 (1867); 2 Halst. Ch. (N. J.) 253 (1847), 625 (1848); 7 C. E. Gr. (N. J.) 138 (1871), 606 (1872); 11 C. E. Gr. (N. J.) 548 (1875); 13 Wend. (N. Y.) 505 (1835); 4 Denio (N. Y.) 104 (1847).

[8] 12 Iowa 364 (1861); 52 Iowa 114 (1879); 7 Vt. 210 (1835).

evade the statute.[1] So, after usurious securities have been destroyed by mutual consent, a promise by the borrower to repay the principal and interest is founded on a sufficient consideration and is binding.[2]

A transfer by the creditor to the debtor's wife of the property of the debtor which is held as security for an usurious debt, and the taking of a new security from the debtor and his wife on the same property for the same debt does not remove the taint of usury.[3]

But a mortgage given to secure an usurious note cannot be validated by crediting the note with the amount of the usury.[4] Where the holder of a note after suit brought, without knowledge of the maker, and without actually receiving anything, indorses on it a sum insufficient to reduce it to the amount of the principal and legal interest, it is still usurious.[5]

(*b*) *By payment.* To be a payment it must be so intended by the parties.[6] The borrower of money on an usurious consideration may waive the benefit of the statute by making payment; and if he pay the usurious debt to a third party, a new security given by such third party, in consideration thereof, will, in the absence of a contrivance to evade the statute, be valid.[7]

A settlement by note is a good defence to a suit for usury, if none of the usury enters into the new one,[8] unless it is a device to cover usury, when it is not a defence.[9]

[1] 5 G. & J. (Md.) 23 (1832); 2 Md. Ch. 201 (1850). See page 228.
[2] 17 Ark. 138 (1856); 91 N. Y. 124 (1883).
[3] 37 Minn. 182 (1887).
[4] 35 Ark. 217 (1879); 4 Denio (N. Y.) 104 (1847).
[5] 5 Hubb. (Me.) 544 (1861).
[6] 83 N. C. 211 (1880).
[7] 2 Conn. 276 (1817); 5 Conn. 154 (1823); 18 Grat. (Va.) 909 (1868).
[8] 125 Ill. 91 (1888); 11 Bush (Ky.) 393 (1875).
[9] 88 N. Y. 62 (1882).

If payment is made by a conveyance of land the title is good,[1] if it is an absolute conveyance and given in satisfaction of the debt;[2] but otherwise if it is only given to secure the debt.

A new note given for the principal and legal interest only, by the maker to the holder, who is other than the payee, for an usurious note is valid[3] and will purge the usury. But the remission of a part of the usury and giving a note for the balance will not purge it.[4]

To be conclusive, accord and satisfaction in settlement for usury must not leave the debtor *in vinculis* to the creditor.[5] Even though the sum advanced is less than the usury paid, if it is accepted as a full discharge of the borrower's claim it is good;[6] but if it is for only a part of the usury it is not sufficient, that is, to defeat a subsequent claim by the creditor,[7] though it is agreed to be so.[8] If the payment is in property reckoned at much more than its vendable value there can be no reclamation of the usury if such be the agreement;[9] and it is also true if in addition to the price there is an agreement that the value of the property over and above the amount of the principal and legal interest shall be in satisfaction of the usury in the claim, and the creditor gives a note for the excess over the legal amount due and pays it.[10]

Free and voluntary performance, by payment of money

[1] 67 Ga. 713 (1881); 78 Ga. 220 (1886).

[2] 31 N. E. Rep. (Ill.) 503 (1892); 17 Ind. 77 (1861).

[3] 3 J. J. Mar. (Ky.) 683 (1830); 7 Wend. (N. Y.) 256 (1831); 20 Wis. 671 (1866). See pages 228 and 229.

[4] 4 B. Mon. (Ky.) 372 (1844).

[5] 63 Ga. 78 (1879).

[6] 54 Ga. 15 (1875).

[7] 24 Pa. St. 215 (1855).

[8] 54 Ga. 15 (1875); 39 Pa. St. 361 (1861).

[9] 10 B. Mon. (Ky.) 220 (1849).

[10] 54 Ga. 15 (1875).

or otherwise, of an usurious contract bars relief in the courts:[1] but it must not be done to evade the usury statute.[2] Such payment may be followed by another loan; but such payment must not be by another obligation of the same parties, although there is an engagement of a new surety, except only where an innocent third person intervenes.[3]

A mercantile account rendered and accepted is deemed, by the Louisiana court, a payment of all the items that make it up; so it is settled, and only such usurious payments included therein as were made within the statutory period can be recovered.[4]

When a lender refunds the usury paid, it purges the contract of the usury, if it is agreed that from that time only lawful interest shall be charged.[5]

The foreclosure of an usurious mortgage by sale under the power does not prevent equitable relief from the usury.[6]

X. RELIEF FROM USURY.

Neither party will be held to an usurious contract while it is executory.[7] Usury is not an unconscionable defence;[8] and equity will cause equity to be done in giving relief.[9] Relief is generally given in proper cases; but where a debtor gives an usurious bond with the creditor, he has no relief against the latter.[10]

[1] 67 Mich. 237 (1887); 62 Pa. St. 481 (1869).

[2] 62 Pa. St. 481 (1869).

[3] 62 Pa. St. 481 (1869).

[4] 39 La. Ann. 788 (1887).

[5] 53 Iowa 719 (1880).

[6] 37 Minn. 182 (1887).

[7] 8 C. E. Gr. (N. J.) 554 (1872).

[8] 1 Stew. (N. J.) 398 (1877).

[9] 69 Miss. 770 (1892); 2 Desau. (S. C.) 333 (1806); 2 Rich. Eq. (S. C.) 63 (1845).

[10] 6 Munf. (Va.) 541 (1820).

(*a*) *Directly in equity.* Usury is not regarded as peculiarly an equitable defence;[1] it can be set up in defence of a suit at law against the debtor.[2]

Equity will relieve from usury only when, from the form of the security, the defence cannot be made available at law, or when the interest sought to be avoided is a cloud upon the title to land, or some other necessity for the interposition of a court of equity is shown.[3]

Equity will not aid if the remedy at law was not embraced when it could have been.[4] The Maryland court, however, holds that even then a party can have relief if he comes in within a reasonable time.[5]

1. *By borrowers.* Until the borrower asks to be relieved from paying usurious interest the other party may regard the whole contract as valid.[6] The borrower can only obtain relief by offering in his bill to pay the amount of the principal and legal interest due,[7] even if the stat-

[1] 2 Beas. (N. J.) 253 (1861); 3 C. E. Gr. (N. J.) 481 (1867).

[2] 8 S. & M. (Miss.) 131 (1847); 11 S. & M. (Miss.) 140 (1848); 2 Cush. (Miss.) 509 (1852).

[3] 49 N. Y. 373 (1872), reversing 3 Lans. (N. Y.) 492.

[4] 2 Stew. (Ala.) 420 (1830); 3 Port. (Ala.) 436 (1836); 10 Ala. 579 (1846); 37 Ala. 573 (1861); 27 Ill. 15 (1861); 17 Kas. 514 (1877); 1 Johns. Ch. (N. Y.) 49 (1814); 3 Johns. Ch. (N. Y.) 395 (1818); 17 Johns. (N. Y.) 436 (1819); 22 Tenn. 63 (1842); 45 Tenn. 497 (1868); 51 Tenn. 300 (1874).

[5] 6 Md. 218 (1854), when a period of seven years was deemed too long a time to wait.

[6] 10 Gray (Mass.) 37 (1858).

[7] 10 Pet. (U. S.) 497, 521 (1836); 23 Ala. 537 (1853); 28 Ala. 580 (1856); 32 Ala. 456 (1858); 38 Ala. 323 (1862); 50 Ala. 587 (1874); 64 Ala. 527 (1879); 18 Ark. 369 (1857); 32 Ark. 346 (1877); 34 Ark. 628 (1879); 30 Conn. 119 (1861); 5 Del. Ch. 180 (1877); 10 Ga. 389 (1851); 75 Ga. 159 (1885); 37 Ill. 216 (1865); 42 Ill. 256 (1866); 75 Ill. 215 (1874); 90 Ill. 245 (1878); 95 Ill. 11 (1880); 69 Miss. 770 (1892); Sax. (N. J.) 358 (1831); 2 Beas. (N. J.) 66 (1860); 5 Johns. Ch. (N. Y.) 122 (1821); 8 Paige (N. Y.) 518 (1841); 7 Hill (N. Y.) 391 (1844); 4 Sandf. Ch. (N. Y.) 312 (1846); 5 Barb. (N. Y.) 130 (1849); 13 Barb.

ute only allows the principal to be recovered at law.[1] Several courts hold that the debtor must make a tender of the principal and legal interest due,[2] and must bring the money into court if it is not accepted.[3]

If the debt is secured by a mortgage, the mortgage remains security for the amount that equity decides to be due.[4] In a certain case, a borrower encumbered his property to secure an usurious debt, then became a bankrupt, and was afterward discharged from his debts under the bankrupt act. He afterward acquired title to the same property by purchase from the assignee in bankruptcy, and on a bill filed by him to have the incumbrance cancelled on account of the usury, it was held that he was not entitled to relief unless he paid the principal and legal interest.[5]

If a borrower defends, this rule does not apply, and he can then have relief without paying or offering to pay what is equitably due on the debt.[6]

(N. Y.) 561 (1852); 2 Hawks (N. C.) 465 (1823); 82 N. C. 134 (1880); 104 N. C. 219 (1889); 109 N. C. 539 (1891); 32 Tenn. 265 (1852); 8 Leigh (Va.) 93 (1837); *contra*, 36 Minn. 460 (1887).

[1] 89 Ill. 123 (1878).

[2] 79 Ga. 790 (1887); 3 Gilm. (Ill.) 547 (1846); 75 Ill. 215 (1874); 89 Ill. 123 (1878); 1 Blf. (Ind.) 382 (1825); 7 Blf. (Ind.) 337, 423 (1845); 4 Ind. 539 (1853); 6 G. & J. (Md.) 18 (1833); 1 Md. Ch. 66 (1847); 7 Gill (Md.) 158 (1848); 8 Gill (Md.) 1 (1849); 9 Gill (Md.) 299 (1850); 24 Neb. 79 (1888); 2 Beas. (N. J.) 66 (1860); 1 C. E. Gr. (N. J.) 468 (1864), 550 (1862); 8 C. E. Gr. (N. J.) 554 (1872); *contra*, 11 Iowa 419 (1860); 12 Iowa 185 (1861); 46 Iowa 84 (1877). In a New Jersey case, a bill was filed against a trustee, but not against the *certui que trust*, and the latter afterward came in as complainant setting up the usury. Sax. (N. J.) 358 (1831). If the bill does not state that an offer to pay has been made, it is demurrable. 2 Beas. (N. J.) 66 (1860).

[3] 1 Blf. (Ind.) 382 (1825); 7 Blf. (Ind.) 337, 423 (1845); 4 Ind. 539 (1853).

[4] 23 Ala. 537 (1853).

[5] 14 N. Y. (4 Kern.) 93 (1856).

[6] 5 Johns. Ch. (N. Y.) 122 (1821); 10 O. St. 200 (1863); 37 Wis. 364 (1875).

The doctrine of equity that the party complaining may be relieved from excess only of interest applies to the case of a claimant of priority of a fund, another claimant, defendant, being an alleged usurer.[1]

The remedy against usury in a trust deed is also in equity.[2]

a. Cancellation. A bill praying for cancellation of securities for usury need not offer to repay the principal with legal interest.[3] A mortgage void for usury cannot be foreclosed;[4] but if the mortgagor seeks its cancellation he must pay the valid debts secured by it.[5] A devisee of the mortgagor must first pay,[6] and so must a surety for the loan at least tender the exact amount due,[7] if he would have the instrument cancelled.

b. Discovery. A discovery may be had in equity,[8] and the payment of the money into court is not a condition to it.[9] A party cannot have a discovery in equity to aid his defence at law,[10] unless he is so situated that he cannot avail himself of the witness in the suit at law.[11]

c. Injunction. Equity will enjoin a lender from endeavoring to collect usurious interest,[12] even on a bond[13] and an execution.[14] It also lies to restrain a sale and transfer of the indebtedness;[15] and a bill to enjoin a sale

[1] 1 Wall. (U. S.) 604 (1863).
[2] 91 Ill. 539 (1879).
[3] 36 Minn. 460 (1887).
[4] 36 Minn. 460 (1887).
[5] 37 N. Y. 444 (1867).
[6] 13 Hun (N. Y.) 126 (1878).
[7] 16 Hun (N. Y.) 311 (1878).
[8] 95 Ill. 11 (1880).
[9] 10 Ga. 389 (1851).
[10] 3 Lit. (Ky.) 109 (1823).
[11] 2 Sandf. Ch. (N. Y.) 187 (1843); 1 Barb. Ch. (N. Y.) 404 (1846).
[12] 19 Kas. 601 (1878).
[13] 1 Grat. (Va.) 153 (1844).
[14] 4 J. J. Mar. (Ky.) 88 (1830).
[15] 12 S. & M. (Miss.) 631 (1849); 4 Geo. (Miss.) 299 (1857); 25 Neb. 481 (1889).

on account of usury may be filed even after the lender's death.[1] Relief will also be given to a party enjoining a sale under an usurious deed of trust.[2]

d. Reconveyance. If the valid portion of a note is paid, it does not then represent any legal indebtedness, and the borrower will be entitled to a reconveyance of the security.[3]

e. Recovery of usury paid. A borrower may be relieved in equity, and usury collected by law may be recovered in equity,[4] even upon a judgment,[5] says the Maryland court of chancery; but see page 295.

2. *By lenders.* If a lender seeks relief in equity, he can recover only the principal;[6] as in the case of a bill for the foreclosure of a mortgage.[7] He must offer to abate all the interest.[8] And rests will not be allowed to convert interest into principal.[9]

Equity will not aid in the recovery of a note that is void under the usury statute.[10]

The Kentucky court will not entertain a bill in favor of a lender to recover money lent on an usurious contract;[11]

[1] 17 Grat. (Va.) 21 (1861).

[2] 8 Grat. (Va.) 22 (1851). Where a widow, who was not her late husband's personal representative, brought a bill to enjoin the foreclosure of a mortgage, which included usurious interest, it was held that she could not maintain the bill without showing that she had an estate in the premises. 37 Wis. 364 (1875).

[3] 34 Iowa 483 (1872).

[4] 4 Mon. (Ky.) 488 (1827).

[5] 1 Md. Ch. 127 (1847).

[6] 22 S. C. 279 (1884). And the Tennessee court holds that a lender cannot sue on an usurious contract, if he admits the usury. 27 Tenn. 605 (1848).

[7] 73 Ala. 111 (1882).

[8] 11 So. Rep. (Ala.) 304 (1892).

[9] 38 Ala. 323 (1862); 50 Ala. 587 (1874).

[10] 10 Wheat. (U. S.) 367 (1825).

[11] 4 Bibb (Ky.) 460 (1816).

and the North Carolina court, sitting in equity, will never assist a creditor who has been guilty of usury.[1] The South Carolina court will not declare a contract usurious and void in favor of him for whose gain the usury was intended, in order to restore to him the rights he surrendered in consideration of the contract.[2]

(*b*) *Recovery of usury paid.* Usury paid may be recovered in three ways: 1. By suit; 2. By set-off; and 3. By forfeiture.

1. *By suit.* Usurious interest paid cannot be recovered by an independent suit brought therefor, unless the statute gives the right,[3] or such contracts are declared void by the statute.[4] The usury need not have been paid in pursuance of an usurious agreement made at the time the contract was entered into, in order to recover it.[5] Interest paid on collateral security cannot be recovered;[6] though the Kentucky court holds that the borrower may recover usury even if it is paid on a judgment, and may recover it at either law or equity,[7] the argument of the

[1] 2 Dev. Eq. (N. C.) 75 (1831); 1 Dev. & Bat. Eq. (N. C.) 50 (1834).

[2] 1 Bail. (S. C.) 4 (1828).

[3] 18 Wall. (U. S.) 375 (1873); 35 Ill. 40 (1864); 2 La. 428 (1831); 14 La. 34 (1839); 19 La. 151, 185 (1841); 16 La. Ann. 217 (1861); 125 Mass. 562 (1878); 43 Mo. App. 300 (1891); 44 Mo. App. 406 (1891); 2 N. H. 333 (1821); 16 N. H. 479 (1845); 34 N. H. 82 (1856); 61 N. H. 157 (1881); 62 N. H. 300 (1882); 46 Barb. (N. Y.) 21 (1866); 102 N. C. 137 (1889); 11 O. 417 (1842); 63 Pa. St. 108 (1869); 20 Vt. 201 (1848); 35 Vt. 476, 503 (1863); *contra*, 34 Md. 389 (1871); 10 Vr. (39 N. J. L.) 22 (1876); 76 Va. 419 (1882).

[4] 12 Iowa 300 (1861). The supreme court of the United States, in the case cited 18 Wall. (U. S.) 375 (1873), allowed illegal interest paid to be recovered, but stated that it was within the discretion of the court of equity.

[5] 23 Vt. 272 (1851).

[6] 24 Ill. 381 (1860); 28 Ill. 519 (1862); 29 Ill. 184 (1862).

[7] 85 Ky. 71 (1887).

court being that the money was paid without consideration, and that it was extorted from the borrower.[1] This right has no cast of a penalty.[2]

The foregoing rule relates to voluntary payments of usury, which prevents usurious interest paid from being recovered or set off in courts of equity, unless the statute gives the right.[3] The court in Virginia, however, holds that the borrower and lender at usurious rates are not *in pari delicto*, but that the former acts under a *quasi* duress, and the maxim, "*In pari delicto, potior est conditio defendentis,*" does not apply.[4]

If the payment is involuntary it can be recovered on common law principles.[5] What constitutes a voluntary payment is sometimes difficult to determine. Where the maker of a note given for an usurious consideration deposited with the holder certain negotiable paper as collateral security, which was to be collected and the proceeds applied to the payment of the note, the money collected on such collateral is to be regarded as voluntarily paid on the note by the maker.[6] So if it is made by a foreclosure and sale of mortgaged property without objection.[7] The Ohio court went so far as to hold that the payment of

[1] 5 B. Mon. (Ky.) 319 (1845).

[2] 63 Pa. St. 108 (1869).

[3] 24 Ill. 381 (1860); 34 Ill. 505 (1864); 39 Ill. 539 (1864); 103 Ill. 600 (1882); 14 Bradw. (Ill.) 340 (1883); 12 Iowa 300 (1861); 40 Iowa 304 (1875); 15 La. 378 (1840); 38 Mich. 200 (1878); 5 Minn. 382 (1861); 22 Minn. 341 (1876); 26 Minn. 547 (1880); 39 Mo. 445 (1867); 55 Mo. 389 (1874); 58 Hun (N. Y.) 575 (1891); 12 O. 153 (1843); 17 O. 605 (1848); 26 O. St. 207 (1875); *contra*, 1 Kelley (Ga.) 241 (1816); 35 Pa. St. 470 (1860); 14 Tenn. 398 (1834); 22 Tenn. 66 (1842); 43 Tenn. 477 (1866).

[4] 4 Barb. (N. Y.) 346 (1848); 11 Barb. (N. Y.) 159 (1850); 9 N. Y. (5 Seld.) 241 (1853); 76 Va. 419 (1882). See 24 Ill. 381 (1860).

[5] 67 Ind. 478 (1879).

[6] 39 Ill. 539 (1864).

[7] 26 Minn. 547 (1880).

usury was voluntary when it was exacted by the creditor before delivery of certain securities belonging to the debtor which he held.[1] The court in Indiana holds that the maker's payment of a judgment recovered on his note payable in bank, by a *bona fide* indorsee for value and before maturity, is not voluntary, and that the maker can recover from the payee the usurious interest so paid.[2]

But usurious interest cannot be recovered before it is paid.[3]

Neither law nor equity will permit the recovery of more than the excess of usury paid;[4] but that can be sued for,[5] even though the contract has passed into a judgment,[6] when it is not included in the judgment.[7]

An accommodation maker and an accommodation indorser can recover only the amount of usury actually paid by them,[8] in Louisiana.

If the recovery of usury paid is allowed, and the remedy is not fixed by the statute, an action at law will lie,[9] as, for instance, an action for debt,[10] and the approved form is *assumpsit* on a count for money had and received.[11] If the statute gives two remedies the neglect to take advantage of one is not a bar to the second.[12]

[1] 26 O. St. 207 (1875).
[2] 67 Ind. 478 (1879).
[3] 6 Ga. 228 (1849); 79 Ga. 416 (1887); 84 Ga. 452 (1889).
[4] 9 Gill (Md.) 299 (1850).
[5] 22 Vt. 581 (1849); 51 Vt. 378 (1879).
[6] 53 Vt. 33 (1880).
[7] 53 Vt. 33 (1880).
[8] 6 Rob. (La.) 120 (1843).
[9] 60 Miss. 319 (1882).
[10] 15 Shepl. (Me.) 215 (1848).
[11] 7 Blf. (Ind.) 105 (1844); 5 Ind. 308 (1854); 12 Shepl. (Me.) 33 (1845); 34 Md. 389 (1871); 6 W. & S. (Pa.) 179 (1843); 63 Pa. St. 108 (1869); 23 Vt. 272 (1851); 21 W. Va. 523 (1883).
[12] 22 Vt. 581 (1849); 51 Vt. 378 (1879); 53 Vt. 33 (1880); 61 Vt. 65 (1888).

If usurious interest is paid on a note after its execution, it amounts to a payment on the principal; and if it exceeds the amount of the principal, the Indiana court holds that the excess beyond the principal can be recovered.[1]

Where payments of usurious interest had more than discharged the debt, and a sum was due to the defendant, he was permited to file a cross bill to recover the amount due him, although he might also have recovered at law.[2]

If payments of usurious interest have been made in the course of mutual dealings between the parties, and they have had no final settlement, the statute of limitations does not begin to run from the dates of payment of the usurious interest, but from the time the principal and legal interest is fully paid.[3]

Interest on usury paid runs from the time the borrower elects by demand, or suit, to reclaim the usury.[4]

A contract founded upon usury paid is good if it can be recovered.[5]

If a borrower delivers property in part payment of a loan, he cannot recover it on the ground of usury in the loan. His only remedy is an action to recover the excess of interest. But when chattels are pledged or mortgaged to secure the payment of an usurious debt, the borrower has an immediate right to recover them,[6] if the usurious contract is void.

2. *By set-off.* Although usurious interest voluntarily paid cannot be recovered by an independent suit at common law, yet it can be set off by plea against a suit brought

[1] 23 Ind. 4 (1864).
[2] 24 Atl. Rep. (Vt.) 131 (1892).
[3] 54 Ga. 190 (1875).
[4] 1 B. Mon. (Ky.) 314 (1841); 5 B. Mon. (Ky.) 93 (1844).
[5] 21 Vt. 38 (1848).
[6] 7 Cow. (N. Y.) 290 (1827).

on the contract, if any part of the legal amount due remains unpaid,[1] but not otherwise. The fact that the usury was voluntarily paid, or the statute of limitations, can be pleaded in defence to such set-off.[2] It must be usury paid on the contract sued on.[3] It cannot be recovered after the transaction is closed;[4] and the contract must still be in the hands of him who received the usury sought to be set off, or in the hands of an assignee with notice.[5] The New Hampshire court has recently decided, however, that where the defendant has paid the plaintiff usurious interest on a note which the plaintiff afterward sold, it may be set off in an action on another note.[6]

All payments of usurious interest made may, at the payor's option, be regarded as partial payments made on the principal and valid interest, and reckoned by the partial payment rule.[7] The rule is the same in recoupment.[8]

No allowance for supposed over-valuation of property received in payment of an usurious loan can be made in taking account of usury.[9]

[1] 74 Ala. 604 (1882); 100 Ill. 611 (1881); 19 Ill. 467 (1857); 39 Ind. 305 (1872); 70 Ind. 373 (1880); 2 Rob. (La.) 99 (1842); 22 La. Ann. 418 (1870); 30 Neb. 99 (1890); 2 Johns. Ch. (N. Y.) 182 (1816); 17 O. 605 (1848); 31 O. St. 142 (1877); 110 Pa. St. 60 (1885); 24 Tenn. 406 (1844); 43 Vt. 400 (1871); 55 Vt. 415 (1883); *contra*, 55 Mo. 389 (1874); 58 Hun (N. Y.) 575 (1891).

[2] 18 Tex. 794 (1857).

[3] 46 Ga. 422 (1872); 73 Ill. 213 (1874); 97 Ill. 568 (1881); 103 Ill. 600 (1882); 9 Iowa 376 (1859); 53 Iowa 396 (1880); 58 Iowa 728 (1882); 24 Kas. 679 (1881); 3 N. H. 185 (1825); 11 N. H. 66 (1840); 24 Pa. St. 215 (1855); 12 R. I. 344 (1879); 43 Vt. 400 (1871).

[4] 37 Ill. 331 (1865); 44 Ill. 405 (1867).

[5] 60 Ill. 367 (1871).

[6] 21 Atl. Rep. (N. H.) 221 (1890).

[7] 7 B. Mon. (Ky.) 442 (1847); 11 Bush (Ky.) 396 (1875); 33 W. Va. 159 (1889).

[8] 75 Ind. 318 (1881).

[9] 22 Tenn. 666 (1842).

It is within the election and discretion of the payor whether he will bring a separate suit for the usury (if the statute allows it), or ask to have it applied to the payment of the principal when sued,[1] or plead it in part payment,[2] or in settlement.[3]

Several courts hold that usurious interest paid cannot be recovered by suit so long as any part of the amount legally due remains unpaid, because the creditor is presumed to have applied it to the payment of the legal portion of the debt.[4] But if a balance remains to the debtor's credit, he can recover it by suit.[5]

If it appears upon the petition of the plaintiff that he is seeking to recover usurious interest, it is held in Kentucky that it is the duty of the court to purge the usury before rendering judgment.[6]

Courts hold generally that payments of usurious interest are technically payments made on the legal portion of the debt,[7] which if the parties appear the court will thus apply without plea or answer.[8] Against such application the

[1] 28 Ill. 352 (1862); 35 Ill. 40, 66 (1864); 37 Ill. 331 (1865); 44 Ill. 405 (1867); 77 Ill. 182, 525 (1875); 97 Ill. 568 (1881); 103 Ill. 600 (1882); 22 Vt. 581 (1849); 35 Vt. 476 (1863); 53 Vt. 539 (1881); *contra*, he cannot charge the usurious interest paid to the payment of the principal of the debt, 12 R. I. 344 (1879).

[2] 15 Vt. 115 (1843); 19 Vt. 496 (1847); 22 Vt. 581 (1849); 53 Vt. 202 (1880), 491, 539 (1881); 60 Vt. 209 (1887).

[3] 51 Vt. 378 (1879); 53 Vt. 33 (1880).

[4] 15 Vt. 115 (1843); 19 Vt. 496 (1847); 22 Vt. 581 (1849); 53 Vt. 202 (1880), 491, 539 (1881); 60 Vt. 209 (1887); 80 Va. 379 (1885); 21 W. Va. 523 (1883).

[5] 53 Vt. 202 (1880).

[6] 12 W. P. D. Bush (Ky.) 298 (1876); 79 Ky. 346 (1881).

[7] 1 Kelley (Ga.) 108 (1846); 35 Ill. 40 (1864); 77 Ill. 182 (1875); 86 Ill. 197, 513 (1877); 53 Vt. 33 (1880); 61 Vt. 65 (1888); *contra*, 98 U. S. 555 (1878); 104 U. S. 52 (1881). See 34 O. St. 142 (1877).

[8] 29 O. St. 587 (1876); 53 Vt. 501 (1881); *contra*, 53 Hun (N. Y.) 93 (1889).

statute of limitations is no defence.[1] If the court has thus applied the usury paid, it cannot afterward be recovered by suit.[2]

When over-due notes are transferred, the usurious interest paid to the original owner may be deducted.[3] And when a new note and a new mortgage are given for old ones, the usury paid on the first may be deducted on the second,[4] in foreclosing. It is the same debt or loan. In defence to a foreclosure, it must be shown, however, that the usurious excess was received by the mortgagee or his agent.[5]

In an action for the principal debt the excess of usurious interest can be recouped only to the legal amount remaining due to the lender.[6]

The Arkansas court says that where the statute gives the right of a suit at law to recover usurious interest paid that remedy is exclusive, and no such interest can be recouped.[7]

Payments made without direction as to their application to the usurious or legal interest or the principal are not appropriated, and therefore the statute of limitations will run against each payment from its date, says the Georgia court.[8]

Where the purchaser of a mortgage has received a bonus in excess of lawful interest paid by the borrower for an extension of time of payment of principal, the borrower, when sued in foreclosure, is entitled to have such excess credited on the mortgage, as a payment.[9]

[1] 5 Dana (Ky.) 83 (1837).
[2] 53 Vt. 33 (1880).
[3] 53 Vt. 501 (1881).
[4] 53 Vt. 501 (1881).
[5] 1 Stew. (N. J.) 345 (1877).
[6] 57 Ind. 539 (1877).
[7] 47 Ark. 54 (1885). See 26 O. St. 75 (1875).
[8] 71 Ga. 519 (1883).
[9] 70 N. Y. 63 (1877).

National banks cannot recoup usurious interest paid in advance, says the Indiana court.[1]

3. *By forfeiture.* When a forfeiture for usury is allowed by the statute, the statute must be followed in the recovery of it. It must be ascertained judicially upon an issue between the parties before it can be applied to the reduction of the debt so as to affect the title of the lender to property held by him as collateral security.[2]

To recover the penalty by the statute against usury, the plaintiff need not show that the principal has been paid,[3] unless the statute requires it. But if the statute requires the usury to have been received before the penalty is incurred, then of course its receipt by the defendant must be shown.[4] A return of judgment satisfied on an execution by a sheriff is not sufficient evidence of receipt in such cases.[5] Neither is it necessary to show that usurious interest has been received, unless the penalty lies only when usury has been received.

Interest on a note, in forfeiture, should be computed from the time the money was borrowed, though several successive notes have been given.[6]

A forfeiture to the school fund, under the laws of Oregon, will carry the securities with it;[7] and in Iowa, where the forfeiture goes to the school fund, the court will decree it in spite of the parties.[8]

Before judgment, the penalty allowed for taking or re-

[1] 44 Ind. 298 (1873).

[2] 1 Allen (Mass.) 399 (1861).

[3] 2 Murph. (N. C.) 200 (1812).

[4] 4 Ired. L. (N. C.) 296 (1844); 6 Ired. L. (N. C.) 390 (1846).

[5] 7 Dev. & Bat. (N. C.) 474 (1837).

[6] 14 Iowa 125 (1862).

[7] 5 Ore. 432 (1875).

[8] 17 Iowa 439 (1864); 60 Iowa 289 (1882).

ceiving usurious interest by a national bank does not bear interest.[1]

(c) *Who may recover, or plead usury.* As the usury law exists for the protection of the borrower,[2] the courts always lean in his favor. A stranger cannot object to usury in a loan,[3] unless it is void by statute,[4] except with the debtor's consent.[5] Neither can the lender[6] set up usury in the loan,—that right is given only to the borrower[7] and certain parties claiming under him. The lender can avoid his agreement on the ground of usury in the contract in order to make the contract legal,[8] but only in equity, as already detailed.

The right to recover usury is assignable,[9] and such an assignment is contained in an absolute and unconditional sale of all interest in a judgment that might be recovered;[10]

[1] 26 O. St. 75 (1875).

[2] 45 Ala. 429 (1871); 27 Conn. 142 (1858); 32 Conn. 550 (1865); 95 Ill. 493 (1880); 33 Vt. 553 (1861); 31 Wis. 673 (1873); 42 Wis. 631 (1877).

[3] 8 Wheat. (U. S.) 339 (1823); 59 Ala. 172, 419 (1877); 9 Ind. 135 (1857); 11 Ind. 398 (1858); 15 Ind. 50 (1860); 37 Iowa 325 (1873); 8 Paige (N. Y.) 639 (1841); 78 Va. 100 (1883).

[4] 8 Wheat. (U. S.) 339 (1823).

[5] 9 Ind. 135 (1857); 11 Ind. 398 (1858); 15 Ind. 50 (1860).

[6] 36 Ark. 248 (1880); 3 Gilm. (Ill.) 547 (1846); 75 Ind. 318 (1881); 4 Barb. (N. Y.) 346 (1848); 11 Barb. (N. Y.) 159 (1850); 9 N. Y. (5 Seld.) 241 (1853).

[7] 22 Ala. 262 (1853); 45 Ala. 429 (1871); 27 Conn. 142 (1858); 32 Conn. 550 (1865); 66 Ga. 398 (1881); 95 Ill. 493 (1880); 123 Ill. 510 (1888); 55 Ind. 341 (1876); 75 Ind. 318 (1881); 14 Iowa 125, 251 (1862); 32 Iowa 418 (1871); 37 Iowa 325 (1873); 1 Mich. 84 (1848); 11 Mich. 59 (1862); 38 Mich. 200 (1878); 9 N. Y. (5 Seld.) 73 (1853); 29 Barb. (N. Y.) 401 (1859); 33 N. Y. 31 (1865); 36 N. Y. 141, 319 (1867); 37 N. Y. 218 (1867); 25 Hun (N. Y.) 490 (1881); 33 Vt. 553 (1861); 78 Va. 100 (1883); 21 W. Va. 108 (1882); 31 W. Va. 410 (1888).

[8] 15 Hun (N. Y.) 564 (1878); 20 Hun (N. Y.) 153 (1880).

[9] 3 J. J. Mar. (Ky.) 13 (1829); 49 Tenn. 454 (1873).

[10] 49 Tenn. 454 (1873).

but a mortgage of "all my estate" does not convey the right to sue for usury.[1]

In a suit on a note where usury may be pleaded by the consent of the maker, it is not necessary that he should be a party to the suit.[2]

When property is mortgaged to secure several debts, some of which are legal and others usurious, and the proceeds of the sale of the property are insufficient to pay all, it must be divided without regard to the illegal interest if the mortgagor assents.[3]

If a borrower waive the privilege of the defence of the usury law, no one else, claiming under him, can take advantage of it.[4]

If a party to an usurious contract be made a party to an action against his vendee to foreclose a mortgage securing it, he may set up usury as a ground of equitable relief to himself.[5]

Where an action of replevin is brought by a chattel mortgagee with general averment of title, the defendant, under a general denial, may show usury in the mortgage.[6]

A plaintiff in replevin suing as mortgagee of a renewal mortgage, which was proved on trial to be usurious, cannot recover under the original mortgage.[7]

Usury cannot be set up as a defence by one who has converted a note and collected the full amount when sued by the true owner for the amount so collected.[8]

Where a debtor had no actual notice of the suit (though the statutory *subpœna* had been served) she was granted a

[1] 3 J. J. Mar. (Ky.) 13 (1829).
[2] 19 Ind. 110 (1862).
[3] 45 Ala. 429 (1871).
[4] 3 Ala. 643 (1842).
[5] 8 Ind. 352 (1856).
[6] 45 Minn. 448 (1891).
[7] 43 Minn. 270 (1890).
[8] 25 Iowa 56 (1868).

motion to set aside the execution, the property having been advertised for sale, that she might be heard;[1] but otherwise, if she had had notice by publication and was represented by her trustee.[2]

A debtor of an estate allowed usurious interest on his debt, and he gave in payment therefor his notes to a legatee, who accepted them in part payment of his legacy. In an action on the notes, the debtor could not set up the usury allowed the estate in defence, although the legatee was one of the executors who made the settlement.[3]

A creditor is not allowed to show that an obligation, which he has taken in satisfaction of a prior demand, is usurious, and therefore void, in order to avoid the effect of such obligation as a satisfaction of the prior demand. The parties do not stand *in pari delicto*. There is oppression on one side, and submission on the other.[4]

Assignees. It is generally held that assignees in insolvency can take advantage of usury paid by their insolvents,[5] providing the statute does not give the exclusive right of recovery to other persons or classes of persons.

If a debtor assigns for the benefit of his creditors, having previously mortgaged his real estate, and the assignee, at the debtor's special request, pays the mortgage, which is usurious, the debtor can recover the usury thus paid, as he furnished the funds with which it was paid.[6]

A general assignment for the benefit of creditors made

[1] 12 C. E. Gr. (N. J.) 356 (1876).

[2] 1 Stew. (N. J.) 398 (1877).

[3] 24 O. St. 486 (1874).

[4] 9 N. Y. (5 Seld.) 241 (1853); 4 Barb. (N. Y.) 346 (1848); 11 Barb. (N. Y.) 159 (1850).

[5] 99 Mass. 63 (1868); 44 Minn. 218 (1890); 64 N. Y. 242 (1876); 43 O. St. 220 (1885); 96 Pa. St. 327 (1880); 23 Vt. 739 (1848); *contra*, 55 Ala. 344 (1876); 22 Vt. 581 (1849); 32 Vt. 93 (1859); 56 Vt. 332 (1883).

[6] 36 Vt. 183 (1863). In this case the time in which the assignee could bring his action had run out.

by a mortgagor to his mortgagee, naming the mortgage as a valid lien, does not estop the mortgagor from setting up usury against foreclosure. Such an assignment is only additional security.[1]

The mortgagor can plead usury paid to the mortgagee in an action brought by an assignee of the mortgage.[2]

The assignee of a judgment may repel the defendant coming into equity for a set-off on notes against the judgment, by alleging the usurious consideration of the notes set up in the bill.[3]

The assignment to a husband of an usurious mortgage made by his wife, and the giving a new mortgage by both for the same and additional consideration, does not preclude the wife from interposing the defence of usury.[4]

A debtor whose note, including usurious interest, has been assigned, when sued in chancery, may bring in the assignor by a cross-bill, and recover any usury that has been paid and which is not barred by the lapse of time.[5]

The obligor of a bond, or other writing under seal, cannot take advantage of the usury practised upon the assignor by the assignee in obtaining the assignment of the instrument,[6] nor reclaim it.[7]

Creditors. One creditor cannot, during his debtor's lifetime, plead usury to defeat the claim of another creditor, in whole or in part.[8]

A judgment creditor of the mortgagor cannot take ad-

[1] 23 Hun (N. Y.) 12 (1880).
[2] 22 S. C. 169 (1884).
[3] 7 Mon. (Ky.) 191 (1828).
[4] 46 Barb. (N. Y.) 272 (1866).
[5] 7 B. Mon. (Ky.) 276 (1847)
[6] Hardin (Ky.) 87 (1807); 4 Dana (Ky.) 181 (1836).
[7] 4 Dana (Ky.) 181 (1836).
[8] 21 W. Va. 10 8 (1882).

vantage of the usury in the mortgage.[1] He may set up usury, however, to avoid title and subject the debtor's property to the debt.[2]

A creditor cannot set up usury in favor of his debtor;[3] neither can he recover it.[4] Nor can a judgment creditor of an insolvent debtor set up usury in behalf of his debtor in a proceeding to which he is not a party.[5]

A judgment creditor cannot attack a prior judgment on the ground that it contains usurious interest, without proof of an intent to defraud him thereby.[6] And such payment of usury is not fraud, necessarily.[7]

Usury paid by an insolvent debtor to one creditor is not recoverable by another;[8] the debtor must assert his own right; *aliter*, if not paid over, and it remains in the hands of the trustee to be paid over.[9] So one creditor cannot enjoin another judgment creditor from enforcing an usurious contract.[10]

Devisees. Devisees cannot take advantage of usury in their testator's contracts.[11] The court in Kentucky holds, however, that a claim against the testator may be purged of usurious interest on demand of any one of the devisees in an action against them to subject the estate to the payment of a debt of the testator.[12]

[1] 45 Ala. 582 (1871); 31 N. E. Rep. (Ill.) 503 (1892); *contra*, 68 Tenn. 104 (1873).

[2] 66 Ga. 398 (1881).

[3] 17 Ind. 77 (1861); 55 Ind. 341 (1876).

[4] 7 B. Mon. (Ky.) 54 (1846); 10 B. Mon. (Ky.) 118 (1849).

[5] 32 Iowa 418 (1871).

[6] 93 Pa. St. 298 (1880).

[7] 93 Pa. St. 301 (1880); 96 Pa. St. 160 (1880).

[8] 37 Ill. 45 (1865).

[9] 78 Ga. 269 (1886).

[10] 48 Ga. 55 (1873).

[11] 33 N. Y. 31 (1865).

[12] 12 W. P. D. Bush (Ky.) 401 (1876).

Where a residuary devisee received usurious notes of the executor, and the debtor gave new notes to the devisee, it was held that the debtor did not deprive himself of the right to have the usury purged from the demand.[1]

Guarantors. A guarantor can set up usury in a suit on the guaranty,[2] whenever an indorser[3] can, says the New York court.

The defence of usury is not available to one who has guaranteed an usurious obligation of a foreign corporation, contracted in New York, says the court in that state,[4] the statute prohibiting corporations setting up the defence of usury.

Heirs. A borrower's heirs can take advantage of the ancestor's usurious contracts.[5] It seems that when land incumbered with an usurious mortgage descends to an heir, the right of action is in the heir and not in the administrator of the deceased. So the heir of the borrower paying the lender usurious interest, to remove an incumbrance of a security deed of the ancestor, may recover it.[6]

Indorsers. Indorsers may take advantage of the maker's usurious contract;[7] but not if he is sued by the indorsee,[8] unless the usury is in their contract.[9]

If a banking corporation cannot set up usury, its indorser cannot.[10]

[1] 15 B. Mon. (Ky.) 466 (1854).

[2] 67 Iowa 13 (1885); 20 Me. (2 Appl., 7 Shepl.) 28 (1841).

[3] 37 Barb. (N. Y.) 189 (1862).

[4] 63 Barb. (N. Y.) 415 (1866).

[5] 55 Ind. 341 (1876); 33 N. Y. 31 (1865).

[6] 78 Ga. 635 (1887).

[7] 1 Greenl. (Me.) 167 (1821); 12 Shepl. (Me.) 33 (1845).

[8] 6 Hill (N. Y.) 492 (1844).

[9] 2 Brev. (S. C.) 199 (1807); *contra*, 55 Tex. 167 (1881).

[10] 60 N. Y. 612 (1875); 11 Hun (N. Y.) 139 (1877); 74 N. Y. 85 (1878).

Accommodation indorsers. An accommodation indorser may set up usury in the maker's contract.[1]

An accommodation indorser of a note who takes it up at maturity, in ignorance of the fact that it has been discounted at an usurious rate, may maintain an action against the maker for re-imbursement.[2]

When a note is discounted at an usurious rate for the payee, who then indorses it, the defence of usury is available both for maker and indorser, the note being accommodation, and assigned with notice of that fact;[3] otherwise, if it is business paper.

An indorser of a note is not estopped from setting up usury, by a certificate to the effect that the note is business paper, given for a full consideration and subject to no defences, when its holder had knowledge that it was indorsed for the accommodation of the maker, and had its inception when so transferred.[4]

Makers. Where an indorsee buys a valid note of the payee, on an usurious consideration, the maker (who was the party sued) has a right to set up such intermediate usury to impeach the plaintiff's title to sue.[5] The Texas court holds that the rule is applicable only to accommodation paper.[6] See beyond under *Purchasers from mortgagors.*

The maker cannot defend on the ground that the debt for which the note was pledged as security was tainted with usury.[7]

Accommodation makers. Accommodation makers are

[1] 22 Ala. 262 (1853); 2 Met. (Mass.) 8 (1840).
[2] 11 Hun (N. Y.) 119 (1877).
[3] 55 Tex. 167 (1881).
[4] 106 N. Y. 70 (1887).
[5] 2 Conn. 175 (1817).
[6] 55 Tex. 167 (1881).
[7] 9 Gill (Md.) 137 (1850).

not "borrowers," and therefore cannot set up usury, where the statute confers that right upon borrowers only.[1]

Oppressed parties. Some courts hold to the broad principle that any oppressed party to a contract can take advantage of the usury in it.[2]

Partners. In an action on a firm note, either partner may set up usury, without the consent of the other, and so may a partner who has undertaken to pay the firm's debts, in a suit brought against him alone after dissolution. If usury is set up by either partner, the penalty should be enforced against both. A renewal of the partnership note by one of the partners will not deprive him of the right to set up usury as to such note.[3]

Payors. He who pays the usury can recover it, generally speaking.[4]

Privies. All privies to the borrower can set up usury in defence.[5] The New York rule is as follows: "All privies to the borrower, whether in blood, representation, or estate, both in law and equity, by the appropriate legal and equitable remedies and defences, may attack or defend against a contract or security given by the borrower

[1] 16 How. Pr. (N. Y.) 142 (1857).

[2] 47 Ala. 363 (1872); 7 Conn. 409 (1829); 111 Ill. 328 (1884); 14 Iowa 125, 251 (1862); 32 Iowa 418 (1871); 37 Iowa 325 (1873); 8 Shepl. (Me.) 195 (1842); 17 Shepl. (Me.) 118 (1849); 50 Vt. 67 (1877); 51 Vt. 77 (1878).

[3] 15 Iowa 49 (1863).

[4] 13 Mass. 104 (1816); 3 Pick. (Mass.) 184 (1825); 35 N. H. 421 (1857); 60 N. H. 17, 100 (1880); 32 Vt. 89 (1859); 33 Vt. 553 (1861); 49 Vt. 400 (1877); 50 Vt. 67 (1877); 51 Vt. 77 (1878); 53 Vt. 33 (1880), 491, 501 (1881).

[5] 36 Ark. 243 (1880); 84 Ga. 748 (1890); 22 Ill. 327 (1859); 123 Ill. 510 (1888); 14 Iowa 125, 251 (1862); 32 Iowa 418 (1871); 37 Iowa 325 (1873); 8 Paige (N. Y.) 639 (1841); 49 N. Y. 635 (1872); 22 Hun (N. Y.) 208, 218 (1880); 25 Hun (N. Y.) 490 (1881); 1 Coop. (Tenn.) 459 (1873). See 2 Hill (N. Y.) 522 (1842).

which is tainted with usury, on the ground of such usury, when such contract or security affects the estate derived by them from the borrower."[1]

Purchasers from mortgagors. A purchaser of an equity of redemption may avail himself of the defence of usury paid by the mortgagor,[2] unless it is purchased subject to the mortgage,[3] in which case he cannot do so, as he thus affirms the mortgage,[4] and waives the right of defence.[5] This is true in equitable relief,[6] and in defence to a writ of entry on the mortgage.[7] The Illinois court holds that the purchaser of property subject to a mortgage, cannot recover usury if he was ignorant of its existence in the mortgage at the time of his purchase,[8] and the Wisconsin court says that it makes no difference whether he knew it or not.[9] The purchaser must have paid full price for the land, and it must have been foreclosed and the money paid before the purchase.[10]

If the purchaser of the equity agrees to pay the mortgage as part of the consideration of the conveyance, the maker may upon the face of the note maintain an action

[1] 22 Hun (N. Y.) 208, 218 (1880).

[2] 86 Ill. 513 (1877); 1 Md. Ch. 127 (1847): 20 N. H. 100 (1849): 1 Stock. (N. J.) 867 (1852); 4 Halst. Ch. (N. J.) 789 (1852); *contra*, 53 Ind. 341 (1876); 13 Mass. 515 (1816); 1 Mich. 84 (1848); 11 Mich. 59 (1862); 27 Neb. 401 (1889).

[3] 45 Ill. 322, 462 (1867); 86 Ill. 513 (1877): 36 Md. 181 (1872); 10 S. & M. (Miss.) 89 (1848); 34 Barb. (N. Y.) 336 (1861); 36 N. Y. 144, 319 (1867); 94 N. Y. 221 (1883).

[4] 45 Ill. 322 (1867).

[5] 1 McCart. (N. J.) 56 (1861); 9 C. E. Gr. (N. J.) 120 (1873).

[6] 24 Md. 62 (1865); 30 Md. 485 (1869).

[7] 86 Ill. 513 (1877); 20 N. H. 100 (1849); 4 N. Y. (4 Comst.) 225 (1850); 10 Wis. 333 (1860); 21 Wis. 239 (1866); *contra*, 13 Mass. 515 (1816).

[8] 45 Ill. 322, 462 (1867).

[9] 10 Wis. 333 (1860); 21 Wis. 239 (1866).

[10] 58 Ga. 158 (1877).

(if the statute allows it) against the payee of the note to recover the forfeiture,[1] that is, payment by the maker's vendee is deemed to be payment by himself. This is specially true if the purchaser agrees to pay the mortgage except the usurious interest;[2] but he cannot set it up in an action to foreclose;[3] and the Minnesota court holds that he is estopped from setting up usury in any case.[4]

In Maine, the rule that the party giving an usurious security is entitled, at some time, to avoid it by showing the usury, receives a very broad construction.[5] A mortgagor was allowed to do so there, even after the equity of redemption had been sold at sheriff's sale, and the purchaser had taken an assignment of the mortgage, the time for redemption having elapsed,[6] it being set up against a writ of entry, the mortgagor remaining in possession. But in a case where the title was absolutely vested by deed of bargain and sale it was not allowed to be disturbed by showing usury in the consideration.[7]

If the purchaser of an equity of redemption assumes and agrees to pay the mortgage he cannot set up usury in it, on the principle that a person contracting to pay the debt of another, and receiving property out of which it is to be paid, cannot oppose the plea of usury, or go into the consideration of the debt, and retain the means placed in his hands to pay it.[8] The New York court holds, how-

[1] 7 Gray (Mass.) 559 (1856).

[2] 62 Ill. 461 (1872).

[3] 10 Iowa 385, 491 (1860); 13 Iowa 174 (1862); 15 Iowa 470 (1863); 32 Iowa 354 (1871); 38 Iowa 112 (1874); 55 Iowa 424 (1880).

[4] 36 Minn. 57 (1886).

[5] 6 Greenl. (Me.) 35 (1829); 5 Hubb. (Me.) 312 (1860).

[6] 6 Greenl. (Me.) 35 (1829).

[7] 7 Greenl. (Me.) 435 (1831).

[8] 11 South. Rep. (Ala.) 836 (1892); 19 La. 154 (1841); 71 Md. 456 (1889); 27 Wis. 414 (1870).

ever, that a grantee of mortgaged land, where the deed warrants against the mortgage, is not estopped from setting up usury in the mortgage, even when he retains part of the purchase money to pay it, and the mortgagor has failed to set aside the bond, which it secured, for usury in the mortgage.[1]

The purchaser of an equity of redemption at an execution sale may set up usury in the mortgage,[2] if it is sold subject to the mortgage,[3] unless the purchaser is a judgment creditor.[4]

Where a mortgagor releases for the sole purpose of creating a trust in favor of himself, the releasee cannot set up usury, having no personal interest in the premises.[5]

A mortgage may be assailed for usury, says the Minnesota court, by a sheriff who holds the mortgagor's interest under an attachment.[6]

Representatives. A borrower's personal representatives may generally take advantage of usury in his contracts.[7]

If an executor gives his own note for usury claimed against his testator, the Kentucky court holds that he may sue as executor for its reclamation.[8]

Second mortgagees. A second mortgagee cannot defend against usury in the first mortgage,[9] unless the owner

[1] 40 Barb. (N. Y.) 359 (1863).

[2] 1 Stock. (N. J.) 807 (1852); 4 Halst. Ch. (N. J.) 789 (1852).

[3] 2 Halst. Ch. (N. J.) 73 (1846); 1 Stock. (N. J.) 807 (1852); 10 C. E. Gr. (N. J.) 188 (1874).

[4] 1 Stock. (N. J.) 807 (1852); *contra*, 2 Halst. (N. J.) 73 (1846).

[5] 11 C. E. Gr. (N. J.) 357 (1875).

[6] 44 Minn. 218 (1890).

[7] 3 Ala. 458 (1842); 55 Ala. 344 (1876); 72 Ala. 294 (1882); 55 Ind. 341 (1876); 75 Ind. 318 (1881); 29 Barb. (N. Y.) 401 (1859); 33 N. Y. 31 (1865).

[8] 12 B. Mon. (Ky.) 89 (1851).

[9] 123 Ill. 510 (1888); 17 Kas. 355 (1876); 26 Hun (N. Y.) 209 (1882); 46 Wis. 692 (1879); *contra*, 26 Conn. 241 (1857); 26 Ind. 94 (1866); 1 Stock. (N. J.) 807 (1852); 4 Halst. Ch. (N. J.) 789 (1852).

of the equity consents,[1] or all the parties are in court.[2] A junior mortgagee, in an action to redeem from the judgment in a foreclosure proceeding to which he was not made a party, and in which usury was not pleaded, cannot set up the defence of usury and compel the holder of the judgment to accept less than the amount of his lien.[3]

A purchaser of real property under a foreclosure sale of a valid mortgage may set up usury against a prior mortgage given by the same mortgagor, and which is an apparent lien,[4] says the New York court, which applies the same rule to a purchaser at a sale in foreclosure of a mechanics' lien.[5]

One who holds a mortgage upon real estate subject to the lien of a prior judgment, is not a "borrower," and therefore cannot maintain a bill to set aside the judgment, on the ground that it was confessed for an usurious debt, without offering to pay the sum equitably due.[6]

Sureties. A surety on a note can set up usury,[7] even though the maker will not join with him,[8] if the contract is usurious in itself.[9] And the rule is the same if the note is in renewal of another on which the interest was paid.[10]

[1] 1 C. E. Gr. (N. J.) 550 (1862).

[2] 2 C. E. Gr. (N. J.) 87 (1864), 517 (1866).

[3] 11 Iowa 430 (1860).

[4] 22 Hun (N. Y.) 208, 218 (1880).

[5] 3 Hun (N. Y.) 577 (1875).

[6] 3 Barb. Ch. (N. Y.) 640 (1847); 2 N. Y. (2 Comst.) 131 (1848); 14 N. Y. (4 Kern.) 93 (1856).

[7] 22 Ala. 262 (1853); 22 Ill. 327 (1859); 89 Ill. 123 (1878); 75 Ind. 318 (1881); 47 Iowa 62 (1877); 67 Iowa 13 (1885); 3 Dana (Ky.) 595 (1835); 12 B. Mon. (Ky.) 307 (1851).

[8] 22 Ill. 327 (1859).

[9] 44 N. H. 227 (1862); 32 Vt. 89 (1859); *contra*, if the usury has been paid by the principal, 50 Vt. 105 (1877).

[10] 39 Ind. 106 (1872).

Wives. A wife may set up usury in her husband's note in an action to foreclose a mortgage of his homestead.[1]

(*d*) *Who is liable to return usury paid.* To charge one with usury, he must know of and be a party to the intent to violate the usury law; as where a note and mortgage were bought of the payee, who was the mortgagee, believing him to be the owner, though he was in fact merely acting for the mortgagor.[2]

Whoever receives usurious interest is liable to pay it back: as an executor,[3] and also an administrator who has exacted usury on debts due his intestate, he being held personally liable to refund, even though he has settled the estate, and accounted for it to those entitled to the estate.[4] So, in order to constitute usury a defence on the foreclosure of a mortgage, it must be shown that the usurious excess was received by the mortgagee or his agent.[5]

A claim for usury paid survives against the estate of the person to whom it was paid.[6]

The assignee of a mortgage, even without notice of the usury, takes it subject to the defence of usury;[7] and a sale under the power in an usurious mortgage puts the purchaser in the same plight as the original mortgagee.[8] A purchaser from the mortgagor may set up the defence of usury to defeat the action of the assignee of the mortgagee.[9]

Where the payee of a note transfers the same before

[1] 20 Iowa 578 (1866).
[2] 42 Minn. 438 (1890).
[3] 8 B. Mon. (Ky.) 452 (1848).
[4] 5 B. Mon. (Ky.) 145 (1844).
[5] 1 Stew. (N. J.) 345 (1877).
[6] 8 B. Mon. (Ky.) 452 (1848); 27 Vt. 396 (1855).
[7] 8 C. E. Gr. (N. J.) 174 (1872).
[8] 31 Minn. 495 (1884).
[9] 1 Md. Ch. 127 (1847).

maturity to a *bona fide* purchaser so that the maker is compelled to pay the usury, he can recover the usury from the payee, if the payment of the usury is the motive for doing it.[1]

The New Jersey court holds that if a contract between an indorser and his indorsee is usurious, the latter can maintain no action against the maker or any prior party to the instrument, although it was good in its creation.[2]

An accommodation indorser of a note who takes it up at maturity, in ignorance of the fact that it has been discounted at an usurious rate, may maintain an action against the maker for reimbursement.[3]

A principal is presumed to know the manner in which his general agent transacts his business, and is chargeable with usury if he authorizes or sanctions the taking by his agent of such usury, even for the agent's own benefit,[4] says the Minnesota court; but see page 240.

(*e*) *Pleading and practice.* The following rules and principles apply to the general usury practice in the courts.

1. *Pleading.* Usury may be set up by plea, or relied upon in answer.[5] The general rule is, that when usury is pleaded in defence it must be done specifically, and in detail, setting out all the facts necessary to sustain the claim,[6]

[1] 27 Ill. 301 (1862); 40 Ill. 131 (1865).

[2] 2 Harr. (N. J.) 191 (1839).

[3] 11 Hun (N. Y.) 119 (1877).

[4] 46 Minn. 360 (1891).

[5] 2 Md. Ch. 510 (1849).

[6] 61 Ala. 492 (1878); 81 Ala. 464 (1886); 85 Ala. 368 (1888); Kirby (Conn.) 143 (1786); 26 Conn. 211 (1857); 1 Kelley (Ga.) 108 (1846); 55 Ga. 412 (1875), 691 (1876); 65 Ga. 386 (1880); 68 Ga. 628 (1882); 69 Ga. 722 (1882); 24 Ill. 381 (1860); 37 Ill. 253 (1865); 40 Ill. 519 (1866); 83 Ill. 519 (1876); 86 Ill. 197 (1877); 6 Blf. (Ind.) 133 (1842), 378 (1843); 16 Ind. 189 (1861); 6 Mon. (Ky.) 81 (1827); 7 Mon. (Ky.) 53, 263 (1828); 1 J. J. Mar. (Ky.) 10 (1828); 2 Duv. (Ky.) 153, 154 (1865); 9 Gray (Mass.) 64 (1857); 53 N. W. Rep. (Minn.) 647 (1892);

unless the contract sued on, which is included in the plaintiff's pleadings, shows the usury on its face.[1] This is true at both law and equity.[2] But unusual strictness is not required in pleading in usury.[3] The plea must also show the amount of illegal interest paid.[4] But in every case it must conform to the statutory requirements.[5] Some courts hold that if the contract set out in the pleadings of the plaintiff is usurious on its face its usurious nature need not be pleaded,[6] or proved,[7] and the court of its own motion will purge the usury.[8] The court will not extend the time for answering in usury.[9] The statute must be pleaded specially;[10] usury cannot be shown under the general issue;[11] though it may be under the plea of

16 Neb. 689 (1884); 50 N. W. Rep. (Neb.) 271 (1891); 3 Harr. (N. J.) 258 (1841); 1 McCart. (N. J.) 326 (1862); 1 C. E. Gr. (N. J.) 415 (1863); 7 C. E. Gr. (N. J.) 438 (1871). 606 (1872); 9 C. E. Gr. (N. J.) 125, 135, 230, 312 (1873); 10 C. E. Gr. (N. J.) 418 (1874); 11 C. E. Gr. (N. J.) 357 (1875); 12 C. E. Gr. (N. J.) 360 (1876), 484 (1875); 2 Stew. (N. J.) 551 (1878); 5 Stew. (N. J.) 456 (1880); 3 Ore. 389 (1872); 50 Tenn. 242 (1873); 8 Leigh (Va.) 330 (1837).

1 2 J. J. Mar. (Ky.) 428 (1829); 80 Va. 379 (1885).

2 Where a bill in equity showed the usury, the respondent might demur. 1 G. Gr. (Iowa) 121 (1848); 3 W. Va. 86 (1868).

3 29 Ind. 158 (1867).

4 13 Ind. 448 (1859).

5 63 Ga. 373 (1879).

6 56 Ga. 210 (1876); 12 W. P. D. Bush (Ky.) 298 (1876); 79 Ky. 346 (1881).

7 9 Pet. (U. S.) 378, 418 (1835).

8 12 W. P. D. Bush (Ky.) 298 (1876); 79 Ky. 346 (1881).

9 2 Beas. (N. J.) 43 (1860).

10 19 Wall. (U. S.) 548 (1873); 65 Ala. 133 (1880); 70 Ala. 406 (1881); 2 Conn. 161 (1817); 19 Ill. 132 (1857); 2 Md. Ch. 510 (1849); 70 Md. 42 (1888); 109 N. C. 539 (1891). See 48 Md. 455 (1877).

11 65 Ala. 133 (1880); 70 Ala. 406 (1881); 7 Ark. 146 (1846); 17 Ark. 138 (1856); 22 Ark. 409 (1860); 26 Ark. 356 (1870); *contra*, 3 Day (Conn.) 68 (1808); 1 McM. (S. C.) 225 (1841). The Connecticut court, however, holds that it may be shown under the general issue, even without notice. 4 Conn. 436 (1822).

non-assumpsit, say the courts of South Carolina and West Virginia.[1] Usury may be shown if it is not pleaded, if the plaintiff puts in evidence showing that it was stipulated for.[2]

If the usury paid equals or exceeds the debt lawfully due, a plea in bar of the action may be made;[3] but if it does not amount to as much, a plea should be made only for a deduction from the sum due.[4] A plea that the consideration is entirely usurious, if the facts shown do not prove it, is not good.[5]

A plea in set-off must state that the money was paid as usury.[6]

A note with illegal interest may be declared on as a note without interest.[7]

An agreement to withdraw a plea of usury is against public policy.[8]

In trover, a bill of sale, or other contract, can be attacked on the ground of usury, without pleading it.[9]

A contract made in another state, bearing upon its face a rate of interest illegal at the *forum*, will not be declared void, without a plea of usury.[10] If the law of another state is necessary to be proven to sustain the allegation of usury, it must be pleaded and proved as a fact in all its

[1] 3 Brev. (S. C.) 54 (1812); 5 W. Va. 540 (1872); *contra*, not good without notice, 66 Tenn. 618 (1873). Notice may be waived, 66 Tenn. 618 (1873).

[2] 7 La. 198 (1834).

[3] 4 Hous. (Del.) 473 (1873); 17 Ind. 521, 528 (1861); 39 Ind. 305 (1872); 3 N. H. 185 (1825).

[4] 17 Ind. 521, 528 (1861); 9 N. H. 531 (1838); 36 N. H. 73 (1858).

[5] 23 Ind. 119 (1864).

[6] 23 Ind. 119 (1864).

[7] 1 Ind. 32 (1848).

[8] 14 Kas. 398 (1875).

[9] 81 Ga. 81 (1888); 50 Mich. 320 (1883); *contra*, 71 Ala. 271 (1882).

[10] 36 Minn. 333 (1887).

necessary details as far as it affects the case.[1] The New York court holds that the law of a foreign state is presumptively the same as that of the *forum*.[2] See, however, a full discussion of this rule under "Conflict of laws," chapter nine.

A legal contract cannot be made usurious by the prayer of the plaintiff for usurious interest, when he seeks to enforce it.[3]

The plaintiff must fully negative the defendant's plea of usury in his answer to it.[4] An evasive answer may be deemed an admission of usury.[5] If only a general denial of the usury is given, but slight evidence will be required to establish it.[6]

The plea of usury must be verified by affidavit if the statute requires it.

Usury is a legal defence,[7] and, although, says the New York court, it is not encouraged,[8] it should be regarded as any other legal defence, and not be treated with disfavor, as being unconscientious.[9]

A plea of usury will be received in equity at any time before the final decree.[10]

When a bill is entered for the foreclosure of a mort-

[1] 1 Halst. Ch. (N. J.) 17 (1845); 1 McCart. (N. J.) 56 (1861), 229, 355 (1862); 2 McCart. (N. J.) 476 (1863); 1 C. E. Gr. (N. J.) 42 (1863); 12 C. E. Gr. (N. J.) 360 (1876); 17 Grat. (Va.) 47 (1861); 4 W. Va. 4 (1870); 23 Wis. 383 (1868).

[2] 29 Barb. (N. Y.) 325 (1859).

[3] 10 La. Ann. 610 (1855).

[4] 49 Md. 516 (1878).

[5] Lit. Sel. Cas. (Ky.) 378 (1821).

[6] Lit. Sel. Cas. (Ky.) 484 (1821); 7 Mon. (Ky.) 383 (1828); 4 J. J. Mar. (Ky.) 90 (1830); 5 Dana (Ky.) 85 (1837).

[7] 9 Cow. (N. Y.) 65 (1828).

[8] 3 Wend. (N. Y.) 573 (1829); 1 Paige (N. Y.) 429 (1829).

[9] 3 Johns. Cas. (N. Y.) 206 (1802); 4 Denio (N. Y.) 264 (1847).

[10] 4 Munf. (Va.) 66 (1813).

gage, the mortgagor may set up usury in defence, and need not file a cross-bill.[1]

It is not necessary generally to show a corrupt intent to evade the statute.

The debtor must distinctly raise the defence of usury, but not necessarily by plea or answer, it may be by written exception to the report of commissioners;[2] but a mere request to have it done is insufficient.[3] So, in a bill seeking relief on the ground of usury, the usury must be put directly in issue.[4]

Where a written contract on its face purports to be usurious, allegations and proof that the contract was not usurious, must be explicit and clear of all doubt.[5]

It is not error to reject pleas that set forth specifically the manner by which a contract is alleged to have been executed usuriously, when a plea is also filed alleging usury, under the statute, by which any defence can be made that could have been made if the pleas had not been rejected.[6]

In an action of debt for a statutory penalty, a promissory note taken being the only legal evidence of the contract of loan, it should be declared on accordingly.[7]

The law will not apply a general payment, nor authorize the creditor to apply it, without the consent of the debtor, to the payment of usury.[8] If the debtor neglects to apply it, the creditor may do so.[9] When payments have been made, which are merely credited on

[1] 2 C. E. Gr. (N. J.) 87 (1864), 547 (1866).
[2] 31 W. Va. 410 (1888).
[3] 31 W. Va. 410 (1888).
[4] 5 Rand. (Va.) 543 (1827).
[5] 7 O. St. 387 (1857).
[6] 5 W. Va. 540 (1872).
[7] 4 Pa. St. 317 (1846).
[8] 16 Tex. 200 (1856).
[9] 80 Va. 379 (1885).

the bond, and not applied specially, the borrower is entitled to have such payments deducted from the principal sum loaned on forfeiture.[1]

A defendant may plead usury in the original contract to a *scire facias* brought to revive a decree obtained by default, says the Virginia court.[2]

2. *Proof.* Usury must be clearly proved[3] by evidence of a satisfactory character;[4] it will never be presumed,[5] as it is a violation of the law. If the instrument sued on shows the usury, its production is sufficient proof of it.[6] If intent is necessary to constitute the usury it must be proved;[7] the law will, however, infer a corrupt agreement if the parties entered into it knowingly.[8] If the evidence, or contract, is capable of two constructions, by fairness and reason, the court will lean in favor of that which makes it legal and valid.[9]

The court in Kentucky holds that taking interest by a separate note stamps the contract as usurious.[10]

The Illinois court says that the taking of usurious interest is *prima facie* evidence that the contract was originally usurious.[11]

[1] 80 Va. 279 (1885).

[2] 4 H. & M. (Va.) 504 (1810).

[3] 53 Hun (N. Y.) 63 (1889); 8 Leigh (Va.) 330 (1837).

[4] 16 Hun (N. Y.) 209 (1878); 80 N. Y. 198 (1880); 81 N. Y. 352 ([illegible]).

[5] 88 Ill. 566 (1878); 53 N. W. Rep. (Iowa) 124 (1892); 5 La. Ann. 682 (1850); 2 Doug. (Mich.) 230 (1846); 39 Minn. 339 (1888); 53 Hun (N. Y.) 63 (1889); 85 Tenn. 127 (1886); 1 Wash. (Va.) 368 (1794); 21 Wis. 329 (1867).

[6] 6 Rand. (Va.) 661 (1828).

[7] 52 N. W. Rep. (Minn.) 135 (1892).

[8] 2 Harr. (N. J.) 487 (1840); 2 Beas. (N. J.) 351, 357 (1861).

[9] 5 La. Ann. 682 (1850); 3 Gr. Ch. (N. J.) 128 (1837); 2 Beas. (N. J.) 253 (1861); 10 C. E. Gr. (N. J.) 491 (1875); 2 Dick. (N. J.) 8 ([illegible]); 66 N. Y. 214 (1876).

[10] 1 J. J. Mar. (Ky.) 49 (1829).

[11] 77 Ill. 182 (1875).

A defendant, who has pleaded usury, cannot take out a commission to have himself examined.[1]

A variation between a note and a mortgage given to secure it, affords no evidence that the difference is usury, when the sum secured by the mortgage is greater than that named in the consideration with accruing interest.[2]

It cannot be shown that the plaintiff has previously been guilty of usury.[3]

It is sufficient if the usury proved be substantially the same as that averred in the pleadings;[4] but it will not avail the defendant that the case proved makes out usury, if it is not the case set out by the answer.[5]

If an answer denies the allegation of usury, and there is no proof of it, the bill will of course be dismissed.[6] Where a bill, brought to set aside a judgment on the ground of usury, simply says that the debt is usurious, without stating the usurious interest taken, and the charge of usury is not sustained by competent evidence, the court will not, after long delay, set aside the judgment and grant a new trial.[7]

Oral evidence. Oral evidence is admissible to show usury in written contracts.[8] A bill of sale[9] or an absolute deed[10] may thus be shown to be a mortgage. Evidence

[1] 4 McC. (S. C.) 254 (1827).

[2] 16 N. H. 479 (1845).

[3] 76 N. C. 314 (1877).

[4] 6 O. St. 19 (1856).

[5] 1 McCart. (N. J.) 326 (1862); 9 C. E. Gr. (N. J.) 124 (1873).

[6] 9 Grat. (Va.) 294 (1852).

[7] 75 Va. 475 (1881).

[8] 97 U. S. 13 (1877); 11 Ark. 16 (1850); 25 Ark. 191 (1868); 47 Ark. 287 (1886); 6 Mon. (Ky.) 155 (1827); 7 Mon. (Ky.) 252 (1828); 43 Minn. 307 (1890); 12 S. & M. (Miss.) 334 (1849); 31 Neb. 328 (1891); 8 W. & S. (Pa.) 31 (1844).

[9] 7 Mon. (Ky.) 252 (1828).

[10] 39 Iowa 549 (1874); 7 Dana (Ky.) 300 (1838).

of any facts establishing the purpose and intent of the loan is admissible.[1]

It may also be shown orally that a mistake was made in a written instrument, and that although it is written for an usurious rate of interest it was not so intended.[2]

The usury law is very broad and will search deeply into contracts.[3] The particulars of a dissolved partnership transaction can be entered into, if it is necessary in order to expose usury, even though it was dissolved before the note was given.[4] A contract for the sale and purchase of property is scrutinized sharply as it is often a device to cover usury.[5] Where a note did not stipulate for usurious interest, an oral promise to pay usury is not admissible, although it was afterward reduced to writing.[6]

Burden of proof. The burden of proving the usury is on the party alleging it.[7]

Quantity of evidence. Usury, like other civil actions, must be proved by a fair preponderance of evidence.[8] The weight of the evidence should not be disregarded.[9]

Character of proof. Usury must be proved clearly by

[1] 25 O. St. 420 (1874).

[2] 3 Gr. (N. J.) 255, 258 (1836).

[3] 6 Mon. (Ky.) 534 (1828).

[4] 22 Ga. 193 (1857).

[5] 1 Mar. (Ky.) 530 (1817); 4 Lit. (Ky.) 302 (1823); 7 Mon. (Ky.) 423 (1828).

[6] 83 Ala. 323 (1887).

[7] 21 S. W. Rep. (Ark.) 432 (1893); 57 Iowa 359 (1881); 59 Iowa 723 (1882); 20 Kas. 285 (1878); 11 Neb. 487 (1881); 1 Gr. Ch. (N. J.) 453 (1841); 2 C. E. Gr. (N. J.) 460 (1864); 3 C. E. Gr. (N. J.) 481 (1867); 5 C. E. Gr. (N. J.) 139 (1869); 7 C. E. Gr. (N. J.) 438 (1871), 606 (1872); 2 Dick. (N. J.) 8 (1890); 66 N. Y. 544 (1876); 81 N. Y. 363 (1880); 36 O. St. 361 (1880); 6 Grat. (Va.) 287 (1849); 21 Wis. 320 (1867).

[8] 73 Ill. 213 (1874); 37 Minn. 441 (1887); 2 Stew. (N. J.) 380 (1878); 2 Dick. (N. J.) 8 (1890).

[9] 52 N. W. Rep. (Minn.) 135 (1892); 10 C. E. Gr. (N. J.) 188 (1874).

cogent evidence.[1] So in proving the usury laws of another state.[2]

Costs. When the lender refuses a tender of the principal and legal interest, before the action is brought, he must pay the costs.[3]

Miscellany. In a suit on two drafts, where the defence was usury, and the verdict was for a sum less than the amount due, it was held by the Maine court that such verdict established the fact of usury.[4]

The mere fact that a debtor has paid usurious interest for several years annually does not support the allegation, under a statute calling for a contract.[5] Neither is it evidence having any legitimate tendency to show the inclusion of usury in notes subsequently given for the debt.[6]

Evidence of a usage with other banks organized under the same law, to discount more than the legal rate of interest upon the acquisition of business paper, is not admissible.[7]

A note given for an usurious consideration is illegal and not evidence of a lawful contract.[8] But where usury is pleaded to a suit on a note, deeds of even date with the note and executed to vest the title in the lender as security for the loan, are admissible as evidence for the plaintiff to show the intention of the parties as to the real *situs*

[1] 4 Halst. Ch. (N. J.) 789 (1852); 1 McCart. (N. J.) 229 (1862); 1 C. E. Gr. (N. J.) 537 (1863); 2 C. E. Gr. (N. J.) 160 (1864); 7 C. E. Gr. (N. J.) 438 (1871), 606 (1872); 9 C. E. Gr. (N. J.) 124 (1873); 10 C. E. Gr. (N. J.) 418 (1874); 12 C. E. Gr. (N. J.) 484 (1875); 13 Stew. (N. J.) 281 (1885).

[2] 5 C. E. Gr. (N. J.) 288 (1869).

[3] 5 Mon. (Ky.) 92 (1827).

[4] 20 Me. (2 Appl., 7 Shepl.) 144 (1841).

[5] 36 O. St. 361 (1880).

[6] 26 Atl. Rep. (Vt.) 67 (1892).

[7] 15 O. St. 68 (1864).

[8] 3 Brev. (S. C.) 54 (1812).

of the contract, and what state or country they had reference to in fixing the rate of interest.[1] So an usurious bond is admissible in evidence to show the amount of money advanced.[2]

The indorsee of a note, originally usurious, cannot recover from the maker on it, though it is in his hands for value in the way of trade. Such indorsee may, however, recover of the indorser if he sues on a count for money had and received.[3]

3. *Recovery of security.* If the valid portion of a note is paid, it does not then represent any legal indebtedness; and the borrower will be entitled to a reconveyance of the property securing the loan.[4]

A privy in estate may recover property pledged under an usurious contract.[5]

If a borrower delivers property in part payment of a loan he cannot recover it on the ground of usury in the loan. The only remedy is an action to recover the excess of interest. But where chattels are pledged or mortgaged simply to secure payment of an usurious debt, the borrower has a right to recover them.[6]

The right to have collateral security cancelled or restrained in equity will not be recognized without the payment of the principal sum; and in such a case an assignee must show that the principal has been paid.[7]

4. *Law and fact.* Whether a certain contract is usurious or not is a mixed question of law and fact.[8] The

[1] 15 S. E. Rep. (Ga.) 812 (1892).
[2] 11 Leigh (Va.) 113 (1840).
[3] 2 Bay (S. C.) 23 (1796).
[4] 34 Iowa 483 (1872).
[5] 49 N. Y. 635 (1872).
[6] 7 Cow. (N. Y.) 290 (1827).
[7] 64 N. Y. 212 (1876).
[8] 17 Grat. (Va.) 21 (1866).

jury must determine upon the evidence what the facts are,[1] and the court decide whether or not such facts bring the contract within the usury law.[2] As is the common practice the jury are to be instructed in the law of the case by the court and then asked to determine whether or not the facts which they find bring the contract within the law.[3]

The question of the consideration of forbearance is one of fact for the jury.[4] So is the question of corrupt intent.[5]

If it is a written contract, and the instrument is the only evidence offered, then it is entirely for the court.[6] If a note is usurious on its face and no other evidence is offered, the court may render judgment for the principal and legal interest.[7]

The law of a foreign state, where a bill was discounted, etc., must be proved to establish usury.[8]

5. *Who may be witnesses.* At common law parties to suits cannot testify as they are interested in the event of the action, but the usury statutes generally give them the right to give evidence as to the usury in the contract, and they can testify, not only to the particular transaction involved in the suit, but to all transactions that have or have had any connection with the usurious contract,[9] or its consideration.[10] The endowment of certain parties

[1] 22 Tex. 120 (1858).

[2] 2 Rich. (S. C.) 73 (1845).

[3] 7 Johns. (N. Y.) 196 (1810).

[4] 12 Wall. (U. S.) 226 (1870); 93 U. S. 344 (1876); 5 Fla. 504 (1854); 77 Ill. 182 (1875); 3 Met. (Mass.) 211 (1841).

[5] 13 Ired. L. (N. C.) 454 (1852).

[6] 3 Cranch (U. S.) 180 (1805); 3 How. (U. S.) 62 (1845).

[7] 20 Ind. 262 (1863).

[8] 78 Ga. 229 (1886); 3 Dana (Ky.) 497 (1835).

[9] 8 Ala. 53 (1845); 25 Ala. 433 (1854); 1 McArt. (D. C.) 232 (1873).

[10] 18 Ill. 101 (1856).

with this privilege of testifying does not exclude those that had such right at common law.[1]

Borrowers may testify that interest is included in the note without producing it.[2]

It is held under the usury statute, generally, that the privilege of testifying to usury in a contract is given only to that class of parties who allege it;[3] that is, where one of two defendants is defaulted, the defaulted one cannot testify to the usury. Where money is borrowed by two persons for the benefit of one, and a joint note is given, on which both are sued, both are competent witnesses to prove the usury in the note.[4] But a borrower cannot give evidence of a distinct and independent fact, and then prove the usury by other witnesses;[5] that is, he must testify to the fact of the offence, as that is the only evidence he can give under the statute.

When there are two defendants, one of them cannot be compelled against his will to be examined as a witness.[6]

Neither the indorser of a security,[7] the drawer of a bill,[8] nor a defendant's administrator, although the estate is insolvent,[9] are competent witnesses, where the statute makes certain parties witnesses to prove usury.

The Massachusetts court held that the maker was not a competent witness where a note was made and discounted for his benefit at an usurious rate of interest, and thus first placed in circulation, the action being against the in-

[1] 4 McC. (S. C.) 397 (1827); 1 Bail. (S. C.) 83 (1828); 45 Tenn. 558 (1868).

[2] 106 Mass. 34 (1870).

[3] 13 Ala. 121 (1848); 2 Heath (Me.) 190 (1853).

[4] 25 Ala. 433 (1854).

[5] 13 Ala. 121 (1848).

[6] 4 Ala. 169 (1842).

[7] 4 Mass. 156 (1808).

[8] 1 Root (Conn.) 129 (1789), 267 (1791).

[9] 16 Mass. 118 (1819).

dorser;[1] but if the suit is against the maker of an accommodation note, the party accommodated is a competent witness to prove that he negotiated it upon an usurious consideration in another state, whose laws render usurious contracts void, to a party from whom the plaintiff took it after maturity.[2]

In a suit between the assignee and obligor of a bond, the obligee is not a competent witness to prove usury.[3]

In an action by or against the representative of a decedent on a contract made between the adverse party and another who had assigned it to the decedent, such adverse party is a competent witness on his own account to prove the contract usurious.[4]

Generally, any disinterested person may testify to the usury in the contract; that is, any one who is not interested in the result of the action. As, in an action between creditors, the debtor is a competent witness.[5] In an action on a note against an indorser, the maker is a competent witness for the defendant.[6] An indorser of a note is a competent witness to prove usury in the inception of the note in a suit against the maker.[7] A surety is a competent witness,[8] when the suit is brought by an indorsee against the maker. The maker of a note made for the accommodation of the payee is competent to prove usury in it, if he is released by the payee, who is the defendant in the suit.[9] In an action by an indorsee against the

[1] 17 Mass. 94 (1821).
[2] 10 Gray (Mass.) 349 (1858).
[3] 9 Grat. (Va.) 294 (1852).
[4] 45 Minn. 1 (1890).
[5] 1 McC. Ch. (S. C.) 431 (1826).
[6] 2 Hous. (Del.) 499 (1862); 4 Hous. (Del.) 473 (1873).
[7] 2 G. Gr. (Iowa) 217 (1849).
[8] 16 Mass. 118 (1819); 2 Rich. (S. C.) 1 (1845).
[9] 12 Pick. (Mass.) 565 (1832); 10 Tenn. 1 (1820), 35 (1821); 40 Tenn 389, 392 (1859); 45 Tenn. 568 (1868).

drawer, the indorser is a competent witness to prove usury.[1] And in an action on a bill, both drawer and indorser are competent witnesses to show usury to which the holder was a party,[2] the suit being against the drawee.

A broker negotiating business between the borrower and lender is a competent witness to prove the usurious nature ot the transaction.[3]

Where a subsequent judgment-creditor is made a party and defends against a mortgage, on the ground that it is tainted with usury, the mortgagor, who has confessed the bill, is held to be a competent witness for the creditor by the court in New York.[4]

The principal of a bond is not a competent witness for the surety to prove that the bond is usurious, or that he has made payments thereon.[5]

One of two partners, who made an usurious contract without the knowledge of the other, is a competent witness for his co-partner, when sued upon a contract he has individually made with the creditor, in which the usurious contract is merged, the partner who is sued having released the other.[6]

When a purchaser of an equity of redemption can have relief in equity for usury in the mortgage, the mortgagor may testify,[7] if he has sold his entire interest in the property.

(*f*) *Defences to claim for usury.* There are several defences that may be set up against claims for usury.

1. *Bona fide holder.* The fact that the plaintiff is

[1] 3 McC. (S. C.) 71 (1825).
[2] 103 Mass. 318 (1869).
[3] 2 Bay (S. C.) 23 (1796).
[4] 8 Paige (N. Y.) 639 (1841).
[5] 1 Rich. Eq. (S. C.) 41 (1844).
[6] 13 Ala. 121 (1848).
[7] 24 Md. 62 (1865).

a *bona fide* holder of negotiable paper for value before maturity[1] is generally a good defence to a plea of usury,[2] even though it was purchased at a discount,[3] and that it was accommodation paper in its inception;[4] if the statute is a penal one, adds the New Hampshire court.[5] The Arkansas court holds that an act of the legislature to make usurious notes in the hands of *bona fide* holders for value valid is unconstitutional and void.[6]

But an assignment of an usurious debt to a third person will not shield it from usury.[7] Neither will the transfer of a note from an old to a new firm, which is essentially the same, have any effect on its usurious character.[8]

If the holder knew of the usury at the time of the transfer, the plea of usury is good; otherwise not.[9] And this is true even though the maker assured the holder before the transfer that he had no defence against it, if he actually knew that it contained usury.[10] Taking a note

[1] 20 Kas. 655 (1878); 3 J. J. Mar. (Ky.) 13 (1829); 9 Neb. 221 (1879); 10 Neb. 83 (1880); 14 Neb. 415 (1883); 18 Neb. 515 (1886); 20 Neb. 128 (1886); 2 McC. (S. C.) 178 (1822); *contra*, 4 Iowa 490 (1857). See 17 Iowa 436 (1864).

[2] 64 Ala. 250 (1879); 24 Ill. 346 (1860); 4 Iowa 490 (1857); 31 Iowa 444 (1871); 122 Mass. 67 (1877); 52 N. W. Rep. (Neb. 693 (1892); 7 C. E. Gr. (N. J.) 606 (1872); 23 Tenn. 244 (1843); 58 Tenn. 340 (1871); 60 Tex. 679 (1884); *contra*, 70 Ala. 406 (1881); 41 Ark. 331 (1883); 31 Ill. 188 (1863); 10 Tenn. 255 (1829), 350 (1831); 23 Tenn. 246 (1843). See 17 Iowa 436 (1864).

[3] 24 Ill. 346 (1860); 58 Tenn. 340 (1871).

[4] 31 Iowa 444 (1871); 7 C. E. Gr. (N. J.) 606 (1872); *contra*, 70 Ala. 406 (1881).

[5] 2 N. H. 410 (1821); 3 N. H. 119 (1824). But the plaintiff must not demur.

[6] 41 Ark. 331 (1883).

[7] 3 Johns. Ch. (N. Y.) 395 (1818); 17 Johns. (N. Y.) 436 (1819).

[8] 17 Iowa 436 (1864).

[9] 8 Ark. 157 (1847).

[10] 10 S. & M. (Miss.) 69 (1848).

from an agent of the indorser and maker is not evidence of notice.[1]

If a note was originally valid, no intermediate usurious transaction will affect it in the hands of a subsequent fair holder not privy to the usury.[2] And any note, after having passed through the hands of a *bona fide* holder, against whom no charge of usury could be sustained, can be used as though it were originally valid.[3]

If such a holder receives a new note in the place of the usurious one, on terms which are valid, the new instrument cannot be impeached for usury in the original one.[4]

Equity will not relieve the borrower against a *bona fide* assignee of an usurious bond, who was induced to take the assignment upon the promise of the borrower to pay it; but it will afford him relief against the lender.[5]

The South Carolina court holds that when a person innocent of usury indorses a note as an accommodation, and the note is then usuriously discounted, the indorsement is void.[6] An earlier case was decided by the same court, in which it was held that the plaintiffs, who were indorsees without notice, had not sufficient reason to repel a charge of usury,[7] when the contract was originally usurious.

The maker of a note, not governed by the law merchant, cannot sell it for a sum less than its face, so as to preclude himself from setting up want of consideration to the extent of the discount, except possibly in the case of estoppel, where the sale is by an agent.[8]

[1] 58 Tenn. 340 (1871).

[2] 1 Bay (S. C.) 486 (1795).

[3] 9 Neb. 454 (1880).

[4] 7 Wend. (N. Y.) 256 (1831); 1 Barb. Ch. (N. Y.) 43 (1845).

[5] 4 Bibb (Ky.) 40 (1815); 7 J. J. Mar. (Ky.) 176 (1832); 9 Dana (Ky.) 593 (1840).

[6] 2 McC. (S. C.) 178 (1822).

[7] 3 Brev. (S. C.) 51 (1812).

[8] 23 Ind. 4 (1864).

A purchaser in good faith and for value at a sale by power of attorney in a mortgage, cannot be defeated in his title by usury in the original debt.[1]

In Virginia, it was held in slavery days that a sale of slaves under an usurious deed of trust could not be disturbed.[2]

A *bona fide* holder does not lose the benefit of a security because he retained usurious interest in the contract it secures,[3] as the usury only affects the interest in the *forum*.

The title of an innocent purchaser of land at a judicial sale under an usurious mortgage is not affected by the usury.[4]

A transfer before maturity, however, upon an usurious consideration, though in the usual course of business and without notice, will not make the indorsee a *bona fide* holder.[5] It is subject to equities. If the note was usurious in its origin only, he is a *bona fide* holder, unless it is a transaction to evade the statute.[6] Where a note is wrongfully signed by a partner in the firm's name, the fact of purchasing it from a broker, to whom he entrusted it for sale, does not afford a conclusive presumption that the purchaser does not take it in good faith against the other members of the firm.[7]

He who claims to be a *bona fide* holder of an usurious note has the burden of proof upon him.[8]

[1] 10 Johns. (N. Y.) 185 (1813); 4 Cow. (N. Y.) 266 (1825).

[2] 1 Leigh (Va.) 147 (1829).

[3] 100 U. S. 239 (1879).

[4] 5 Del. Ch. 302 (1880).

[5] 73 Ala. 558 (1883).

[6] 16 Ala. 398 (1848); 73 Ala. 558 (1883).

[7] 6 Allen (Mass.) 313 (1863).

[8] 9 Neb. 221 (1879); 24 Neb. 630 (1888); 25 Neb. 380 (1889); 52 N. W. Rep. (Neb.) 693 (1892).

Accommodation paper. The first real holder of negotiable paper cannot recover upon it if it is made to raise money on and is purchased at an usurious discount,[1] because it is deemed to be a loan made by him;[2] but he must know of the purpose of the paper,[3] or that it was originally tainted with usury.[4] It makes no difference whether the suit is brought against the indorser or maker,[5] if he had notice.[6] Such holder for value may sell it for any price,[7] but no prior holder can.[8] And such a holder is one who can maintain an action on the note against the maker when it is due.[9] But subsequent holders for value and without notice can buy and sell for any price, and it is not usurious.[10] It is then the same as business paper.[11]

[1] 22 N. Y. (8 Smith) 312 (1860); 44 Barb. (N. Y.) 87 (1865); 7 Hun (N. Y.) 576 (1876); 9 Hun (N. Y.) 263 (1876); 16 Hun (N. Y.) 307 (1878); 72 N. Y. 108 (1878); 111 N. Y. 441 (1888); 4 Jones L. (N. C.) 399 (1857); 2 Bail. (S. C.) 59 (1830); 23 Tenn. 374 (1843); *contra*, 11 N. Y. (1 Kern.) 368 (1854); 10 How. Pr. (N. Y.) 315 (1854). The indorsee must not know of the existence of the usury. 5 Rand. (Va.) 333 (1827); 76 Va. 419 (1882); 77 Va. 492 (1883).

[2] 122 N. Y. 385 (1890).

[3] 10 B. Mon. (Ky.) 12 (1849); 55 Tex. 167 (1881); Gil. (Va.) 42 (1820); 5 Rand. (Va.) 333 (1827); 76 Va. 419 (1882); 77 Va. 492 (1883); 14 Wis. 571 (1861); 28 Wis. 198 (1871).

[4] 1 Stew. (Ala.) 255 (1827); 3 Ala. 158 (1841); 16 Ala. 398 (1849); 5 Hubb. (Me.) 312 (1860); 5 Allen (Mass.) 134 (1862); 7 Allen (Mass.) 407 (1863); 10 Paige (N. Y.) 326 (1843); 2 Denio (N. Y.) 621 (1846); 4 Duer (N. Y.) 408 (1855); *contra*, 31 Iowa 444 (1871); 3 Mon. (Ky.) 289 (1826).

[5] 2 Johns. Cas. (N. Y.) 60 (1800).

[6] 55 Tex. 167 (1881).

[7] 15 Johns. (N. Y.) 44 (1818); 8 Cow. (N. Y.) 669 (1826); 7 Wend. (N. Y.) 256, 569 (1831).

[8] 8 Cow. (N. Y.) 669 (1826).

[9] 15 Johns. (N. Y.) 44 (1818); 8 Cow. (N. Y.) 669 (1826); 7 Wend. (N. Y.) 256, 569 (1831); 2 Denio (N. Y.) 621 (1846); 17 How. Pr. (N. Y.) 566 (1859); 29 Barb. (N. Y.) 576 (1859); 9 Hun (N. Y.) 263 (1876); 72 N. Y. 108 (1878).

[10] 130 N. Y. 6 (1891); 26 Pa. St. 259 (1856).

[11] 6 O. St. 37 (1856).

Where the holder and apparent owner of negotiable securities sells them at a discount to a *bona fide* purchaser, who supposes them to be business paper, it is not usurious to the maker,[1] but is to the seller. If it is accommodation paper, the maker could defend against the first indorsee.[2]

A note endorsed for the accommodation of the maker and passed by him as a security for an usurious loan, is an usurious contract in its inception, and the lender is the first holder.[3]

A party who transfers a note upon a sufficient consideration by delivery, knowing it to be usurious, to one who is ignorant of the defect, can be compelled to repay the usury he has received; and the cause of action is complete at the moment the fraudulent contract is consummated.[4] Usury still attaches to it, unless the holder received it through the fraud of the maker.[5]

Taking a note bearing unpaid instalments of interest before the principal is due, is taking it before it is due, as as far as equities are concerned, if it is done in good faith.[6]

Usury in a debt secured by mortgage does not affect the validity of the mortgage and is not available at law, in defence of an action founded on the mortgage.[7]

An exchange of notes is binding, thus making the payees holders for value.[8]

The time of the inception of notes is a question of fact.[9]

[1] 2 Denio (N. Y.) 621 (1846).
[2] 10 Paige (N. Y.) 326 (1843); 2 Denio (N. Y.) 621 (1846).
[3] 1 H. & G. (Md.) 477 (1827).
[4] 12 Ga. 371 (1853).
[5] 23 Ala. 537 (1853).
[6] 108 Mass. 497 (1871).
[7] 64 Ala. 501 (1879).
[8] 12 Ired. L. (N. C.) 334 (1851).
[9] 7 Hun (N. Y.) 576 (1876).

Banks are also governed by these rules relating to usury in the transfer of business and accommodation paper.[1]

2. *Estoppel.* A party may by his representations estop himself from setting up the defence of usury in an action against him by the party to whom such representations were made. Where the maker represents to the purchaser that the instrument sued on is not usurious, he is estopped.[2] Also, where upon an assignment of a mortgage, the mortgagor gave a written certificate that the mortgage was a good and valid lien upon the premises, and that there then existed no legal or equitable defence thereto, he was estopped.[3] In each of these cases the party purchasing must take the note upon the representations of the maker made at that time. The rule applies to all parties.[4]

Where an illegal reservation was made by the mortgagee, and the mortgagor afterward effected a new loan by the assignment of the mortgage, representing it to be good, he is precluded from setting up the original usury against the assignee and those claiming under him.[5]

If a mortgagor induces his mortgagee to secure a third person's chose in action, etc., to be assigned to him on account of the mortgage, he is estopped from setting up usury in such chose in action, etc., as a defence against his mortgagee.[6]

But the maker of an usurious note is not barred of the defence of usury by silently standing by when it was trans-

[1] 6 O. St. 527 (1856).

[2] 15 Iowa 563 (1864); 21 Iowa 441 (1868); 9 Hun (N. Y.) 263 (1876); 72 N. Y. 108 (1878).

[3] 39 Amer. Rep. 669, *note* (1881); 1 C. E. Gr. (N. J.) 210 (1863); 85 N. Y. 294 (1881).

[4] 3 Keyes (N. Y.) 609 (1867); 35 How. Pr. (N. Y.) 477 (1867).

[5] 8 C. E. Gr. (N. J.) 126 (1872).

[6] 85 Ala. 391, 417, 459 (1888).

ferred to an innocent holder, and not disclosing the fact of the usury;[1] nor by his subsequent promise to pay it, the plaintiffs having parted with nothing on the strength of the promise;[2] nor is a borrower precluded from setting up usury in a prior mortgage, because he has meanwhile conveyed away the premises with warranty, by a deed intended only as security, and a reconveyance to him having been subsequently made.[3]

The Ohio court has decided that where a national bank loans one of its directors a sum of money, which loan is usurious, the borrower is not estopped from the recovery of the usurious interest which he paid because he is an officer of the bank.[4]

3. *Judgment.* A judgment rendered is conclusive upon the question of the legality of the action,[5] unless the suit is brought to evade the usury law;[6] and if the judgment is satisfied the usury included therein cannot be recovered,[7] even in equity,[8] although the judgment was obtained by

[1] 1 Kelley (Ga.) 392 (1846).

[2] 16 Iowa 278 (1864).

[3] 65 Barb. (N. Y.) 30 (1873); 16 Hun (N. Y.) 487 (1879).

[4] 34 O. St. 142 (1877).

[5] 48 Ga. 55 (1873); 66 Ga. 102 (1880); 74 Ga. 701 (1885); 29 Ill. 184 (1862); 83 Ind. 147 (1882); 9 Iowa 201 (1859); 22 Iowa 543 (1867); 37 Iowa 325 (1873); 58 Iowa 529 (1882); 2 Red. (Me.) 17 (1850); 12 Mass. 268 (1815); 2 Cai. (N. Y.) 150 (1804); 20 Johns. (N. Y.) 285 (1822); 1 N. Y. (1 Comst.) 274 (1848); 5 N. Y. Leg. Obs. 226; 21 S. W. Rep. (Tex.) 69 (1893); 19 Vt. 496 (1847).

[6] 46 Iowa 386 (1877); 50 Iowa 671 (1879); 55 Iowa 386 (1880); 58 Iowa 529 (1882). It must be shown that it was done to evade the usury law in such a case. 58 Iowa 529 (1882).

[7] 2 Red. (Me.) 17 (1850); 12 Mass. 268 (1815); 83 Pa. St. 109 (1876); 99 Pa. St. 265 (1881); 121 Pa. St. 582 (1888); 19 Vt. 496 (1847); *contra*, 3 Lit. (Ky.) 109 (1823); 4 J. J. Mar. (Ky.) 88 (1830); 8 B. Mon. (Ky.) 28 (1847); 3 Met. (Ky.) 275 (1860); 6 Bush (Ky.) 95 (1869).

[8] 9 Paige (N. Y.) 165 (1841); *contra*, 4 Mon. (Ky.) 488 (1827).

default,[1] or confession.[2] The Pennsylvania court, however, will, if the debtor has paid usurious interest upon a judgment, and confessed a judgment of revival, nevertheless open the judgment, and allow him a credit for the usurious interest paid upon the principal.[3] If the statute allows usury paid to be recovered, it may be recovered even though it has been paid on a judgment.

When the court has authorized and approved an usurious mortgage, it will not afterward entertain a bill to question its validity.[4]

A new note given in payment of an usurious judgment is a final settlement of the judgment and the usury cannot be recovered.[5] If the note is given at about the time the judgment is recovered, the court may consider it a device to evade the usury law.[6]

A creditor must first establish his claim by judgment, before he can recover against third persons who receive the usury from the debtor.[7]

Where courts allow usury to be recovered after having been paid upon a judgment, the judgment is not otherwise impeached.[8]

An award is not conclusive, that is, if it gives illegal interest, on a suit to recover the amount of the award usury can be pleaded.[9]

[1] 12 Mass. 268 (1815).

[2] 55 Ark. 536 (1892); 18 S. W. Rep. (Ark.) 931 (1892); 2 Bail. (S. C.) 51 (1830); *contra*, 50 Tenn. 89 (1873).

[3] 86 Pa. St. 457 (1878).

[4] 66 Md. 171 (1886).

[5] 99 Pa. St. 265 (1881); 121 Pa. St. 582 (1888).

[6] 126 Pa. St. 415 (1889).

[7] 50 Tenn. 23 (1873).

[8] 105 N. C. 498 (1890).

[9] 12 Ind. 187 (1859).

Where a judgment on an usurious debt was obtained, and a sheriff's sale took place under it, his deed is not infected with the usury, the creditor being the purchaser.[1]

If usurious interest is paid on a note after execution, it amounts to a payment on the principal; and if the amount thus paid exceeds the principal, it may be recovered,[2] says the Indiana court.

A note executed for a judgment obtained upon an usurious consideration is void, and by pleading the usury in an action on it may be defeated; judgments on usurious considerations not being embraced within the words of the statute.[3]

A written statement authorizing the entry of judgment does not before the judgment is entered estop the party from pleading usury.[4]

Where a judgment is given on two notes, one of which is usurious and the other valid, it does not consolidate them, and they will afterward be distinctly regarded in usury proceedings.[5]

4. *Laches.* Laches in setting aside a judgment, as for two years, is a bar to the recovery of usury paid.[6]

5. *Novation.* A novation does not relieve the contract of usury, but usury paid and the entire debt discharged by a novation, before usury is reclaimed, its recovery is barred if the statute of limitations has run out.[7] See page 232.

6. *Payment.* A free and voluntary payment of usury bars any right of recovery,[8] unless the statute provides

[1] 74 Ga. 465 (1885).
[2] 23 Ind. 4 (1864).
[3] 1 Mon. (Ky.) 266 (1824).
[4] 20 Iowa 578 (1866).
[5] 91 Pa. St. 516 (1879).
[6] 135 U. S. 304 (1889).
[7] 11 Bush (Ky.) 393 (1875).
[8] 67 Mich. 237 (1887); 62 Pa. St. 481 (1869).

otherwise. As where an usurious debt has been settled by the creditor taking in satisfaction thereof property mortgaged to secure its payment, equity will not open the transaction on the ground of usury alone.[1]

A subsequent loan is valid, but the jury must be satisfied that it is not a device to evade the usury statute.[2]

Such payment of usurious interest cannot be by another obligation of the same borrower to the same lender, although the engagement of a new surety, except only where an innocent third party intervenes.[3]

An absolute conveyance of land upon trust to sell and pay certain debts, cannot be avoided on the ground that the debts are usurious; such conveyance being more than a mere security for the payment of the debts; it is in the nature of a payment, and is so treated.[4]

When a testatrix in her lifetime submitted accounts to arbitration and was satisfied with the award and performed it, her representatives cannot open the settlement on the ground of usury in the accounts.[5]

For usury paid on judgments, see page 295.

7. *Release.* The possessor of a right to claim usury can release it;[6] as by a discharge under seal;[7] but to be effectual it must be subsequent to the usurious contract;[8] as, if done at the same time, it is deemed a device to evade the statute.[9]

8. *Repeal of usury law.* If the usury statute is repealed

[1] 18 Ala. 698 (1851).
[2] 62 Pa. St. 481 (1869).
[3] 62 Pa. St. 481 (1869).
[4] 1 Johns. Cas. (N. Y.) 158 (1799).
[5] 1 McC. Ch. (S. C.) 408 (1826).
[6] 32 Vt. 98 (1859).
[7] 54 Vt. 215 (1881).
[8] 54 Vt. 215 (1881), 568 (1882).
[9] 13 B. Mon. (Ky.) 389 (1852).

before a suit for the recovery of usury paid is brought, or, if brought, before judgment is rendered, or before or during the pendency of a suit in which usury is pleaded in defence, the claim for, or defence of, usury will be gone. But if a constitution repeals the usury laws existing usurious contracts are not thereby legalized.[1]

9. *Statute of limitations.* Usury paid must be sued for within the time allowed by the statute, or the right of recovery will be barred.[2] The statute runs from the time that the money is paid.[3] The rule is the same in suing to recover a penalty.[4]

While any part of an usurious debt remains unpaid, the statute of limitations will not cut off the right of the party who has paid the usurious interest to recover it.[5]

See chapter twelve, for further rules and decisions.

10. *Waiver.* The borrower may by his own act or neglect forfeit his right to recover usury.[6] Usury will not be considered when a mortgagor, having tendered the amount of the mortgage debt, and demanded its discharge, asks for the statutory penalty for not discharging the mortgage.[7]

The borrower must take advantage of the defence at his first opportunity,—he will not be allowed to set it up afterward.[8]

The defence may be waived,[9] but only by a subsequent

[1] 39 Tex. 365 (1873).

[2] 61 N. H. 147 (1881).

[3] 59 Ga. 546 (1877); 61 N. H. 147 (1881).

[4] 61 N. H. 147 (1881).

[5] 18 Tex. 794 (1857); 39 Tex. 365 (1873).

[6] 3 Ala. 643 (1842); 82 Ala. 363 (1886); 6 Greenl. (Me.) 35 (1829); 5 Hubb. (Me.) 312 (1860).

[7] 41 Mich. 371 (1879).

[8] 13 Pet. (U. S.) 65 (1839).

[9] 38 Mich. 200 (1878).

agreement:[1] as where a mortgagor conveys land subject to an usurious mortgage, the purchaser cannot set it up.[2]

A forfeiture may also be waived, and the debtor may insist upon its application to the payment of the debt.[3]

The New York supreme court holds that an agreement to waive and abandon the defence of usury and never set it up is void and cannot be enforced; nor does it create an estoppel as between the parties.[4]

The debtor is not obliged to avail himself of the defence of usury, and his omission to do so is not a fraud upon other creditors; it is a personal defence, which he may waive.[5]

The defendant can waive in court the privilege of setting up usury in defence when sued, expressly or impliedly.[6] But a borrower by a contemporaneous agreement cannot waive the right to retain or recover usurious interest.[7]

Where in equity a mortgagor seeks to restrain his mortgagee from selling mortgaged property because of usury, an injunction will be dissolved if the mortgagee waives the usury.[8] The mortgagor must pay the principal and legal interest, however.

[1] 28 Ind. 435 (1867); 72 Pa. St. 54 (1872).

[2] 9 C. E. Gr. (N. J.) 120 (1873); 1 McCart. (N. J.) 56 (1861); *contra*, 1 Stock. (N. J.) 807 (1852).

[3] 78 Ky. 367 (1880); 7 O. St. 387 (1857).

[4] 22 Hun (N. Y.) 264 (1880).

[5] 9 N. Y. (5 Seld.) 73 (1853).

[6] 21 Tex. 441 (1858).

[7] 72 Pa. St. 54 (1872).

[8] 92 N. C. 45 (1885).

CHAPTER XI.

INTEREST IN EQUITY.

THE rule in England for the allowance of interest in equity appears to be narrower than it is in America at law.[1] Here, upon demands bearing interest at law, the court of equity is bound to allow it,[2] but where the demand does not bear interest at law, it will or will not be allowed according to the equity of the case, in the discretion of the court.[3] It is generally deemed equitable to allow interest on all sums which are due and payable;[4] but it will not decree current interest unless the law would.[5]

Compound interest is not allowable in equity as a general rule,[6] as it is deemed inequitable; but where it is necessary to reach certain profits and to do justice in a case annual rests are allowed.[7]

Wherever the law prohibits the payment of the principal, interest is not demandable during the existence of the prohibition, and the rule is the same in courts of equity as in courts of law.[8]

[1] 11 N. H. 501 (1841).

[2] 23 Ala. 296 (1853); 52 Ala. 444 (1875); 1 Mon. (Ky.) 150 (1824); 6 J. J. Mar. (Ky.) 535 (1831); 3 Dana (Ky.) 297 (1835).

[3] 3 Rich. Eq. (S. C.) 465 (1851); 4 Rich. Eq. (S. C.) 92 (1851).

[4] 11 N. H. 501 (1841).

[5] 6 J. J. Mar. (Ky.) 535 (1831).

[6] Conf. (N. C.) 435 (1800).

[7] 11 N. H. 501 (1841).

[8] 2 Dall. (Pa.) 102 (1789).

In equity, interest is allowed on the balance due on a building contract, though the contract was never fully performed.[1]

Although equity cannot carry interest beyond the penalty of a bond, yet it does not suffer the mortgagor to redeem without paying all that is due.[2]

[1] 7 Dana (Ky.) 240 (1838).
[2] McM. Eq. (S. C.) 157 (1841).

CHAPTER XII.

EFFECT OF STATUTE OF LIMITATIONS UPON INTEREST.

THE statute of limitations has the same effect, generally, upon interest due as it has on other debts. All the interest that has accrued during the statutory period next preceding the beginning of the suit to recover it, is within the recoverable period, whether it is contractual interest, or interest allowed as damages.[1] As, for instance, if a note due four years from date, bearing interest, is sued on after it has been due five years, no part of the interest is barred (although the statute fixes the time within which suits must be brought at six years), and interest for the nine years can be collected.[2] But if interest is payable on a note annually, so much as accrued thereon prior to six years before the commencement of the action to recover it is barred by the statute, although the note itself, being on time, together with the interest which accrued within the statutory period is not barred.[3]

Interest coupons are held, however, not to be barred until the bonds themselves are.[4]

Within the confederate states, the statute of limitations was suspended during the Rebellion, whether in actions

[1] 1 Y. & Coll. Ch. Cas. (Eng.) 151 (1841).
[2] 2 Cush. (Mass.) 92 (1848).
[3] 5 Greenl. (Me.) 81 (1827).
[4] 65 Cal. 67 (1884); 19 Minn. 338 (1873).

between belligerents or between residents within those states.[1]

In an action brought to recover usurious interest paid at different times, it was held that all interest that had been paid within the statutory period before bringing the suit could be recovered;[2] that is, the statute begins to run at the time it is paid.[3] But while any part of the usurious debt remains unpaid, the statute will not cut off the right of recovery.[4]

Extension. Where interest has been paid in advance, and the time thus extended for a contract's maturity, the statute of limitations does not begin to run until the end of the period for which the interest was thus paid.[5]

The payment of interest by one of several promissors in a note takes it out of the statute of limitations as to all the others.[6] The court in Pennsylvania holds, however, that this rule does not apply to a joint and several note.[7]

The payment of interest and indorsement on a joint and several note by a deceased co-maker, in a suit brought against the living maker, and the admission of its validity by the maker sued, takes it out of the statute of limitations.[8]

Revival. The payment of interest on a debt is a sufficient recognition of the debt, as due at the time of such payment to take the case out of the statute of limitations.[9]

[1] 37 Ark. 463 (1881).
[2] 3 N. H. 489 (1826).
[3] 59 Ga. 546 (1877); 61 N. H. 147 (1881).
[4] 18 Tex. 794 (1857); 39 Tex. 365 (1873).
[5] 15 N. H. 520 (1844).
[6] 51 Mo. 31 (1872).
[7] 89 Pa. St. 331 (1879).
[8] 55 Md. 384 (1880).
[9] 19 Conn. 591 (1849); 1 Bail. (S. C.) 148 (1829).

A debt barred by the statute and revived by an acknowledgment, bears interest for the whole time, as though it had never been barred.[1] It is, however, held in England that the payment of the principal of a debt barred by the statute of limitations does not revive the creditor's claim for interest thereon, especially when the debtor says he does not intend to revive the interest.[2]

[1] 1 Sw. Dig. 715; 79 Ga. 301 (1887); 16 Vt. 297 (1844).

[2] 12 Moore (Eng.) 557 (1827); 4 Bing. (Eng.) 313 (1827).

CHAPTER XIII.

INTEREST STATUTES.

LEGISLATIVE acts to regulate interest are in derogation of the common law, and must be strictly construed.[1] So with usury statutes.[2] Each state's construction of its own statutes controls in other states.[3]

Force in other states. If a contract is not usurious where it is made and is to be performed, it is good everywhere.[4] If a statute declares usurious contracts void or voidable, they are so regarded everywhere; but if the statute makes it simply a penal offence to take or contract for usury, the usury is not regarded in another jurisdiction.[5]

While the courts of one state do not enforce the penal statutes of another state, yet when a contract made with reference to the laws of another state is usurious there, the forfeiture provided by such laws is enforced.[6]

A statute that relates to the remedy merely can have no force in another state,[7] and penalties given by the usury laws of one state are not recoverable in the courts of

[1] 11 Cal. 14 (1858).
[2] 111 U. S. 31 (1884).
[3] 59 Vt. 120 (1886).
[4] 33 Conn. 570 (1866); 14 Bradw. (Ill.) 405 (1883).
[5] 4 Gilm. (Ill.) 521 (1847); 59 Vt. 120 (1886).
[6] 22 Iowa 194 (1867). See 59 Vt. 120 (1886).
[7] 32 N. H. 560 (1856); 43 N. H. 518 (1862); 12 Vt. 464 (1840).

another state,[1] that is, in a state other than that in which the contract was made.

Change of statute. Existing contracts for interest are not affected by changes in the statute, whether usurious or not.[2] The law in force when the contract is made governs as to rights of parties.[3]

The right to interest on interest when it exists, cannot be impaired by legislation declaring the true intent and meaning of a statute previously existing.[4]

Interest allowed as damages, however, varies with the statute.[5] So, if no rate of contractual interest has been agreed upon it varies with the statute.[6]

A statute regulating the rate of interest after maturity of a debt does not affect existing contracts that became due before the law was passed.[7]

By the repeal of a penal statute all penalties fall, even if given to individuals, and a suit is pending for them.[8]

The parties to usurious contracts hold any right they have to the penalties given by the law, subject to a modification or repeal by the legislature, and a consequent direct or indirect validation of the contracts.[9]

Statutes making valid a void contract,[10] or imposing a

[1] 59 Vt. 120 (1886). See 22 Iowa 194 (1867).

[2] 1 Fla. 356 (1847); 5 Fla. 345 (1853); 61 Ga. 458 (1878); 62 Ga. 86 (1878); 7 Allen (Mass.) 139 (1863); 27 Neb. 644 (1889); 28 Neb. 210 (1889); 58 Hun (N. Y.) 575 (1891); 3 Ore. 129 (1869); 29 Grat. (Va.) 1 (1877).

[3] 17 Neb. 491 (1885).

[4] 104 U. S. 668 (1881).

[5] 9 C. E. Gr. (N. J.) 451 (1874); 4 Stew. (N. J.) 91 (1879); 12 Vr. (N. J.) 349 (1879); 28 O. St. 266 (1876).

[6] 17 Stew. (N. J.) 56 (1888).

[7] 12 La. Ann. 793 (1857); 15 La. Ann. 17 (1860).

[8] 30 Conn. 149 (1861).

[9] 30 Conn. 149 (1861).

[10] 30 Conn. 149 (1861).

penalty for receiving interest on an existing usurious contract,[1] or reducing the penalty for receiving usurious interest, do not impair the obligation of a contract within the meaning of the United States constitution;[2] neither are they retroactive.[3]

TEXT OF THE GENERAL INTEREST STATUTES.

Below is given the text of the general interest statutes in force in the states and countries named.

ENGLAND.

"Upon hearing the Appeal if it shall appear to the House of Lords to be just to decree or adjudge the payment of interest, simple or compound, by any of the parties in the cause to which such appeal relates, it shall be competent to the said House to decree or adjudge the payment thereof, as the said House in its sound discretion shall think meet."[4]—48 *Geo. III*, *ch.* 151, § 19.

"From and after the passing of this Act, it shall and may be lawful to and for the said Chief Justices, Chief Baron, Justices and Barons, in all cases now depending, or which hereafter shall depend in the said court, where the defendant in error shall have got judgment for any sum of money, whether for debt, damages or costs, or all or any two of them, and such judgment shall be affirmed by the said court, then not only to give such judgment of affirmance, but also to order that interest be forthwith computed in open court, at such rate, not exceeding the legal interest for the time being, as such court shall direct, from the day of the allowance of the writ of error on which they shall so give judgment to the day of so giving the same, on the sum so adjudged to the defendant in error as aforesaid; and to order that the amount of such interest shall be included in their judgment, in addition to the sum so theretofore adjudged, and to the costs, if they shall think proper to award costs as aforesaid."[5]—1 *Geo. IV*, *ch.* 68, § 7.

[1] 27 S. C. 110 (1887).

[2] 81 Ill. 331 (1868).

[3] 27 S. C. 110 (1887).

[4] This statute relates to Scotland, and is applicable to any appeal to the House of Lords.

[5] This statute relates to Ireland, and applies to appeals in the Court of Exchequer Chamber.

"Upon all debts or sums certain, payable at a certain time or otherwise, the jury on the trial of any issue, or on any inquisition of damages, may, if they shall think fit, allow interest to the creditor at a rate not exceeding the current rate of interest, from the time when such debts or sums certain were payable, if such debts or sums be payable by virtue of some written instrument at a certain time, or if payable otherwise, then from the time when demand of payment shall have been made in writing, so as such demand shall give notice to the debtor that interest will be claimed from the date of such demand until the term of payment; provided that interest shall be payable in all cases in which it is now payable by law."[1]—3 & 4 *Wm. IV*, *ch.* 42, § 28.

"The jury on the trial of any issue, or on any inquisition of damages, may, if they shall think fit, give damages in the nature of interest, over and above the value of the goods at the time of the conversion or seizure, in all actions of trover or trespass de bonis asportatis, and over and above the money recoverable in all actions on policies of assurance made after the passing of this act."[2]—3 & 4 *Wm. IV*, *ch.* 42, § 29.

"Every judgment debt shall carry interest at the rate of four pounds *per centum per annum* from the time of entering up the judgment, or from the time of the commencement of this act in cases of judgments then entered up and not carrying interest, until the same shall be satisfied, and such interest may be levied under a writ of execution on such judgment."—1 & 2 *Vict.*, *ch.* 110, § 17.

An execution ordered to be registered with the "Executions of Charge and Denunciation, . . . shall have the effect to accumulate the debt and interest into a capital sum, whereon interest shall thereafter become due."[3]—1 & 2 *Vict.*, *ch.* 114, §§ 5, 10.

"Every judgment debt due upon any judgment not confessed or recovered for any penal sum for securing principal and interest shall carry interest at the rate of four pounds *per centum per annum* from the time of entering up the judgment, or from the time of the commencement of this act in cases of judgments then entered up and not carrying interest, until the same shall be satisfied, and such interest may be levied under a writ of execution as such judgment."[4]—3 & 4 *Vict.*, *ch.* 105, § 26.

[1] This and the following section were reënacted for Ireland 3 & 4 Vict., ch. 105, §§ 53, 54, to which was then added a clause providing that interest be allowed for not more than six years.

[2] See preceding foot note.

[3] This statute concerns Scotland.

[4] This statute concerns Ireland.

"If any person shall sue out any writ of error upon any judgment whatsoever given in any court in any action personal, and the court of error shall give judgment for the defendant thereon, then interest shall be allowed by the court of error for such time as execution has been delayed by such writ of error for the delaying thereof."[1]—3 & 4 *Vict., ch.* 105, § 55.

"From and after the passing of this act every bank in Scotland with which any money shall have been or shall be deposited or lodged by any judicial factor, tutor, or curator, or under authority of any court in Scotland, or with reference to any suit in any court in Scotland, whether on deposit receipt or on account current, or otherwise, shall once at least in every year accumulate the interest with the principal sum, so that both shall thereafter bear interest together as principal; and any bank failing so to do shall be liable to account as if such money had been so accumulated."[2]—12 & 13 *Vict., ch.* 51, § 37.

"In any case in which duty payable in respect of any legacy or residue under the legacy duty acts now in force, or in respect of any succession under the succession duty act, 1853, is or shall be in arrear, the person by whom the arrears of duty may be payable shall be liable to pay interest thereon at the rate of four pounds *per centum per annum;* and such interest shall be recoverable by the commissioners of inland revenue in the same manner as the arrears of duty, and as part thereof." —31 & 32 *Vict., ch.* 124, § 9.

The general usury statute of England was repealed in 1854.

CANADA.

"Except as otherwise provided by this or by any other Act of the Parliament of Canada, any person may stipulate for, allow and exact, on any contract or agreement whatsoever, any rate of interest or discount which is agreed upon."—*R. S. Can., ch.* 127, § 1.

"Whenever interest is payable by the agreement of parties or by law, and no rate is fixed by such agreement or by law, the rate of interest shall be six per centum per annum."—*R. S. Can., ch.* 127, § 2.

"Whenever any principal money or interest secured by mortgage of real estate is, by the same, made payable on the sinking fund plan, or on any plan under which the payments of principal money and interest are blended, or on any plan which involves an allowance of interest in stipulated repayments, no interest whatever shall be chargeable, payable or recoverable,

[1] This statute concerns Ireland.

[2] This statute concerns Scotland.

on any part of the principal money advanced, unless the mortgage contains a statement showing the amount of such principal money and the rate of interest chargeable thereon, calculated yearly or half-yearly, not in advance."—*R. S. Can., ch.* 127, § 3.

"Whenever the rate of interest shown in such statement is less than the rate of interest which would be chargeable by virtue of any other provision, calculation or stipulation in the mortgage, no greater rate of interest shall be chargeable, payable or recoverable, on the principal money advanced, than the rate shown in such statement."—*R. S. Can., ch.* 127, § 4.

"No fine or penalty or rate of interest shall be stipulated for, taken, reserved or exacted on any arrear of principal or interest secured by mortgage of real estate which has the effect of increasing the charge on any such arrear beyond the rate of interest payable on principal money not in arrear; but nothing in this section contained shall have the effect of prohibiting a contract for the payment of interest on arrears of interest or principal at any rate not greater than the rate payable on principal money not in arrear."—*R. S. Can., ch.* 127, § 5.

"If any sum is paid on account of any interest, fine or penalty not chargeable, payable or recoverable under the three sections next preceding, such sums may be recovered back, or deducted from any other interest, fine or penalty chargeable, payable or recoverable on the principal."—*R. S. Can., ch.* 127, § 6.

"Whenever any principal money or interest secured by mortgage of real estate is not, under the terms of the mortgage, payable till a time more than five years after the date of the mortgage, then, if at any time after the expiration of such five years, any person liable to pay or entitled to redeem the mortgage tenders or pays to the person entitled to receive the money, the amount due for principal money and interest to the time of payment, as calculated under the four sections next preceding, together with three months further interest in lieu of notice, no further interest shall be chargeable, payable or recoverable at any time thereafter on the principal money or interest due under the mortgage."—*R. S. Can., ch.* 127, § 7.

"The provisions of the five sections next preceding shall only apply to moneys secured by mortgage on real estate executed after the first day of July, in the year one thousand eight hundred and eighty."—*R. S. Can., ch.* 127, § 8.

ONTARIO AND QUEBEC.

"The two sections next following apply to the Provinces of Ontario and Quebec."—*R. S. Can., ch.* 127, § 9.

"Except as otherwise provided by this or any other Act or law, no corporation or company or association of persons, not being a bank, authorized by law before the sixteenth day of August, one thousand eight hundred and fifty-eight, to lend or borrow money, shall, upon any contract, take directly or indirectly, for loan of any moneys, wares, merchandise or other commodities whatsoever, above the value of six dollars for the advance or forbearance of one hundred dollars for a year, and so after that rate for a greater or less sum or value, or for a longer or shorter time.

"Provided that any insurance company incorporated by Act of the legislature of the late Province of Canada, or of either of the late Provinces of Upper or of Lower Canada, or by charter from Her Majesty, or by an act of the Parliament of the United Kingdom, and any corporation constituted for religious, charitable or educational purposes, in the Provinces of Ontario or Quebec, authorized by law to lend or borrow money, may stipulate for, allow and exact, on any contract or agreement whatsoever, any rate of interest or discount which is agreed upon, not exceeding eight per centum per annum."—*R. S. Can., ch.* 127, § 10.

"All bonds, bills, promissory notes, contracts and assurances whatsoever made or executed in violation of the provisions of the section next preceding, whereupon or whereby a greater interest is reserved and taken than authorized by this or any other Act or law, shall be void; and every corporation, company and association of persons, not being a bank, authorized to lend or borrow money as aforesaid, which, directly or indirectly, takes, accepts and receives a higher rate of interest, shall incur a penalty equal to treble the value of the moneys, wares, merchandise, or other commodities, lent or bargained for:

"Such penalty may be recovered by action in any court of competent jurisdiction, and one moiety thereof shall belong to Her Majesty for the public uses of Canada, and the other moiety to the person who sues for the same."—*R. S. Can., ch.* 127, § 11.

NOVA SCOTIA.

"The five sections next following apply to the Province of Nova Scotia, but shall not extend to any hypothecation or agreement in writing entered into for money advanced upon the bottom of a ship or vessel, her cargo or freight."—*R. S. Can., ch.* 127, § 12.

"Any person may stipulate and agree in writing for any rate of interest not exceeding seven per centum per annum, for the loan or forbearance of money to be secured on real estate or chattels real; and any person may stipulate in writing for or may receive in advance any rate of interest not exceeding ten per centum per annum, whenever the security for the payment of the money consists only of personal property or the personal responsibility of the person to whom forbearance is given, or of others."—*R. S. Can., ch.* 127, § 13.

"In any action brought on any contract whatsoever, in which there is, directly or indirectly, taken or reserved a rate of interest exceeding that authorized in the next preceding section, the defendant may, the same being duly pleaded, as in other cases, prove such excessive interest, and it shall be deducted from the amount due on such contract."—*R. S. Can., ch.* 127, § 14.

"No person shall, upon any contract or security, made or entered into, given or taken before the twenty-third day of May, one thousand eight hundred and seventy-three, take, directly or indirectly, for the loan of moneys or goods, above the rate of six per centum per annum, and every such contract and security whereby a greater rate of interest is reserved shall be void; and every person who takes or receives, upon any such contract or security, a greater rate, shall incur a penalty equal to treble the value of the moneys or goods in such contract or security contracted for or secured; but no prosecution for any such penalty shall be commenced except within twelve months from the commission of the offence."—*R. S. Can., ch.* 127, § 15.

"Nothing in the three sections next preceding shall apply to any chartered bank."—*R. S. Can., ch.* 127, § 16.

"Any person may contract for the loan or hire of grain or live stock, upon halves or otherwise, upon the lender taking upon himself all risk of such stock; but if it appears that the same, or any part thereof, perished or was lost through the wilful neglect of the borrower, he shall make good to the lender the full value thereof."—*R. S. Can., ch.* 127, § 17.

NEW BRUNSWICK.

"The five sections next following apply to the Province of New Brunswick with respect to,—

"(*a*) Banks which are not subject to '*The Bank Act;*'

"(*b*) Other incorporated companies, but subject to any special provision in any other Act; and —

"(c) Contracts made between the thirteenth day of April in the year one thousand eight hundred and fifty-nine, and the eighth day of April, in the year one thousand eight hundred and seventy-five."—*R. S. Can., ch.* 127, § 18.

"No person shall, directly or indirectly, receive on any contract for the loan of any money or goods, more than six dollars for the forbearance of one hundred dollars for one year, and after that rate for a greater or lesser sum, and a longer or shorter time."—*R. S. Can.*, *ch.* 127, § 19.

"No deed or contract for payment of any money loaned, or for the forbearance of anything undertaken, upon or by which more than such rate of interest is reserved or received, shall be void by reason thereof."—*R. S. Can.*, *ch.* 127, § 20.

"In any action brought on any contract whatsoever, in which there is, directly or indirectly, taken or reserved a rate of interest exceeding six per centum per annum, the defendant, or his attorney, may, under the general issue, with notice of defence as in other cases, prove such excessive interest, and it shall be deducted from the amount due on such contract."—*R. S. Can.*, *ch.* 127, § 21.

"Every bank not subject to '*The Bank Act*,' which, upon any such deed or contract, receives or reserves, by means of any loan, bargain, exchange or transfer of any money or goods, or by any deceitful means, for the forbearing or giving day of payment beyond a year, of its money or goods, more than six dollars for one hundred dollars for one year, and after that rate for a greater or lesser sum and longer or shorter time, shall incur a penalty equal to the value of the principal sum or goods so loaned, bargained, exchanged or transferred, and all interest and other profits accruing therefrom; and such penalty may be recovered by action in any court of record in the county in which the offence was committed, — which action shall be brought within twelve months from the time of such offence and not afterwards; and one moiety of such penalty shall belong to Her Majesty for the public uses of Canada, and the other moiety to the person who sues for the same."—*R. S. Can.*, *ch.* 127, § 22.

"Nothing in the four sections next preceding, shall apply to bottomry bonds or contracts on the bottom of any vessel, damages on protested bills, allowed by law, penalties incurred for the non-fulfilment of any contract, if such penalties are mutually binding, and contracts for the loan or hire of any grain, cattle, or live stock, let out as the parties agree, if the lender takes the risk of casualties upon himself,—in which case the borrower shall not avail himself of any loss suffered through his wilful neglect, or any voluntary damage which is committed by him."—*R. S. Can.*, *ch.* 127, § 23.

BRITISH COLUMBIA.

"The three sections next following apply to the Province of British Columbia."—*R. S. Can.*, *ch.* 127, § 24.

"In all cases where interest is chargeable or recoverable by law or by any contract expressed or implied, or upon any judgment of any court in British Columbia, if the rate of interest has not been agreed upon in writing, such rate shall be six per centum per annum."—*R. S. Can., ch.* 127, § 25.

"In all cases in which judgment is recovered upon any contract in writing in or by which interest at a higher rate than six per centum per annum has been agreed to be paid, the amount awarded by such judgment shall bear interest at the rate agreed upon, not however exceeding twelve per centum per annum."—*R. S. Can., ch.* 127, § 26.

"The provisions of the two sections next preceding shall not extend to contracts entered into before the second day of June, one thousand eight hundred and eighty-six."—*R. S. Can., ch.* 127, § 27.

PRINCE EDWARD ISLAND.

"The following provisions apply to the Province of Prince Edward Island."—*R. S. Can., ch.* 127, § 28.

"No person shall recover, in any court, more than six per centum per annum interest on any account, contract or agreement, unless it appears to the court that a higher rate of interest was agreed to in writing between the parties."—*R. S. Can., ch.* 127, § 29.

"Nothing herein shall prejudice or affect the rights or remedies of any person, or diminish or alter the liabilities of any person, in respect of any act done previously to the fifteenth day of April, in the year one thousand eight hundred and seventy, and if interest was payable at that date upon any contract, express or implied, for the payment of the legal or current rate of interest or upon any debt or sum of money by any rule of law, the same shall be recoverable as if the provisions of the next preceding section had not been enacted."—*R. S. Can., ch.* 127, § 30.

UNITED STATES.

"Upon all bonds, on which suits are brought for the recovery of duties, interest shall be allowed, at the rate of six per centum a year, from the time when said bonds became due."—*Rev. St.*, § 963.

"In all suits for balances due to the Post-Office Department, interest thereon shall be recovered, from the time of the default, at the rate of six per centum a year."—*Rev. St.*, § 964.

"In suits upon debentures, issued by the collectors of the customs under any act for the collection of duties, interest shall be allowed at the rate of six per centum per annum, from the time when such debenture became due and payable."—*Rev. St.*, § 965.

"Interest shall be allowed on all judgments in civil causes, recovered in a circuit or district court, and may be levied by the marshal under process of execution issued thereon, in all cases where, by the law of the State in which such court is held, interest may be levied under process of execution on judgments recovered in the courts of such State; and it shall be calculated from the date of the judgment, at such rate as is allowed by law on judgments recovered in the courts of such State."—*Rev. St.*, § 966.

"In cases where the judgment appealed from is in favor of the claimant, and the same is affirmed by the Supreme Court, interest thereon at the rate of five per centum shall be allowed from the date of its presentation to the Secretary of the Treasury for payment as aforesaid, but no interest shall be allowed subsequent to the affirmance, unless presented for payment to the Secretary of the Treasury as aforesaid."—*Rev. St.*, § 1090.

"No interest shall be allowed on any claim up to the time of the rendition of judgment thereon by the Court of Claims, unless upon a contract expressly stipulating for the payment of interest."—*Rev. St.*, § 1091.

If internal revenue taxes are not paid at the end of ten days after demand of payment by the collector, they shall be increased five per cent and shall bear interest at the rate of one per cent a month.—*Rev. St.*, § 3184. The next section of the statute says that in such cases no interest for a fraction of a month shall be demanded.

Revenue stamps can be affixed to documents after the time they ought to have been affixed by paying six per cent interest on the amount of the tax from the time the stamps should have been to the time they were affixed.—*Rev. St.*, § 3422.

"Any association may take, receive, reserve, and charge on any loan or discount made, or upon any note, bill of exchange, or other evidence of debt, interest at the rate allowed by the laws of the State, Territory, or district where the bank is located, and no more, except that where by the laws of any State a different rate is limited for banks of issue organized under State laws, the rate so limited shall be allowed for associations organized or existing in any such State under this Title.[1] When no rate is fixed by the laws of the State, or Territory, or district, the bank may take, receive, reserve, or charge a rate not exceeding seven per centum, and such interest may be taken in

[1] Pertaining to national banks.

advance, reckoning the days for which the note, bill, or other evidence of debt has to run. And the purchase, discount, or sale of a bona-fide bill of exchange, payable at another place than the place of such purchase, discount, or sale, at not more than the current rate of exchange for sight drafts in addition to the interest, shall not be considered as taking or receiving a greater rate of interest."—*Rev. St.*, § 5197.

"The taking, receiving, reserving, or charging a rate of interest greater than is allowed by the preceding section, when knowingly done, shall be deemed a forfeiture of the entire interest which the note, bill, or other evidence of debt carries with it, or which has been agreed to be paid thereon. In case the greater rate of interest has been paid, the person by whom it has been paid, or his legal representatives, may recover back, in an action in the nature of an action of debt, twice the amount of the interest thus paid from the association taking or receiving the same; provided such action is commenced within two years from the time the usurious transaction occurred."—*Rev. St.*, § 5198.

ALABAMA.

"Every bill of exchange, note, bond, or instrument of any description, whatever may be its form or device, issued with the intent to circulate as money, without authority of law, is an absolute, unconditional promise of the association or person putting such bill, note, or other instrument in circulation, and may be sued on by the holder thereof, without transfer or assignment, and without demand, protest, or notice, and the amount thereof recovered, with interest thereon at the rate of fifty per cent. per annum from the date thereof, or from the time the same was put in circulation."—*Code*, § 1193.

"The rate of interest upon the loan or forbearance of money, goods, or things in action, is eight dollars upon one hundred dollars for one year; and at that rate for a greater or less sum, or a longer or shorter time."—*Code*, § 1750.

"All contracts, express or implied, for the payment of money, or other thing, or for the performance of any act or duty, bear interest from the day such money, or thing, estimating it at its money value, should have been paid, or such act, estimating the compensation therefor in money, performed."—*Code*, § 1751.

"Judgments and decrees for the payment of money, other than costs, bear interest from the day of rendition."—*Code*, § 1752.

"When partial payments are made, the interest due is first

to be paid, and the balance applied to the payment of the principal."—*Code*, § 1753.

"All contracts for the payment of interest upon the loan, or forbearance of goods, money, things in action, or upon any contract whatever, at a higher rate than is prescribed in this chapter, are usurious and cannot be enforced, except as to the principal; and if any interest has been paid, the same must be deducted from the principal, and judgment rendered for the balance only."—*Code*, § 1754.

"All change bills and notes for a sum not exceeding one dollar, issued or circulated in this state without authority of law, bear interest at the rate of one hundred per cent. per annum, from the day of their date, or time of issue, or circulation; and may be sued by the holder thereof, without regard to the person to whom the same are payable, and a recovery had against the person issuing or giving circulation to the same."—*Code*, § 1755.

"Damages on protest for non-payment are in place of all charges except costs of protest incurred previous to, and at the time of giving notice of non-payment, but the holder may recover legal interest upon the aggregate amount of the principal sum specified in such bill, and of the damages thereon, from the time at which payment of the principal sum has been demanded, and costs of protest."—*Code*, § 1772.

"When a bill of exchange is protested for non-acceptance, the same rate of damages is allowed as in the case of a protest for non-payment; and such damages are in the place of all charges, except costs of protest, incurred previous to, and at the time of giving notice of non-acceptance, but the holder is entitled to recover legal interest, exclusive of the damages, upon the amount of the principal sum, from the time when the same would have become payable, if accepted, interest on the damages from the demand of acceptance, and costs of protest."—*Code*, § 1775.

"If on such sale [of collateral securities or pledges], after paying the costs and expenses thereof, and the debt, there remains any balance of the proceeds of sale, the same must be paid to the debtor or person from whom such security was taken or received, or to his assignee or transferee. If on demand, after receiving the proceeds of sale, the creditor, or his transferee, or the personal representative of the creditor or transferee, fail or neglect to pay such balance, the same shall bear interest at the rate of five per cent. per month."—*Code*, § 1787.

"If any executor or administrator uses any of the funds of the estate for his own benefit, he is accountable for any profit made thereon, or legal interest; and in making out his account for a settlement, he must state the sum so used, the time, and the profit resulting from such use, if over legal interest; or he must expressly deny on oath that he has so used such funds; and any party interested may contest the same."—*Code*, § 2142.

"All contracts made with guardians, verbal or written, for the payment of money, bear compound interest after maturity, if not otherwise expressed; and judgments rendered thereon also bear compound interest."—*Code*, § 2113.

"In all actions founded on any instrument of writing, ascertaining the plaintiff's demand, if judgment by default, nil dicit, or on demurrer, be rendered for the plaintiff, such judgment may be entered up by the clerk, under the direction of the court, without the intervention of a jury; and the clerk must compute the interest, and, in case of a bill of exchange, the damages, if any be due thereon."—*Code*, § 2740.

"The secretary of state must cause to be printed, in the pamphlet acts of each session of the general assembly, the rate of interest of each state and territory; and such publication must be received as presumptive evidence of such interest."—*Code*, § 2791.

"Any banker, who discounts any note, bill of exchange, or draft at a higher rate of interest than eight per cent. per annum, not including the difference of exchange, is guilty of a misdemeanor."—*Code*, § 4140.

ARIZONA.

"The rate of interest in any other State, territory or country, is presumed to be the same as that established by law in this territory, and may be recovered accordingly without allegation or proof of the rate of interest in such other state, territory or country, unless the rate of interest in such other country be alleged and proved."—*R. S.* § 1876.

"When there is no express agreement fixing a different rate of interest, interest shall be allowed at the rate of seven per cent per annum on all moneys after they become due on any bond, bill, promissory note or other instrument in writing, or any judgment recovered in any court in this territory, for money lent, for money due on any settlement of accounts from the day on which the balance is ascertained and for money received for the use of another."—*R. S.* § 2161.

"Parties may agree in writing for the payment of any rate of interest whatever on money due or to become due on any contract; any judgment rendered on such contract shall conform thereto, and shall bear the rate of interest agreed upon by the parties, and which shall be specified in the judgment."—*R. S.*, § 2162.

"Every pawnbroker who charges or receives interest at the rate of more than four per cent per month, or who by charging commission, discount, storage or other charge, or by compounding, increases or attempts to increase such interest, is guilty of a misdemeanor."—*R. S., Penal Code*, § 558.

ARKANSAS.

"In addition to the damages allowed in the two preceding sections[1] to the holder of any bill of exchange protested for non-payment or non-acceptance, he shall be entitled to costs of protest and interest at the rate of ten per centum per annum on the amount specified in the bill, from the date of the protest until the amount of such bill shall be paid."—*Dig. of Stat.*, § 468.

"If any guardian fail to loan the money of his ward on hand. . . . . under the provisions of this act, he shall be accountable for the interest thereon."—*Dig. of Stat.*, § 3513.

"All contracts for a greater rate of interest than ten per centum per annum shall be void as to principal and interest, and the general assembly shall prohibit the same by law, but when no rate of interest is agreed upon, the rate shall be six per centum per annum."—*Dig. of Stat.*, § 4732.

"The parties to any contract, whether the same be under seal or not, may agree in writing for the payment of interest not exceeding ten per centum per annum on money due or to become due."—*Dig. of Stat.*, § 4733.

"No person or corporation shall, directly or indirectly, take or receive in money, goods, things in action, or any other valuable thing, any greater sum or value for the loan or forbearance of money or goods, things in action, or any other valuable thing, than is in section 4733 prescribed."—*Dig. of Stat.*, § 4734.

"All bonds, bills, notes, assurances, conveyances, and all other contracts or securities whatever, whereupon or whereby there shall be reserved, taken or secured, or agreed to be taken or reserved, any greater sum or greater value for the loan or forbearance of any money, goods, things in action, or any other valuable thing, than is prescribed in this act shall be void."—*Dig. of Stat.*, § 4735.

"It shall be lawful for all parties loaning money in this state

[1] Certain per centum forfeitures.

to reserve, or discount, interest upon any commercial paper, mortgages or other securities, at any rate of interest agreed upon by the parties, said rate of interest not to exceed ten per centum per annum, whether such paper or securities for principal or interest be payable in this state, or any other state, kingdom or country."—*Dig. of Stat.*, § 4736.

"For the purpose of calculating interest, a month shall be considered the twelfth part of a year, and as consisting of thirty days; and interest for any number of days less than a month shall be estimated by the proportion which such number of days shall bear to thirty."—*Dig. of Stat.*, § 4737.

"In calculating interest, where partial payments may have been made, the interest shall be calculated to the time when the first payment shall have been made, and such payment shall be applied to the payment of such interest; and if such payment exceed the interest, the balance shall be applied to diminish the principal, and the same course shall be observed in all subsequent payments; but in no case when a payment shall fall short of paying the interest due at the time of making such payment shall the balance of such interest be added to the principal."—*Dig. of Stat.*, § 4738.

"Whenever any certain interest is or may be mentioned, and no period of time is stated for such rate of interest to be calculated, interest shall be calculated at the rate mentioned by the year, in the same manner as if the words 'per annum' or 'by the year' had been added to such rate."—*Dig. of Stat.*, § 4739.

"Creditors shall be allowed to receive [interest] at the rate of six per cent. per annum on any judgment before any court or magistrate authorized to enter up the same, from the day of signing judgment until the effects are sold, or satisfaction be made."—*Dig. of Stat.*, § 4740.

"Judgments or decrees upon contracts bearing more than six per cent. interest shall bear the same interest as may be specified in such contracts, and the rate of interest shall be expressed in all such judgments and decrees, and all other judgments and decrees shall bear interest at the rate of six per cent. per annum, until satisfaction is made as aforesaid."—*Dig. of Stat.*, § 4741.

"If default be made in the regular payment of interest due upon money loaned, or for lands sold by any common school commissioner or township treasurer, or in the payment of the principal, interest at the rate of ten per cent. per annum shall be charged upon the principal and interest from the day of default, which shall be included in the assessment of damages, or in the judgment, in suits or actions brought upon the obligation to enforce payment thereof; and interest, as aforesaid, may be recovered in actions brought to recover interest only."—*Dig. of Stat.*, § 6130.

"When any bond, bill or note for the payment of money or delivery of property shall not be paid by the principal debtor, according to the tenor thereof, and such bond, bill or note, or any part thereof, shall be paid by the surety, the principal debtor shall refund to the surety the amount or value, with interest thereon at the rate of ten per centum per annum from the time of such payment."—*Dig. of Stat.*, § 6401.

"When such payment by a surety shall be made in money, such surety may recover the same, with interest, in an action for so much money paid to the use of the defendant; and when payment is made in property, he may recover the value, with the interest, in an action for so much property sold to the defendant."—*Dig. of Stat.*, § 6402.

Taxes bear interest at ten per cent under certain conditions. —*Acts of* 1885, *ch.* 71.

"Every lien created or arising by mortgage, deed of trust or otherwise, as real or personal property, to secure the payment of a contract for a greater rate of interest than ten per centum per annum, either directly or indirectly, and every conveyance made in furtherance of any such lien is void; and every such lien or conveyance may be cancelled and annulled at the suit of the maker of such usurious contract, or his vendees, assigns or creditors. The maker of a usurious contract may by suit in equity against all parties asserting rights under the same, have such contract and any mortgage, pledge or other lien, or conveyance executed to secure the performance of the same, annulled and cancelled, and any property, real or personal, embraced within the terms of said lien or conveyance, delivered up if in possession of any of the defendants in the action, and if the same be in the possession of the plaintiff, provision shall be made in the decree in the case removing the cloud of such usurious lien, and conveyances made in furtherance thereof, from the title to such property. And any person who may have acquired the title to, or an interest in, or lien upon such property by purchase from the makers of such usurious contract, or by assignment or by sale under judicial process, mortgage or otherwise, either before or after the making of the usurious contract, may bring his suit in equity against the parties to such usurious contract, and any one claiming title to such property by virtue of such usurious contract, or may intervene in any suit brought to enforce such lien, or to obtain possession of such property under any title growing out of such usurious contract, and shall by proper decree have such mortgage, pledge or other lien, or conveyance made in furtherance thereof, cancelled and annulled in so far as the same is in conflict with the rights of the plaintiff in the action."—*Acts of* 1887, *ch.* 39, § 1.

"That any creditor whose debtor has given a lien by mortgage, pledge or otherwise, on real or personal property, subject to execution to secure the payment of a usurious contract, may bring his suit in equity against the parties to such usurious contract, and recover judgment for his debt against the debtor, and a decree cancelling and annulling such usurious lien, and directing the sale of the property to satisfy the plaintiff's judgment and costs, and any surplus that may remain after satisfying the plaintiff's judgment, shall be paid to the debtor."—*Acts of* 1887, *ch.* 39, § 2.

"That neither the maker of a usurious contract nor his vendees, assigns or creditors, or any other person who may have or claim an interest in any property embraced within the terms of said usurious contract, shall be required to tender or pay any part of the usurious debt or interest as a condition of having such contract, and any conveyance, mortgage, pledge or other lien given to secure its payment or executed in furtherance thereof, enjoined, cancelled and annulled, and any rule of law, equity or practice to the contrary is hereby abrogated."—*Acts of* 1887, *ch.* 39, § 3.

"That this act shall apply to all usurious contracts and securities, whether executed before or after its passage, and shall be in force from and after its passage."—*Acts of* 1887, *ch.* 39, § 4.

CALIFORNIA.

"If the debt for which the mortgage, lien, or incumbrance is held is not all due, so soon as sufficient of the property has been sold to pay the amount due, with costs, the sale must cease; and afterwards, as often as more becomes due, for principal or interest, the court may, on motion, order more to be sold. But if the property cannot be sold in portions, without injury to the parties, the whole may be ordered to be sold in the first instance, and the entire debt and costs paid, there being a rebate of interest where such rebate is proper."—*Code of Civil Procedure*, § 728.

"The clerk must include in the judgment entered up by him, any interest on the verdict or decision of the court, from the time it was rendered or made."—*Code of Civil Procedure*, § 1035.

"In case of a bequest of the interest or income of a certain sum or fund, the income accrues from the testator's death." —*Civil Code*, § 1366.

"Legacies bear interest from the time when they are due and payable, except that legacies for maintenance, or to the testator's widow, bear interest from the testator's decease."[1]—*Civil Code*, § 1369.

Money paid on a claim, if not specially stated what its payment is to be applied to, will be first applied to the payment "of interest due at the time of the performance."—*Civil Code*, § 1479.

"An offer of payment or other performance, duly made, though the title to the thing offered be not transferred to the creditor, stops the running of interest on the obligation, and has the same effect upon all its incidents as a performance thereof."—*Civil Code*, § 1504.

"Whenever a loan of money is made, it is presumed to be made upon interest, unless it is otherwise expressly stipulated at the time in writing."—*Civil Code*, § 1914.

"Interest is the compensation allowed by law or fixed by the parties for the use, or forbearance, or detention of money."—*Civil Code*, § 1915.

"When a rate of interest is prescribed by a law or contract, without specifying the period of time by which such rate is to be calculated, it is to be deemed an annual rate."—*Civil Code*, § 1916.

"Unless there is an express contract in writing, fixing a different rate, interest is payable on all moneys at the rate of seven per cent per annum after they become due, on any instrument of writing, except a judgment, and on moneys lent, or due on any settlement of account, from the day on which the balance is ascertained, and on moneys received to the use of another and detained from him. In the computation of interest for a period less than a year, three hundred and sixty days are deemed to constitute a year."—*Civil Code*, § 1917.

"Parties may agree in writing for the payment of any rate of interest, and it shall be allowed, according to the terms of the agreement, until the entry of judgment."—*Civil Code*, § 1918.

"The parties may, in any contract in writing whereby any debt is secured to be paid, agree that if the interest on such debt is not punctually paid it shall become a part of the prin-

[1] Section 1370 says that this section is controlled by the testator's expressed intention.

cipal, and thereafter bear the same rate of interest as the principal debt."—*Civil Code*, § 1919.

"Interest is payable on judgments recovered in the courts of this state at the rate of seven per cent per annum, and no greater rate, but such interest must not be compounded in any manner or form."—*Civil Code*, § 1920.

"A trustee who uses or disposes of the trust property, contrary to section 2229, may, at the option of the beneficiary, be required to account for all profits so made, or to pay the value of its use, and, if he has disposed thereof, to replace it, with its fruits, or to account for its proceeds, with interest."—*Civil Code*, § 2237.

"If a trustee omits to invest the trust moneys [as fast as he collects a sufficient amount], he must pay simple interest thereon if such omission is negligence merely, and a compound interest if it is willful."—*Civil Code*, § 2262.

"Upon a contract of bottomry, the parties may lawfully stipulate for a rate of interest higher than that allowed by the law upon other contracts. But a competent court may reduce the rate stipulated when it appears unjustifiable and exorbitant."[1] —*Civil Code*, § 3022.

"From the time of notice of dishonor and demand of payment, lawful interest must be allowed upon the aggregate amount of the principal sum specified in the bill, and the damages mentioned in the preceding section."—*Civil Code*, § 3236.

"Every person who is entitled to recover damages certain, or capable of being made certain by calculation, and the right to recover which is vested in him upon a particular day, is entitled also to recover interest thereon from that day, except during such time as the debtor is prevented by law, or by the act of the creditor from paying the debt."—*Civil Code*, § 3287.

"In an action for the breach of an obligation not arising from contract, and in every case of oppression, fraud, or malice, interest may be given, in the discretion of the jury."—*Civil Code*, § 3288.

"Any legal rate of interest stipulated by a contract remains chargeable after a breach thereof, as before, until the contract is superseded by a verdict or other new obligation."—*Civil Code*, § 3289.

"Accepting payment of the whole principal, as such, waives all claim to interest."—*Civil Code*, § 3290.

"Interest at the rate of two per cent per month must be collected on . . delinquent taxes from the time they were first delinquent until paid."—*Political Code*, § 3803.

[1] By section 3039, this applies also to loans on respondentia.

"When any warrant is presented to the [county] treasurer for payment and the same is not paid for want of funds, the treasurer must indorse thereon, 'not paid for want of funds,' annexing the date of presentation, and sign his name thereto; and from that time until paid the warrant bears seven per cent per annum interest."—*Political Code*, § 4148.

COLORADO.

"Debts not due [in an assignment for the benefit of creditors] may be claimed, but if the same are not bearing interest, a suitable rebate shall be made. Interest shall be computed to the date of the assignment, and not afterward."—*Mill's St.*, § 187.

County bonds bear "interest at the rate of not exceeding ten per cent per annum from their date until paid, said interest being payable on the first day of April of each year," etc.—*Mill's St.*, § 935.

"State warrants shall bear interest at the rate of six (6) per cent per annum from the date of their presentation for payment," but compound interest shall not be paid.—*Mill's St.*, §§ 1814, 1850.

"The [state] treasurer shall keep a record of the number and amount of the warrants so presented and indorsed for non-payment, and when there are funds in the treasury for the payment to an account [of an amount] sufficient to render it advisable, he shall give notice to what number of warrants the funds will extend and which he will pay, by the insertion in a newspaper printed at the seat of government. At the expiration of thirty days from the day of the last insertion, interest on the warrants so named as being payable shall cease. When interest is paid upon the warrants, the amount shall be indorsed upon the warrant and be signed by the party receiving it."—*Mill's St.*, § 1852.

"The legal rate of interest on the forbearance or loan of any money when there is no agreement between the parties, as specified in section three of this act,[1] shall be at the rate of eight per centum per annum."—*Mill's St.*, § 2251.

"Creditors shall be allowed to receive interest when there is no agreement as to the rate thereof, at the rate of ten per centum per annum, for all moneys after they become due, on any bond, bill, promissory note or other instrument of writing, or any judgment recovered before any court or magistrate authorized to enter up the same within this state, from the day of entering up said judgment until satisfaction thereof be made; also on money due on mutual settlement of accounts from the date of such set-

[1] § 2253 beyond.

tlement on money due on account from the date when the same became due, and on money received to the use of another and detained without the owner's knowledge."—*Mill's St.*, § 2252.

"The parties to any bond, bill or promissory note, or other instrument of writing, may stipulate therein for the payment of a greater or higher rate of interest than eight per centum per annum, and any such stipulation may be enforced in any court of competent jurisdiction in the state."—*Mill's St.*, § 2253.

"County orders and warrants, town and city orders and warrants, and other like evidences or certificates of indebtedness, shall bear interest at the rate of eight per centum per annum from the date of the presentation thereof for payment at the treasury where the same may be payable, until there is money in the treasury for the payment thereof, except when otherwise specially provided by law, and every county treasurer, town treasurer and city treasurer to whom any such county, town or city order or warrant is presented for payment, and who shall not have on hand the funds to pay the same, shall indorse thereon the rate of interest said order or warrant will draw, and the date of such presentation, and subscribe such indorsement with his official signature."—*Mill's St.*, § 2254.

"In all executions, to be issued upon judgments recovered upon contracts expressed or implied, it shall be lawful to direct the collection of interest on the said judgment from the time of recovering the same until paid, at the rate of ten per cent per annum."—*Mill's St.*, § 2536.

"It shall be lawful for any defendant, his heirs, executors, administrators or grantees, whose lands or tenements shall be sold by virtue of any execution within six months from such sale, to redeem such lands or tenements by paying to the purchaser thereof, his executors, administrators or assigns, or the sheriff or other officer who sold the same, for the benefit of such purchaser, the sum of money which may have been paid on the purchase thereof,[1] or the amount given or bid if purchased by the plaintiff in the execution, together with the interest thereon at the rate of ten per cent. from the time of such sale; and on such sum being paid as aforesaid, the said sale and the certificate thereupon granted shall be null and void."—*Mill's St.*, § 2547.

If "judgment be rendered upon any note or bond, or for a balance due upon a settled account, the justice shall allow interest from the time when the same became due, and include the same in the said judgment; and in all cases the judgment shall

[1] The next section (2548) gives proceedings for redemption after six months.

bear interest at the rate of ten per cent per annum until paid." —*Mill's St.*, § 2647.

If constables fail to return executions within ten days after the return day, or if the claims are wholly or partially lost, etc., they shall be charged interest from the date of the judgment.—*Mill's St*, § 2676.

Suit may be begun when the subject of it is not payable. In such a case, "a rebate of interest from the time when the judgment is rendered until the maturity of the debt shall be allowed in all cases when a judgment in favor of the plaintiff is rendered under the provisions of this section."—*Mill's St.*, § 2703.

"On the first day of March the unpaid taxes of the preceding year become delinquent, and shall draw interest at the rate of twenty-five per cent. per annum; but the treasurer shall continue to receive payments of the same with interest after the first day of March until the day of sale for taxes."—*Mill's St.*, § 3864.

"Real property, sold under the provisions of this act,[1] may be redeemed by the owner, his agent, assignee or attorney, at any time before the expiration of three years from the date of sale, and at any time before the execution of the deed to the purchaser, his heirs or assigns, by the payment to the treasurer of the proper county, to be held by him subject to the order of the purchaser of the amount for which the same was sold, with interest thereon at the rate of twenty-five per cent. per annum from the date of sale, and fifteen per cent. on the sum if redeemed after three months and within one year from the date of sale, and forty per cent. if redeemed after one year and within two years from the date of sale, and fifty per cent. if redeemed after two (2) years and within three (3) years together with the amount of all taxes accruing on such real estate after the first sale, paid by the purchaser and indorsed on his certificate of purchase, with interest on the same at the rate of twenty-five per cent. per annum on such taxes paid subsequent to such sale; but if said subsequent taxes should be paid before the time when unpaid taxes levied for that year would become delinquent, interest shall only be computed from the time of their delinquency."— *Mill's St.*, § 3905.

"If the court shall direct that the executor or administrator raise money by mortgage of any of the real estate, the order shall specify a rate of interest not exceeding which, and a period for not less than which such loan shall be made."—*Mill's St.*, § 4763.

If shares in a deceased person's estate are not paid over for any reason, the county treasurer shall hold the funds without interest.—*Mill's St.*, § 4801.

[1] For collection of taxes.

CONNECTICUT.

"The treasurer of any town may, at any time, give notice to all persons holding orders drawn by the selectmen on the treasurer of such town to present them for payment on or before a certain day to be fixed in said notice, which shall be at least thirty days after the date thereof. Such notice shall be advertised for three weeks successively in a newspaper printed or having circulation in said town, and be posted on the sign-posts therein. If any person holding an order, outstanding at the time of such notice, shall fail to present it for payment on or before the day fixed in said notice, no interest shall be allowed on it after said day."—*G. S.*, § 86.

"The rate of interest on all existing loans of the school fund in this State, and upon all hereafter made, shall not be more than six per cent. per annum, payable semi-annually."—*G. S.*, § 354.

"When the semi-annual interest due on any bond or note given for moneys loaned from the school fund shall remain fifteen days or more after it shall have become due, the School Fund Commissioner is authorized to charge interest thereon from the time the same became due, and if the semi-annual interest shall remain unpaid six months after it shall have become due, the interest charged shall be at the rate of nine per cent. per annum, until the same is paid."—*G. S.*, § 355.

"On every execution issued on a judgment, legal interest on the amount of the judgment shall be collected."—*G. S.*, § 1154.

"No savings bank shall demand or receive on any loan, either as bonus, commission, or tax, or in any other way, directly or indirectly, more than the value of six dollars for the forbearance of one hundred dollars a year, and at that rate for a greater or less sum, or for a longer or shorter period; but the taking of interest in advance for a period not to exceed six months, and the reimbursement of any money paid by said bank for insurance on property mortgaged to them, shall not be deemed a violation of this section."—*G. S.*, § 1810.

"The compensation for forbearance of property loaned at a fixed valuation, or for money, shall, in the absence of any agreement to the contrary, be at the rate of six per cent. a year; and, in computing interest, three hundred and sixty days may be considered a year."—*G. S.*, § 2941.

"Interest at the rate of six per cent. a year, and no more, may be recovered and allowed in civil actions, including actions to recover money loaned at a greater rate as damages for the detention of money after it becomes payable. But judgment may be given in any court for the recovery of taxes assessed and paid upon the loan, and the insurance upon the estate mortgaged to secure the loan whenever the borrower has agreed in writing to pay such taxes or insurance, or both. And whenever the maker of any contract is a resident of another State, or the mortgage security is located in another State, any obligee or holder of such contract, residing in this State, may lawfully recover any agreed rate of interest, or damages on such contract until it is fully performed, not exceeding the legal rate of interest in the State where such contract purports to have been made, or such mortgage security is located."—*G. S.*, § 2942.

"No borrower of money shall be permitted to set off or recover back, by any proceeding in court, any sum of money paid by way of interest, discount, or damages, for the detention of money, in excess of the rate of six per cent. a year."—*G. S.* § 2943.

"Pawnbrokers and loan-brokers, and all persons who lend money on the pledge of personal property, are prohibited from taking or receiving, directly or indirectly, any more than at the rate of twenty-five per cent. per annum, for the use of money loaned on personal property."—*G. S.*, § 3003.

"If any tax laid by any town, city, borough, or school district, except the town and city of New Haven, and any school district within the limits of said town of New Haven, shall remain unpaid for one month, or in said town or city of New Haven, or in any school district within the limits of said town of New Haven for two months after the same shall become due and payable, interest at the rate of nine per cent. shall be charged from the time when such tax becomes due until the same shall be paid, which shall be collectible as a part of said tax; and said collectors shall keep an accurate and separate account of all such additions, and the time when the same may be received, and shall pay over the same as a part of said tax."—*G. S.*, § 3886.

DELAWARE.

"The legal rate of interest is six per centum per annum; and if any person shall, directly or indirectly, take for the loan, or use of money, more than six dollars for the loan, or use, of one hundred dollars, for one year, and in that proportion, he shall forfeit and pay, to any one who will sue for the same, a sum equal to the money lent — one half for the use of the person so suing, and the other half for the use of the State."—*Code, ch.* 63, § 1.

"If any bank incorporated by any law of this State shall hereafter, either directly or by or through the agency or employment of any person, be in anywise concerned in any paper or security of any description whatever, whereby the amount of profit to said bank to arise from said transaction shall exceed the rate of one per cent., for sixty days, such bank shall be deemed and taken to have forfeited its charter; and furthermore, the directors or managers of the affairs of said bank who knowingly and intentionally assent to the violation of the foregoing provision, shall severally be guilty of a misdemeanor, and on conviction thereof, by indictment, shall be fined at the discretion of the court: Provided, however, That in case of a draft or bill drawn upon a place between which and the city of Philadelphia there shall be, at the time of the negotiation of such paper a rate of exchange below the par thereof, the bank negotiating such paper shall be allowed to add the exchange to the profit before mentioned and take the whole amount of such profit and exchange and no more; and provided also, That when application shall be made for the purchase of a draft on any place other than that where the business of said bank is transacted, it shall be lawful for the said bank to charge for the accommodation, a reasonable exchange. Nothing herein contained shall be held or taken to contravene the usage with banks of taking discount or interest in advance."—*Laws*, 1855, *ch*. 227.

DISTRICT OF COLUMBIA.

"The rate of interest upon judgments or decrees, and upon the loan or forbearance of any money, goods, or things in action, shall continue to be six dollars upon one hundred dollars for one year, and after that rate for a greater or less sum, or for a longer or shorter time, except as provided in this chapter."—*R. S.*, § 713.

"In all contracts made it shall be lawful for the parties to stipulate or agree in writing that the rate of ten per centum per annum, or any less sum, of interest shall be taken and paid upon every one hundred dollars of money loaned, or in any manner due and owing from any person or corporation in the District."—*R. S.*, § 714.

"If any person or corporation shall contract to receive a greater rate of interest than ten per cent. upon any contract in writing, or six per cent. upon any verbal contract, such person or corporation shall forfeit the whole of the interest so contracted to be received, and shall be entitled only to recover the principal sum due to such person or corporation."—*R. S.*, § 715.

"If any person or corporation within the District shall directly or indirectly take or receive any greater amount of interest than is provided for in this chapter, upon any contract or agreement whatever, it shall be lawful for the person, or his personal representative, or the corporation paying the same, to sue for and recover all the interest paid upon any such contract or agreement from the person or his personal representatives, or from the corporation receiving such unlawful interest; but the suit to recover back such interest shall be brought within one year after such unlawful interest shall have been paid or taken."[1]—*R. S.*, § 716.

"Upon all judgments rendered on the common-law side of the court in actions founded on contracts, interest at the rate of six per centum per annum shall be awarded on the principal sum due until the judgment shall be satisfied, and the amount which is to bear interest and the time from which it is to be paid shall be ascertained by the verdict of the jury sworn in the cause."—*R. S.*, § 829.

"Judgments [of justices of the peace] shall bear interest from their date until paid or satisfied."—*R. S.*, § 1007.

FLORIDA.

"All judgments (and decrees) shall bear interest at the rate of eight per centum per annum."—*R. S.*, § 1176.

"In all cases where interest shall accrue without a special contract for the rate thereof, the rate shall be eight per cent. per annum."—*R. S.*, § 2320.

"All contracts for the payment of interest upon any loan, advance of money, or forbearance to enforce the collection of any debt, or upon any contract whatever, at a higher rate of interest than ten per centum per annum, are hereby declared usurious."—*Laws*, 1891, *ch.* 4022, § 1.

"It shall not be lawful for any person, company or corporation, to reserve, charge or take, for any loan or advance of money, or forbearance to enforce the collection of any sum of money, a rate of interest greater than ten per centum per annum, either directly or indirectly, by way of commissions for advances, discounts, exchange, or by any contract, contrivance or device whatever, whereby the debtor is required or obligated to pay a greater sum than the actual principal sum received, together with interest at the rate of ten per centum per annum as aforesaid" (excepting loans of building, loan and other mutual benefit associations to their members).—*Laws*, 1891, *ch.* 4022, § 2.

[1] Section 717 provides that this section has no effect on the operation of the National Bank law.

"Any person, company or corporation, violating the provisions of this act, shall forfeit the entire interest so charged, or taken or contracted to be charged, reserved, or taken, and only the actual principal sum of such usurious contracts can be enforced at law or in equity: *Provided, however*, That no *bona-fide* endorsee or transferee, of negotiable paper, purchased before maturity, shall be affected by any usurious interest, exacted by any former holder of such paper, unless the usurious character should appear on its face, or the said endorsee or transferee shall have had actual notice of the same before the purchase of such paper, but double the amount of such usurious interest, may, in such cases, be recovered after payment, by action against the party originally exacting the same in any court of competent jurisdiction, provided such action be commenced within one year from the maturity of such paper."—*Laws*, 1891, *ch.* 4022, § 3.

GEORGIA.

"The legal rate of interest shall remain seven per centum per annum, where the rate per cent. is not named in the contract, and any higher rate must be specified in writing, but in no event to exceed eight per cent. per annum."—*Code*, § 2050.

"Usury is the reserving and taking, or contracting to reserve and take, either directly or by indirection, a greater sum for the use of money than the lawful interest."—*Code*, § 2051.

"Interest from date, when stipulated, if the debt is not punctually paid at maturity, may be recovered: *Provided*, interest has not already been included in the principal amount." —*Code*, § 2052.

"Every contract bears interest according to the law of the place of the contract at the time of the contract, unless upon its face it is apparent that the intention of the parties referred the execution of the contract to another forum: in this case, the law of the forum shall govern."—*Code*, § 2053.

"All judgments in this State bear lawful interest upon the principal amount recovered."—*Code*, § 2054.

"When a payment is made upon any debt, it shall be applied first to the discharge of any interest due at the time, and the balance, if any, to the reduction of the principal. If the payment does not extinguish the interest then due, no interest shall be calculated on such balance of interest, but only on the principal amount up to the time of the next payment."—*Code*, § 2055.

"All liquidated demands, where by agreement or otherwise the sum to be paid is fixed or certain, bear interest from the time the party is liable and bound to pay them; if payable on demand, from the time of the demand. In case of promissory notes payable on demand, the law presumes a demand instantly, and gives interest from date."—*Code*, § 2056.

"All accounts of merchants, tradesmen, mechanics, which by custom become due at the end of the year, bear interest from that time upon the amount actually due whenever ascertained."—*Code*, § 2057.

"It shall not be lawful for any person, company or corporation to reserve, charge or take for any loan or advance of money, or forbearance to enforce the collection of any sum of money, any rate of interest greater than eight per centum per annum, either directly or indirectly, by way of commission for advances, discount, exchange, or by any contract or contrivance or device whatever."—*Code*, § 2057*a*.

"Any person, company or corporation violating the provisions of the foregoing section, shall forfeit the excess of interest so charged or taken, or contracted to be reserved, charged or taken."—*Code*, § 2057*b*.

"The amount of forfeit as aforesaid may be plead as a set-off in any action for the recovery of the principal sum loaned or advanced by the defendant in said action."—*Code*, § 2057*c*.

"No contrivance or arrangement between the parties to any such unlawful transaction, or their privies, shall have the effect to discharge such forfeiture, except it be an actual and full payment of the amount so forfeited."—*Code*, § 2057*d*.

"Any plea or suit for the recovery of such forfeiture shall not be barred by lapse of time shorter than one year."—*Code*, § 2057*e*.

"All titles to property made as a part of an usurious contract, or to evade the laws against usury, are void."—*Code*, § 2057*f*.

"Every provision in the charter of any corporation, granted since the 1st day of January, 1863, inconsistent with the foregoing provisions of this Article, is hereby repealed."—*Code*, § 2057*g*.

"All contracts for rent shall bear interest from the time the rent is due, and judgments upon suits for rent may be rendered at the first term."—*Code*, § 2288.

"A general legacy usually bears interest from the expiration of twelve months from the death of the testator. But when the condition of the estate at that time, as to the payment of debts and legacies, is doubtful, or the fund out of which the legacy is to be paid, is unavailable for all the charges made upon it, or any other equitable circumstance intervenes, the general rule yields to the equity and necessity of the particular case. A general legacy, to be paid at a future time or event, bears no interest until such time or event."—*Code*, § 2460.

"A reasonable time, according to the facts in each case, should be allowed to the trustee to invest funds coming into his hands before charging him with interest thereon; and, in like manner, disbursements made by the trustee should, as a general rule, bear interest from some period anterior to the date of payment, according as he may have retained funds to meet them. In every case, the object is to charge the trustee with such interest as a diligent man would make, and to see that the trust fund is not used for private benefit."—*Code*, § 2601.

The interest to be charged against trustees appointed since the first of January, 1848, and hereafter appointed, shall be at the rate of seven per cent. per annum, without compounding, for six years, from the date of their qualification; and after that time at the rate of six per cent. per annum, annually compounded. But any trustee may relieve himself from this rule by returning annually the interest actually made and accounting for the balance of the fund. Any distributee may recover greater interest by showing that the trustee actually received more, or that he used the funds himself to greater profit."—*Code*, § 2603.

"In all cases where an amount ascertained would be the damages at the time of the breach, it may be increased by the addition of legal interest from that time till the recovery."—*Code*, § 2945.

"The plea of usury must set forth the sum upon which it was paid, or to be paid, the time when the contract was made, when payable, and the amount of usury agreed upon, taken or reserved."—*Code*, § 3470*a*.

"As a general rule, a party who is prevented from paying over money by process of law is not liable for interest: but if a garnishee resists the payment of the fund in his hands, or controverts his indebtedness, he is liable for interest thereon—but he may relieve himself from interest by paying the fund into Court."—*Code*, § 3546

"In all cases where judgment may be obtained, such judgment shall be entered up for the principal sum due, with interest: *Provided* the claim upon which it was obtained draws interest; but no part of such judgment shall bear interest except the principal which may be due on the original debt."—*Code*, § 3570.

"If any Sheriff, coroner, Justice of the Peace, constable, Clerk of the Superior Court, or attorney at law, shall fail, upon application, to pay to the proper person, or his attorney, any money they may have in their hands, which they may have collected by virtue of their office, the party entitled thereto, or his attorney, may serve said officer with a written demand for the same, and if not then paid, for such neglect or refusal the said officer shall be compelled to pay at the rate of twenty per cent. per annum upon the sum he has in his hands, from the date of such demand, unless good cause be shown to the contrary."—*Code*, § 3950.

Executions for state, county and municipal taxes bear seven per cent interest, except in municipalities assessing other damages upon delinquents.—*Acts of* 1890, *No.* 97.

IDAHO.

"When there is no express contract in writing fixing a different rate of interest, interest is allowed at the rate of ten cents on the hundred by the year, on:

"1. Money due by express contract;

"2. Money after the same becomes due;

"3. Money lent;

"4. Money due on the judgment of any competent court or tribunal;

"5. Money received to the use of another, and retained beyond a reasonable time without the owner's consent, express or implied;

"6. Money due on the settlement of mutual accounts from the day the balance is ascertained;

"7. Money due upon open accounts after six months from the date of the last item."—*R. S.*, § 1263.

"Parties may agree in writing for the payment of any rate of interest on money due or to become due on any contract, not to exceed the sum of one and one-half per cent. per month; any judgment rendered on such contract bears interest at the rate of ten per cent. per annum until satisfied."—*R. S.*, § 1264.

"Compound interest is not allowed, but a debtor may agree in writing to pay interest upon interest over-due at the rate of such agreement."—*R. S.*, § 1265.

"If it is ascertained in any suit brought on any contract, that a rate of interest has been contracted for greater than is authorized by this chapter, either directly or indirectly, in money or in property, such contract works a forfeiture of ten cents on the hundred by the year, and at that rate, upon the amount of such contract, to the School Fund of the county in which the suit is brought and the plaintiff must have judgment for the principal sum less all payments of principal or interest theretofore made and without interest or cost. The court must render judgment in said action for ten per cent. per annum upon the entire principal of said contract, against the defendant in favor of the Territory [State] for the use of the School Fund of the county, whether the unlawful interest is contested or not; and in no case where unlawful interest is contracted for, must the plaintiff have judgment for more than the principal sum less the payments already made, whether the unlawful interest be incorporated with the principal sum or not. But no indorsee in due course of negotiable paper, is affected by any usury exacted by any former holder of such paper unless he have actual notice of the usury previous to his purchase; but in no such case the judgment above provided in favor of the School Fund must be entered against the drawer or maker, if a party to the action, and he may recover back the usury paid from the party who received the same."—*R. S.*, § 1266.

"Interest at the rate of two per cent. per month must be collected on such delinquent taxes[1] from the time they were first delinquent until paid."—*R. S.*, § 1573.

"When any warrant is presented to the [County] Treasurer for payment and the same is not paid for want of funds, the Treasurer must endorse thereon, 'Not paid for want of funds,' annexing the date of presentation and sign his name thereto; and from that time until paid the warrant bears seven per cent. per annum interest."—*R. S.*, § 1844.

"From the time of notice of dishonor and demand of payment [of bills of exchange], lawful interest must be allowed upon the aggregate amount of the principal sum specified in the bill, and the damages mentioned in the preceding section."[2]—*R. S.*, § 3563.

"If the debt for which the mortgage, lien or incumbrance is held is not all due, so soon as sufficient of the property has been sold to pay the amount due, with costs, the sale must cease; and afterwards, as often as more becomes due, for principal or interest, the court may, on motion, order more to be sold. But if the property cannot be sold in portions, without injury to the parties, the whole may be ordered to be sold in the first instance, and the entire debt and costs paid, there being a rebate of interest where such rebate is proper."—*R. S.*, § 4522.

"The Clerk must include in the judgment entered up by him, any interest on the verdict or decision of the court, from the time it was rendered or made, and the costs, if the same have

[1] Taxes not paid and cancelled on the collector's book.

[2] The preceding section specifies certain damages instead of interest after notice of dishonor, etc.

been taxed or ascertained; and he must, within two days after the same are taxed or ascertained, if not included in the judgment, insert the same in a blank left in the judgment for that purpose, and must make a similar insertion of the costs in the copies and docket of the judgment."—*R. S.*, § 4914.

Municipal bonds are not to bear more than six per cent interest.—*Acts of* 1891, *p.* 54.

ILLINOIS.

"All moneys, bonds, notes and credits which any administrator or executor may have in his possession or control as property or assets of the estate, at a period of two years and six months from the date of his letters testamentary or of administration, shall bear interest, and the executor or administrator shall be charged interest thereon from said period at the rate of ten per cent., or after two years and six months from any subsequent time that he may have discovered and received the same, unless good cause is shown to the court why such should not be taxed."—*R. S. ch.* 3, § 113.

"The rate of interest upon the loan or forbearance of any money, goods, or thing in action, shall be five dollars ($5) upon one hundred dollars ($100) for one year, and after that rate for a greater or less sum, or for a longer or shorter time, except as herein provided."—*Laws of* 1891, *p.* 149.

"Creditors shall be allowed to receive at the rate of five (5) per centum per annum for all moneys after they become due on any bond, bill, promissory note or other instrument of writing; on money lent or advanced for the use of another; on money due on the settlement of account from the day of liquidating accounts between the parties and ascertaining the balance, on money received to the use of another, and retained without the owner's knowledge, and on money withheld by an unreasonable and vexatious delay of payment."—*Laws of* 1891, *p.* 149.

"Judgments recovered before any court or magistrate, shall draw interest at the rate of five (5) per centum per annum from the date of the same until satisfied. When judgment is entered upon any award, report or verdict, interest shall be computed at the rate aforesaid, from the time when made or rendered to the time of rendering judgment upon the same, and made a part of the judgment."—*Laws of* 1891, *p.* 150.

"In all written contracts it shall be lawful for the parties to stipulate or agree that seven (7) per cent. per annum, or any less sum of interest, shall be taken and paid upon every one hundred ($100) dollars of money loaned or in any manner due and owing from any person or corporation to any other person or corporation in this State, and after that rate for a greater or less sum, or for a longer or shorter time, except as herein provided."—*Laws of* 1891, *p.* 150.

"If any person or corporation in this State shall contract to receive a greater rate of interest or discount than seven (7) per cent. upon any contract, verbal or written, such person or corporation shall forfeit the whole of said interest so contracted to be received, and shall be entitled only to recover the principal sum due to such person or corporation. And all contracts executed after this act shall take effect, which shall provide for interest or compensation at a greater rate than herein specified, on account of non-payment at maturity, shall be deemed usurious, and only the principal sum due thereon shall be recoverable."—*Laws of* 1891, *p.* 150.

"The defense of usury shall not be allowed in any suit, unless the person relying upon such defense shall set up the same by plea, or file in the cause a notice in writing, stating that he intends to defend against the contract sued upon or set off, on the ground that the contract is usurious."—*R. S.*, *ch.* 74, § 7.

"When any written contract, wherever payable, shall be made in this State, or between citizens or corporations of this State, or a citizen or corporation of this State and a citizen or corporation of any other State, territory or country (or shall be secured by mortgage or trust deed on lands in this State), such contract may bear any rate of interest allowed by law, to be taken or contracted for by persons or corporations in this State, or which is or may be allowed by law on any contract for money due or owing in this State: *Provided, however*, that such rate of interest shall not exceed seven per cent. per annum. And if any such person or corporation shall contract to receive a greater rate of interest or discount than seven per cent. upon any such contract, such person or corporation shall forfeit the whole of said interest so contracted to be received, and shall be entitled only to recover the principal sum due to such person or corporation."—*Laws of* 1891, *p.* 150.

"Whenever, in any statute, act, deed, written or verbal, contract, or in any public or private instrument whatever, any certain rate of interest is or shall be mentioned, and no period of time is stated for which such rate is to be calculated, interest shall be calculated at the rate mentioned, by the year, in the same manner as if 'per annum' or 'by the year' had been added to the rate."—*R. S.*, *ch.* 74, § 9.

"In all computations of time, and of interest and discounts, a month shall be considered to mean a calendar month, and a year shall consist of twelve calendar months; and in computations of interest or discount for any number of days less than a month, a day shall be considered a thirtieth part of a month, and interest or discount shall be computed for such fractional parts of a month upon the ratio which such number of days shall bear to thirty."—*R. S., ch.* 74, § 10.

"No corporation shall hereafter interpose the defense of usury in any action."—*R. S., ch.* 74, § 11.

"Every execution issued upon a judgment shall direct the collection of interest thereon, from the date of the recovery of the judgment until the same is paid, at the rate of six per centum per annum."—*R. S., ch.* 77, § 7.

Pawnbrokers cannot charge more than three per cent per month for loans.—*R. S., ch.* 107, § 2.

INDIANA.

"No bank shall receive, directly or indirectly, a greater rate of interest than shall be allowed by law to individuals loaning money."—*Const., Art.* 11, § 9.

"In any case when a surety on any bill, note, bond, or other instrument in writing shall be compelled to pay the debt or obligation of the principal debtor, such surety shall recover such rate of interest on the amount so paid by him for his principal as was originally provided for in such bill, note, bond, or other instrument in writing, held against such principal debtor; and the judgment therein shall bear the same rate of interest, not exceeding ten per cent. per annum."—*R. S.*, § 1219.

"Cities shall, in all cases, be liable to pay interest on their orders or other liabilities payable on demand from and after such demand, which shall be indorsed on the same by the Treasurer when presented."—*R. S.*, § 3040.

"The principal of all moneys, whether belonging to the common school fund or to the congressional township school fund, received into the county treasury, shall be loaned at eight per cent. per annum, payable annually in advance, and the interest paid out as prescribed in this act, and not otherwise: and any judgment upon any note or mortgage for any part of said fund shall bear eight per cent. interest from the date thereof till the same is paid."—*R. S.*, § 4369.

"The rate of interest required [on loans of the funds of the university] shall be seven per cent. in advance, payable annually. On failure to pay any installment of interest when due, the principal shall forthwith become due; and the note and mortgage may be collected."—*R. S.*, § 4600.

"The interest on loans or forbearance of money, goods, or things in action, when the parties do not agree on the rate, shall be six dollars a year on one hundred dollars, and at that rate for a greater or less sum, or for a shorter or longer time; but it may be taken yearly, or for a shorter period, in advance. No agreement to pay a higher rate shall be valid, unless the same be in writing, signed by the party to be charged thereby; and, in such case, it shall not be lawful to contract for more than eight per centum per annum."—*R. S.*, § 5198.

"Interest on judgments for money, hereafter rendered, shall be from the date of the return of the verdict or finding of the Court, until the same shall be satisfied, at the rate per cent. agreed upon by the parties in the original contract, not exceeding six per cent.; and if there be no contract by the parties, at the rate of six dollars a year on one hundred dollars."—*R. S.*, § 5199.

"On money due on any instrument in writing, on any account stated from the day of settlement, or an account closed upon the day an itemized bill shall have been rendered and payment demanded, or on money had and received for the use of another, and retained without his consent, interest shall be allowed at the rate of six dollars a year on one hundred dollars."—*R. S.*, § 5200.

"When a greater rate of interest than is hereby allowed shall be contracted for, the contract shall be void as to the usurious interest contracted for; and in an action on such contract, if it appear that interest at a higher rate than eight per cent. has been directly or indirectly contracted for, the excess of interest over six per cent. shall be deemed usurious and illegal, and in an action on a contract affected by such usury, the excess over the legal interest may be recouped by the debtor, whenever it has been reserved or paid before the beginning of the suit."—*R. S.*, § 5201.

"If an action be instituted on a contract in which illegal interest shall have been directly or indirectly contracted for, and the defendant shall have, before the commencement of the suit, tendered to the plaintiff his principal, with six per cent. interest, the defendant shall recover costs."—*R. S.*, § 5202.

"When, in any law or contract, a rate of interest is specified, but no period of time is mentioned for which such rate is to be calculated, it shall be deemed to be by the year."—*R. S.*, § 5203.

"The provisions of this Act shall apply to all contracts made within this State, although they are to be performed without this State; and when a contract shall be made without the State, and a rate of interest greater than that herein allowed shall be directly or indirectly contracted for, and a mortgage shall be executed, to secure the performance of the contract, on lands in this State, such lands shall not be liable for a higher rate of interest than is provided for in this Act."—*R. S.*, § 5204.

"Interest on public funds, purchase-money of canal, college, school, or saline lands, and upon the permanent school fund, shall be at the rate of eight dollars a year on one hundred dollars. But nothing herein contained shall be construed as affecting existing contracts,[1] except after verdicts as herein provided, nor a right to defend in a suit upon such contracts for excessive interest, as is now provided by law."—*R. S.*, § 5205.

"Beyond such damages,[2] no interest, or charges accruing prior to protest shall be allowed; but interest from the date of the protest may be recovered."—*R. S.*, § 5508.

"Whenever it shall be necessary to construct, complete, or repair the court-house, jail, or other county buildings, or whenever it may be desirable to fund or average any existing debt incurred for county purposes, and the revenues afforded by reasonable taxation are insufficient to do the same, the County Commissioners may borrow, for that purpose, any sum of money not exceeding one per centum on the assessed valuation of the real and personal property of the county, and issue bonds therefor in amounts of not less than twenty-five dollars each, and bearing a rate of interest not exceeding the legal rate in the State or Territory where the same are negotiated, not exceeding the rate of ten per centum per annum: *Provided*, That no second or subsequent loan shall be made or authorized by said Commissioners, as above provided, so long as any former loan, made under the provisions of this Act, shall remain unpaid." — *R. S.*, § 5749.

Each county treasurer "shall pay all orders of the Auditor when presented, if there be money in the treasury for that purpose, and write on the face of each order the date of redemption, over his signature. If there be no funds to pay such order when presented, he shall endorse thereon 'Not paid for want of funds,' and the date of such presentment, over his signature; which shall entitle such order to draw, thenceforth, legal interest: *Provided*, That such interest shall cease from the date of notice by publication in some newspaper printed or circulated in his county, to be given by the Treasurer, that there are funds to redeem such outstanding orders; which notice the Treasurer shall give." — *R. S.*, § 5920.

"Where bonds or stocks are now, or may hereafter be, exempt from taxation, the accrued interest on such bonds or dividends

[1] Existing when this act was passed.

[2] Certain liquidated damages stipulated for in the preceding section (5507) of the statute.

on such stock shall be listed, unless otherwise exempt, as personal property, without regard to the time when the same is to be paid."— *R. S.*, § 6304.

IOWA.

"The rule of interest shall be six cents on the hundred by the year, on:

" 1. Money due by express contract;

" 2. Money after the same becomes due;

" 3. Money lent;

" 4. Money received to the use of another, and retained beyond a reasonable time without the owner's consent, express or implied;

" 5. Money due on settlement of matured accounts from the day the balance is ascertained;

" 6. Money due upon open accounts after six months from the date of the last item;

" 7. Money due, or to become due, where there is a contract to pay interest, and no rate is stipulated. In all of the cases above contemplated parties may agree in writing for the payment of interest not exceeding eight cents on the hundred by the year."—*Rev. Code*, § 2077, *amended by Acts of* 1890, *ch.* 40.

"Interest shall be allowed on all moneys due on judgments and decrees of any competent court or tribunal, at the rate of six cents on the hundred by the year, unless a different rate is fixed by the contract on which the judgment or decree is rendered; in which case the judgment or decree shall draw interest at the rate expressed in the contract, not exceeding ten cents on the hundred by the year, which rates must be expressed in the judgment or decree."—*Rev. Code*, § 2078.

"No person shall, directly or indirectly, receive in money, goods, or things in action, or in any other manner, any greater sum or value for the loan of money, or upon contract founded upon any bargain, sale, or loan of real or personal property, than is in this chapter prescribed."—*Rev. Code*, § 2079.

"If it shall be ascertained in any suit brought on any contract, that a rate of interest has been contracted for greater than is authorized by this chapter, either directly or indirectly, in money or property, the same shall work a forfeiture of ten cents on the hundred by the year upon the amount of such contract, to the school fund of the county in which the suit is brought, and the plaintiff shall have judgment for the principal sum without either interest or cost. The court in which said suit is prosecuted shall render judgment for the amount of interest forfeited as aforesaid against the defendant, in favor of the state of Iowa for the use of the school fund of said county, whether the said suit is contested or not; and in no case where unlawful interest is contracted for, shall the plaintiff have judgment for more than the principal sum, whether the unlawful interest be incorporated with the principal or not."—*Rev. Code*, § 2080.

"Nothing in this chapter shall be so construed as to prevent the proper assignee, in good faith and without notice, of any usurious contract, recovering against the usurer the full amount of the consideration paid by him for such contract, less the amount of the principal money, but the same may be recovered of the usurer in the proper action before any court having competent jurisdiction."—*Rev. Code*, § 2081.

KANSAS.

Premiums bid for priority of loan in building and saving or trust associations organized under the corporation laws of Kansas, by the members of such associations, shall not be deemed usurious, etc.—*G. S.*, § 1121.

"Creditors shall be allowed to receive interest at the rate of six per cent. per annum, when no other rate of interest is agreed upon, for any money after it becomes due; for money lent or money due on settlement of account, from the day of liquidating the same and ascertaining the balance; for money received for the use of another, and retained without the owner's knowledge of the receipt; for money due and withheld by an unreasonable and vexatious delay of payment or settlement of accounts; for all other money due and to become due, for the forbearance of payment whereof an express promise to pay interest has been made; and for money due from corporations and individuals to their day or monthly employés, from and after the end of each month, when the same shall be paid within fifteen days thereafter."—*G. S.*, § 3497.

"The parties to any bond, bill, promissory note or other instrument of writing for the payment or forbearance of money, may stipulate therein for interest receivable upon the amount of such bond, bill, note, or other instrument of writing, at a rate not to exceed ten per cent. per annum: *Provided*, that any person so contracting for a greater rate of interest than ten per cent. per annum shall forfeit all interest so contracted for in excess of such ten per cent.; and in addition thereto shall forfeit a sum of money, to be deducted from the amount due for principal and lawful interest, equal to the amount of interest contracted for in excess of ten per cent. per annum."—*G. S.*, § 3498.

"All payments of money or property made by way of usurious interest or of indorsement to contract for more than ten per cent. per annum, whether made in advance or not, shall be deemed and taken to be payments made on account of the principal and ten per cent. interest per annum, and the courts shall render judgment for no greater sum than the balance found due after deducting the payments of money or property made as aforesaid: *Provided*, that no *bona fide* indorsee of negotiable paper, purchased before due shall be affected by any usury exacted by any former holder of such paper, unless he shall have actual notice of the usury previous to his purchase. But double the amount of such excess incorporated into negotiable paper, may, in such cases, after payment, be recovered back by action against the party exacting the usury, in any court of competent jurisdiction: *Provided farther*, That such action shall be brought within ninety days from the maturity of such paper."—*G. S.*, § 3499.

"All judgments of courts of record and justices of the peace shall bear interest from the day on which they are rendered, at the rate of six per cent. per annum, except as herein otherwise provided."—*G. S.*, § 3500.

"When a rate of interest is specified in any contract, that rate shall continue until full payment is made, and any judgment rendered on any such contract shall bear the same rate of interest mentioned in the contract, which rate shall be specified in the judgment; but in no case shall such rate exceed ten per cent. per annum, and any bond, note, bill, or other contract for the payment of money, which in effect provides that any interest or any higher rate of interest shall accrue as a penalty for any default shall be void as to any such provisions."—*G. S.*, § 3501.

KENTUCKY.

"If any bill of exchange, drawn on any person out of the United States, shall be protested for non-payment or non-acceptance, it shall bear ten per cent. per year interest from the day of protest, but not longer than eighteen months, unless payment be sooner demanded from the party to be charged, or unless by the contract a rate greater than six per cent. is stipulated for. Such interest shall be recovered to the time of the judgment, and the judgment shall bear six per cent. interest thereafter. Damages on all other bills are disallowed."—*G. S., ch.* 22, § 10.

"A personal representative, after the expiration of two years from the time he qualifies, shall be charged with interest on the surplus assets in his hands from that period."—*G. S., ch.* 39, § 25.

"All demands against the estate of a decedent shall be verified by the written affidavit of the claimant, or in his absence from the State by his agent, or, if dead, by his personal representative, stating that the demand is just, and has never, to his knowledge or belief, been paid, and that there is no offset or discount against the same, or any usury therein."—*G. S., ch.* 39, § 35.

"If any part of the demand has been paid, or there be any offset or discount against the same, or any usury therein, the affidavit shall state the amount of the payment or usury, when the payment was made, and when the offset or discount was due, to the best of the affiant's knowledge and belief. This verification shall not be held to dispense with other proof of the demand, as required by law."—*G. S., ch.* 39, § 36.

"Before such affidavit is made, no action shall be brought, or recovery had, on any such demand, nor until demand of payment thereof has been made of the personal representative, accompanied by affidavit of its justice."—*G. S., ch.* 39, § 37.

"In a proceeding to coerce a claim against the estate of a decedent, his personal representative shall have the right to compel the attendance of the claimant, the original obligee, or intermediate assignors, and interrogate any of them touching the usury embraced in the claim, a payment of all or a part thereof, or of the existence of an offset or discount against the same."—*G. S., ch.* 39, §40.

"No personal representative shall pay, or be adjudged to pay, any more of any demand against the decedent's estate than what remains due of the same after the usury embraced therein, and the payments made thereon, and the offsets and discounts against the same, are deducted."—*G. S., ch.* 39, § 41.

"When a personal representative shall pay to a creditor an undue proportion of his demands, or to a distributee a part, or all of his share or legacy, under a mistake as to the solvency of the estate or otherwise, such personal representative may recover from the creditor, distributee, or devisee, the amount of the over-payment, with interest thereon."—*G. S., ch.* 39, § 42.

"No interest accruing after his death shall be allowed or paid on any claim against a decedent's estate, unless the claim be verified and authenticated as required by law, and demanded of the executor, administrator, or curator, within one year after his appointment."—*G. S . ch.* 39, § 53.

"When the heir or devisee shall alien, before suit brought, the estate descended or devised, he shall be liable for the value thereof, with legal interest from the time of alienation, to the creditors of the decedent or testator; but the estate so aliened shall not be liable to the creditors, in the hands of a *bona fide* purchaser for valuable consideration."—*G. S., ch.* 44, § 8.

"If no time is fixed for the payment of a specific pecuniary legacy, it shall be payable one year after the testator's death, and carry interest after due."—*G. S., ch.* 50, *art. II*, § 2.

"Legal interest shall be at the rate of six dollars upon one hundred dollars for one year, and at the same rate for a greater or less sum, and for a longer or shorter time."—*G. S., ch.* 60, § 1.

"All contracts and assurances made, directly or indirectly, for the loan or forbearance of money or other thing of value at a greater rate than legal interest, shall be void as to the excess over the legal interest."—*G. S., ch.* 60, § 2.

"The amount loaned, with legal interest, may be recovered on any such contract or assurance; but if the lender refuse, before suit brought, a tender of the principal, with legal interest, he shall pay the costs of any suit brought on such contract or assurance."—*G. S., ch.* 60, *p.* 797, § 3.

"A court of equity may grant relief for any such excess of interest, and to that end compel the necessary discovery from the lender or forbearer."—*G. S., ch.* 60, *p.* 799, § 3.

"Such excess of interest may be recovered from the lender or forbearer, although the payment thereof was made to his assignee."—*G. S., ch.* 60, § 4.

"Partial payment on a debt bearing interest shall be first applied to the extinguishment of the interest then due."—*G. S., ch.* 60, § 5.

"A judgment shall bear legal interest from its date. A judgment may be for the principal and accrued interest; but if rendered for accruing interest, it shall bear interest only according to its terms."—*G. S., ch.* 60, § 6.

"Any indebtedness incurred, or evidenced by judgment rendered out of the State, shall be presumed, unless the contrary be shown, to bear like interest as if it had been incurred or the judgment rendered in this Commonwealth."—*G. S., ch.* 60, § 7.

"Rent shall bear six per cent. per annum interest from the time it is due."—*G. S., ch.* 66, *art. II* § 3.

"And no action shall be prosecuted in any of the courts of this Commonwealth, for the recovery of usury heretofore paid, for the loan or forbearance of money, or other thing against the the loaner or forbearer, or assignee, or either, unless the same shall have been instituted within one year next after the payment thereof; and this limitation shall apply to all payments made on all demands, whether evidenced by writing or existing in parol."—*G. S., ch.* 71, *art. III*, § 4.

"Judgments, when given against the defendants in the cases

referred to in the two preceding sections,[1] shall be for the principal due, with interest at the rate of ten per cent. per annum from the first day of November preceding and until paid."—*G. S., ch. 92, art. XI*, § 6.

LOUISIANA.

"All debts shall bear interest at the rate of five per cent. from the time they become due, unless otherwise stipulated."—*Voorhie's Rev. Laws*, § 1883.

"The amount of conventional interest shall in no case exceed eight per cent., under pain of forfeiture of the entire interest so contracted."—*V.'s R. L.*, § 1884.

"If any person hereafter shall pay on any contract a higher rate of interest than the above, as discount or otherwise, the same may be sued for and recovered within twelve months from the time of such payment."—*V.'s R. L.*, § 1885.

"The holder of any circulating note which may have been protested for non-payment shall be entitled to damages at the rate of twelve per cent. per annum, in lieu of interest, until final payment, payable out of the general fund of the insolvent party."—*V.'s R. L.*, § 1886.

"Bankers and banking companies shall be entitled to charge and receive discount at a rate not greater than the maximum allowed by law on conventional obligations; and their other contracts shall be regulated by the laws in regard to interest upon contracts between individuals."—*V.'s R. L.*, § 1887.

Tutors of minors are liable to pay their pupils legal interest on the funds which they may have failed to place at interest for their use.—*V.'s R. L.*, § 1888.

"The owner of any promissory note, bond or written obligation for the payment of money, to order or bearer, or transferable by assignment, shall have the right to collect the whole amount of such promissory notes, bonds or written obligations, notwithstanding such promissory notes, bonds or written obligations may include a greater rate of interest or discount than eight per cent. per annum; *provided*, such obligations shall not bear more than eight per cent. interest per annum after their maturities until paid."—*V.'s R. L.*, § 1889.

"The banking institutions of the State of Louisiana be and they are hereby authorized to discount paper at the rate of eight per cent. per annum interest."—*V.'s R. L.*, § 1890.

[1] Sections 4 and 5, which compel sheriffs and others to pay revenue into the treasury.

Tax to be levied by state to pay interest due on state bonds. —V.'s *R. L.*, § 3820.

MAINE.

"The rate of interest upon unpaid state and county taxes, and taxes assessed by county commissioners for opening, making, and repairing roads, shall be twenty per cent., commencing at the expiration of one year from the date of the assessments, except when otherwise provided."—*R. S.*, *ch.* 6, § 86.

"Towns, at their annual meetings, may determine when the lists named in section ninety-seven[1] shall be committed, and when their taxes shall be payable, and that interest shall be collected thereafter."—*R. S.*, *ch.* 6, § 120.

"The rate of such[2] interest, not exceeding one per cent. a month, shall be specified in the vote, and shall be added to, and become part of the taxes."—*R. S.*, *ch.* 6, § 121.

"The person interested in the estate, by purchase at the sale, may pay any tax assessed thereon before or after that so advertised, and for which the estate remains liable, and on filing with the treasurer the receipt of the officer to whom it was paid, the amount so paid shall be added to that for which the estate was liable, and shall be paid by the owner redeeming the estate, with interest at the same rate as on the other sums. After the deed is so delivered, the owner has six months within which to redeem his estate, by paying to the purchaser the sum by him so paid, with interest at the rate of twenty-five per cent. a year."—*R. S.*, *ch.* 6, § 191.

"No pawnbroker shall directly or indirectly receive a rate of interest greater than twenty-five per cent. a year on a loan not exceeding twenty-five dollars, nor more than six per cent. on a larger loan made upon property pawned, under a penalty of one hundred dollars for each offence."—*R. S.*, *ch.* 35, § 3.

"In the absence of an agreement in writing, the legal rate of interest is six per cent. a year."—*R. S.*, *ch.* 45, § 1.

"A bank may allow a certain rate of interest for deposits made therein, if it thinks proper; but shall not issue any note, bill, check or negotiable security payable at a future day, or bearing interest."—*R. S.*, *ch.* 47, § 26.

"No bank shall take a greater interest or discount on any note, draft, or security, than at the rate of six per cent. a year, unless by agreement in writing, whether such loan is made in specie or otherwise, or an agreement is made to pay such loan

[1] Of the town, county and state taxes.

[2] In the preceding section.

in specie or at a place other than such bank; but such interest or discount may be taken according to the established rules of banking; and the bank in discounting drafts, bills of exchange or other negotiable securities payable at another place, may, in addition to interest, charge the existing rate of exchange between the places of discount and payment."—*R. S., ch.* 47, § 31.

One year is allowed receivers of banks to convert the assets into money and "All claims allowed shall bear interest from the time that they are filed, *provided*, that the assets in the hands of the receiver are more than sufficient to pay the principal of all the claims allowed and outstanding when the final dividend is declared."—*R. S., ch.* 47, § 66.

"No deposit shall be received [by savings banks] under an agreement to pay any specified sum of interest for its use, other than the regular semi-annual and extra dividends."—*R. S., ch.* 47, § 107.

"A railroad corporation, to obtain money to build or furnish its road, or to pay debts contracted for that purpose, may issue its bonds in sums not less than one hundred dollars, bearing interest, secured in such manner as it deems expedient, and binding upon it although sold at less than par value; and no defence of usury shall, for that cause, be admitted."—*R. S., ch.* 51, § 56.

"Interest shall be cast on claims [against insolvent estates] allowed, from the death of the debtor to the time of the commissioners' first report, unless the contract otherwise provides. At the expiration of the time limited, the commissioners shall make their report to the judge, who, before ordering distribution, may recommit it for the correction of any error appearing to him to exist."—*R. S., ch.* 66, § 8.

"Interest shall be allowed on verdicts and amounts reported by referees to be due, from the time of finding such verdicts or making such reports, to the time of judgment."—*R. S., ch.* 77, § 51.

In warrants of distress, on judgments legally rendered by the county commissioners, "Interest on the damages shall be included and collected by such warrants as in executions."—*R. S., ch.* 78, § 18.

"In any personal action, the defendant may, in writing entered of record with its date, offer to be defaulted for a specified sum. If accepted, interest may be added from that date to date of judgment."—*R. S., ch.* 82, § 25.

"Interest shall be allowed on the amount found due for damages and costs in actions on judgments of a court of record."—*R. S., ch.* 82, § 31.

"On executions, issued on judgments or acknowledgments of debt, interest shall be collected from the time of judgment, or payment, and the form of the execution be varied accordingly."—*R. S.*, *ch.* 82, § 142.

"In all cases, any mill or building seized and sold on execution as a chattel personal, may be redeemed within one year, as land levied upon by appraisement may be; and the remedies and rights of the parties are the same as those of mortgagor and mortgagee, except the rate of interest, which shall be ten per cent. a year."—*R. S. ch.* 84, § 11.

The treasurer of the hospital for the insane "shall charge and collect interest on all debts due to said hospital, for board and clothing of patients, after thirty days from the time when they become due."—*R. S* , *ch.* 143, § 22.

Maine has no usury law now, the usury statute that had been in force there for many years having been repealed in 1870.

MARYLAND.

All judgments by confession, on verdict, or by default, shall be so entered as to carry interest from the time they are rendered."—*G. Laws*, *art.* 26, § 16.

"Interest may be charged or deducted at the rate of six per centum per annum, and the same may be calculated according to the standard laid down in Rowlett's tables."—*G. Laws*, *art.* 49, § 1.

"No plea of usury shall be available against any legal or equitable assignee or holder of any bond, bill obligatory, bill of exchange, promissory note, or other negotiable instrument, where such assignee or endorsee or holder shall have received the same for a *bona fide* and legal consideration, without notice of any usury in the creation or subsequent assignment thereof." *G. Laws*, *art.* 49, § 2.

"If any person shall exact, directly or indirectly, for loan of any money, goods or chattels, to be paid in money above the value of six dollars for the forbearance of one hundred dollars for one year, and so after that rate for a greater or lesser sum, or for a longer or shorter time, he shall be deemed guilty of usury."—*G. Laws*, *art.* 49, § 3.

"Any person guilty of usury shall forfeit all the excess above the real sum or value of the goods and chattels actually lent or advanced, and the legal interest on such sum or value, which forfeiture shall enure to the benefit of any defendant who shall plead usury and prove the same."—*G. Laws*, *art.* 49, § 4.

"Every plea of usury shall state the sum of money or the value of the goods or chattels lent or advanced, with the time at which the same was or were so lent or advanced, and the plaintiff shall be entitled to recover the sum of money or the value of the goods and chattels actually lent or advanced, with legal interest from the time the same was so lent or advanced." —*G. Laws, art.* 49, § 5.

"Nothing in the preceding sections of this article shall be so construed as to make usury a cause of action in any case when the bond, bill obligatory, promissory note, bill of exchange, or other evidence of indebtedness, has been redeemed or settled for by the obligor or obligors, in money or other valuable consideration, except that of a renewal in whole or in part of the original indebtedness."—*G. Laws, art.* 49, § 6.

MASSACHUSETTS.

"When a city or town has fixed a time within which taxes assessed therein shall be paid, such city by its city council, and such town at the meeting when money is appropriated or raised, may vote that, on all taxes remaining unpaid after a certain time, interest shall be paid at a specified rate, not exceeding seven per cent per annum; and may also vote that, on all taxes remaining unpaid after another certain time, interest shall be paid at another specified rate, not exceeding seven per cent per annum; and the interest accruing under such vote or votes shall be added to, and be a part of such taxes."—*P. S., ch.* 11, § 67.

"The legal voters of any fire, water-supply, improvement, or school district, organized under the laws of the commonwealth, may, at the meeting when money is appropriated or raised, fix a time within which all taxes assessed therein shall be paid, and may vote that, on all taxes remaining unpaid after a certain time, interest shall be paid at a specified rate, not exceeding one per cent per month, and may also vote that, on all taxes remaining unpaid after another certain time, interest shall be paid at another specified rate, not exceeding one per cent per month; and the interest accruing under such vote or votes shall be added to and be a part of such taxes."—*P. S., ch.* 11, § 68.

Taxes assessed on corporations whether assessed before or after the tenth day of December "shall bear interest at the rate of twelve per cent per annum from that date until they are paid." —*P. S., ch.* 13, § 35.

"In all cases where a time is fixed for the payment of moneys due to a county, the persons, cities, towns, or corporations from whom such moneys are due shall pay interest to the county at the rate of twelve per cent per annum for the period which may elapse after such time until the time of payment: *provided*, that notice is given by the county treasurer to such debtors seven days at least previous to the time fixed for such payment. All interest received from such debtors shall be paid into the county treasury."—*P. S.*, *ch.* 23, § 19.

"A town making such purchase[1] may issue, in payment therefor, bonds, bearing interest at a rate not exceeding seven per cent, payable semi-annually, and redeemable at a time not exceeding twenty years from their date; and may, for the purpose of purchasing materials, laying pipes, and doing other work necessary for so supplying water, issue additional similar bonds; and a town making such contract as aforesaid may, for the purpose named in this section, issue similar bonds."—*P. S.*, *ch.* 27, § 28.

"Where there is no agreement for a different rate, the interest of money shall be at the rate of six dollars upon each hundred dollars for a year, but it shall be lawful to pay, reserve, or contract for any rate of interest or of discount; but no greater rate than that before mentioned shall be recovered in any action, unless the agreement to pay such greater rate is in writing, and no bond issued by a corporation shall bear interest at a yearly rate exceeding seven dollars on each hundred."—*P. S.*, *ch.* 77, § 3.

"When a bill of exchange, drawn or indorsed within the commonwealth and payable beyond the limits of the United States, is duly protested for non-acceptance or non-payment, the party liable for the contents of such bill shall, on due notice and demand thereof, pay such contents at the current rate of exchange at the time of the demand, and damages at the rate of five per cent upon such contents, together with interest on the contents to be computed from the date of the protest; and said amount of contents, damages, and interest shall be in full of all damages, charges, and expenses."—*P. S.*, *ch.* 77, § 18.

"In an action on a contract, other than a bill of exchange, for the payment of money beyond the limits of the United States, the debt or damages recovered by the creditor shall be determined by the current rate of exchange at the time when such contract falls due, and to such amount interest from such time shall be added."—*P. S.*, *ch.* 77, § 19.

"The board of officers licensing pawnbrokers in any place may fix the rate of interest which such pawnbrokers may receive on loans, and may fix different rates which may be received for different amounts of money lent; and no licensed pawnbro-

[1] Of a corporation the right to take water to supply the inhabitants of the town.

ker shall charge or receive a greater rate of interest than that so fixed. Any such pawnbroker who violates any provision of this or the preceding section shall be punished by fine not exceeding fifty dollars for each offence."—*P. S., ch.* 102, § 34.

Railroad bonds are to bear "interest not exceeding seven per cent a year, payable annually or semi-annually."—*P. S., ch.* 112, § 62.

Savings banks and institutions for savings "may receive deposits from any person until they amount to one thousand dollars; and may allow interest upon such deposits, and upon the interest accumulated thereon, until the principal, with the accrued interest, amounts to sixteen hundred dollars; and thereafter upon no greater sum than sixteen hundred dollars; but the limitations contained in this section shall not apply to deposits by religious or charitable corporations, or to deposits[1] made by direction of a probate court by virtue of the sixteenth section of the one hundred and forty-fourth chapter of the Public Statutes."— *P. S., ch.* 116, § 19; *Acts of* 1889, *ch.* 86.

"No bank shall make or issue a note, bill, check, draft, acceptance, certificate, or contract, in any form whatever, for the payment of money at a future day certain or with interest, except for money borrowed of the commonwealth or of an institution for savings incorporated under authority of the commonwealth, or money [2] deposited by an assignee as provided in section fifty-three of chapter one hundred and fifty-seven; and except also that all debts due to one bank from another, including bills of the bank indebted, may draw interest; and banks may contract with cities and towns in this commonwealth for the payment or receipt of interest, upon an account current of money deposited with and drawn from them by said cities and towns."— *P. S., ch.* 118, § 40.

"When judgment is made up upon an award of county commissioners, a committee, or referees, or on the report of an auditor or master in chancery, or on a verdict of a jury, interest shall be computed upon the amount of the award, report, or verdict, from the time when made to the time of making up the judgment. Every judgment for the payment of money shall bear interest from the day of the rendition thereof. The warrant or execution issued on a judgment for the payment of money shall specify the day upon which judgment is rendered, and shall require the collection or satisfaction thereof with interest from the day of its rendition."— *P. S., ch.* 171, § 8.

[1] Of money unclaimed six months after decree of distribution.

[2] The assets of the estate.

"When it appears to the court [in a suit for the redemption of a mortgage] that the mortgagee has not unreasonably neglected or refused to render a true account of the rents and profits of the mortgaged estate, the court may award to him the balance found due on the mortgage, with interest thereon at a rate not exceeding twelve per cent a year from the expiration of three years after such entry to the time of rendering judgment in the suit."— *P. S., ch.* 181, § 34.

"The clause [in the statutory form of recognizance for debt] as to the payment of interest may be altered or wholly omitted according to the agreement of the parties; but interest shall always be allowed for any delay after the time of payment, unless the recognizance contains an express agreement to the contrary." — *P. S., ch.* 193, § 3.

"If upon the hearing of an appeal or exceptions by the full [supreme judicial] court, whether in an action at law or suit in equity or other proceeding, it appears that the appeal or exceptions are frivolous, immaterial, or intended for delay, the court may, either upon motion or without any motion therefor, award against the appellant or party taking exceptions double costs from the time when the appeal or exceptions were taken, and interest from the same time at the rate of twelve per cent. by the year on any sum which has been found due for debt or damages, or which he has been ordered to pay, or for which judgment has been recovered against him, or the court may award any part of such additional costs and interest."—*Acts of* 1883, *ch.* 223, § 15.

"All assessments on account of betterments and other public improvements which are a lien upon real estate shall bear interest from the thirtieth day after assessment, until paid."—*Acts of* 1884, *ch.* 237.

"When judgment is rendered upon any such complaint against a corporation,[1] the court may issue a warrant of distress to compel the payment of the penalty prescribed by law, together with costs and interest."—*Acts of* 1886, *ch.* 87, § 4.

"A special partner [in a limited partnership] may withdraw interest on the capital contributed by him at any rate agreed on not exceeding six per cent. per annum, provided that such withdrawal is out of profits and does not impair the capital of the partnership, without any liability to refund the same in any event."— *Acts of* 1887, *ch.* 248, § 2.

"All sums of money hereafter deposited in savings banks, institutions for savings or trust companies in the name of a judge

[1] For not paying wages weekly.

of probate court, as trustee, or by order of any court, shall draw interest or dividends at the same rate as other deposits in the same bank, institution or company, while they remain therein without regard to the amount deposited."—*Acts of* 1889, *ch.* 449, § 1.

"The probate court, court of insolvency or other court, respectively, shall, upon the application of any person interested or of the attorney-general and after such public notice as the court or any judge or justice thereof may deem proper to be given, order and decree that all sums of money heretofore or hereafter deposited in a savings bank, institution for savings or trust company, by authority of either of said courts or any judge or justice thereof, and which shall have remained unclaimed for a period of more than five years from the date of such deposit, with the increase and proceeds thereof, to be paid to the treasurer of the Commonwealth, to be held and used by him, according to law, subject for fifteen years only to be paid with interest at the rate of three per cent. per annum from the time it is so paid to said treasurer to the time it is paid by him to the person or persons having, and established, a lawful right thereto."—*Acts of* 1889, *ch.* 449, § 2.

"Interest, whether arising as damages for the detention of money or otherwise, may be declared on, in addition to the forms of pleading now authorized by law, by including in any count which is followed by an account annexed, or bill of particulars, the words 'and interest,' and setting forth as an item in the account annexed or bill of particulars the times and amounts for and upon which interest is claimed, and the amount of interest so claimed."—*Acts of* 1890, *ch.* 398.

"All loans hereafter contracted, for less than one thousand dollars, shall be dischargeable by the debtor upon payment or tender of the principal sum actually borrowed and interest at the rate of eighteen per centum per annum, from the time said money was borrowed, together with a sum, for the actual expenses of making the loan and securing the same, not exceeding five dollars, provided that the lender shall be entitled to interest for six months at said rate when the debt is paid before the expiration of that period. And all payments in excess of said rate shall be applied to the discharge of the principal and the borrower shall only be obliged to pay or tender the balance of the principal and interest, at said rate, due after such application. All acts and parts of acts inconsistent herewith are hereby repealed: *provided*, that nothing in this act shall be construed to affect any loan made at a less rate than at the rate of eighteen per centum per annum, nor shall it be construed to repeal so much of section three of chapter seventy-seven of the Public Statutes as provides that when there is no agreement for a different rate the interest of money shall be at the rate of six dollars upon each hundred dollars for a year."—*Acts of* 1892, *ch.* 428, § 1. If the security is household furniture, and the loan less than a thousand dollars, and at or more than eighteen per cent. interest, the mortgage must state the amount of the loan, rate of interest, etc. This act does not apply to licensed pawnbrokers, and it does not affect Public Statutes, ch. 102, § 31.

MICHIGAN.

"In any action brought on any bill of exchange, or promissory note payable in money, and to order or bearer, originally given or made for, or upon any usurious consideration or contract, if it shall appear that the plaintiff became, in good faith, the indorsee or holder of such bill of exchange or promissory note, for a valuable consideration, before the same became due, then and in such case, unless it shall further appear that the plaintiff, at the time of becoming such indorsee or holder, had actual notice that such bill or note was given for, or upon a usurious consideration or contract, he shall be entitled to recover thereon, in the same manner, and to the same extent, as if such usury had not been alleged and proved."—*H.'s A. S.*, § 1596.

"Interest may be allowed and received upon all judgments at law, for the recovery of any sums of money, and upon all decrees in chancery for the payment of any sums of money, whatever may be the form or cause of action or suit in which such judgment or decree shall be rendered or made; and such interest may be collected on execution, at the rate of seven per centum per annum: *Provided*, that on a judgment rendered on any written instrument, having a different rate, the interest shall be computed at the rate specified in such instrument, not exceeding ten per centum."—*H.'s A. S.*, § 1597.

"In all actions founded on contracts express or implied, whenever in the execution thereof any amount in money shall be liquidated or ascertained in favor of either party, by verdict, report of referees, award of arbitrators, or by any other mode of assessment according to law, it shall be lawful, unless such verdict, report, award, or assessment shall be set aside, to allow and receive interest upon such amount so ascertained or liquidated, until payment thereof, or until judgment shall be thereupon rendered; and in making up and recording such judgment, the interest on such amount shall be added thereto, and included in the judgment."—*H.'s A. S.*, § 1598.

"When any installment of interest upon any note, bond, mortgage, or other written contract, shall have become due, and the same shall remain unpaid, interest may be computed and collected on any such installment so due and unpaid, from the time at which it became due, at the same rate as specified in any such note, bond, mortgage, or other written contract, not exceeding ten per cent.; and if no rate of interest be specified in such instrument, then at the rate of seven per centum per annum."—*H.'s A. S.*, § 1599.

"It shall be lawful for any person or corporation, borrowing money in this state, to make notes, bills, bonds, drafts, acceptances, mortgages, or other securities, for the payment of principal or interest, at the rates authorized by the laws of this state, payable at the place where the parties may agree, although the legal rate of interest in such place may be less than in this state; and such notes, bonds, bills, drafts, or other securities, shall not be regarded or held to be usurious, nor shall any securities taken for the same, or upon such loans, be invalidated in consequence of the rate of interest of the state, kingdom or country, where the paper is made payable, being less than in this state, nor of any usury or penal law therein." —*H.'s A. S.*, § 1600.

"No plea of usury, nor defense founded upon an allegation of usury, shall be sustained in any court in this state, nor shall any security be held invalid on an allegation of usury, when the rate of interest reserved, discounted or taken, does not exceed that allowed by the laws of this state, in consequence of such security being payable in a state, kingdom or country, where such rate of interest is not allowed."—*H.'s A. S.*, § 1601.

"It shall be lawful for all parties loaning money in this state, to take, reserve or discount interest upon any note, bond, bill, draft, acceptance, or other commercial paper, mortgage, or other security, at any rate authorized by the laws of this state, whether such paper or securities, for principal or interest, be payable, in this state, or in any other state, kingdom or country, without regard to the laws of any other state, kingdom or country; and all such notes, bonds, bills, drafts, acceptance, or other commercial paper, mortgages or other security, shall be held valid in this state, whether the parties to the same reside in this state or elsewhere."—*H.'s A. S.*, § 1602.

"When any contract or loan shall be made in this state, or

between citizens of this state and any other state or country, bearing interest at any rate which was or shall be lawful according to any law of the state of Michigan, it shall and may be lawful to make the amount of principal and interest of such contract or loan payable in any other state or territory of the United States, or in England; and in all such cases, such contract or loan shall be deemed and considered as governed by the laws of the state of Michigan, and shall not be affected by the laws of the state or country where the same shall be made payable; and no contract or loan, which may have heretofore been made or entered into, in this state, or between citizens of this state and of any other country, bearing interest at a rate which was legal according to the laws of this state at the time when the same was made or entered into, shall be invalidated or in anywise impaired or affected by reason of the same having been made payable in any other state or country."—*H.'s A. S.*, § 1603.

Land sold for taxes may be redeemed by paying "interest thereon at the rate of twenty per cent. per annum" from the date of the certificate of sale.—*H.'s A. S.*, § 3015.[1]

"It shall not be lawful for any such association[2] to take or receive more than the legal rate of interest, in advance on its loans and discounts."—*H.'s A. S.*, § 3138.

"It shall be the duty of the board of directors or trustees [of savings banks], from time to time, to regulate the rate of interest to be allowed to depositors, and pay the same at regular and stated periods."—*H.'s A. S.*, § 3202.

Savings associations may "receive deposits of money and pay interest on the same at such rates as shall be agreed upon, but in no case exceeding seven per cent. per annum."—*H.'s A. S.*, § 3215. So of money loaning and investing societies.—*Ibid.*, § 3254. Borrowers in the last-named societies may pay their loans in instalments by paying not over ten per cent interest. —*Ibid.*, § 3260.

"When execution shall be issued upon any judgment, interest on the amount of the judgment, from the time of entry of the same until such amount shall be paid, shall be collected thereon."—*H.'s A. S.*, § 7672.

"If it shall appear upon the trial of the cause, or upon the assessment of damages, that the amount so tendered[3] was sufficient to pay the plaintiff's demand, or was a sufficient amends for the injury done, and the costs of the suit or proceeding up

[1] See act of 1889 below.

[2] Bank.

[3] Provided for by § 7764.

to the time of such tender, the plaintiff shall not be entitled to recover or collect any interest on such demand from the time of such tender, or any costs incurred subsequent to that time, but shall be liable to the defendant for the costs incurred by him subsequent to such time."—*H.'s A. S.*, § 7765.

"When judgment shall be rendered against any incorporated bank, for the amount of any bills or other evidences of debt, payable absolutely, the payment of which shall have been refused by such bank, and no measure of damages shall be specified in the act incorporating such bank, the plaintiff shall recover interest on such amount from the time of such refusal, at the rate of ten per cent. a year, instead of the rate established by law."—*H.'s A. S.*, § 8139.

To all unpaid taxes shall be added interest at the rate of one per cent. for every month or part of a month during which such taxes remain unpaid.—*Acts of* 1889, *No.* 195, § 74.

"The interest of money shall be at the rate of six dollars upon one hundred dollars for a year, and at the same rate for a greater or less sum, and for a longer or shorter time, except that in all cases, it shall be lawful for the parties to stipulate in writing, for the payment of any rate of interest not exceeding eight per cent. per annum: *Provided*, That this act shall not apply to existing contracts whether the same be either due, not due, or post due."—*Acts of* 1891, *No.* 156, § 1.

"No bond, bill, note, contract or assurance, made or given for or upon a consideration or contract, whereby or whereon a greater rate of interest has been, directly or indirectly, taken or received, than is allowed by law shall be thereby rendered void; but in any action brought by any person on such usurious contract or assurance, except as is provided in the following section, if it shall appear that a greater rate of interest has been, directly or indirectly, reserved, taken or received, than is allowed by law, the defendant shall not be compelled to pay any interest thereon."—*Acts of* 1891, *No.* 156, § 2.

"Whenever it shall satisfactorily appear by the admission of the defendant, or by proof that any bond, bill, note, assurance, pledge, conveyance, contract, security, or any evidence of debt has been taken or received in violation of this act, the court shall declare the interest thereon to be void."—*Acts of* 1891, *No.* 156, § 3.

MINNESOTA.

"The interest for any legal indebtedness shall be at the rate of seven (7) dollars upon one hundred (100) dollars for a year, unless a different rate is contracted for in writing, and no person, company, or corporation shall directly or indirectly take or receive in money, goods or things in action or in any other way, any greater sum or any greater value for the loan or forbearance of money, goods, or things in action than ten (10) dollars on one hundred (100) dollars for one year. And in the computation of interest upon any bond, note or other instrument or agreement, interest shall not be compounded. But any contract to pay interest not usurious upon interest overdue shall not be construed to be usury. *Provided*, that all contracts hereafter made shall bear the same rate of interest after they become due as before, and that any provision in any contract, note or instrument providing for an increase of the rate of interest upon maturity or any increase therein after the making and delivery thereof, shall work a forfeiture of the entire interest thereon. *Provided, further*, that the foregoing proviso shall not apply to notes or contracts which bear no interest before maturity."—*G. S.*, § 2089.

"Every person who for any such loan or forbearance shall have paid or delivered any greater sum or value than is above allowed to be received, may by himself or his personal representatives, recover in an action against the person who shall have taken or received the same, or his personal representatives, the full amount of interest or premium so paid, with costs, if such action shall be brought within two (2) years after such payment or delivery: *Provided*, that one-half of the amount so recovered shall be paid by the officer collecting the same into the county treasury of the county where such penalty is collected for the use of the common schools."—*G. S.*, § 2090.

"All bonds, bills, notes, assurances, conveyances, chattel mortgages, and all other contracts and securities whatsoever, and all deposits of goods, or anything whatever, whereupon or whereby there shall be reserved, secured, or taken any greater sum or value for the loan or forbearance of any money, goods, or things in action, than is above prescribed, shall be void, except as to the *bona fide* purchasers of negotiable paper as hereinafter provided in good faith, for a valuable consideration before maturity. *Provided*, that no merely clerical error in the computation of interest made with no intent to avoid the provisions of this act shall constitute usury. *Provided further*, that interest at the rate of one-twelfth of ten per centum for every thirty (30) days, shall be construed not to exceed ten per centum per annum. *Provided further*, that the payment of interest in advance for one year at a rate not to exceed ten per centum per annum, shall not be construed to constitute usury. *Provided further*, that nothing herein shall be so construed to prevent the purchase of negotiable mercantile paper, usurious or otherwise, for a valuable consideration, by an innocent purchaser, free from all equities at any price before the maturity of the same, when there has been no intent to evade the provisions of this act, or where said purchase has not been a part of the original usurious transaction. In any case, however, when the original holder of an usurious note sells the same to an innocent purchaser, the maker of said note or his representatives shall have the right to recover back from the said original holder the amount of principal and interest paid by him on said note."—*G. S.*, § 2091.

"Whenever it satisfactorily appears to a court that any bond, bill, note, assurance, pledge, conveyance, contract, security or evidence of debt, has been taken or received in violation of the provisions of this act, the court shall declare the same to be void, and enjoin any proceeding thereon, and shall order the same to be cancelled and given up."—*G. S.*, § 2092.

"Every person, company or corporation offending against the provisions of this act, shall be compelled to answer on oath any complaint that may be exhibited or filed against him in the district court for the proper county, for the discovery of any sum of money, goods, or things in action so taken, accepted or received in violation of any of the foregoing provisions."—*G. S.*, § 2093.

"Whenever, in any action in any court the defendant shall plead or answer the defense of usury, either party to the action may be a witness in his own behalf on the trial, except in actions in which the opposite party sues or defends as administrator or personal representative of a deceased person; except, also, actions in which the opposite party claims as assignee, and the original assignor is deceased. In case of all notes or other instruments bearing interest, when no rate of interest is specified after maturity, the said note or other instrument shall be construed to bear the same rate of interest after maturity as before, and until fully paid and satisfied."—*G. S.*, § 2094.

The laws against usury do not apply to mutual building associations.—*G. S.*, § 2095.

"Nothing in this act shall be construed as in any way affecting any contract heretofore, or hereafter made, whereby one (1) of the parties thereto has advanced, or may advance, money to be used in money, or other ventures, mutually determined upon, and whereby the other party thereto, the one receiving such money, has refunded, or agrees to refund the same, with interest thereon as stipulated (provided such interest does not exceed a lawful rate) and in addition thereto has shared, or agrees to share equally or otherwise, with the party so advancing the money, the profits, if any there were or may be, of the business or other ventures carried on, or undertaken, in whole or in part with such money."—*G. S.*, § 2096.

Banks may receive interest in advance.—*G. S.*, § 2329.

Savings banks are not required to pay their depositors more than four per cent interest per annum.—*G. S.*, § 2384.

"All awards for compensation and damages for the taking of land for public use on behalf of railroad corporations, where no appeal is taken, shall draw interest at the rate of seven per cent. per annum from the date of the filing of such awards until paid; and where an appeal is taken, the verdict in such appeal shall draw the like rate of interest until paid."—*G. S.*, § 2482.

"After the order allowing any claim is made [by the probate court] . . , the claim as allowed shall draw the same rate of interest as judgments recovered in the district courts."—*G. S.*, § 5722.

MISSISSIPPI.

The county board of supervisors may hire money for public buildings, etc., for a rate of interest not exceeding seven per cent."—*An. Code*, § 311.

"The legal rate of interest on all notes, accounts, and contracts shall be six per centum per annum; but contracts may be made, in writing, for the payment of a rate of interest as great as ten per centum per annum. And if a greater rate of interest than ten per centum shall be stipulated for or received in any case, all interest shall be forfeited, and may be recovered back, whether the contract be executed or executory; but this section shall not apply to a building and loan association domiciled in this state, dealing only with its members."—*An. Code*, § 2348.

Usurious contracts of banks or their officers, etc., having an interest therein, "shall, as to the whole of the discount or interest allowed or paid, or agreed to be allowed or paid, be void, and the discount or interest may be recovered back by the person suffering such discount or paying such interest."—*An. Code*, § 2349.

"All judgments and decrees founded on any contract, shall bear interest after the rate of the debt on which the judgment or decree was rendered. All other judgments and decrees shall bear interest at the rate of six per centum per annum."—*An. Code*, § 2350

"When partial payments are made, the interest that has

accrued to the time of payment, if any, shall be first paid, and the residue of such partial payment shall be placed to the payment of the principal."—*Ia. Code*, § 2351.

MISSOURI.

The court may adjust claims against estates of deceased persons not yet due, by rebating therefrom the interest thereon from the time of trial until their maturity.—*R. S.*, § 203.

Executors and administrators are obliged to state amount and rate of interest received in their annual accounts. — *R. S.*, § 215.

"All interest received by executors or administrators on debts due to the deceased shall be assets in their hands; and if they lend the money of the deceased, or use it for their own private purposes, they shall pay interest thereon to the estate." —*R. S.*, § 221.

"The court shall, at each settlement, exercise an equitable control in making executors and administrators account for interest received by them on debts due the estate, and for interest accruing on money belonging to the estate, loaned or otherwise employed by them; and, for that purpose, may take testimony or examine the executor or administrator on oath." —*R. S.*, § 225.

"The jury on the trial of any issue, or on any inquisition of damages, may, if they shall think fit, give damages, in the nature of interest, over and above the value of the goods at the time of the conversion or seizure."—*R. S.*, § 4430.

"Creditors shall be allowed to receive interest at the rate of six per cent per annum, when no other rate is agreed upon, for all moneys after they become due and payable, on written contracts, and on accounts after they became due and demand of payment is made; for money recovered for the use of another, and retained without the owner's knowledge of the receipt, and for all other money due or to become due for the forbearance of payment whereof an express promise to pay interest has been made."—*R. S.*, § 5972.

"The parties may agree, in writing, for the payment of interest, not exceeding eight per cent. per annum, on money due or to become due upon any contract."—*R. S.*, § 5973, *amended by act of* 1891.

"Interest shall be allowed on all money due upon any judgment or order of any court, from the day of rendering the same until satisfaction be made by payment, accord or sale of property; all such judgments and orders for money upon contracts bearing more than six per cent. interest shall bear the same interest borne by such contracts, and all other judgments and orders for money shall bear six per centum per annum until satisfaction made, as aforesaid."—*R. S.*, § 5974.

"No person shall directly or indirectly take, for the use or loan of money or other commodity, above the rates of interest specified in the three preceding sections, for the forbearance or use of one hundred dollars, or the value thereof, for one year, and so after those rates for a greater or less sum, or for a longer or shorter time, or according to those rates or proportions, for the loan of any money or other commodity."—*R. S.*, § 5975.

"Parties may contract, in writing, for the payment of interest upon interest; but the interest shall not be compounded oftener than once in a year. When a different rate is not expressed, interest upon interest shall be at the same rate as interest on the principal debt."—*R. S.*, § 5977.

"Where tender and no deposit shall be made, . . . , the tender shall only have the effect, in law, to prevent the running of interest or the accumulation of damages from and after the time such tender was made."—*R. S.*, § 6211.

One hundred per cent per annum interest is allowed on an execution against a defaulting constable.—*R. S.*, § 6320.

"After the return of an execution, satisfied in whole or in part out of the property of the surety, such surety shall be entitled to a judgment, upon motion, against the principal, for the amount paid by him, together with the interest thereon at ten per cent per annum, from the time of the payment."—*R. S.*, § 6351.

"Usury may be pleaded as a defense in civil actions in the courts of this state, and upon proof that usurious interes has been paid, the same, in excess of the legal rate of interest, shall be deemed payment, shall be credited upon the principal debt, and all costs of the action shall be taxed against the party guilty of exacting usurious interest, who shall in no case recover judgment for more than the amount found due upon the principal debt, with legal interest, after deducting therefrom all payments of usurious interest made by the debtor, whether paid as commission or brokerage, or as payment upon the principal, or on interest on said indebtedness."— *Usury act of* 1891, § 1.

"In actions for the enforcement of liens upon personal property pledged or mortgaged to secure indebtedness, or to maintain or secure possession of property so pledged or mortgaged, or in any other case where the validity of such lien is drawn in question, proof upon the trial that the party holding or claiming to hold any such lien has received or exacted usurious interest for such indebtedness shall render any mortgage or pledge of personal property, or any lien whatsoever thereon given to secure such indebtedness, invalid and illegal."—*Usury act of 1891*, § 2.

MONTANA.

"Whenever any payment of principal or interest has been or shall be made upon an existing contract, whether it be bill of exchange, promissory note, bond, or other evidence of indebtedness, if such payment shall be made after the same shall have become due, the limitation [of time in which an action shall be brought] shall commence from the time the last payment was made."— *C. S.*, § 51.

"Legacies bear interest from the time when they are due and payable, except that legacies for maintenance, or to the testator's widow, bear interest from the testator's decease."—*C. S.*, § 521.

"All state warrants issued by the proper authorities of this state, after the first day of March, A. D. 1881, shall draw interest at the rate of six per centum per annum from and after the date of their presentation until there are funds to pay said warrants in the hands of the state treasurer."—*C. S.*, § 1129, *as amended by the state constitution.*

"The legal rate of interest on the forbearance or loan of any money, when there is no agreement between the parties, as specified in section 1238 of this chapter, shall be ten per centum per annum."— *C. S., ch.* 73, § 1236.

"Creditors shall be allowed to collect and receive interest when there is no agreement as to the rate thereof, at the rate of ten per cent. per annum for all moneys after they become due, on any bond, bill, promissory note, or other instrument of writing, and on any judgment rendered before any court or magistrate authorized to enter up the same, within the territory, from the day of entering up such judgment until satisfaction of the same be made; likewise on money lent, or money due on the settlement of accounts, from the day of such settlement of accounts, between the parties, and ascertaining the balance due; on money received to the use of another, and retained without the owner's knowledge, and on money withheld by an unreasonable and vexatious delay."— *C. S., ch.* 73, § 1237.

"The parties to any bond, bill, promissory note or other instrument of writing, may stipulate therein the payment of a greater or higher rate of interest than ten per centum per annum, and any such stipulation contained in any such instrument of writing may be enforced in any court of law or equity of competent jurisdiction in this territory. And when any instrument provides for a certain rate of interest, from date until paid, or after due until paid, or in words to like effect, it shall be construed to mean interest at the stipulated rae until the same is paid."— *R. S., ch.* 73, § 1238.

NEBRASKA.

"Any rate of interest which may be agreed upon, not exceeding ten dollars per year upon one hundred dollars, shall be valid upon any loan or forbearance of money, goods, or things in action; which rate of interest so agreed upon may be taken yearly or for any shorter period, or in advance, if so expressly agreed." — *C. S.*, § 2021.

"Interest upon the loan or forbearance of money, goods, or things in action shall be at the rate of seven dollars per year upon one hundred dollars, unless a greater rate, not exceeding ten per cent per annum. be contracted for by the parties."—*C. S.*, § 2022.

"Interest on all decrees and judgments for the payment of money shall be from the date of the rendition thereof, at the rate of seven dollars upon each one hundred dollars annually until the same shall be paid; *Provided*, That if said judgment or decree shall be founded upon any contract, either verbal or written, by the terms of which a greater rate of interest, not exceeding the amount allowed by law, than seven per centum shall have been agreed upon, the rate of interest upon such judgment or decree shall be the same as provided for by the terms of the contract upon which the same was founded."— *C. S.*, § 2023.

"On money due on any instrument in writing, or on settlement of the account from the day the balance shall be agreed upon, on money received to the use of another, and retained without the owner's consent, express or implied, from the receipt thereof, and on money loaned or due, and withheld by unreasonable delay of payment, interest shall be allowed at the rate of seven per cent per annum. Unsettled accounts between parties shall bear interest after six months from the date of the last item thereof."— *C. S.*, § 2024.

"If a greater rate of interest than is hereinbefore allowed shall be contracted for or received or reserved, the contract shall not, therefore, be void; but if in any action on such contract proof be made that illegal interest has been directly or indirectly contracted for, or taken, or reserved, the plaintiff shall only recover the principal, without interest, and the defendant shall recover costs; and if interest shall have been paid thereon, judgment shall be for the principal, deducting interest paid; *Pro-*

vided. The acts and dealings of an agent in loaning money shall bind the principal, and in all cases where there is illegal interest by the transaction of the agent, the principal will be held thereby as if he had done the same in person. Where the same person acts as agent for the borrower who obtains the money from the lender, he shall be deemed to be the agent of the loaner also."— *C. S.*, § 2025.

"Any person charged with taking illegal interest may be required to answer touching the same, on oath, in any civil proceeding."— *C. S.*, § 2026.

"Relief to a complain[an]t in case of an usurious loan, may be given without payment or tender by him of the principal sum."— *C. S.*, § 2027.

"Any officer or agent of a person or a corporation, whether interested or not, may be summoned as witness in any action for usury against such person or corporation, and required to disclose all the facts of the case, but the testimony of such witness, or the answer of a party as required in section 6 [2026] shall not be used against such witness or party in any criminal prosecution for perjury."— *C. S.*, § 2028.

"When in any law, or in any instrument in writing specifying a rate of interest, no period of time is mentioned for which such rate is to be calculated, it shall be deemed to be by the year." — *C. S.*, § 2029.

"All warrants issued by the proper authorities of the state, county, city, town, or other municipal subdivision less than a county, shall draw interest from and after the date of their presentation for payment at the rate of seven per cent. per annum, and all bonds issued by any county, city, township, precinct, or school district, shall not draw interest at a rate exceeding eight per cent per annum."— *C. S.*, § 2030.

"The rate of interest fixed by this chapter shall not affect interest on purchase money of school, university, and agricultural college lands, or on lands delinquent or sold for the non-payment of taxes."— *C. S.*, § 2031.

Taxes bear ten per cent interest.— *C. S.*, § 4004.

Any treasurer failing to pay money due to the state shall pay interest thereon "at the rate of ten per cent. per annum from the time the same became due until the same is paid."— *C. S.*, § 4066.

Mutual loan and building associations are exempt from the applications of the usury law.—*Acts of* 1891, *ch.* 14, § 9.

NEVADA.

"Where there is no express contract in writing fixing a different rate of interest, interest shall be allowed at the rate of twenty-four per cent. per annum for all moneys after the same become due on any bond, bill, promissory note, or other instrument in writing, executed, drawn, or payable to or in favor of any banking association[1] mentioned in section one of this Act, and upon any overdrawn bank account had with such association, and on any judgment recovered on any such bond, bill, promissory note, other instrument in writing, or overdrawn bank account in any court in this state."—*G. S.*, § 947.

"The Clerk shall include in the judgment entered up by him, any interest in the verdict or decision of the court or referee, from the time it was rendered or made."—*G. S.*, § 3509.

Certain damages are allowed in lieu of interest for non-payment of bills of exchange.—*G. S.*, §§ 4892, 4893.

"When there is no express contract, in writing, fixing a different rate of interest, interest shall be allowed at the rate of seven per cent. per annum for all moneys after they become due on any bond, bill or promissory note, or other instrument of writing, on any judgment recovered before any court in this state for money lent, for money due on the settlement of accounts from the day on which the balance is ascertained, and from money received to the use of another."—*G. S.*, § 4903, *as amended by Acts of* 1887, *ch.* 77.

"Parties may agree, in writing, for the payment of any rate of interest whatever on money due, or to become due, on any contract. Any judgment rendered on such contract, shall conform thereto, and shall bear the interest agreed upon by the parties, and which shall be specified in the judgment; *provided*, only the amount of the original claim or demand shall draw interest after judgment."—*G. S.*, § 4904.

NEW HAMPSHIRE.

"Interest at ten per cent shall be charged upon all taxes not paid on or before the first day of December, after their assessment, from that date, which shall be collected with the taxes as incident thereto."—*P. S.*, *ch.* 59, § 8.

"If any such [savings bank, etc.] corporation shall not pay its taxes when due, it shall pay interest thereon from that time at the rate of ten per cent per annum."—*P. S.*, *ch.* 65, § 13.

"The state treasurer shall issue his extent against any such corporation which fails to pay its taxes when due for the sum

[1] Any banking association formed under Act of Congress, providing for a national currency and its circulation and redemption, approved Feb. 25, 1863.

unpaid and interest; and all property owned by the corporation on the first day of April preceding shall be holden for the payment thereof."—*P. S., ch.* 65, § 14.

The redeemer of proprietors' land sold for assessments laid thereon under the statute must pay "interest at the rate of twelve per cent per annum thereon from the day of sale, which shall be for the benefit of the purchaser."—*P. S., ch.* 151, § 13.

"If a bank chartered by this state shall neglect or refuse to pay in specie, upon demand therefor, any bill or note issued by it as currency, the holder may recover the amount thereof, with interest at the rate of two per cent a month from the time of demand, in an action of assumpsit against the bank, and treble costs of suit."—*P. S., ch.* 163, § 6.

In claims against insolvent estates, the commissioner "shall allow interest, on demands carrying interest, to the expiration of the commission, and on demands not ordinarily carrying interest, to the same time, from the death of the testator or intestate; but from demands not payable and not on interest he shall discount such sum as will reduce them to their just present value."—*P. S., ch.* 192, § 9.

"In rendering judgments, and in all business transactions where interest is paid or secured, it shall be computed and paid at the rate of six dollars on a hundred dollars for one year, unless a lower rate is expressly stipulated."—*P. S., ch.* 203, § 1.

"If any person, upon a contract, receives interest at a higher rate than six per cent, he shall forfeit three times the sum so received in excess of six per cent to the person aggrieved who will sue therefor."—*P. S., ch.* 203, § 2.

"No contract shall be rendered invalid by reason of the securing thereby, or the paying or receiving thereon, a higher rate of interest than as aforesaid; but the money secured thereby, and actually advanced or loaned thereon, may be recovered, with interest at six per cent, after applying thereto as payments any excess of interest above six per cent received thereon, as of the dates of such receipts. The right to such application shall exist and may be enforced so long as a right of action upon the contract may be maintained."—*P. S., ch.* 203, § 3.

"If a person has recovered the excess above six per cent so paid by him, he shall not thereafter be entitled to have it applied as provided in the preceding section."—*P. S., ch.* 203, § 4.

"Nothing in this chapter shall extend to the letting of cattle, or other usages of like nature in practice among farmers, or to maritime contracts, as bottomry, insurance, or course of exchange, as heretofore used."—*P. S., ch.* 203, § 5.

"Judgments for debt, damages, or costs shall be rendered in dollars and cents; and in rendering judgment for the debt or damages found by verdict, report of an auditor, or otherwise, interest shall be added from the time of such finding to the rendition of judgment."—*P. S., ch.* 228, § 1.

"Interest is payable on executions in civil actions from the time of judgment rendered."—*P. S., ch.* 231, § 9.

NEW JERSEY.

Claims against estates of deceased persons and insolvent debtors not yet due may be proved, "deducting only a rebate of legal interest for what he shall receive on such debt, to be computed from the actual payment thereof to the time such debt would have become due."—*R. S., p.* 51, § 51, *p.* 501, § 27, *and p.* 761, § 61.

"No person or corporation shall, upon contract, take directly or indirectly, for loan of any money, wares, merchandise, goods and chattels, above the value of six dollars for the forbearance of one hundred dollars for a year, and after that rate for a greater or less sum or for a longer or shorter time."—*R. S., p.* 519, § 1, *as amended by P. L.*, 1878, *p.* 30.

"In all cases of suits at law or in equity to enforce any note, bill, bond, mortgage, contract, covenant, conveyance, or assurance, which shall be hereafter made for the payment or delivery of any money, wares, merchandise, goods, or chattels lent, and on which a higher rate of interest shall be reserved or taken than was or is allowed or taken by the law of the place where the contract was made or is to be performed, the amount or value actually lent, without interest or costs of suit, may be recovered, and no more; and if any premium or illegal interest shall have been paid to the lender, the sum or sums so paid shall be deducted from the amount that may be due as aforesaid, and recovery had for the balance only."—*R. S., p.* 519, § 2.

"Every person offending against the first section of this act, may be compelled to answer as a witness in any suit that he may bring, either at law or in equity, as to his agreement to receive, or the receipt by him, of any money, wares, merchandise, goods or chattels, in violation of the provisions of said first section." *R. S., p.* 519, § 3.

"Any borrower of money, wares, merchandise, goods or chattels, may exhibit a bill in chancery against the lender, and compel him or her to discover, upon oath or affirmation, the money or wares, merchandise, goods or chattels, really lent, and all agreements, devices, shifts, bargains, contracts and conveyances which shall have passed between them relative to such loan, or the repayment thereof, and the interest or consideration for the same, and if thereupon it shall appear that more than lawful interest was taken or reserved, the lender shall be obliged to accept his principal money, or the wares, merchandise, goods or chattels, or the value thereof, without any interest or other consideration, and to pay costs."—*R. S., p.* 519, § 4.

"Every solicitor, scrivener, broker, or driver of bargains, who shall directly or indirectly, take or receive more than the rate or value of fifty cents for brocage, or soliciting or procuring the loan or forbearance of one hundred dollars for a year, and so in proportion for a greater or less sum, making or renewing the bond or bill for such loan or forbearance, or for any counter bond or bill concerning the same, shall, for every such offence, forfeit sixteen dollars, to be recovered by action of debt, with costs, by any person who shall sue for the same; the one moiety to the prosecutor, and the other to the state."—*R. S., p.* 519, § 5.

"No bond, mortgage or other security for the payment of money heretofore made or issued, or that may hereafter be made or issued by any railroad or canal corporation created by or under the laws of this state, shall be held, deemed or considered invalid, because such bond, mortgage or other security may have been made, issued, sold, assigned or otherwise disposed of by such corporation below the par value thereof; *provided*, such bond, mortgage or other security shall be valid on its face."—*R. S., p.* 519, § 6.

All contracts for the loan of any money, wares, merchandise, goods or chattels, hereafter made in the county of Monmouth in this state, whereby above the value of seven dollars for the forbearance of one hundred dollars for a year or above that rate for a greater or less sum, or for a longer or shorter period, shall be taken directly or indirectly, shall be utterly void."—*R. S., p.* 520, § 7 (1).

Interest on unpaid taxes is allowed at a rate not to exceed twelve per cent per annum from the fifteenth of October after they are assessed; and if land is sold for the taxes such land may be redeemed by paying a rate of interest of from seven to twelve per cent per annum as determined by the board of aldermen or the common council.—*R. S., p.* 711, § 1, *p.* 712, § 5, *and p.* 1159, § 85.

"Where executors, administrators, guardians or trustees use the money of minors or others which shall come to their hands, they shall be accountable not only for the principal, but for the interest thereon."—*R. S., p.* 777, § 115.

"Not more than the rate of twenty five per centum per annum interest shall be charged on any sum not exceeding twenty-five dollars loaned upon any pledged or pawned goods and on sums exceeding twenty-five dollars not more than ten per centum interest shall be charged, and such interest at such rate shall be in lieu of all other charges and demands."—*R. S., p.* 812, § 3.

Not more than five per cent interest is to be paid to depositors in savings banks.—*Acts of* 1878, *p.* 393.

Mutual savings associations cannot take for any loan more than seven per cent interest.—*R. S., p.* 1069, § 62.

Mutual building and loan associations do not come under the usury statute.—*P. L.,* 1876, *p.* 243.

NEW MEXICO.

Guardians must loan money, if they can, or else pay interest. *C. L.,* §§ 1019, 1034.

"The rate of interest, in the absence of a written contract fixing a different rate, shall be six per cent. per annum, in the following cases:

"*First*—On money due by contract.

"*Second*—On judgments and decrees for the payment of money when no other rate is expressed.

"*Third*—On money received to the use of another, and retained without the owner's consent expressed or implied.

"*Fourth*—On money due upon the settlement of matured accounts from the day the balance is ascertained.

"*Fifth*—On money due upon open account, after six months from the date of the last item."—*C. L.,* § 1734.

"Judgments and decrees for the payment of money shall draw the same rate of interest with the contract on which they are rendered; and such rate, if other than six per cent., shall be expressed in the judgment or decree, but no judgment or decree shall draw more than twelve per cent. interest."—*C. L.,* § 1735.

"In current or open accounts in commercial houses there shall not be collected more than six per cent. interest thereon, six months after the delivery of the last article: *Provided,* that in written contracts for the payment of money, it shall not be legal to recover more than twelve per cent. interest per annum." —*C. L.,* § 1736.

"Any person, persons, or corporation, who shall hereafter charge, collect, or receive from any person a higher rate of interest than twelve per cent. per annum, shall be guilty of a misdemeanor, and upon conviction thereof before the district court or a justice of the peace, shall be fined in a sum of not less than twenty-five dollars nor more than one hundred dollars; and such person, persons, or corporation, shall forfeit to the person of whom such interest was collected or received, or to his executors, administrators, or assigns, double the amount so collected or received upon any action brought for the recovery of the same within three years after such cause of action accrued."—*C. L.*, § 1737.

"The provisions of this act shall also apply to any person, persons, corporation, or officer of the same, who may charge, receive, or collect a higher rate of interest than twelve per cent. per annum by means of discount, commission, agency, or any other subterfuge."—*C. L.*, § 1738.

"All persons who shall purchase grain, of any kind whatsoever, from one or more laborers, in case of any general injury or particular accident, such as inundation, devouring insects, scarcity of water, damage, or any other unavoidable accident, in such cases the purchaser or purchasers of grain shall not have the right to exact of their debtors their pay in grain, but only exact the amount they may have paid for the same, adding thereto twelve per cent., annually, on said amount."—*C. L.*, § 1739.

Pawnbrokers are not to collect more than ten per cent a month interest under penalty of indictment for obtaining money under false pretences.—*C. L.*, §§ 1818, 1819.

NEW YORK.

"The legislature shall not pass a private or local bill . . regulating the rate of interest on money."—*N. Y. Const., art.* 3, § 18.

"All taxes or assessments which shall remain unpaid for thirty days after the final return of said warrant [for collection] shall bear interest at the rate of twelve per centum per annum, from and after the date of said return."—*R. S., p.* 899, § 5.

"If any tax charged on lands of non-residents, or lands returned [unpaid] shall remain until the first day of August following the year in which they shall have been assessed, they shall thereafter be subject to a yearly interest, at the rate of ten per cent., until the same shall be duly paid on the lands sold."—*R. S., p.* 1023, § 26.

"No corporation shall hereafter interpose the defence of usury in any action."—*R. S., p.* 1537, *ch.* 172, § 1.

"The rate of interest upon the loan or forbearance of any money, goods, or things in action shall be six dollars upon one hundred dollars, for one year, and after that rate, for a greater or less sum, or for a longer or shorter time. But nothing herein contained shall be so construed as to in any way affect any contract or obligation made before the passage of this act."—*R. S., p.* 2253, § 1.

"No person or corporation shall, directly or indirectly, take or receive in money, goods or things in action, or in any other way, any greater sum or greater value, for the loan or forbearance of any money, goods or things in action, than is above prescribed."—*R. S., p.* 2253, § 2.

"Every person who, for any such loan or forbearance, shall pay or deliver any greater sum or value than is above allowed to be received, and his personal representatives, may recover in an action against the person who shall have taken or received the same, and his personal representatives, the amount of the money so paid or value delivered, above the rate aforesaid, if such action be brought within one year after such payment or delivery."—*R. S., p.* 2253, § 3.

"If such suit be not brought within the said one year, and prosecuted with effect, then the said sum may be sued for and recovered with costs, at any time within three years after the said one year, by any overseer of the poor of the town where such payment may have been made, or by any county superintendent of the poor of the county, in which the payment may have been made."—*R. S., p.* 2253, § 4.

"All bonds, bills, notes, assurances, conveyances, all other contracts or securities whatsoever (except bottomry and respondentia bonds and contracts), and all deposits of goods or other things whatsoever, whereupon or whereby there shall be reserved or taken, or secured or agreed to be reserved or taken, any greater sum, or greater value, for the loan or forbearance of any money, goods or other things in action, than is above described, shall be void; but this act shall not affect such paper as has been made and transferred previous to the time it shall take effect."—*R. S., p.* 2254, § 5.

"Every person offending against the provisions of this title, shall be compelled to answer on oath any bill that may be exhibited against him in the court of chancery, for the discovery of any sum of money, goods or things in action so taken, accepted, or received, in violation of the foregoing provisions, or either of them."—*R. S., p.* 2254, § 6.

"Every person who shall discover and repay or return the money, goods, or other things so taken, accepted or received, or the value thereof, shall be acquitted and discharged from any other or further forfeiture, penalty or punishment, which he may have incurred, by taking or receiving the money, goods or other thing so discovered and repaid, or returned, as aforesaid."—*R. S., p.* 2254, § 7.

"Whenever any borrower of any money, goods or things in action, shall file a bill in chancery for a discovery of the money, goods or things in action, taken or received, in violation of either of the foregoing provisions, it shall not be necessary for him to pay, or offer to pay, any interest whatever on the sum or thing loaned; nor shall any court of equity require or compel the payment or deposit, of the principal sum, or any part thereof, as a condition of granting relief, to the borrower, in any case of a usurious loan forbidden by this chapter."—*R. S., p.* 2254, § 8.

"For the purpose of calculating interest, a month shall be considered the twelfth part of a year, and as consisting of thirty days; and interest for any number of days, less than a month, shall be estimated by the proportion which such number of days shall bear to thirty."—*R. S., p.* 2254, § 9.

"Whenever, in any statute, act, deed, written or verbal contract, or in any public or private instrument whatever, any certain rate of interest is or shall be mentioned, and no period of time is stated for which such rate is to be calculated, interest shall be calculated at the rate mentioned, by the year, in the same manner as if the words 'per annum' or 'by the year,' had been added to such rate."—*R. S., p.* 2251, § 10.

"Whenever in an action at law the defendant shall plead or give notice of the defence of usury, and shall verify the truth of his plea or notice by affidavit, he may, for the purpose of proving the usury, call and examine the plaintiff as a witness, in the same manner as other witnesses may be called and examined."—*R. S., p.* 2255, § 2.

"Every person offending against the provisions of the said title, or of this act, may be compelled to answer on oath any bill that shall be exhibited against him, in the court of chancery, for relief, or discovery, or both."—*R. S., p.* 2255, § 3.

"Whenever any borrower of money, goods or things in action, shall file a bill in chancery for relief or discovery, or both, against any violation of the provisions of the said title or of this act, it shall not be necessary for him to pay or offer to pay any interest or principal on the sum or thing loaned; nor shall any court of chancery require or compel the payment or deposit of the principal sum or interest, or any portion thereof, as a condition of granting relief or compelling or discovering to the borrower in any case, usurious loans forbidden by said title or by this act."—*R. S., p.* 2255, § 4.

"Whenever it shall satisfactorily appear by the admissions of the defendant, or by proof, that any bond, bill, note, assurance, pledge, conveyance, contract, security, or any evidence of debt, has been taken or received in violation of the provisions of said title or of this act, the court of chancery shall declare the same to be void, and enjoin any prosecution thereon, and order the same to be surrendered and cancelled."—*R. S., p.* 2255, § 5.

"An accumulation of the interest of money, the produce of stock or other income or profits arising from personal property, may be directed by any instrument sufficient in law to pass such personal property as follows:

"1. If the accumulation be directed to commence from the date of the instrument, or from the death of the person executing the same, such accumulation must be directed to be made for the benefit of one or more minors then in being, or in being at such death, and to terminate at the expiration of their minority:

"2. If the accumulation be directed to commence at any period subsequent to the date of the instrument, or subsequent to the death of the person executing such instrument, it must be directed to commence within the time allowed [two lives in being] in the first section of this title, for the suspension of the absolute ownership of personal property, and at some time during the minority of the persons for whose benefit it is intended, and must terminate at the expiration of their minority."—*R. S., p.* 2257, § 3.

All other accumulations of interest, etc., than as above stated are void for the excess.—*R. S., p.* 2257, § 4.

"All interest received by any special administrator, on all moneys which may come to his hands, shall be accounted for and paid over by him in the same manner as the principal sum in his hands."—*R. S., p.* 2305, § 12.

"If it appears, upon the trial, that the sum so tendered[1] was sufficient to pay the plaintiff's demand, or to make amends for the injury, and also to pay the costs of the action, to the time of the tender, the plaintiff cannot recover costs or interest, from the time of the tender, but must pay the defendant's costs from that time."—*R. S., Civ. Proc.*, § 733.

"A judgment for a sum of money, rendered in a court of record, or not of record, or a judgment rendered in a court of record, directing the payment of money, bears interest from the time when it is entered. But where a judgment directs that money paid out shall be refunded or repaid, the direction includes interest from the time when the money was paid, unless the contrary is expressed."—*R. S., Civ. Proc.*, § 1211.

[1] To the plaintiff or his attorney after suit is brought.

"Where final judgment is rendered for a sum of money, awarded by a verdict, report or decision, interest upon the sum awarded, from the time when the verdict was rendered, or the report or decision was made, to the time of entering judgment, must be computed by the clerk, added to the sum awarded, and included in the amount of the judgment."—*R. S., Civ. Proc.*, § 1235.

In actions for causing death by negligence, "when final judgment for the plaintiff is rendered, the clerk must add to the sum so awarded, interest thereupon from the decedent's death, and include it in the judgment. The inquisition, verdict, report, or decision, may specify the day from which interest is to be computed; if it omits so to do, the day may be determined by the clerk, upon affidavits."—*R. S., Civ. Proc.*, § 1904.

"A cause of action to cancel, or otherwise affect, an instrument executed, or an act done, as security for a usurious loan or forbearance, can be thus transferred,[1] when the instrument or act creates a specific charge upon property, which is also transferred in disaffirmance thereof, and not otherwise; but, in that case, the transferee does not succeed to the right, conferred by statute upon the borrower, to procure relief, without paying, or offering to pay, any part of the sum or thing loaned." —*R. S., Civ. Proc.*, § 1911.

NORTH CAROLINA.

"All bonds, bills, notes, bills of exchange, liquidated and settled accounts, shall bear interest from the time they become due, provided such liquidated and settled accounts be signed by the debtor, unless it be specially expressed that interest is not to accrue until a time mentioned in the said writings or securities."—*Code*, § 44.

"All bills, bonds, or notes payable on demand, shall be held and deemed to be due when demandable by the creditor, and shall bear interest from the time they are demandable, unless otherwise expressed."—*Code*, § 45.

"All securities for the payment or delivery of specific articles shall bear interest as moneyed contracts, and the articles shall be rated by the jury at the time they become due." —*Code*, § 46.

"Bills of exchange which shall be drawn or indorsed in the state, and shall be protested, shall carry interest, not from the date thereof, but from the time of payment therein mentioned." —*Code*, § 47.

[1] So as to sue in the transferee's own name.

"When the judgment is for the recovery of money, interest from the time of the verdict or report until judgment be finally entered shall be computed by the clerk and added to the costs of the party entitled thereto."—*Code*, § 529.

"All sums of money due by contract of any kind whatsoever, excepting money due on penal bonds, shall bear interest, and when a jury shall render a verdict therefor they shall distinguish the principal from the sum allowed as interest; and the principal sum due on all such contracts shall bear interest from the time of rendering judgment thereon until it be paid and satisfied. In like manner, the amount of any judgment or decree, except the costs, rendered or adjudged in any kind of action, though not on contract, shall bear interest till paid, and the judgment and decree of the court shall be rendered according to this section."—*Code*, § 530.

"Whenever a suit shall be instituted on a single bond, a covenant for the payment of money, bill of exchange, promissory note, or a signed account, and the defendant shall not plead to issue thereon, upon judgment, the clerk of the court shall ascertain the interest due by law, without a writ of inquiry, and the amount shall be included in the final judgment of the court as damages, which judgment shall be rendered therein in the manner prescribed by the preceding section."—*Code*, § 531.

"The legal rate of interest shall be six per cent. *per annum* for such time as interest may accrue, and no more: *Provided*, that upon special contract in writing, signed by the party to be charged therewith, or by his agent, so great a rate as eight per cent. may be allowed."—*Code*, § 3835.

"The taking, receiving, reserving, or charging a rate of interest greater than is allowed by the preceding section, when knowingly done shall be deemed a forfeiture of the entire interest which the note, or other evidence of debt. carries with it, or which has been agreed to be paid thereon; and in case a greater rate of interest has been paid, the person by whom it has been paid, or his legal representative, may recover back, in an action in the nature of an action of debt twice the amount of interest paid: *Provided*, such action shall be commenced within two years from the time the usurious transaction occurred."—*Code*, § 3836.

NORTH DAKOTA.

The statutes given under *South Dakota* are still in force in North Dakota, except so far as they have been repealed and amended by the following statutes, which have been passed since North Dakota became a state.

"Interest for any legal indebtedness shall be at the rate of 7 per centum per annum, unless a different rate is contracted for in writing, and all contracts shall bear the same rate of interest after they become due as before; unless it clearly appears therefrom that such was not the intention of the parties; and no contract for a greater rate of interest than 12 per centum per annum shall be valid."—*Acts of* 1890, *ch.* 181, § 1.

"No person, company or corporation shall directly or indirectly take or receive, or agree to take or receive, in money, goods or things in action, or in any other way, any greater sum, or any greater value for the loan or forbearance of money, goods, or things in action than 12 per centum per annum; and in the computation of interest upon any bond, note or other instrument or agreement, interest shall not be compounded, but any contract to pay interest not usurious upon interest overdue shall not be construed to be usury."—*Acts of* 1890, *ch.* 181, § 2.

"All bonds, bills of exchange, promissory notes, mortgages, contracts and securities whatsoever, and all deposits or pledges of goods, wares, merchandise, or property of any kind, or things in action whereby or whereupon there shall be directly or indirectly taken, reserved or secured, or agreed to be taken, reserved or secured, any greater sum or value for the use, loan or forbearance of money or things in action than is provided in Section 1 of this act, whether the sum or value so secured, reserved or taken or agreed to be taken shall appear in or from such bond, bill, note, assurance, mortgage, contract, or otherwise, shall be deemed usurious, and are hereby declared to be void from the beginning; *Provided*, That the provisions of this section shall not apply to nor invalidate the collection of any negotiable bill of exchange or promissory note purchased of the original holder in good faith for a valuable consideration before the maturity of the same; and *Provided*, *further*, That the payment of interest in advance for any time not exceeding ninety days at a rate not exceeding 12 per cent. per annum shall not be deemed to be usury within the meaning of this act."—*Acts of* 1890, *ch.* 181, § 3.

"In all written contracts for the loan of money the exact amount agreed upon to be received for the use, by the borrower, shall be stated in the contract, and separately therefrom, the rate per cent. thereon of interest contracted to be charged, and if in any contract, either verbal or written, for the loan of money, the borrower receives a less sum than the principal sum so agreed upon and contracted to be loaned to and received by the borrower, the said contract shall be deemed to be usurious except as otherwise herein provided."—*Acts of* 1890, *ch.* 181, § 4.

"In all cases where the original owner or receiver of any usurious bill of exchange or promissory note, shall sell or part with the same before maturity thereof, or without giving notice to the purchaser or receiver of such bill of exchange or promissory note of its usurious character, the maker of such usurious negotiable bill of exchange or promissory note, or his legal representatives or assigns may recover of such original owner or receiver, or from any broker or agent or person who procured or aided or assisted in inducing and procuring the execution and delivery of the same, jointly or severally, the full amount of the principal and interest named in and represented by such bill of exchange or promissory note, the interest in case of recovery to be computed to the time when such bill of exchange or promissory note shall become due and payable according to the terms thereof."—*Acts of* 1890, *ch.* 184, § 5.

"The right of action to recover from the original owner or receiver, or from any broker, agent or person who aided or assisted in inducing and procuring the execution and delivery by any person, of an usurious negotiable bill of exchange or promissory note, the amount of the principal sum named in such bill or note, with interest thereon at the rate specified in such bill or note until the maturity thereof shall arise and accrue and be complete to the maker of such usurious negotiable bill of exchange or promissory note, or to his legal representatives or assigns, on and after the sale before maturity of such bill of exchange or promissory note by such original owner or receiver; and in such action it shall not be necessary for the plaintiff to allege or prove the payment of such usurious negotiable bill of exchange or promissory note; nor shall the payment of such usurious bill of exchange or promissory note be a condition precedent to the collection, from the original owner or receiver of such bill of exchange or note, or from any broker, agent or person in anywise a party to, or aiding and abetting in the soliciting or procuring of the execution and delivery of such bill of exchange or promissory note sold before maturity, of the full amount specified in such bill of exchange or promissory note, with interest as specified therein to the date of maturity thereof; *Provided*, That the provisions of this section shall not apply to nor prevent the collection of any bond, bill of exchange, promissory note, mortgage, conveyance or other contract of security while in the hands of the original or any holder who has not participated in such fee or compensation, nor authorized the taking of the same."—*Acts of* 1890, *ch.* 184, § 6.

"The receipt of or any agreement by any broker, loan agent or person to receive from any person a sum of money or other consideration as a fee or compensation for obtaining a loan or forbearance of money, or an extension of time on an existing loan or forbearance of money, where such sum of money or other consideration received or agreed to be received, as a fee or compensation by such broker, loan agent or person, when added to the rate of interest expressed and reserved in the bond, bill of exchange, promissory note, mortgage or other security made or given to evidence or to secure such loan, exceeds in the aggregate the rate of 12 per centum per annum, interest shall be deemed and is hereby declared to be usury within the meaning of this act, and all and every bond, bill of exchange, promissory note, mortgage or other contract or security, thus or in like manner tainted with usury or usurious purposes, shall be void from the beginning and subject to the same provisions and liabilities and provisos, and the maker of such usurious bill of exchange, promissory note, mortgage, security or other contract shall have the same remedy in the law against the original owner or receiver of any such usurious bond, bill, note, mortgage, or other contract or security, or against any broker, agent, or person who procured, or aided or assisted in procuring the execution and delivery of any such usurious bond, bill, note, mortgage or other contract or security, as is provided for by the preceding sections of this act."—*Acts of* 1890, *ch.* 184, § 7.

"Every person, company or corporation offending against this act shall be compelled by an order of court to answer on oath any complaint that may be exhibited or filed against him in the district court for the proper county for the discovery of any sum of money, goods, or things so taken, accepted, or received in violation of any of the foregoing provisions."—*Acts of* 1890, *ch.* 184, § 8.

"Whenever in any action in any court the question of usury shall be raised either by complaint or answer, either party to the action may be a witness in his own behalf on the trial, except in actions in which the opposite party sues or defends as administrator or personal representative of a deceased person; except, also, actions in which the opposite party claims as assignee and the assignor is deceased."—*Acts of* 1890, *ch.* 184, § 9.

"Whenever it shall satisfactorily appear to a court that any bond, bill, note, assurance, pledge, mortgage, contract, security or other evidence of debt has been received in violation of the provisions of this act, the court shall declare the same to be void, and enjoin any proceedings thereon, and shall order the same to be cancelled and delivered up."—*Acts of* 1890, *ch.* 184, § 10.

"None of the provisions of this act shall apply to any building and loan association incorporated under the provisions of any law of this State."—*Acts of* 1890, *ch.* 184, § 11.

"The taking, receiving or accepting of a greater rate of interest upon any bond, bill of exchange, promissory note, mortgage or contract for the use, loan or forbearance of money or things in action, than is provided by law is usury."—*Acts of* 1891, *ch.* 124, § 1.

"Any person or persons, company or corporation, which shall take, receive or accept of usury, or sell, assign, transfer, or in any manner dispose of any usurious bond, bill of exchange or contract whatsoever, knowing the same to be usurious without first giving such purchaser or assignee notice of its usurious character, shall be deemed guilty of a misdemeanor, and upon conviction thereof in any court having competent jurisdiction shall be fined not less than twenty-five (25) nor more then two hundred (200) dollars, or by imprisonment in the county jail not less than ten nor more than sixty days, or both fine and imprisonment in the discretion of the court for each and every such offence."—*Acts of* 1891, *ch.* 124, § 2.

OHIO.

"When any warrant is presented to the county treasurer for payment, and the same is not paid, for want of money belonging to the particular fund on which the same is drawn, the treasurer shall indorse said warrant, 'Not paid for want of funds,' annexing the date of its presentment, and shall sign his name thereto; and said warrant shall thenceforth bear interest at the rate of six per centum per annum; and a memorandum of all such warrants shall be kept by the treasurer in a book used for that purpose."—*R. S.*, § 1108.

"So soon as there are sufficient funds in the treasury of the county, to redeem the warrants drawn thereon, and on which interest is accruing, the county treasurer shall give notice in some newspaper printed in his county, or circulating therein, that he is ready to redeem such warrants; and from the date of such notice, the interest on such warrants shall cease."—*R. S.*, § 1109.

"The parties to a bond, bill, promissory note, or other instrument of writing for the forbearance or payment of money at any future time, may stipulate therein for the payment of interest upon the amount thereof at any rate not exceeding eight per centum per annum, payable annually."—*R. S.*, § 3179.

"Upon all judgments, decrees, or orders, rendered upon any bond, bill, note, or other instrument of writing containing stipulations for the payment of interest in accordance with the provisions of the preceding section, interest shall be computed till payment at the rate specified in such instrument."—*R. S.*, § 3180.

"In cases other than those provided for in the two preceding sections, when money becomes due and payable upon any bond, bill, note, or other instrument of writing hereafter made, upon any book account, or settlement hereafter made between parties, upon all verbal contracts hereafter entered into, and upon all judgments, decrees, and orders of any judicial tribunal for the payment of money arising out of a contract hereafter made, or other transaction which hereafter occurs, the creditor shall be entitled to interest at the rate of six per cent. per annum, and no more."—*R. S.*, § 3181.

"All creditors shall be entitled to collect and receive interest on all bonds, bills, notes, and other written instruments heretofore entered into, upon all balances struck on settlements heretofore made, upon book accounts heretofore accrued, upon all verbal contracts heretofore made, and upon all judgments, decrees, and orders of courts heretofore rendered, precisely as if this chapter had not passed."—*R. S.*, § 3182.

"Payments of money or property made by way of usurious interest, whether made in advance or not, shall be deemed and taken, as to the excess of interest above the rate allowed by law at the time of making the contract, to be payments made on account of principal; and judgment shall be rendered for no more than the balance found due, after deducting the excess of interest so paid. No debtor shall be deemed a particeps criminis, on account of having paid, or having agreed to pay, such exorbitant interest, but he shall have like remedy and relief in either case; and no bona fide indorsee of negotiable paper purchased before due, shall be affected by any usury exacted by any former holder of such paper, unless he have actual notice of the usury previous to his purchase; but in such cases, the amount of such excess, if incorporated into negotiable paper, may, after payment, be recovered back, by action against the party who originally exacted the usury."—*R. S.*, § 3183.

"Whenever usurious interest shall have been charged or taken in this state by any bank, whether incorporated by the laws of this state or elsewhere, it shall be lawful for any party or parties to an action brought upon any bond, bill, note, or other instrument of writing in which such usurious interest shall have been charged or included, at any time before or after judgment to set up and prove the taking or demand of such usurious interest, without tendering to such bank the legal amount of debt and interest due on such obligation."—*R. S.*, § 7590.

"In all cases in which judgment shall have been heretofore rendered in favor of such bank or banks upon default, or upon a warrant of attorney to confess judgment, it shall be the duty of the court in which such judgment was rendered, at any time before such judgment shall have been satisfied, upon affidavit of any defendant against whom such judgment was rendered, setting forth the facts constituting such usurious demand, to set aside such judgment, and permit such defendant or defendants to file his or their answer in said action, setting up such usurious demand, without tendering to such bank the legal amount of debt and interest due on the bond, bill, note, or other obligation upon which said action was founded.—*R. S.*, § 7591.

OKLAHOMA.

"Whenever a loan of money is made, it is presumed to be made upon interest, unless it is otherwise expressly stipulated at the time in writing."—*St.*, § 910.

"Interest is the compensation allowed for the use or forbearance, or detention of money, or its equivalent."—*St.*, § 911.

"When a rate of interest is prescribed by a law or contract, without specifying the period of time by which such rate is to be calculated, it is to be deemed an annual rate."—*St.*, § 912.

"Under an obligation to pay interest, no rate being specified, interest is payable at the rate of seven per centum per annum, and in the like proportion for a longer or shorter time; but in the computation of interest for less than a year, three hundred and sixty days are deemed to constitute a year."—*St.*, § 913.

"The highest rate of interest which it shall be lawful for any person to take, receive, retain, or contract for in this Territory, shall be twelve per cent per annum, and at the same rate for a shorter time.

"Unless, within the above limitation, there is an express contract in writing fixing a different rate, interest is payable on all moneys at the rate of seven per cent per annum, after they become due on any instrument of writing, except a judgment, and on moneys lent, or due on any settlement of accounts, from the day on which the balance is ascertained, and on moneys received to the use of another and detained from him."—*St.*, § 914.

"The interest which would become due at the end of the term for which a loan is made, not exceeding one year's interest in all, may be deducted from the loan in advance if the parties thus agree."—*St.*, § 915.

"A person taking, receiving, retaining, or contracting for any higher rate of interest than the rate of twelve per cent per annum, shall forfeit all the interest so taken, received, retained, or contracted for; it being the intent and meaning of this section not to provide a forfeiture of any portion of the principal. When a greater rate of interest has been paid than twelve per cent per annum, the person paying it, or his personal representatives, may recover the excess from the person taking it, or his personal representative, in an action in the proper court."—*St.*, § 916.

"Interest is payable on judgments recovered in the courts of this Territory, at the rate of seven per cent. per annum, and no greater rate, but such interest must not be compounded in any manner or form."—*St.*, § 917.

"Any legal rate of interest, stipulated by a contract, remains chargeable, after a breach thereof, as before, until the contract is superseded by a verdict or other new obligation."—*St.*, § 918.

OREGON.

"The legislative assembly shall not pass special or local laws in any of the following enumerated cases, that is to say, — . . in relation to interest on money."—*Const., art. IV*, § 23.

"The rate of interest in this state shall be eight per centum per annum, and no more, on all moneys after the same become due; on judgments and decrees for the payment of money; on money received to the use of another and retained beyond a reasonable time without the owner's consent, expressed or implied, or on money due upon the settlement of matured accounts from the day the balance is ascertained; on money due or to become due when there is a contract to pay interest and no rate specified. But on contracts, interest at the rate of ten per centum per annum may be charged by express agreement of the parties, and no more."—*Laws*, § 3587.

"No person shall, directly or indirectly, receive in money, goods, or things in action, or in any other manner, any greater sum or value for the loan or use of money, or upon contract founded upon any bargain, sale, or loan of wares, merchandise, goods, chattels, lands and tenements, than in this chapter prescribed."—*Laws*, § 3588.

"If it shall be ascertained in any suit brought on any contract that a rate of interest has been contracted for greater than is authorized by this chapter, either directly or indirectly, in money, property, or other valuable thing, or that any gift or donation of money, property, or other valuable thing has been made or promised to be made to a lender or creditor, or to any person for him, directly or indirectly, either by the borrower or debtor, or any person for him, the design of which is to obtain for money so loaned or for debts due, or to become due a rate of interest greater than that specified by the provisions of this chapter, the same shall be deemed usurious, and shall work a forfeiture of the entire debt so contracted to the school fund of the county where such suit is brought. The court in which such suit is prosecuted shall render judgment for the amount of the original sum loaned or the debt contracted, without interest, against the defendant and in favor of the state of Oregon, for the use of the common-school fund of said county, and against the plaintiff for costs of suit, whether such suit be contested or not."—*Laws*, § 3589.

"Nothing in this act shall be construed to prevent the proper *bona fide* assignee of any usurious contract recovering against his immediate assignor, or the original usurer, the full amount paid by him for such contract, but the same may be recovered by proper action, in any court having competent jurisdiction; *provided*, that such assignee had no notice of the usury affecting the contract."—*Laws*, § 3590.

"Judgments and decrees for money upon contracts bearing more than six per centum interest, and not exceeding ten per centum per annum, shall bear the same interest borne by such contracts; *provided, however*, that this act shall not be so construed as to affect or change the rate of interest to be received by virtue of any contract entered into before this act shall take effect."—*Laws*, § 3591.

"This act shall not be construed so as to affect or change the rate of interest to be received by virtue of any contract entered into before this act shall take effect."—*Laws*, § 3592.

"All contracts made and entered into in this state by and between borrower and lender, debtor and creditor, or mortgagor and mortgagee, on which the rate of interest is eight per cent or under, whereby one party shall agree to pay the taxes on the debt, credit, or mortgage existing or entered into between such parties, be and the same are hereby declared legal and valid, and shall not be deemed or taken to be usurious."—*Laws*, § 3593.

"All contracts entered into under section 3593 may be enforced by the parties thereto in the courts of this state; *provided*, that in making the assessments of credits, loans, or mortgages the same shall be assessed to the holder thereof as now provided by law."— *Laws*, § 3594.

PENNSYLVANIA.

Mutual building associations do not come within the restrictions of the usury law.—*B.'s P.'s Dig.*, *p.* 223, § 2.

"No executor or administrator shall be liable to pay interest but for the surplusage of the estate remaining in his hands or power when his accounts are or ought to be settled and adjusted in the register's office: *Provided*, that nothing herein contained shall be construed to exempt an executor or administrator from liability to pay interest, when he may have made use of the funds of the estate for his own purposes, previously to the time when his accounts are or ought to be settled as aforesaid."—*B.'s P.'s Dig.*, *p.* 550, § 207.

"The amount of interest to be paid in all cases by executors, administrators and guardians, shall be determined by the orphans' court, under all the circumstances of the case; but shall not, in any instance, exceed the legal rate of interest for the time being."—*B.'s P.'s Dig.*, *p.* 550, § 208.

"The lawful rate of interest for the loan or use of money in all cases where no express contract shall have been made for a less rate, shall be six per cent. per annum."—*B.'s P.'s Dig.*, *p.* 926, § 1. This includes banking corporations by act of May 23, 1878.

"When a rate of interest for the loan or use of money exceeding that established by law shall have been reserved or contracted for, the borrower or debtor shall not be required to pay the creditor the excess over the legal rate, and it shall be lawful for such borrower or debtor, at his option, to retain and deduct such excess from the amount of any such debt; and in all cases where any borrower or debtor shall heretofore, or hereafter, have voluntarily paid the whole debt or sum loaned, together with interest exceeding the lawful rate, no action to recover back any such excess shall be sustained in any court of this commonwealth, unless the same shall have been commenced within six months from and after the time of such payment: *Provided always*, That nothing in this act shall affect the holders of negotiable paper taken *bona fide* in the usual course of business."—*B.'s P.'s Dig.*, *p.* 927, § 2.

"Commission-merchants and agents of parties not residing in this commonwealth, be and they are hereby authorized to enter into an agreement to retain the balances of money in their hands, and pay on the same a rate of interest not exceeding seven per centum per annum, and receive a rate of interest not exceeding that amount, for any advance of money made by them on goods or merchandise consigned to them for sale or disposal: *Provided*, That this act shall only apply to moneys received from or held on account of, and advances made upon goods consigned from importers, manufacturers and others living and transacting business in places beyond the limits of the state."—*B.'s P.'s Dig., p.* 927, § 5.

"Whenever any railroad or canal company has borrowed money and given to the lender thereof a bond or other evidence of indebtedness in a larger sum than the amount actually received, such transactions shall not be deemed usurious, or in violation of any law of this commonwealth prohibiting the taking of more than six per cent. interest."—*B.'s P.'s Dig., p.* 927, § 6.

"Lawful interest shall be allowed to the creditor for the sum or value he obtained judgment for, from the time the said judgment was obtained till the time of sale, or till satisfaction be made."—*B.'s P.'s Dig., p.* 928, § 9.

"It shall be lawful for any party or parties, in whose favor any verdict may be rendered for a specific sum of money, to collect and receive interest upon such sum from the date of the verdict; and every general judgment entered upon such verdict, whether by a court of original jurisdiction, or by the supreme court, shall be deemed and held to be a judgment for the sum found by the verdict, with interest thereon from the date of such finding: *Provided*, That nothing in this act contained shall prevent any court from directing special verdicts, or entering special judgments, whenever the same shall be deemed just and proper."—*B.'s P.'s Dig., p.* 928, § 10.

RHODE ISLAND.

Interest is allowed on taxes.—*P. S., ch.* 41, § 21.

"Interest in the rendition of judgments and in all business transactions where interest is secured or paid shall be computed at the rate of six dollars on a hundred dollars for one year unless a different rate is expressly stipulated."—*P. S., ch.* 141, § 1.

"Whenever any foreign bill of exchange is or shall be drawn or endorsed within this state for the payment of any sum of money, and such bill is or shall be returned from any place or country without the limits of the United States, protested for non-acceptance or non-payment, the drawer or endorser shall be subject to the payment of ten per centum damages thereon and charges for protest, and the bill shall carry an interest of six per centum per annum from the date of the protest."—*P. S., ch.* 142, § 1.

"Any person having a right to demand any sum of money upon a foreign protested bill of exchange as aforesaid may commence and prosecute an action for principal, damages, interest and charges of protest against the drawers and endorsers, jointly or severally, or against either of them separately; and judgment shall and may be given for such principal, damages and charges and interest upon such principal after the rate aforesaid, to the time of such judgment, together with costs of suit."—*P. S., ch.* 142, § 2.

"Whenever any inland bill of exchange shall be drawn or endorsed within this state for the payment of any sum of money without the same, and such bill shall be protested for non-acceptance or non-payment, the drawer or endorser shall be subject to the payment of five per centum damages thereon and charges of protest, and the bill shall carry an interest of six per centum per annum from the date of the protest."—*P. S., ch.* 142, § 3.

Corporations, whose franchises have been sold on execution, "may, at any time within three months from the time of such sale, redeem the franchise by paying or tendering to the purchaser thereof the sum that he shall have paid therefor, with twelve per centum interest thereon, but without any allowance for toll which he may have received; and upon such payment or tender, the said franchise and all the rights and privileges thereof shall revert and belong to said corporation as if no such sale had been made."—*P. S., ch.* 152, § 11.

Executors "may be compelled to pay interest for the detention of money in their hands, if in the opinion of such [probate] court it shall be reasonable."—*P. S., ch.* 190, § 9.

"Every judgment for debt or damages shall draw interest on such debt or damages from the time of its rendition to the time of its discharge."—*P. S., ch.* 216, § 9.

"Verdicts, awards of referees and reports of masters in chancery or of auditors, ascertaining amounts due from party to party by way of debt or damages, shall, if and in so far as confirmed by judgment or decree, draw interest on such debt or damages; if a verdict, from the time the same is rendered, and if an award or report, from the time the same is dated or made up: *Provided*, there be nothing in the verdict, award or report to the contrary thereof or plainly inconsistent therewith."—*P. S., ch.* 216, § 10.

"The appellee in any case appealed from the court of common

pleas to the supreme court, brought upon any bond or promissory note for money or upon any bill of exchange against the acceptor thereof, whether interest be payable thereon or not, who shall recover in the supreme court, shall recover double costs in said court and double interest on the debt from the day of the judgment of the court of common pleas appealed from to the time of the final trial in the supreme court: *Provided*, that if the supreme court on such final trial shall be satisfied that the appellant had reasonable ground of defence and that such appeal was not solely for delay, they shall allow only simple interest from the day of the judgment of the court of common pleas appealed from to the time of such final trial, with single costs." —*P. S., ch.* 217, § 13.

"If in any action for such cause originally brought in the supreme court, a verdict be recovered by the plaintiff, and a motion for a new trial be filed therein by the defendant and allowed as of course, and judgment be afterwards rendered in favor of the plaintiff upon verdict, by default or on submission, the defendant may, in the discretion of the court, be adjudged to pay double costs and double interest on the debt accruing or taxable after the filing of such written motion."—*P. S., ch.* 217, § 14.

"If the appellant [from the court of common pleas to the supreme court] shall neglect to enter his appeal, as by law required, the adverse party, in case he did not also appeal, may at any time during the term appealed to, or at the next succeeding term, enter his complaint and obtain a confirmation of the former judgment, as of the third day of the said term, with double interest from the time of the rendition of the judgment appealed from, to said third day, if damages were therein given, and double costs."—*P. S., ch.* 218, § 9.

"In case of such neglect, if the court appealed to shall be satisfied that the appellant had reasonable grounds of appeal and that the appeal was not taken solely for delay, single interest on the damages and single costs only shall be required of him."—*P. S., ch.* 218, § 10.

"Every sheriff, deputy sheriff and town sergeant, charged with the service of any execution issued by the supreme court or court of common pleas, for any debt or damages, shall levy, collect, receive and pay over interest on the same debt or damages, from the date entered on the margin, up to the time of its discharge by him."—*P. S., ch.* 223, § 27.

SOUTH CAROLINA.

"In all money decrees and judgments of courts enrolled or entered, in all cases of accounts stated, and in all cases wherein any sum or sums of money shall be ascertained and, being due, shall draw interest according to law, the legal interest shall be at the rate of seven per centum per annum."—*G. S.*, § 1289.

"Where any bill of exchange is or shall be drawn for the payment of any sum of money, for value received, and such bill shall be protested for non-acceptance or non-payment, the same shall carry interest from the time such bill shall become due and payable, at the rate of seven per cent. per annum, until the money therein drawn for, together with damages and costs, be fully satisfied and paid."—*G. S.*, § 1298.

"No greater rate of interest than seven (7) per centum per annum shall be charged, taken, agreed upon or allowed upon any contract arising in this State for the hiring, lending or use of money or other commodity except upon written contracts, wherein, by express agreement, a rate of interest not exceeding ten per cent. may be charged.

"No person or corporation lending or advancing money or other commodity upon a greater rate of interest shall be allowed to recover in any Court of this State any portion of the interest so unlawfully charged: and the principal sum, amount or value so lent or advanced, without any interest, shall be deemed and taken by the Courts of this State to be the true legal debt or measure of damages to all intents and purposes whatsoever, to be recovered without costs.—*Acts of* 1882, *No.* 21, § 1.

"Any person or corporation who shall receive as interest any greater amount than is herein provided for shall, in addition to the forfeiture herein provided, forfeit also double the sum so received, to be collected by a separate action, or allowed as a counter-claim to any action brought to recover the principal sum."—*Acts of* 1882, *No.* 21, § 2.

SOUTH DAKOTA.

"All county orders hereafter drawn by the proper authorities of any county shall after having been presented to the county treasurer of the respective counties and by him indorsed, 'Not paid for want of funds in the treasury," from said date draw interest at the rate of seven per cent. per annum." — *Comp. Laws*, § 618.

"On the first Monday of February of the year after which taxes shall have been assessed, all unpaid taxes shall become delinquent, and shall draw interest at the rate of ten per cent. per annum from the date of such delinquency."—*Comp. Laws*, § 1610.

Land sold for taxes, may be redeemed by paying the sum mentioned in the certificate of sale, "and interest thereon at the rate of thirty per cent. per annum from the date of purchase, together with all other taxes subsequently paid, whether for any year or years previous or subsequent to said sale, and interest thereon at the same rate from the date of such payment."—*Comp. Laws*, § 1635.

"Legacies bear interest from the time when they are due and payable, except that legacies for maintenance, or to the testator's widow, bear interest from the testator's decease."—*Comp. Laws*, § 3390.

When a partial payment is made it shall be first applied to the payment of interest due at the time.—*Comp. Laws*, § 3457.

"An offer of payment or other performance, duly made, though the title to the thing offered be not transferred to the creditor, stops the running of interest on the obligation, and has the same effect upon all its incidents as a performance thereof."—*Comp. Laws*, § 3477.

"Whenever a loan of money is made, it is presumed to be made upon interest, unless it is otherwise expressly stipulated at the time in writing."—*Comp. Laws*, § 3717.

"Interest is the compensation allowed for the use, or forbearance, or detention of money, or its equivalent."—*Comp. Laws*, § 3718.

"When a rate of interest is prescribed by a law or contract, without specifying the period of time by which such rate is to be calculated, it is to be deemed an annual rate."—*Comp. Laws*, § 3719.

"Under an obligation to pay interest, no rate being specified, interest is payable at the rate of seven per centum per annum, and in the like proportion for a longer or shorter time; but in the computation of interest for less than a year, three hundred and sixty days are deemed to constitute a year."—*Comp. Laws*, § 3720.

"1. The highest rate of interest which it shall be lawful for any person to take, receive, retain, or contract for in this territory [state], shall be twelve per cent. per annum, and at the same rate for a shorter time; except in the counties of Lawrence, Pennington, Custer, Mandan, and Forsythe, wherein it shall be lawful to take, receive, retain, and contract for any rate agreed on between the parties.

"2. Unless, within the above limitation, there is an express contract in writing fixing a different rate, interest is payable on all moneys at the rate of seven per cent. per annum, after they become due on any instrument of writing, except a judgment, and on moneys lent, or due on any settlement of accounts, from the day on which the balance is ascertained, and on moneys received to the use of another and detained from him."—*Comp. Laws*, § 3721.

"The interest which would become due at the end of the term for which a loan is made, not exceeding one year's interest in all, may be deducted from the loan in advance if the parties thus agree."—*Comp. Laws*, § 3722.

"A person taking, receiving, retaining, or contracting for any higher rate of interest than the rate of twelve per cent. per annum, shall forfeit all the interest so taken, received, retained, or contracted for: it being the intent and meaning of this section not to provide a forfeiture of any portion of the principal. When a greater rate of interest has been paid than twelve per cent. per annum, the person paying it, or his personal representative, may recover the excess from the person taking it, or his personal representative, in an action in the proper court."—*Comp. Laws*, § 3723.

"Interest is payable on judgments recovered in the courts of this territory [state], at the rate of seven per cent. per annum, and no greater rate; but such interest must not be compounded in any manner or form."—*Comp. Laws*, § 3724.

"Any legal rate of interest stipulated by a contract, remains chargeable after a breach thereof, as before, until the contract is superseded by a verdict or other new obligation."—*Comp. Laws*, § 3725.

A trustee may, at the option of the beneficiary, be required to account for all profits he has made for himself from the trust fund, "or to pay the value of its use, and, if he has disposed thereof, to replace it, with its fruits, or to account for its proceeds with interest."—*Comp. Laws*, § 3930.

If a trustee omits to invest the trust moneys as fast as he collects a sufficient amount "he must pay simple interest thereon if such omission is negligent merely, and compound interest if it is wilful."—*Comp. Laws*, § 3941.

"Upon a contract of bottomry, the parties may lawfully stipulate for a rate of interest higher than that allowed by the law upon other contracts. But a competent court may reduce the rate stipulated when it appears unjustifiable and exorbitant."—*Comp. Laws*, § 4423.

"Every person who is entitled to recover damages certain, or capable of being made certain by calculation, and the right to recover which is vested in him upon a particular day, is entitled also to recover interest thereon from that day, except during such time as the debtor is prevented by law, or by the act of the creditor, from paying the debt."—*Comp. Laws*, § 4577.

"In an action for the breach of an obligation not arising from contract, and in every case of oppression, fraud, or malice, interest may be given, in the discretion of the jury."—*Comp. Laws*, § 4578.

"Accepting payment of the whole principal, as such, waives all claim to interest."—*Comp. Laws*, § 4579.

"The detriment caused by the breach of an obligation to pay money only is deemed to be the amount due by the terms of the obligation, with interest thereon."—*Comp. Laws*, § 4582.

"The words 'compound interest' mean interest added to the principal as the former becomes due, and thereafter made to bear interest."—*Comp. Laws*, § 4761.

"When the judgment is for the recovery of money, interest from the time of the verdict or report, until judgment be finally entered, must be computed by the clerk and added to the costs of the party entitled thereto."—*Comp. Laws*, § 5196.

If the whole of mortgaged premises are sold, "the proceeds of such sale must be applied as well to the interest or portion or installment of the principal due, as towards the whole or residue of the sum secured by such mortgage, and not due and payable at the time of such sale, and if such residue do not bear interest, then the court may direct the same to be paid, with a rebate of the legal interest for the time during which residue shall not be due and payable, or the court may direct the balance of the proceeds of such sale, after paying the sum due, with costs, to be put out at interest for the benefit of the plaintiff, to be paid to him as the installments or portions of the principal or interest may become due, and the surplus for the benefit of the defendant, his representatives or assigns, to be paid to them by order of the court."—*Comp. Laws*, § 5145.

If the estate of a deceased person "is insolvent, no greater rate of interest shall be allowed upon any claim, after the first publication of notice to creditors, than is allowed by law on judgments obtained in the district court."—*Comp. Laws*, § 5791.

"If there be any debt of the decedent bearing interest, whether presented or not, the executor or administrator may, by order of the probate court, pay the amount then accumulated and unpaid, or any part thereof, at any time when there are sufficient funds properly applicable thereto, whether said claim be then due or not; and interest shall thereupon cease to accrue upon the amount so paid."—*Comp. Laws*, § 5811.

When the real estate of a minor is sold by a guardian, the guardian must apply the proceeds of the sale to the purpose for which the sale was made, "as far as necessary, and put out the residue, if any, on interest, or invest it in the best manner in his power, until the capital is wanted for the maintenance of the ward and his family, or the education of his children, or for the education of the ward when a minor, in which case the capital may be used for that purpose, as far as may be necessary, in like manner as if it had been personal estate of the ward."—*Comp. Laws*, § 6011.

"Every person who directly or indirectly receives any interest, discount or consideration upon the loan or forbearance of any money, goods or things in action greater than is allowed by law is guilty of a misdemeanor."—*Acts of* 1889, *ch.* 155, § 1.

TENNESSEE.

"In taking judgment against a delinquent officer, interest at the rate of six per cent. on the amount which he has failed to pay over shall be added, and twelve and one-half per cent. damages thereon."—*Code*, § 914.

"Interest is the compensation which may be demanded by the lender from the borrower, or the creditor from the debtor for the use of money."—*Code*, § 2700.

"The amount of said compensation shall be at the rate of six dollars for the use of one hundred dollars for one year; and every excess over that rate is usury."—*Code*, § 2701.

"All bills single, bonds, notes, bills of exchange, and liquidated and settled accounts, signed by the debtor, shall bear interest from the time they become due, unless it is expressed that interest is not to accrue until a specific time therein mentioned." —*Code*, § 2702.

"The time from which interest may be computed shall be the day when the debt is payable, unless another day be fixed in the contract itself."—*Code*, § 2703.

"If the debt be payable on demand, the interest shall be computed from the day of the demand; and suing for the debt shall be equivalent to an actual demand."—*Code*, § 2704.

"Interest shall be computed on every judgment from the day on which it was entered up."—*Code*, § 2705.

"The amount upon which interest may be computed shall be the sum expressed in the contract; and if the contract be for the payment or delivery of property, or any specific article or articles, the value of the same in dollars, to be ascertained by the triers of the suit, shall be the amount on which interest shall be computed."—*Code*, § 2706.

"A defendant sued for money may avoid the excess over legal interest, by a plea setting forth the amount of the usury." —*Code*, § 2707.

"If the defendant be the original debtor, his surety, or accommodation endorser, he shall verify the plea by an affidavit that it is true. If the defendant be the personal representative of the original debtor, he may verify the plea by an affidavit that he has good reason to believe, and does believe, the plea to be true."—*Code*, § 2708.

"If the plaintiff be the original creditor, he shall deny the usury, or state the amount of usury in his replication, which he shall verify by an affidavit of its truth. If the plaintiff is an endorsee or other holder, and deny the usury, he shall verify the replication, either by an affidavit of its truth by the original creditor, or, if the original creditor is dead, or removed from the county, or refuses to make the affidavit, that there was no usury in the transaction to his knowledge. And where the plaintiff is a personal representative, if he deny the usury in the replication, it shall be supported by an affidavit that he has no knowledge that there was usury in the contract."—*Code*, § 2709.

"If the replication admit the usury, or is not supported by the affidavit aforesaid, the judgment shall be that the plaintiff recover the principal and legal interest, and no more. If the replication is supported by an affidavit, the judgment shall be that the plaintiff recover the amount claimed, unless the defendant prove the usury, in which case it shall be deducted from the claim, and the judgment shall be for the balance. But if there are other defences, they shall be disposed of."—*Code*, § 2710.

"This remedy at law against usury shall not prevent the party from having relief in equity."—*Code*, § 2711.

"If usurious interest has been paid, the same may be recovered by action at the suit of the party from whom it was taken, or his representative; or it may be subjected by any judgment creditor of such party to the satisfaction of his debt."—*Code*, § 2712.

"In settlements with a guardian, he shall not be chargeable with compound interest, if he can show that he did not and could not have received compound interest on the debts due the estate of his ward."—*Code*, § 3406.

"In all cases of affirmance of the judgment, or dismissal of the writ for any cause, where the original judgment has been superseded, judgment shall be rendered against the plaintiff in error and his sureties for the amount of the former judgment, with interest at the rate of twelve and one-half per cent. per annum from the rendition thereof, and all costs."—*Code*, § 3827.

'Upon affirmance of the judgment or decree below, or recovery of a larger amount, or upon dismissal of the *certiorari* for want of prosecution, or for any other cause, the court shall enter up judgment for the amount recovered against the principal and the sureties to the prosecution bond, with interest at the rate of six per cent. per annum from the date of the judgment or decree below, and all costs."—*Code*, § 3853.

"On affirmance of decrees in equity cases for money, interest shall be recovered at the rate of six per cent. per annum."—*Code*, § 3881.

"If it be made to appear in the action that usurious interest has been intentionally taken or reserved, the person taking or reserving such usury shall pay full costs."—*Code*, § 3930.

"No person shall receive, by way of compensation for the use of money, more than at the rate of six dollars for the use of one hundred dollars for one year."—*Code*, § 5622.

"The punishment of this offence shall be a fine in no case less than ten dollars, nor more than the amount of the usury received, to be ascertained by the jury. In case the defendant plead guilty to the charge, or judgment go against him on a plea in abatement, a jury shall be sworn to ascertain the amount of the usury received."—*Code*, § 5623.

TEXAS.

"The legal rate of interest shall not exceed eight per cent. per annum, in the absence of any contract as to the rate of interest; and by contract parties may agree upon any rate not to exceed twelve per cent. per annum. All interest charged above this last named rate shall be deemed usurious."—*Const.*, *art.* XVI, § 11.

An answer "that the contract sued upon is usurious" "must be verified by affidavit" "unless the truth of the pleadings appear of record."—*S.'s Civ. St.*, § 1265.

"The rate of interest in any other state, territory or country is presumed to be the same as that established by law in this state, and may be recovered accordingly without allegation or proof of the rate of interest in such other state, territory or country, unless the rate of interest in such other country be alleged and proved."—*S.'s Civ. St.*, § 2261.

"If the surplus money in the hands of the guardian belonging to the ward cannot be invested or loaned at interest as directed in this chapter, after due diligence to do so by the guardian, he shall be liable for the principal only of such money. But if the guardian neglects to invest such money or loan the same at interest when he could do so by the use of reasonable diligence, he shall be liable for the principal and also for the highest legal rate of interest upon such principal for the time he so neglects to invest or loan the same."—*S.'s Civ. St.*, § 2567.

"'Interest' is the compensation allowed by law or fixed by the parties to a contract for the use of forbearance or detention of money."—*S.'s Civ. St.*, § 2972.

"'Legal interest' is that interest which is allowed by law when the parties to a contract have not agreed upon any particular rate of interest."—*S.'s Civ. St.*, § 2973.

"'Conventional interest' is that interest which is agreed upon and fixed by the parties to a written contract, not to exceed twelve per cent. per annum."—*S.'s Civ. St.*, § 2974.

"The distinction between legal and conventional interest shall be known and recognized by the laws of this state."—*S.'s Civ. St.*, § 2975.

"On all written contracts ascertaining the sum payable, when no specified rate is agreed upon by the parties to the contract, interest shall be allowed at the rate of six per cent per annum from and after the time when the sum is due and payable."—*S.'s Civ. St.*, § 2976, *as amended by Acts of* 1891, *ch.* 68.

"On open accounts, when no specified rate is agreed upon by the parties, interest shall be allowed at the rate of six per cent per annum from and after the time when such accounts were due and payable."—*S.'s Civ. St.*, § 2977, *as amended by Acts of* 1891, *ch.* 68.

"The parties to any written contract may agree to and stipulate for any rate of interest not exceeding twelve per cent. per annum on the amount or value of the contract."—*S.'s Civ. St.*, § 2978.

"All written contracts whatsoever which may in any way, directly or indirectly, violate the preceding article by stipulating for a greater rate of interest than twelve per cent. per annum shall be void and of no effect for the whole rate of interest only; but the principal sum of money or the value of the contract may be received and recovered."—*S.'s Civ. St.*, § 2979.

"All judgments hereafter obtained in the several courts of this state, shall bear interest at the rate of six per cent per annum from and after the date of the judgment, except when the contract upon which the judgment was founded bears a specified interest greater than six per cent per annum, and not exceeding the highest rate of conventional interest permitted by law, in which case, the judgment shall bear the same rate of interest specified in such contract and after the date of such judgment."—*S.'s Civ. St.*, § 2980, *as amended by Acts of* 1891, *ch.* 68.

"No evidence of usurious interest shall be received on the trial of any case unless the same shall be specially pleaded and verified by the affidavit of the party wishing to avail himself of such defence."—*S.'s Civ. St.*, § 2981.

"If any person shall for himself or as the agent of another, either directly or indirectly, loan any money, and directly or indirectly charge or receive a greater rate of interest thereon, than twelve per cent per annum, he shall be deemed guilty of usury, and upon conviction thereof, shall be fined in any sum not less than one-third nor more than the whole amount of the money so loaned."—*Acts of* 1891, *ch.* 18.

UTAH.

"Hereafter it shall be lawful to take eight per cent interest per annum, when the amount of interest has not been specified or agreed upon. But parties may agree in writing for the payment of any rate of interest whatever on money due, or to become due on any contract. Any judgment rendered on such contract shall conform thereto, and shall bear the interest agreed upon by the parties and which shall be specified in the judgment."—*Acts of* 1890, *ch.* 23.[1]

VERMONT.

"The rate of interest, on the sum allowed for the forbearance or use of money, shall be six dollars for one hundred dollars for one year, at the same rate for a greater or less sum, and for a longer or shorter time; and no higher rate shall be allowed, except in cases specially provided for by law."—*Rev. Laws, ch.* 101, § 1996.

"On notes, bills, or other similar obligations, payable on demand or at a specified time, with interest, when payments are made, such payments shall be applied: first, to liquidate the interest accrued at the time of such payments; and secondly to extinguish the principal."—*Rev. Laws, ch.* 101, § 1997.

"When such obligations are payable on demand or at a specified time, with interest annually, the annual interests that remain unpaid shall bear simple interest from the time they become due to the time of final settlement; but if in any year, reckoning from the time such annual interest began to accrue, payments are made, the amount of such payments at the end of each year, with interest thereon from the time of payment, shall be applied: first, to liquidate the simple interest accrued from the unpaid annual interests; secondly, to liquidate the annual interests due; and thirdly, to extinguish the principal."—*Rev. Laws, ch.* 101, § 1998.

"The two preceding sections shall not affect notes and contracts existing prior to November 19, 1866."—*Rev. Laws. ch.* 101, § 1999.

[1] This takes the place of § 2119 of the Compiled Laws of the territory, which permitted ten per cent.

"When a greater rate of interest than is allowed by law is paid, the person paying the same may recover back the amount so paid above the legal interest, with interest thereon from the time of payment, in an action of assumpsit, declaring for money had and received or goods sold and delivered, as the case may be."—*Rev. Laws, ch.* 101, § 2000.

"The foregoing provisions relating to interest shall not extend to the letting of cattle or other usages of a like nature among farmers, or maritime contracts, bottomry, or course of exchange, as has been customary."—*Rev. Laws, ch.* 101, § 2001.

"Such[1] banking associations shall not receive or demand greater interest or discount on a note, draft, or security, than six per cent. per annum; but such interest or discount may be calculated and taken according to the established rules of banking."—*Rev. Laws, ch.* 160, § 3520.

"Savings banks incorporated under the laws of this state may demand and receive interest on their loans at the rate of six per cent. per annum, payable semi-annually."—*Rev. Laws, ch.* 160, § 3590.

VIRGINIA.

"If any balance, whether of profits received or estimated, or of interest or principal, be due by any guardian, or other person acting as guardian, at the end of any year, which ought to be invested or loaned out within a reasonable time for the benefit of the ward, and the same remain in the hands of such guardian or other person, he shall be charged with interest thereon from the end of the year in which such balance arose, and so on *toties quoties* during the continuance of the trust."—*Code*, § 2606.

"Any person acting as guardian shall have the right to demand and recover of all obligors in bonds, payable to him as guardian, and held by him for the benefit of his ward, not only the principal sum due, with interest thereon after the rate prescribed by law, but also, when the interest on the principal sum is not paid punctually at the end of each year, to demand and recover interest upon the interest so due and unpaid, which has accrued during the continuance of the trust."—*Code*, § 2607.

"Whenever a guardian shall collect any principal or interest belonging to his ward, he shall have thirty days to invest or loan the same, and shall not be charged with interest thereon until the expiration of said time, unless he shall have made the in-

[1] Banks of circulation, discount and deposit organized under chapter 160 of the Revised Laws.

vestment previous thereto: in which case, he shall be charged with interest from the time the investment or loan is made."—*Code*, § 2608.

"Legal interest shall continue to be at the rate of six dollars upon one hundred dollars for a year, and proportionately for a greater or less sum, or for a longer or shorter time; and no person upon any contract shall take for the loan or forbearance of money or other thing above the value of such rate."—*Code*, § 2817.

"All contracts and assurances made, directly or indirectly, for the loan or forbearance of money or other thing, at a greater rate of interest than is allowed by the preceding section, shall be deemed to be for an illegal consideration as to the excess beyond the principal amount so loaned or forborne."—*Code*, § 2818.

"A bank may take interest on its loans or discounts at the rate of one half of one *per cent.* for thirty days, and the interest may be received in advance."—*Code*, § 2819.

"Any licensed banker or broker, and any corporation licensed by law to make loans or to purchase or discount bonds, bills, notes, or other paper, may loan money, or discount bonds, bills, notes, or other paper, at a rate of interest not exceeding one-half of one *per cent.* for thirty days, and may receive such interest in advance."—*Code*, § 2820.

"Any defendant may plead in general terms that the contract or assurance on which the action is brought was for the payment of interest at a greater rate than is allowed by law, to which plea the plaintiff shall reply generally, but may give in evidence, upon the issue made up thereon, any matter which could be given in evidence under a special replication. Under the plea aforesaid, the defendant may give in evidence any fact showing or tending to show that the contract or assurance, or other writing upon which the action was brought, was for an usurious consideration; and when no such plea is made, if the contract or assurance be in writing, and usurious interest be provided for therein, judgment shall be rendered for the principal sum only."—*Code*, § 2821.

"Any borrower of money or other thing may exhibit a bill in equity against the lender and compel him to discover, upon oath, the money or thing really lent, and all bargains, contracts, or other shifts relative to such loan and the interest or consideration of the same; and if it appear that more than lawful interest was reserved, the lender shall recover only his principal money or other thing, without interest, and pay the costs of suit. If property has been conveyed to secure the payment of the debt, and a sale thereof is about to be made, or is apprehended, an injunction may be awarded to prevent such sale pending the suit."—*Code*, § 2822.

"If an excess beyond the lawful interest be paid in any case, the person paying the same may, in a suit brought within one year thereafter, recover it from the person with whom the contract was made or to whom the assurance was given; and it may be so recovered from such person, notwithstanding the payment of the excess be made to his endorsee or assignee."—*Code*, § 2823.

"Any judgment creditor, who apprehends that he is in danger of loss, by reason of usurious dealings on the part of his debtor, may exhibit his bill in equity, verified by affidavit, against the party with whom the dealings were had, and compel him to discover, on oath, all bargains, contracts, or shifts relative to such dealings; and if it appear that more than legal interest has been received, the excess above that rate, or so much thereof as may be necessary, shall be applied to the satisfaction of the plaintiff's demand. Such bill shall be filed within five years after the receipt of the illegal interest."—*Code*, § 2824.

"No corporation shall, by way of defence or otherwise, avail itself of the provisions of the preceding sections of this chapter, to avoid or defeat the payment of any interest which it has contracted to pay; nor shall anything contained in any of said sections be construed to prevent the recovery of such interest, though it be more than legal interest, and though that fact appear on the face of the contract."—*Code*, § 2825.

"Nothing in the act of incorporation of any insurance, banking, or other corporation, shall be construed as giving authority (unless expressly given), to charge, take, or receive, for the loan or forbearance of money or other thing, more than the legal rate of interest."—*Code*, § 2826.

"The jury, in any action founded on contract, may allow interest on the principal due, or any part thereof, and fix the period at which such interest shall commence. And in any action whether on contract or for tort, the jury may allow interest on the sum found by the verdict, or any part thereof, and fix the period at which the interest shall commence. If a verdict be rendered which does not allow interest, the sum thereby found shall bear interest from its date, and judgment shall be entered accordingly."—*Code*, § 3390.

"In any suit in equity, or in an action founded on contract, where no jury is impaneled, judgment or decree may be rendered for interest on the principal sum recovered, until such judgment be paid; and where there is a jury, which allows interest, the judgment shall, in like manner, be for such interest until payment."—*Code*, § 3391.

WASHINGTON.

Certain damages are given on bills of exchange instead of interest.—*St.*, §§ 2396, 2397.

"The legal rate of interest shall be ten per centum per annum." —*St.*, § 2795.

"Any rate of interest agreed upon by parties to a contract, specifying the same in writing, shall be valid and legal."—*St.*, § 2796.

WEST VIRGINIA.

"No corporation shall interpose the defence of usury in any suit or proceeding at law or in chancery; nor shall any bond, note, debt, or contract of a corporation be set aside, impaired, or adjudged invalid by reason of anything contained in the laws prohibiting usury."—*Code, ch.* 52, § 22.

"If any balance, whether of profits received or estimated, or of interest or principal, be due by any guardian, or other person acting as guardian, at the end of any year, which ought to be invested or loaned out within a reasonable time, for the benefit of the ward, and the same remain in the hands of such guardian or other person, he shall be charged with interest thereon from the end of the year in which such balance arose, and so on *toties quoties* during the continuance of the trust."—*Code, ch.* 82, § 10.

"Hereafter any person acting as guardian shall have the right to demand and recover of all obligors in bonds payable to him as guardian, and held by him for the benefit of his ward, not only the principal sum due, with interest thereon after the rate prescribed by law; but also when the interest on the principal sum is not paid punctually at the end of each year, to demand and recover interest upon the interest so due and unpaid." —*Code, ch.* 82, § 11.

"Whenever a guardian shall collect any principal or interest belonging to his ward, he shall have thirty days to invest or loan the same, and shall not be charged with interest thereon until the expiration of said time, unless he shall have made the investment previous thereto, in which case he shall be charged with interest from the time the investment or loan was made." —*Code, ch.* 82, § 12.

"Legal interest shall continue to be at the rate of six dollars upon one hundred dollars for a year, and proportionably for a greater or less sum, or for a longer or shorter time, and no person upon any contract, shall take for the loan or forbearance of money or other thing, above the value of such rate."—*Code*, *ch.* 96, § 4.

"All contracts and assurances made directly or indirectly for the loan or forbearance of money or other thing at a greater rate of interest than six per cent. except where such greater rate is now allowed by law, shall be void as to any excess of interest agreed to be paid above that rate, and no further."—*Code*, *ch.* 96, § 5.

"Any defendant may plead in general terms that the contract or assurance on which the action is brought, was for the payment of interest at a greater rate than is allowed by law, to which plea the plaintiff shall reply generally, but may give in evidence upon the issue made up thereon, any matter which could be given in evidence under a special replication; under the plea aforesaid, the defendant may give in evidence any fact showing, or tending to show, that the contract, or assurance, or other writing upon which the action was brought, was for an usurious consideration. And upon such plea the court shall direct a special issue to try and ascertain:

"I. Whether or not, the contract, assurance or other writing is usurious.

"II. If usurious, to what extent.

"III. Whether or not interest has been paid on said contract, assurance or other writing, above six per cent., and if so, to what extent. And if a verdict be found upon the plea of usury, for the defendant, a judgment shall be rendered for the plaintiff for the principal sum due, with interest at the rate of six per centum per annum, and if any interest has been paid above the rate of six per centum per annum, the excess over and above that rate shall be entered as a credit on the sum due, and if nothing be found due after applying all credits and all excesses of interest paid above six per cent., judgment shall be entered for the defendant."—*Code*, *ch.* 96, § 6.

"Any borrower of money, or other thing may exhibit a bill in equity against the lender, and compel him to discover upon oath the money or thing really lent, and all bargains, contracts, or shifts relative to such loan, and the interest or consideration of the same; and if it appear that more than lawful interest was reserved, the lender shall recover his principal money or other thing with six per cent. interest only, but shall recover no costs. If property has been conveyed to secure the payment of the debt, and a sale thereof is about to be made, or is apprehended, an injunction may be awarded to prevent such sale pending the suit."—*Code*, *ch.* 96, § 7.

"The jury in any action founded on contract, may allow interest on the principal due, or any part thereof, and in all cases they shall find the aggregate of principal and interest due at the time of the trial, after allowing all credits, payments and set-offs, and judgment shall be entered for such aggregate with interest from the date of the verdict."—*Code, ch.* 131, § 14.

"When there is a recovery on a bond conditioned for the payment of money, as well as in all cases where a judgment or decree is rendered or made for the payment of money, it shall be for the aggregate of principal and interest due at the date of the verdict if there be one, otherwise at the date of the judgment or decree, with interest thereon from such date, except in cases where it is otherwise provided."—*Code, ch.* 131, § 16.

"Every judgment or decree for the payment of money, except where it is otherwise provided by law, shall bear interest from the date thereof, whether it be so stated in the judgment or decree or not."—*Code, ch.* 131, § 18.

"The interest on all loans made to individuals under an order of court, shall become due and payable on the first day of January in each year, until the principal is paid; and unless the interest be paid at the time it becomes due and payable, compound interest shall be charged thereon to the borrower from such time until payment thereof is made."—*Code, ch.* 133, § 23.

WISCONSIN.

"No interest shall be allowed to the plaintiff upon any sum allowed by the county board, and for which orders were drawn." —*St.*, § 685.

"The rate of interest upon the loan or forbearance of any money, goods or things in action, shall be seven dollars upon the one hundred dollars, for one year, and after that rate for a greater or less sum, or for a longer or shorter time; but it shall be competent for parties to contract for the payment and receipt of a rate of interest not exceeding ten dollars on one hundred dollars, as aforesaid; in which case, such rate exceeding seven dollars on one hundred dollars shall be clearly expressed in writing."—*St.*, § 1688.

"No person, company or corporation shall, directly or indirectly, take or receive in money, goods, or things in action, or in any other way, any greater sum, or any greater value, for the loan or forbearance of money, goods, or things in action, than at the rate of ten dollars upon one hundred dollars for one year; and in the computation of interest upon any bond, note, or other instrument or agreement, interest shall not be compounded, nor shall the interest thereon be construed to bear interest, unless an agreement to that effect is clearly expressed in writing, and signed by the party to be charged therewith." —*St.*, § 1689.

"All bonds, bills, notes, assurances, conveyances, and all other contracts or securities whatever, whereby there is reserved or secured a rate of interest exceeding ten dollars on one hundred dollars for one year, shall be valid and effectual to secure the repayment of the principal sum loaned; but no interest shall be recovered on such securities, or on any money or other thing loaned by such contract, except upon bottomry and respondentia bonds and contracts; and no corporation shall interpose the defence of usury."—*St.*, § 1690.

"Every person who, for any such loan or forbearance, shall have paid or delivered any greater sum or value than is above allowed to be received, may, by himself or his personal representative, recover in an action against the person who shall have taken or received the same, or his personal representative, treble the amount of the money so paid or value delivered, above the rate aforesaid, if such action shall be brought within one year, after such payment or delivery."—*St.*, § 1691.

"Whenever any person shall apply to any court in this state to be relieved in case of a usurious contract or security, or when any person shall set up the plea of usury in any action instituted against him, such person to be entitled to such relief or the benefit of such plea, shall prove a tender of the principal sum of money or thing loaned to the party entitled to receive the same."—*St.*, § 1692.

No turnpike or other "such corporation shall be allowed to make the defense of usury against the holder of any indebtedness so secured."—*St.*, § 1864.

"No premiums, fines or interest on such premiums[1] that may accrue to any such corporation under the provisions of this chapter shall be deemed usurious."—*St.*, § 2013.

"When the judgment is for the recovery of money, interest from the time of verdict or report until judgment is finally entered shall be computed by the clerk and added to the costs of the party entitled thereto."—*St.*, § 2922.

"It shall be lawful to direct in every execution upon a judgment for the recovery of money, in whole or in part, the collection of interest on the amount recovered, from the date of the rendition thereof until such amount be paid."—*St.*, § 2969.

"The amount adjudged to be due in the judgment shall draw interest at the rate provided to be paid on the mortgage debt,

[1] Of mutual loan and building corporations.

but shall not exceed the minimum legal rate of interest from its date until the date of sale or payment, and all installments which shall become due after the date of such judgment, shall draw interest at the same rate from the time the same shall become due."—*St.*, § 3161, *as amended by Acts of* 1887, *ch.* 186, *and Acts of* 1891, *ch.* 303, § 1.

WYOMING.

"Any rate of interest which may be agreed upon between parties, for the loan or forbearance of money, goods or things in action, shall be valid; *Provided*, that if such agreement be for a higher rate of interest than twelve per cent. per annum, the same shall be in writing."—*R. S.*, § 1310.

"In the absence of any contract between the parties, the rate of interest upon loan or forbearance of money, goods, or things in action, shall be at the rate of twelve per cent. per annum."—*R. S.*, § 1311.

"Interest on all judgments or decrees for money, shall be at the rate of twelve per cent. per annum from the date of the rendition and signing thereof until satisfied."—*R. S.*, § 1312.

"On money due on an instrument in writing, or on settlement of account from the day the balance shall be agreed on, money received to the use of another, and retained without the owner's consent, express or implied, from the receipt thereof, and on money loaned or due and withheld by unreasonable delay of payment, interest shall be allowed at the rate of twelve per cent. per annum. Unsettled accounts between parties shall bear interest after thirty days from the date of the last item thereof." —*R. S.*, § 1313.

"When in any instrument in writing, specifying the rate of interest, no period of time is mentioned for which such is to be calculated, it shall be deemed by the year."—*R. S.*, § 1314.

"All territorial [state], county, school district, town, city or other warrants issued after February eighth, eighteen hundred and eighty-two, for any salary or salaries, fee or fees, or for or on account of any indebtedness, claim or demand whatever, which indebtedness, claim or demand shall have accrued on any contract, transition or liability entered into or arising after February eighth, eighteen hundred and eighty-two, shall draw interest upon the amount expressed in such warrant or warrants at the rate of eight per centum per annum from the date of the presentation thereof for payment at the treasury or other place where the same may be payable, until there is money in the treasury for the payment thereof, and it shall be unlawful to allow or pay any rate of interest upon such warrant or warrants, except as herein specified and expressed, and every territorial [state] or county treasurer to whom such order or warrant is presented for payment, provided he has not sufficient funds in the treasury to pay the same, shall indorse thereon the words 'not paid for want of funds,' and sign and date the same officially."—*R. S.*, § 1315.

"The legal rates of interest in all debts, dues and demands not above specified, shall be at the rate of twelve per cent. per annum, in the absence of any contract by the parties to the contrary."—*R. S.*, § 1316.

"On the thirtieth day of November in each year, the unpaid taxes of that year become delinquent, and shall draw interest at the rate of twenty-five per centum per annum until paid, or collected by distress and sale, and taxes upon real property are hereby made a perpetual lien thereupon, against all persons or corporations except the United States and this territory [state], and taxes due from any person or personal property, shall be a lien on any real property owned by such person."—*R. S.*, § 3819.

Land sold for taxes may be redeemed by paying "the amount for which the same was sold, and thirty per cent. on the sum, with twelve per cent. interest per annum on the whole amount, from the day of sale, and the amount of all taxes accruing after such sale, with twelve per cent. interest per annum on such subsequent taxes," if paid by the then holder.—*R. S.*, § 3829.

"Delinquencies on the part of any county in payment of the territorial [state] tax levy shall bear interest at the rate of eight per centum per annum, after the fifteenth day of January when such tax levy was payable to the territorial [state] treasurer."—*R. S.*, § 3837.

INDEX.

www.ingramcontent.com/pod-product-compliance
Lightning Source LLC
Chambersburg PA
CBHW032258280326
41932CB00009B/608

* 9 7 8 3 3 3 7 2 0 7 4 2 7 *